(Continued from front flap)

Marcan Gospel, in Q, in the Matthean Gospel, and in the Lucan Gospel. In each case, the actual Biblical references are given.

The author argues that the term "Son of Man" denotes the transcendent sovereignty celebrated in apocalyptic literature, and was not applied by Jesus to himself. It was only the Easter revelation that persuaded the Church that this "coming" Perfecter had actually come in the earthly work of Jesus — but the Church was thus persuaded at a very early stage, before the oral tradition developed into Q and Mark.

This study has led Dr. Tödt to conclude that on the one hand the passion-kerygma and on the other hand the "Son of Man" and the Christology of his supreme authority are together the two sources of the Christological discovery. "We have arrived at the conclusion," he says, "that there is a Christology in the synoptic tradition the basis of which is not a Christological concept of Jesus' *person*. This Christology conceives of Jesus' *authority on earth*. It does not conceive of a transcendent person, the Son of Man as immanent in Jesus."

Another valuable contribution of the book is its many references to other scholarly literature, including a new appendix covering recent British work in this field. It also confronts the minister with a challenge: Does his preaching express the spiritual relationship to Jesus' authoritative word which the earliest collection of the Lord's sayings demands?

THE AUTHOR:

Heinz Eduard Tödt is Professor of Theology, University of Heidelberg.

THE SON OF MAN
IN THE SYNOPTIC TRADITION

H. E. TÖDT

THE SON OF MAN IN THE SYNOPTIC TRADITION

The Westminster Press

PHILADELPHIA

Copyright © SCM Press Ltd 1965

Translated by Dorothea M. Barton, M.A., from the German
Der Menschensohn in der synoptischen Überlieferung
2nd edition, published 1963 by
Gütersloher Verlagshaus Gerd Mohn

LIBRARY OF CONGRESS CATALOG CARD No. 65–22392

PUBLISHED BY THE WESTMINSTER PRESS®
PHILADELPHIA 7, PENNSYLVANIA

PRINTED IN GREAT BRITAIN

To the memory of my brother
HANS CHRISTIAN TÖDT

Born March 16, 1924
Wounded February 5, 1944
south-west of Lake Ilmen
I buried him near Solzy

Romans 14.7–9

CONTENTS

PREFACE

THE PROBLEM OF the synoptic Son of Man sayings aroused my interest not long after I had begun to study theology. It was laid before me in a seminar held by Günther Bornkamm at the University of Heidelberg in the winter term of 1951/52. It accompanied me during the course of my studies in which I became acquainted with Rudolf Bultmann's way of listening to the New Testament and with Karl Barth's way of considering the responses of the Christian community. In 1956 the result of my enquiry into the problem of sovereignty and humility in the synoptic Son of Man sayings was accepted as a doctoral dissertation in Heidelberg. In 1959 it was published, with generous financial help from the Carl Bertelsmann Stiftung, under the title *Der Menschensohn in der synoptischen Überlieferung*. In 1963 a second edition was needed and prepared by the Gütersloher Verlagshaus Gerd Mohn; there was no occasion to alter the text of the first edition. Nor was there any intention of altering it for this edition in English. But different languages express things differently. Matthew and Luke were not able to adopt without alteration certain Son of Man sayings transmitted to them by Q or by Mark, since these sayings would have been no longer true when the original words were embedded in the different language of another evangelist. Likewise a German statement may lose its truth when literally translated into English. German formulations often have to be dissolved and reformulated in English. This working-over and expansion of the excellent translation by Mrs D. M. Barton was mainly done by Dr phil. Ilse Tödt. Marlin Miller, of Indiana, USA, watched this procedure and reformulated yet again where he saw a possibility of making the sense clearer to English readers, as did Miss Jean Cunningham of the SCM Press. In another language German concepts appeared in a fresh light. The most conspicuous modification had to do with the term *Verkündigung*. This term revealed itself as expressing a three-dimensional concept. It denotes what happens at present both referring to what has actually happened in the past and to what is to happen in the future. Thus it denotes the utterance of both an indicative and an imperative, a statement as well as a summons. We preferred to render this term in the sense of (the act of) utterance by the verb 'to preach', in the sense of statement by the verb 'to proclaim' and in the sense of summons by the verb 'to teach'. 'Teaching' means to preach the kingdom of God and 'proclamation' means to preach the gospel of Jesus Christ, or the kerygma in the Marcan definition. We are conscious of the fact that although this book now appears in English it still bears the imprint of having been thought in German. But every effort is needed in order both to make oneself understood and to understand in times when contacts are brought about between individuals and peoples to whom it is by no means always self-evident what the other person or group has to say.

Heidelberg, Germany　　　　　　　　　　　　　　HEINZ EDUARD TÖDT
June 1964

INTRODUCTION

WHAT IS THE significance of the title 'Son of Man' in the Gospels? For more than a hundred years synoptic research has attempted to answer this question. Owing to its close connexion with the problem of Jesus' messianic consciousness, great importance has come to be attached to it. But the investigations may have had to pay too high a price for this distinction. We cannot escape the impression that the discussions on the latter problem have overshadowed the former, obstructing any independent study of the sayings concerning the Son of Man. Therefore we shall take these sayings as the starting-point for our enquiry, referring to their Christological relevance at first only in the broadest and most general manner, i.e. by considering the connotations of *sovereignty* and *humility*. The vagueness of this pair of concepts, sovereignty and humility, might arouse objection. The terms *humiliation* and *exaltation* would undoubtedly be more definite. This qualification, however, involves an unnecessary anticipation: the term 'humiliation' suggests a previous state out of which humiliation comes to pass. This term has, in fact, repeatedly served to place the Christological discussion in a frame of reference providing for the descent of a transcendent being and his course through the earthly world toward his resurrection. By using the terms 'humiliation' and 'exaltation', the train of thought is bound to follow the pattern of an itinerary. We wish to avoid such an *a priori* decision. The need for this precaution will become evident from the following review of recent exegesis which treats the synoptic concepts of sovereignty and humility.

The association of sovereignty and humility within the personality of Jesus was primarily the endeavour of *conservative* scholars. It is remarkable how readily, with Phil. 2.6ff. in mind, they inserted the pattern of humiliation-exaltation into the synoptic texts. Adolf Schlatter's commentaries on the Synoptic Gospels, for instance, are permeated by this pattern. Following the Church's traditional teaching, he answers the question of how Jesus' sovereignty and humility belong together by referring to Phil. 2.8 and combining the statements in this passage with the concept of the obedient Son of God, who receives from his Father in his inner life all that he needs to carry out his office in humility, i.e. to renounce any resistance and claim to his supra-terrestrial power. Jesus' sovereignty is therefore basically transcendent in its nature; the humility which he is obliged to assume as part of his office is a renunciation of the exercise of that supra-terrestrial sovereignty which is inherent in the Son of God as such.[1]

William Wrede has shown how problematical it is to use Schlatter's procedure for the exegesis of the synoptic texts. In his book *Das Messiasgeheimnis in den Evangelien* he shows that the Gospels scarcely afford an insight into Jesus' consciousness of his person. According to Wrede the traits of humility in Jesus' activity on earth are located chiefly in those strata of tradition which depend most heavily on actual reminiscences of Jesus' life, and which therefore still preserve the knowledge that Jesus acted without any messianic pretensions, hence in humility. The post-Easter faith of the community, which invested the material concerning Jesus' life with ever greater glory, is the source for the application of the concept of transcendent sovereignty to Jesus. By this theory Wrede gave the decisive stimulus for taking account of the *strata in the history of tradition* when examining the association of sovereignty and humility in Jesus. He thus broke through the customary exegesis which, chiefly following Phil. 2.6–11, approached the synoptic material with a pattern of different origin.

Albert Schweitzer also departed decidedly from the traditional conservative exegesis, even though he did not co-ordinate sovereignty and humility by noting the strata in the history of tradition. Schweitzer related both concepts to the historical course of Jesus' activity on earth. He emphatically turned against critical scholarship in so far as it presupposed that those passages in the Gospels which are governed by a dogmatic point of view must therefore be un-historical. 'The "consequent eschatological" school says that they are dogmatic and therefore historical.'[2] With the key of 'consequent eschatology', Schweitzer felt better equipped to penetrate into Jesus' historical consciousness than was the exegesis bound to the traditional dogma of the Church. Here then the different strata of tradition are not made responsible for coining the contrasting groups of sayings which speak on the one hand of the passion, on the other of the

---

[1] Cf. Schlatter, *Geschichte*, pp. 11, 153, 156, 161; *Glaube*, pp. 120, 125f., 128ff.
[2] Schweitzer, *The Quest of the Historical Jesus*, p. 385. Cf. *The Mystery of the Kingdom of God*, p. 119.

transcendent sovereignty of the Son of Man. Schweitzer seeks to co-ordinate them in Jesus' consciousness. The crisis of Caesarea Philippi which resulted from the failure of the disciples' mission provided the impulse for the development of Jesus' teaching about his suffering. After this crisis, the pre-messianic tribulation was cancelled for all those others who would not be equal to it and concentrated on Jesus himself. Jesus applied Isa. 53 to himself; he died for the many, i.e. for those who are predestined for the kingdom, with the intention of compelling by his death the coming of the kingdom. Jesus' suffering becomes the arm of a lever by means of which he exerts an active influence on God, on the coming of his kingdom.[1]

Schweitzer's theories made a strong impression on German as well as English-speaking scholars. Julius Schniewind, in spite of his vigorous criticism of Schweitzer's ideas, took over the attempt of seeking the co-ordination of sovereignty and humility in Jesus him-self, in his teaching, and not in the development of the tradition. In its basic substance the messianic secret was not a dogmatic product of the community but the real key to every synoptic logion; for the paradox of the unity of veiled sovereignty with manifest humility and poverty on earth constitutes the real messianic secret which pervades Jesus' whole message. The secret is attached to Jesus' offer of salva-tion: In this offer God's reign is already present, yet the one on whom the offer depends is a non-regal Messiah coming with but the *powerless word*. Thus the secret of God's reign is enclosed in the secret of the word.[2]

Vincent Taylor, in his discussion of the Son of Man sayings, adopts to a large extent Schweitzer's approach by making an 'historical reconstruction' the basis of his interpretation of the Son of Man concept. Jesus set out proclaiming the imminence of God's reign and the coming of the Son of Man. In this early period of his activity he probably applied the name Son of Man to himself; the sayings con-cerning his activity on earth give evidence for this statement. After the failure of the mission of the Twelve, Jesus imparted to his disciples at Caesarea Philippi the teaching that the Son of Man must *suffer*.[3] Thus the concepts of sovereignty and humility expressed in the Son of Man sayings were connected by Jesus himself during the course of his life on earth.

---

[1] Cf. Schweitzer, *The Quest of the Historical Jesus*, pp. 385-9.
[2] Cf. Schniewind, *Messiasgeheimnis*, pp. 9-11; *Markus*, cf. on chapter 4.
[3] Cf. Taylor, *Names*, pp. 33f.

An important novel attempt to understand the Son of Man sayings is presented by T. W. Manson in his book *The Teaching of Jesus*. He strives for a 'communal interpretation' of the Son of Man concept. Jesus was sent to create the Son of Man, i.e. the kingdom of the saints of the Most High. ' "Son of Man" in the Gospels is the final term in a series of conceptions, all of which are found in the Old Testament. These are: the Remnant (Isaiah), the Servant of Jehovah (II Isaiah), the "I" of the Psalms, and the Son of Man (Daniel). It has been argued above that it is the idea of the Remnant which is the essential feature about each of these; and it is now suggested that the Son of Man in the Gospels is another embodiment of the Remnant idea. In other words, the Son of Man, like the Servant of Jehovah, is an ideal figure and stands for the manifestation of the Kingdom of God on earth in a people wholly devoted to their heavenly King.'[1] If the designation Son of Man can be used *corporately* for the whole body of the saints of the Most High, how then can Jesus on the other hand apply this expression to himself alone? Manson sees the solution in the nature of Jesus' prophetic office. It was Jesus' task to bring about the embodiment of the Son of Man. At first he attempted to do so by public appeal and by sending forth the disciples. When their failure and unfitness for this task became apparent, Jesus stood alone 'embodying in his own person the perfect human response to the regal claims of God'.[2] Thus Manson too follows Schweitzer in fitting the Son of Man sayings into an historical construction of Jesus' activity on earth. But Manson tries to interpret the Son of Man as a corporate entity. According to this interpretation, Jesus did not summon his disciples to follow him as individuals, but intended to embody a corporality similar to the Remnant in Israel in community with them. And this fellowship with the designation Son of Man was destined to be the 'organ of God's redemptive purpose in the world'. It already displayed features of the Church whose head is Christ: a living organism which reproduces in its life the sufferings and exaltation of the head. The disciples were

[1] Manson, *Teaching*, p. 227. For the collective nature of the Son of Man cf. the bibliography in Schweizer, *Erniedrigung*, nn. 383 and 376; details in McCown, *JR*, 1948, pp. 8ff. In addition, Taylor, *Names*, pp. 31f. Jeremias writes with convincing arguments against the theory that Jesus wished to embody the idea of the Remnant in Israel, in 'Der Gedanke des "Heiligen Restes" im Spätjudentum und in der Verkündigung Jesu', *ZNW*, 1949, pp. 184ff.

[2] Manson, *Teaching*, p. 228.

called to share in this destiny during Jesus' lifetime, but they were not able to carry out their task.[1]

Amongst German scholars this corporate interpretation has met with little response.[2] The theory, however, that a *combination* of the individual figures of the Servant of Jehovah and of the Son of Man determined Jesus' consciousness of his mission was widely accepted. Either the combination had already been accomplished in the Similitudes of I Enoch—in this view, Jesus' consciousness of himself and of his mission was less spontaneous and more dependent on Scripture and tradition; what was new in Jesus was only his transforming into reality the thoughts of long ago—or the combination was discovered and accomplished by Jesus himself. In this alternative view the co-ordination of humility on earth (Servant of Jehovah) and sovereignty (Son of Man) were to be traced to the spontaneity of Jesus' consciousness.[3] This would lead to the solution that Jesus himself conveyed the heavenly sovereignty of the coming Son of Man into his own historical appearance, possibly proleptically, by designating himself on earth with the name of him who he would be post-existentially[4] and of whose activity he was already aware.

The strongest objections to these suppositions are raised by Rudolf Bultmann on the grounds of the historical aspects of the tradition. Bultmann evidently refers to Wrede. Analysis from the point of view of the history of tradition shows that the different groups of sayings concerning the Son of Man are located in different strata in the history of the synoptic tradition. Only the sayings concerning the parousia can be traced to Jesus' teaching and to Q. The sayings concerning the Son of Man's activity and suffering on earth arise within the Hellenistic community where the original meaning of the apocalyptic title Son of Man was no longer understood; for only so could the name be used for Jesus *on earth*.[5] The meaning of the name denoting the transcendent Son of Man in Daniel may therefore not be introduced into the sayings concerning the activity and suffering on earth. The two types of sayings, announcements of the passion and resurrection on the one hand, parousia prophecies on the other

---

[1] Manson, *Teaching*, pp. 231, 233f.
[2] Cf. Kümmel, *Promise*, p. 27 n. 27, pp. 45f.
[3] So also W. Manson, *Jesus the Messiah*, p. 117.
[4] 'We might apply the term "post-existential thinking" to a mode of thinking which places one in (paradoxical, anticipative) relation to a being which has yet to come into existence.' R. Otto, *Kingdom*, p. 175.
[5] Cf. Bultmann, *Tradition*, p. 155; *Theology* I, p. 30.

hand, are rooted in different historical strata of the tradition and cannot be connected or harmonized.[1] Bultmann accordingly refuses any interpretation deviating from the strictly transcendent nature of the Son of Man concept. In the early primitive community Jesus was considered to be only the future Son of Man who would appear at the parousia in heavenly power and glory. The name Son of Man was not yet applied to Jesus' activity and passion. It was the Hellenistic community which first projected this name back into the period of Jesus' activity on earth. The co-ordination of transcendent sovereignty and earthly humility within the person and activity of Jesus of Nazareth did not yet appear as a problem to the pre-Hellenistic community, because it understood the heavenly sovereignty as future and consequently Jesus' life as unmessianic.[2] No tension existed between the concepts of sovereignty and humility until the later community understood Christ from an eschatological understanding of itself.[3] The tension among the different groups of sayings concerning the Son of Man—which occur in the thinking of the later community elsewhere as well—results from the community's self-interpretation. Thus according to Bultmann our problem must be treated not as part of the story of Jesus but in the frame of the history of tradition.

Ernst Lohmeyer in his books *Galiläa und Jerusalem* and *Das Evangelium des Markus*, as well as in *Gottesknecht und Davidssohn*, has placed the Son of Man concept right in the centre of his studies. Like Bultmann he expects to solve the problems not by reconstructing Jesus' activity within history but by research into the great streams of tradition and spheres of thought in the primitive community. Unlike Bultmann, who ascribes a predominant share in the fruitful development of the primitive community's kerygma and concepts to the Hellenistic community, Lohmeyer sees all the essentials conceived and defined, at least in their main features, before they passed into the Hellenistic world, i.e. in the Palestinian stage of the synoptic tradition. Lohmeyer ascribes a most vigorous productivity and dominating significance to the Galilean stream of tradition. He also attributes the development of the Son of Man concept to this stratum. This concept was a fundamental one of the primitive Church, 'a basin . . . into which the different streams of tradition, including

---

[1] Cf. Bultmann, 'Matt. 16.17–19', cols. 278f.
[2] Cf. Bultmann, *Theology* I, pp. 30, 32.
[3] Cf. Bultmann, *Theology* I, p. 38.

those of the Servant of Jehovah, flowed, surrendering in part their particular colour and direction'.[1] The name Son of Man is but one symbol for a definite set of concepts which can be prominent even where the name itself is not employed.[2] This set of concepts is constituted by a peculiar and contradictory duality: the eschatological Son of Man is foremost a completely transcendent figure who belongs to the coming heavenly world, to God's side; at the same time he is unimpeachably a human figure, a Jew, even though directed toward the coming aeon in his activity.[3] This marvellous duality is the fundamental secret of the primitive Christian concepts; the same paradoxical unity of human humility and unrestricted divine sovereignty is the basis of the other Christological concepts, e.g. the Servant of Jehovah concept.[4] It is a distinctive mark of the name Son of Man that the association with the concept 'man' makes itself felt to the extent of veiling the transcendent sovereignty which, in fact, the name is intended to display. Thus the name bears the stamp of a parable.[5] It is an eschatological cipher. Hence Lohmeyer speaks of the *secret of the Son of Man*,[6] which includes the element of the concealment of the Son of Man. Only in concealment could the Son of Man unite with the Jewish rabbi. According to Lohmeyer, however, the Son of Man did not lose his heavenly nature in his concealment. Again and again a few rays of his glory penetrate his secret and thereby intensify it.[7] Precisely that form which is concealed by the secret of the Son of Man is revealed by the names Son of God and *Kyrios*. In the Master that form is already present in concealment; it is immanent in him and constitutes his divine nature.[8] Lohmeyer proceeded in his theological investigations from primary findings in Phil. 2.6–11 to the synoptic problem of the Son of Man. Hence it is not surprising that he interprets the Son of Man concept by means of the *Kyrios* idea and the basic Christological pattern of Phil. 2. In this interpretation, the one exalted to be *Kyrios*/Son of Man was the central figure of the synoptic Son of Man sayings.[9] Undoubtedly the question of how the

---

[1] Lohmeyer, *Gottesknecht und Davidssohn*, p. 58.
[2] Cf. Lohmeyer, *Galiläa*, p. 94.
[3] Cf. Lohmeyer, *Markus*, p. 6.
[4] Cf. Lohmeyer, *Galiläa*, pp. 4, 18 *et passim*.
[5] Lohmeyer, *Markus*, p. 5.
[6] Cf. Lohmeyer, *Gottesknecht*, p. 12 *et passim*.
[7] Cf. Lohmeyer, *Galiläa*, p. 87.
[8] Cf. Lohmeyer, *Galiläa*, pp. 38, 73f.; *Markus*, pp. 4, 7.
[9] Cf. Lohmeyer, *Galiläa*, pp. 23, 38 *et passim*.

concepts of sovereignty and humility are related within the synoptic tradition concerning the Son of Man has been posed by Lohmeyer in a clear-cut manner. We shall have to test the validity of his answers by examining the texts.

From the above survey of recent exegesis treating our problem the following aspects may be selected:

1. We must decide whether our study should be concerned with the *quest of Jesus* or with the exegesis and the *history of the synoptic tradition*. What do those reconstructions of Jesus' historical activity signify for the interpretation of the Son of Man sayings?

2. Do the synoptic concepts of sovereignty and humility fit into the frame of the Christological pattern of Phil. 2.6–11?

3. Are the synoptic Son of Man sayings influenced by the concept of the suffering Servant of Jehovah in Deutero-Isaiah, possibly combined with the Son of Man concept from I Enoch?

4. We must consider the historical element of *tradition* and the logical element of *conception* in the relationship of the three groups of sayings concerning the Son of Man's parousia, activity on earth and passion. In the parousia sayings the concept of transcendent sovereignty appears; in the announcements of the passion the concept of humility prevails. What is their relation?

5. Do the synoptic Son of Man sayings give impetus to a communal interpretation such as T. W. Manson proposes? The clarification of this question is of considerable importance with regard to the origin of the Church and to its possible antecedent forms at the time of Jesus' activity. Does Jesus, when summoning disciples to follow him in view of the coming of God's reign which he has announced with authority, call them into an individual relationship to their Master or into a corporate community? What function is to be assigned to the actual effect of God's reign?

6. The synoptic Son of Man sayings go back into the earliest strata of tradition; they are an important component of the tradition during its formation and development, a part of the primitive community's kerygma. What is their position and function in the synoptic kerygma as a whole? Many scholars consider the passion-kerygma to be the centre of the earliest teaching and tradition. Does the examination of the synoptic Son of Man sayings confirm this theory, or is a modified conception required?

7. Success in interpreting the concepts of sovereignty and humility in the synoptic Son of Man sayings will contribute to the under-

standing of the rise of early Christological ideas. The co-ordination of
sovereignty and humility in Jesus' activity is one of the fundamental
themes of Christology. 'It is not sufficient or profitable for anyone to
know God in his glory and majesty, if he does not at the same time
know him in the humility and shame of his cross.'[1]

[1] Luther, *WA.* I, p. 362 11ff., in *Disputatio Heidelbergae habita,* Probationes
Conclusionum, XX.

I

THE TRANSCENDENT SOVEREIGNTY OF THE SON OF MAN IN JEWISH APOCALYPTIC LITERATURE

(a) The intimate connexion of the synoptic presentation of the Son of Man with that of Jewish apocalyptic literature can no longer be seriously contested. So we will begin by glancing at the features of sovereignty which are attributed to the Son of Man in Jewish apocalyptic literature. The synoptic features will then stand out from this background in more distinct relief.

One of the most important issues which modified the Jewish religion during the pre-Christian, late Hellenistic period was the decisive step taken towards a radically *transcendent* concept of the eschatological saviour. The image of the Perfecter is no longer drawn with lines extended from the course of history which raise earthly traits to a higher level. New attributes originating in a world other than ours are used to depict his sovereignty. The Messiah who is attached to history and nation is overshadowed by the transcendent bringer of salvation; the eschatological event is transferred into dimensions of cosmic and universal proportions.

(b) In **Dan. 7.13f.** a fleeting spotlight touches the figure of a transcendent Perfecter. The seer beholds in a dream, after the great judgement scene has taken place in heaven and the sentence has been executed, a figure coming with the clouds of heaven who is like a (son of) man. This approaching visionary figure is free from the restrictions of an existence on earth. His origin is not indicated, but he arrives upon the heavenly scene in a marvellous and mysteriously significant manner, namely with the clouds of heaven.

The task committed to this Man by the Ancient of Days is not directed at human kingdoms or nations but at an everlasting reign. It is neither stated nor implied that the Man judges the nations. He

merely accepts the office of ruler bestowed on him by the Ancient
of Days at a heavenly enthronement scene. 'It is not stated in the
vision where the "man" will rule in the new era, where the kingdom
of God will be established; whether in heaven, or on earth, or between heaven and earth. This remains in semi-darkness in spite of its
connexion with Israel. The main point is that from now onwards the
kingdom of God and his ruler will dominate in the place of the
demonic world-wide kingdoms to the glory of God and for the benefit
of the people of God.'[1]

How do we have to understand the statement that the appearance
of this marvellous supra-terrestrial being is 'like a man'? The word
'like' (a human being) of the vision hints not only at the similarity
to men but even more at a mysterious dissimilarity. It is not a man
who is appearing but one like a man. Nevertheless in the context of
chapter 7 emphasis is given to the human quality of the figure by
contrasting him with the beasts representing the pagan kingdoms.
The similarity to men may have been emphasized for the following
reasons: several scholars conjecture that the author of Dan. 7.13 'was
influenced by the concept of a half-divine *Urmensch* (primal man)'.[2]

---

[1] Volz, *Eschatologie*, p. 13.

[2] Volz, *Eschatologie*, p. 13, cf. pp. 189f.; Reitzenstein, *Erlösungsmysterium*, pp.
118–23; Kraeling, *Anthropos*, pp. 94ff.; cf. Schweizer, *Erniedrigung*, pp. 88f.: 'It is
certain that in Dan. 7.13 he who appears "like a son of man" represents the
"people of the saints of the Most High" (v. 27).' But probably the interpretation
which follows this passage explains the vision in a new secondary sense. M. Noth
also demands a separate exegesis of the vision and of its interpretation. 'For the
individual parts of the description of the vision—and this applies especially to the
scene of the heavenly court of justice and to the appearance of the one who looked
"like a man"—had developed separately without being planned in view of the
interpretation.' Cf. Noth, *Die Heiligen des Höchsten*, p. 282. W. Manson thinks it
possible that the concept of the heavenly man may have had a more comprehensive
meaning previous to its admission into the book of Daniel. This would accord
with the more elaborate and complete presentation in the Similitudes of Enoch and
in IV Ezra 13. 'While the Son of Man conception may have come to Daniel and
the writer of Enoch from an Iranian source, to Jesus its presence in Daniel made
it part of Holy Writ, and as such to be accepted and understood in the light and
context of all that is made known to him in his personal history concerning the
will of God.' W. Manson, *Jesus the Messiah*, p. 185. But can we be sure that Jesus
himself relied on Dan. 7? Why do we not detect a dependence on Dan. 7 in any
of the Son of Man sayings in Q? Iber, *Überlieferung*, pp. 40ff., adduces arguments
for the view that the vision in Dan. 7.13f. represents an older source introducing
the figure of an individual as contrasted with the collective interpretation in
vv. 18, 27 (cf. also p. 29 n. 1). On the collective conception see especially Manson,
Teaching, pp. 227ff. Critical consideration in Sjöberg, *Verborgener Menschensohn*,
p. 241 n. 1. Preiss, *Fils*, pp. 16ff., tries to combine the messianic and collective
interpretation of Dan. 7.

In case this influence were present it would necessitate the adherence to the human quality even if referring to a heavenly being.[1]

Confining ourselves to the features of sovereignty of this Son of Man without taking account of the secondary interpretation of the vision in 7.15ff., we can only name, in addition to his marvellous advance with the clouds of heaven, the tokens of an everlasting universal ruler. To the Man is given by the Ancient of Days dominion, glory and kingdom[2] for ever and ever. It is striking that no actual activity of the Man is described. The acts of punishment are carried through without him by the Ancient of Days. Thus the image of the Man in the context of the description of the vision attains only a limited prominence. The interpretation in vv. 15ff. robs him 'who is like a man' completely of his individuality and puts 'the people of the saints of the Most High' in his place.

The vision in Dan. 7.13f. furnishes us merely with the somewhat hazy picture of a heavenly figure with an appearance like that of a human being. After the judgement by the Ancient of Days this figure assumes the office of ruler over the eschatological Kingdom of God. Free from all restrictions connected with the earth, he moves in a marvellous manner amongst the heavenly setting.

(c) The **Sixth vision in IV Ezra 13** links up with Dan. 7.13f. The connexion between the two visions can be recognized by the combined motifs of 'a figure like a man' and 'this Man flew with the clouds of heaven'. Yet the vision in IV Ezra takes us into a new context. Daniel 7 merely describes the act of conferring the reign on the Man, whereas IV Ezra 13.1–13 depicts a continuous series of actions brought to an end prior to the stage of conferring the reign.[3]

---

[1] Iber rightly distinguishes between the possible relationship of the Son of Man in Daniel to the Iranian *Urmensch* (primal man) on the one hand, and the relationship of the Son of Man to the 'Iranian *Anthropos*' with the original meaning of a god of the elements, or of the essence of the cosmos, on the other hand. The latter relationship cannot be shown. *Überlieferung*, pp. 8–12; cf. also Bousset, *Religion*, p. 267; Dahl, *Volk Gottes*, p. 90 (references in n. 57); Cullmann, *Christology*, pp. 141ff.

[2] Translation of RSV; cf. W. Baumgärtner in Koehler, *Lexicon, Wörterbuch zum aramäischen Teil des Alten Testaments*. For dominion cf. LXX, *exousia*.

[3] We restrict our statements to the sixth vision without its interpretation. The vision was interpreted by the author in a secondary manner and inserted into the context of the other material. In the interpretation, at variance with the vision, that Man is designated 'my Servant' by the Most High, cf. vv. 32, 37, 52. In translating 'my Servant' instead of 'my Son' I follow the translation of Violet, *Apokalypsen*, pp. 74f., 182, 187. Sjöberg, *Verborgener Menschensohn*, p. 47 n. 1,

The seer of IV Ezra 13 beholds the Man moving up in a tempest from the heart of the ocean and flying with the clouds of heaven. Whatever he looks at, whatever he strikes with the voice from out of his mouth, melts away before him. The space in which he moves with the clouds of heaven must be imagined as a *cosmic* setting. A great act of destruction is sketched with mysterious, indistinct lines (13.3b, 4).

In v. 5 a new section of the vision begins, indicated by: 'And after this, I beheld . . . ' A second act of destruction is described in greater detail. It takes place on earth and its victims are men. An innumerable host of men is crowding to make war against the Man who ascended from the sea. He carves out for himself a great mountain and flies upon it. From it he destroys with the fiery stream out of his mouth the hostile host assaulting him in great fear; it is dissolved into dust of ashes and vapour of smoke (13.5–11).

Verse 12 begins another section of the vision describing the union of the Man with a peaceable multitude which he calls to himself. Many figures draw near, some rejoicing, others sorrowful; some still carrying chains as a sign of their release from captivity, others bringing human beings along as offerings (Isa. 66.20). The procession of those set free ends the whole vision—almost abruptly. Why is not even the establishment of that new marvellous reign mentioned which is essential for traditional Apocalyptic? Why is there no allusion to that assuming of the reign by the Man which might be expected? Why no hint at that bestowal of the blessings of salvation which is about to begin? The whole purport of the vision appears to be the defeat of the hostile powers and the deliverance of the captives which this defeat guarantees.

We are not allowed to attribute the fact that the destruction is performed twice over, in the first and the second act, to the clumsiness of the seer or the author or the editor respectively—blaming him, as it were, for not having succeeded in combining more skilfully the different materials at his disposal into a smooth continuous account. The beginning of v. 5, 'And after this I behold and lo! . . .' separates the two acts of destruction from each other. If it is intended to indicate two different acts in succession, the enemies to be vanquished must be two different groups.

The setting of the first act of destruction in vv. 3b–4 immediately

rightly remarks that by this translation and by the absence of chapter 105 in the Greek text of I Enoch, all evidence for the messianic title 'my Son' or 'Son of God' is excluded from apocalyptic literature.

following the flying with the clouds of heaven, void of any element pertaining to human existence on earth, suggests that the Man after his ascension from the sea first overcomes the cosmic powers. This act would then be comparable to the struggle at the *ascensus* of the *Urmensch* (primal man).[1] After having accomplished the first act the man turns to the host of human foes. Superhuman weapons of war are at his disposal: the stream of flaming fire flowing from his mouth unites with a mighty storm and instantaneously dissolves the hostile host to nothingness.

This second act of destruction undoubtedly stands closer than the first one to traditional Jewish apocalyptic in so far as it takes place in a setting on earth which is somewhat elevated by miraculous traits. If, however, the general train of thought follows an *anabasis* myth influenced by Gnosticism and at the same time employs individual traits from traditional Jewish eschatology, the abrupt ending of the

---

[1] Gressmann, *Messias*, p. 372, concludes: 'In IV Ezra both are clearly distinguishable from each other: the Redeemer (*Soter*) in the vision, the Messiah in the interpretation . . . the Redeemer is a divine being who descends from heaven into the underworld in order to deliver mankind from the dominion of death.' But probably the Man is not intended to be the *sol invictus* as Gressmann supposes but the *ascending* Redeemer. Jeremias, *Erlösung*, p. 110, considers the sea out of which that Man appears to be a symbol indicating the underworld. Sjöberg, *Verborgener Menschensohn*, p. 47 n. 4, objects, in my opinion rightly, to this view: 'But the author of IV Ezra knows nothing of this, even though it might be what this feature meant in the tradition lying behind it. According to him the concealed Messiah is preserved not in Hades but by God in heaven.' Sjöberg's argument remains unsatisfactory in so far as no interpretation is given of the older tradition which does speak of the Man's ascent out of the sea. The concept of that Man is already a part of this tradition which plainly does not emphasize the Man's concealment in heaven. Since even according to Sjöberg's view of IV Ezra 'no man beheld the Redeemer in advance', since 'the manifestation to the elect is not mentioned here' (p. 47), there is no reason at all to speak of the Man's concealment in heaven either in the case of the older tradition in IV Ezra 13 or in the case of its later revision. The dissimilarity to I Enoch must not be overlooked. Joseph Kroll, *Gott und Hölle* (Studien der Bibliothek Warburg 20), 1932, explains the sixth vision as a blurred account of a *descensus*. Our interpretation maintains a view which G. Bornkamm expounded in a study group during the winter term of 1952/53. According to this view the sixth vision is related in its general train of thought as well as in some specific passages to the Gnostic *anabasis* myth; nevertheless the Jewish revision cannot be disputed. The result of our investigation of the Son of Man's traits of sovereignty in Jewish apocalyptic literature however, as we sum it up at the end of Chapter I, does not depend on this particular interpretation of the sixth vision. If one chooses to base the explanation of the sixth vision mainly on those individual traits which link up with the book of Daniel, the following passages will be used predominantly: For IV Ezra 13.3 'flying with the clouds of heaven' in Dan. 7.13; for IV Ezra 13.6f. 'the great mountain' in Dan. 2.34, 35, 45; for IV Ezra 13.3 'the wind out of the heart of the sea' in Dan. 7.2.

vision is easily explained: the description need not go further than the redemption, the deliverance. The emphasis here is on the ascension and the struggle resulting in the deliverance of the enslaved and captive souls. The interest in the heavenly judgement scene and the installation of the Man in the office of ruler which were emphasized in Dan. 7, quite in the spirit of later Jewish eschatology, recedes completely into the background.

It is of no relevance to our investigation whether Gnostic or Jewish apocalyptic motifs are preferred in interpreting the whole vision. We need do no more than point to the peculiar character of this vision. It is distinguished by both its content and its form from the visions of the Son of Man in Dan. 7 and in the Similitudes of I Enoch. The events which are seen are fundamentally different in kind. Only in the sixth vision of IV Ezra is the figure of the Son of Man actively engaged in a complete series of actions.

The traits of sovereignty attributed to the figure of that Man certainly have a *transcendental* nature in all three visions alike. But the area in which they become visible is different. The events of the sixth vision of IV Ezra take place first in mysterious cosmic remoteness and then on a miraculously modified earth. They do not happen immediately under the eyes of the Ancient of Days. Heaven is not affected by them. The figure of the Redeemer is engaged in an independent activity of his own. Sovereignty, power and honour do not have to be bestowed upon him by the Ancient of Days, but are inherent in him from the beginning.[1] The seer of the vision depicts the sovereignty with concrete traits extended into cosmic dimensions: the elements, such as fire and wind, are at the command of 'that Man'.

(d) In the **Similitudes of the Ethiopic I Enoch** we meet with the most detailed account of 'that Man' which has come down to us within Jewish apocalyptic literature. Although much is noted in detail about that figure—his origin, his enthronement, his activities in judging and saving—yet there is nothing which would resemble

[1] Lietzmann, Wellhausen, Dalman and others have denied that in the sixth vision *the Man* is a messianic title. Indeed we cannot speak of a *title*. The figure of the Redeemer is introduced with the phrase: 'I beheld . . . something like a man', and he is spoken of later on as *the man* or *that man* not in the definite manner that one would expect in the case of a title. Nevertheless it is indicated that the supraterrestrial leader to salvation is a distinctly conspicuous *individual*. Manson, *Teaching*, pp. 228ff. does not use the sixth vision to support his 'communal interpretation' of the Son of Man. For literature on this subject see Iber, *Überlieferung*, pp. 45f.

even remotely the general train of thought of the sixth vision in IV Ezra. Throughout I Enoch the Apocalyptists' technique of collecting and compiling dominates to the extent that the account of 'that Man' remains completely subject to it. Fragmentary items concerning this figure are given again and again, but never a continuous complete description of a course of action or part of such a course as we found in IV Ezra 13 which would correspond to the itineraries of Gnostic myths. From this point of view Dan. 7.13f. and the account of I Enoch approach each other in contrast to IV Ezra 13, although in Dan. 7 only a rudimentary portion of the set of concepts about 'that Man' has been adopted.

The Similitudes apparently betray a deeper interest in the *person* of 'that Man'.[1] Although his countenance resembles that of a man, it is full of supra-terrestrial graciousness 'like one of the holy angels' (46.1). Again and again that Son of Man appears with the Lord of Spirits, the Ancient of Days, who has elected him before the creation of the world, before the cosmos existed (48.3–6; 46.3). The Most High previously concealed the Son of Man and preserved him in the presence of his might (62.7). Out of the pre-existence in which he is already seen amidst a community of the righteous under the wings of God, the Son of Man appears at last as the Revealer of all the treasures of the hidden world (46.3).[2] Because he has been placed on the 'throne of his glory' by the Lord of Spirits, the spirit of righteous-

[1] Sjöberg finds in chapter 46 the basic description to which the expression Son of Man each time refers, except for the one passage in 71.14. In his opinion this is valid even in a case where the demonstrative was not predominantly connected with the expression Son of Man in the original text. At any rate the demonstrative in 46.4 and 48.2 is thought to be original; for contrary to the Ethiopic usage the demonstrative in 48.2 stands after the noun. Cf. Sjöberg, *Menschensohn*, pp. 52–57. But even chapter 46 does not really supply us with the description of a scene. That Man full of graciousness like an angel is seen with the Ancient of Days, and the seer is given by the interpreting angel a few hints about the righteousness and election of the Son of Man and about his future function at the judgement on the mighty. From v. 6b onwards there follows a general description of the future fate and the guilt of the rejected. For recent literature see Schweizer, *Erniedrigung*, nn. 167, 172, 383.

[2] For the pre-existence of the Son of Man in Enoch compare Manson, *Teaching*, pp. 228–30. Sjöberg deals exhaustively with this problem. He wishes to show in opposition to other scholars that in the book of Enoch the pre-existence of the Son of Man is meant to be a fact and not a retrospective declaration. He considers only the three passages 48.6; 62.7; 39.6 f. as capable of supporting this interpretation. Proceeding from these passages we must accordingly presuppose this concept of pre-existence also in 40.5 and 46.3. Cf. Sjöberg, *Menschensohn*, pp. 90f., 93. For the connexion between the concept of pre-existence and the motif of concealment cf. our Excursus I on Sjöberg, *Verborgener Menschensohn*.

ness has been poured out over him. Hence he is the judge over the angels in heaven above (61.8f.), over Azazel and all his associates (55.4), and over mankind. He elects the righteous from mankind (51.2) and makes a selection from their works as well (45.3). The negative side of the judgement in particular is depicted in full detail. The mere word of his mouth slays all the sinners and unrighteous (62.2). The heavy wrath of the judgement smites the kings, the mighty and lofty ones, who held sway over the earth unlawfully (62.3). Innumerable evil deeds which will not be kept secret cling to them. What weighs most heavily against them is the fact that they persecute the congregation of the elect and deny the name of the Lord of Spirits (41.2; 45.1f.). The sentence as well as its execution lies in the hands of 'that Son of Man'.

On the positive side, the Son of Man is described as the bringer of salvation; he is the deliverer from the ordeals of the judgement, the staff to support the righteous, the light of the Gentiles, the hope of the oppressed (48.4). He is the central figure of the future holy community of the righteous who are to be saved and live and eat together (62.14).[1]

In Dan. 7 we saw that Man merely as the ruler over God's kingdom. In IV Ezra 13 we saw him ascending out of the sea, defeating the hostile cosmic and terrestrial powers and delivering those whom he called to himself. In I Enoch the traits of sovereignty are grouped around the traditional Last Judgement and its execution. The mightiness of this Son of Man is supra-terrestrial throughout; he is acting in a transcendent place rather than within the boundaries of the existing world. The throne of his glory is mentioned again and again (e.g. 55.4; 51.3; 61.8; 62.2, 3, 5; 69.27). Even in those passages where the existing world is regarded as the scene of judgement and salvation there is a tendency to conceive of it as a modified, transfigured world, or as passing through judgement into another state (I Enoch chapters 46 and 48).

---

[1] Manson likewise claims the figure of the Son of Man in the book of Enoch for his 'communal interpretation', cf. *Teaching*, p. 229. Taylor doubts this interpretation for the book of Enoch, though he agrees with it for Mark 8.38; Luke 12.8f. = Matt. 10.32f. and other passages; cf. Taylor, *Names*, pp. 31ff. Sjöberg, *Menschensohn*, pp. 96–98, 101, decisively rejects the 'communal interpretation' for the book of Enoch. In Enoch the idea found several times is that the Son of Man is *connected* with a community which is a corporate group, but not that he is its personification. The importance of the idea of connexion becomes especially clear with regard to table-fellowship (62.14). For the evaluation of chapters 70f. cf. Otto, *Kingdom*, pp. 201ff., opposed by Bultmann in *ThR* 9, 1937, pp. 22ff.; Dibelius in *GGA*, 1935, pp. 209ff.; Sjöberg, *Menschensohn*, pp. 147–89; Manson, *Teaching*, p. 229.

In I Enoch we see the figure of the visionary Son of Man equipped
with an increased number of traits of sovereignty and in a more
intimate relationship with the community of the saved. In spite of this
we may doubt the vitality of this figure. Is not the visionary imagination—in so far as it is still at work with the material accumulated
during the course of its tradition—preoccupied in painting with
ardour, desire and anguish the judicial procedures and intimating
the blessed state of salvation? Is not the figure of the Son of Man interpolated almost as an afterthought to embody these images instead of
being their primary source? In the sixth vision of IV Ezra the figure
of the Redeemer determines by his appearance the whole series of
events. In I Enoch on the contrary we get the impression that individual actions depicted apart from the figure of the Son of Man are
hung like ready-made clothes on a lifeless form. The figure of the
Perfecter is fitted into eschatological events already provided.

Nevertheless the traits of sovereignty which we have mentioned
exalt the one who embodies them to a thoroughly transcendent
figure who springs from pre-cosmic origins, annihilates the sinners and
leads the elect and righteous to a supra-terrestrial salvation.[1]

(e) With regard to the deep-rooted differences which separate the
figure of the Son of Man in the sixth vision of IV Ezra on the one
hand from the Man in I Enoch and Dan. 7 on the other hand, it
may be doubted whether a definite set of concepts concerning the
Son of Man was generally accepted in Jewish apocalyptic literature.
The spirit which lives in the visions issued from very different
contexts. And yet it is possible that to the earliest Christian congregations these different figures of a Son of Man appeared to draw
together. Since they were seen in a fresh light the differences could

[1] Recently Dodd has once more stressed the problems encountered when the
book of Enoch is used for elucidating the concept of the Son of Man in the New
Testament. 'Until we know more about this, it cannot be accepted as certain that
the Similitudes are pre-Christian at all. However this may be, the Similitudes are
in any case an isolated and probably eccentric authority for the association of the
title "Son of Man" with an "Apocalyptic Messiah", and cannot be used with any
confidence to elucidate the New Testament.' In view of the corresponding passages
in Ps. 8; Ps. 80; Dan. 7, Dodd arrives at the conclusion: 'The New Testament
use of the title "Son of Man" for Christ results from the individuation of this corporate conception [of the Son of Man representing a community, namely Israel,
or mankind visited by God]' (According to the Scriptures, pp. 116–18). Evidently
British scholars combine a strong bias in favour of the communal interpretation
with the argument that Jesus had Dan. 7 in mind when he spoke of the Son of Man.

recede into the background in favour of the similarities in several of the specific traits of the visions.[1]

All the seers alike tended to borrow the traits of sovereignty which we have delineated not from the dimensions of man but from heavenly beings. According to the spirit of those times they did not consider the figure of an angel to be adequate for the Perfecter. So they could hardly help adopting traits of the sovereignty of the Most High for the figure of the Son of Man. Attributes and actions of God were delegated to him. This might have easily led to placing him in competition with God. The apocalyptists themselves may have sensed the danger of a *deus otiosus*; maybe this is the reason for their alluding to activities of the Most High without a clear motive for doing so (I Enoch 62.10). When traits of sovereignty are adopted from the Most High the transcendent figure of that Man obviously cannot be depicted in lowliness and hemmed in by earthly restrictions, as would to a certain extent be possible for the figure of the Messiah whose traits are delineated by exalting historical and earthly realities. The figure of a transcendent Perfecter, however, is exalted above all earthly sufferings. His power and sovereignty, untroubled by any earthly condition, accordingly lie in the future as part of the coming, the second aeon. A strict dualism which radically separates the present from the coming aeon (IV Ezra 7.50) determines this transcendent concept of the sovereignty of the Perfecter. How could this transcendent figure be related to Jesus, who lived on earth and in history? At any rate fundamental changes were necessary, the traces of which we wish to pursue in the differing groups of the synoptic sayings concerning the Son of Man.

[1] We shall see in Chapter II C, pp. 67ff. and 79, that Matthew's Gospel, for instance, does fit particular traits from different apocalyptic traditions into the sayings concerning the Son of Man and yet by this means brings into prominence a clear-cut concept of the author's own. The authors of Jewish apocalypses were hardly aware of how little they conformed to the original meanings of the differing traditional material which they combined and used in a new manner. Likewise the members of the earliest congregations hardly paid attention to the correlation within the whole system of thought inherent in the traditional visions and other material when accepting those isolated elements which they could use.

II

THE SAYINGS CONCERNING THE COMING
SON OF MAN IN THE SYNOPTIC GOSPELS

SAYINGS CONCERNING THE coming Son of Man are contained in
those strata of the synoptic tradition which undoubtedly count
amongst the most primary, i.e. in Q and in the early material
peculiar to Matthew. To a large extent scholars today have arrived
at the consensus that some of these sayings can be traced back with a
high degree of probability to authentic utterances of Jesus.[1] Since
for this group of sayings the history of their tradition can be followed
up with comparative certainty, we shall deal with them first, before
the groups of sayings about the activity on earth and the suffering
and rising of the Son of Man. In doing so we shall be guided by the
following considerations.

1. The synoptic concepts of the Son of Man cannot be examined
without comparing them with the various Jewish apocalyptic concepts. Some scholars stress the dependence on Dan. 7.13f., and wish to
look upon a close relationship with any other Jewish apocalyptic
text as unproven. But a primary dependence on Dan. 7.13f. would
determine the interpretation in advance. Thus, for example, this
text yields decisive support for the 'communal interpretation' of the
Son of Man.[2] Other scholars search for a dependence on the combination of Dan. 7.13f. and the Son of Man concept in the Similitudes

---

[1] Recently, after our investigation had been completed, Vielhauer in his essay
'Gottesreich und Menschensohn' has defended the position that 'There is a
probability verging on certainty that none of the sayings concerning the coming
Son of Man did originate with the historical Jesus' (p. 71). This view, for which
the whole body of the synoptic Son of Man sayings should be taken into account,
is discussed in Excursus VI at the end of our study, pp. 329ff. Excursus V, pp.
319ff., is devoted to the examination of the Son of Man problem which Cullmann
submitted in his book *The Christology of the New Testament*, Part II, chapter 6,
pp. 137–92.

[2] See above in the introduction and also p. 29 n. 1.

of I Enoch, paying less attention to IV Ezra 13 as well as to the deep-rooted differences between those texts.

In view of such conflicting interpretations it will be important to refer to the inlets within the history of the synoptic tradition through which earlier concepts of the Son of Man were channelled. In addition the channelling process itself must be analysed. For it makes a great difference whether it was Jesus himself who referred to Dan. 7 in his teaching, or whether it was the scribes in the post-Easter community who established this relationship for the synoptic sayings concerning the Son of Man.

2. The Son of Man concept has commonly been treated as a constant entity possessing the same meaning throughout the synoptic tradition. But this tradition passed through an eventful history from the time when the material of Jesus' teaching was received until it was collected, arranged and edited by the evangelists. The Son of Man concept shared fully in this process. Therefore it will not suffice to pay attention to the way in which Jesus modified the Son of Man concept in his teaching. In addition we shall have to examine whether the post-Easter tradition continued to develop the Son of Man concept *productively*.

3. In order to take account of the fact that the Son of Man concepts are tied up with the synoptic kerygma as a whole we arrange the sayings about the coming Son of Man as follows: (A) sayings in the Gospel of Mark, (B) sayings according to Q, (C) sayings in the Gospel of Matthew, (D) sayings in the Gospel of Luke. By this procedure the investigation will show whether the Son of Man concept within the synoptic tradition was explained in its meaning, modified in its use, and associated with specific ideas of the individual evangelists or spheres of tradition.

A. THE SAYINGS CONCERNING THE COMING SON OF MAN IN THE GOSPEL OF MARK

The Gospel of Mark transmits only three sayings about the coming Son of Man. Amongst these Mark 13.26f. undoubtedly conforms most closely to the sphere of Jewish apocalyptic thought. Mark 8.38 stands farthest away from it, whilst Mark 14.62 occupies a certain midway position.

I. Analysis of the Son of Man sayings in Mark

(a) **Mark 13.26f.** The direct reference to Dan. 7.13f. in this saying can be recognized without difficulty. In both passages it is said that the Son of Man comes with the clouds of heaven. The terms 'with great power and glory' in Mark 13.26 evidently depend on Dan. 7.14. In Mark 13.27 it is stated that the Son of Man will send out his angels to gather his elect. The same concept of the activity of the Perfecter at the end of time occurs frequently in the Old Testament as well as in apocalyptic literature.[1]

In the scene sketched in Mark 13.26f. as a whole, however, we cannot recognize much that accords with Dan. 7.13f. The vision in Daniel tells of the everlasting rule being conferred; its heavenly nature is described in 7.14. In Mark 13.26f., however, the subject is the arrival of the Son of Man on earth. At the very moment when the earth is dissolving amidst cosmic convulsions the Son of Man shows himself with great power and glory and commands his angels to rescue his elect from the desolation. Thus he appears as their helper and saviour at the end of time. Likewise I Enoch speaks of the activity of the coming Son of Man: 'And the righteous and elect shall be saved on that day, and they shall never thenceforward see the face of the sinners and unrighteous. And the Lord of Spirits will abide over them, and with that Son of Man shall they eat and lie down and rise up for ever and ever' (I Enoch 62.13f.). Yet the text in the Gospel of Mark contrasts remarkably with the description in I Enoch in so far as it lacks any allusion to the Son of Man's traditional activity as a *judge*. This is particularly true of the negative side of the judgement, namely the authoritative sentence on the unjust, the sinners and the mighty of this earth, as well as the execution of the verdict. Mark 13.26f. describes merely the positive side of the activity at the end of time. The author of the Gospel of Matthew, who is more intimately attached to Jewish apocalyptic literature, deems this to be one-sided and adds an allusion to the negative side of the Son of Man's appearance. The passage from Zechariah which he quotes in Matt. 24.30 points indirectly but clearly to the seriousness of the judgement at the parousia. He does not actually describe the Son of Man acting as a judge, but he definitely states that all the tribes of the earth will mourn when the sign of the Son of Man appears in heaven.[2]

We have seen that Mark 13.26f. clearly links up with Dan. 7.13f.,

---

[1] Cf. the references in Klostermann, *Markus*, p. 137. In addition, e.g., IV Ezra 13.12f. and 13.39ff.

[2] The positive antithesis to these laments, namely the praise of the Son of Man, occurs in I Enoch 48.5; 61.8 and elsewhere.

yet presupposes a different scene and advances ideas of a very different kind. Now Dodd is certainly right when he maintains that Dan. 7 belongs to those particular parts of the Old Testament which were considered significant by early Christian thinkers in view of the fulfilment of the Scriptures and which they therefore used as a mine of scriptural evidence.[1] Dan. 7 is echoed not only in Mark 13.26f. and 14.62 but also in Rev. 1.7 and probably also in Rev. 1.13 and 14.14. So we can assume that the forming of Mark 13.26f. was influenced by a scribe's intentional reference to Dan. 7; moreover, the context is permeated by scriptural allusions.[2]

Besides the wish to establish a connexion with the Scriptures, there are other tendencies which must be taken into account. These tendencies show up in the ideas diverging from Dan. 7.13f. The Son of Man concept which was at work in Mark 13.26f. had not been adopted from but rather secondarily confirmed by Dan. 7. Obviously the concept underlying Mark 13.26f. is closely related to the ideas of I Enoch—as we saw above—even though only the positive side of the Son of Man's appearance is emphasized in Mark. The context also corresponds to this relationship.

Bultmann includes Mark 13.24–27 in the 'Jewish apocalyptic sayings which comprised a context that had been preserved intact before it was worked into Mark'.[3] Although the question of Jewish or Christian authorship may not yet be finally settled, it is evident in any case that in these verses a series of eschatological events is described quite in the spirit and with the literary technique of Jewish apocalyptic. This fact forbids the assumption that this Son of Man saying is an authentic saying from Jesus' own lips.[4]

There is no need to demonstrate in detail that the chronological arrangement of the eschatological events in Mark 13.24–27 conflicts with the material of Jesus' teaching.[5] It is noteworthy, however, that even Mark 13.26f., by omitting details of the eschatological events as well as the negative side of the judgement, in which the apocalyptists were eagerly interested, departs from the apocalyptic trend.

Moreover, the saying Mark 13.26f. is alien to Jesus' own teaching in so far as no authentic saying of Jesus refers to a scriptural saying

---

[1] Dodd, *According to the Scriptures*, pp. 67–69.
[2] Cf. Lohmeyer, *Markus*, p. 279 nn. 1–4.
[3] Bultmann, *Tradition*, p. 122. Hölscher reconstructs in *ThBl*, 1933, cols. 195f. the text of the '*Vorlage*' (original) of which he considers Mark 13.26f. to be a part.
[4] Cf. Kümmel, *Promise*, pp. 97 and 103f.
[5] Cf. Luke 17.20f.

concerning the Son of Man, whether it be Dan. 7.13f. or any other apocalyptic passage in the Scriptures. The first clear references by scribes which we discover within the synoptic tradition occur in Mark 13.26 and 14.62. We may therefore infer that Mark 13.26f. was not received directly from Jesus' preaching and still presume that the inclusion of this Son of Man saying in the context of Mark 13.24ff. was occasioned indirectly by Jesus' preaching which announced the coming of the Son of Man.

(b) **Mark 14.62.** This saying concerning the coming of the Son of Man, pronounced by Jesus as a threat against the men judging him, is certainly linked to Dan. 7.13 (cf. Theodotion). In addition it refers to Ps. 110.1, a scriptural passage which the primitive community valued as evidence for Jesus' messiahship; there is sufficient proof for this in the discussion about Christ the son of David in Mark 12.35ff. In the formulation of the Son of Man saying addressed to the Sanhedrin, the scribes' study of the Scriptures is likely to have played a part. It is not likely that Jesus himself formulated the sayings about the coming of the Son of Man with reference to the Scriptures. Authentic sayings of Jesus (e.g. Luke 12.8f. and parallels; Matt. 24.27, 37, 39 and parallels) do not refer to scriptural sayings concerning the Son of Man, as we already observed above on Mark 13.26f. Moreover, the manner in which Jesus uses biblical quotations elsewhere in his preaching renders this assumption improbable.[1]

Scholarly criticism has questioned the accuracy of the description of Jesus' judicial examination.[2] Dibelius summarizes his objections in the sentence:'. . . it can hardly be assumed that the Christian communities had at their service an eye-witness who could have reported to them that Jesus said, "I am He", which means, I am the Messiah, as it is reported to us in Mark 14.62.' We accord with these doubts because it is improbable indeed that the community had at its disposal detailed reports about the course of the examination in which Jesus' words were repeated accurately. Besides, the community was not much interested in historical details, but preferred to describe the passion by means of the words of Scripture. In particular the debate with the Jews required the community to turn their attention to the Old Testament. There they also found the pertinent

---

[1] See below in Chapter V C III b, pp. 266ff.
[2] Cf. Lietzmann, *Prozess*, p. 314; Bultmann, *Tradition*, pp. 269ff.; Dibelius, *Tradition*, pp. 192ff. The following quotation is from Dibelius, *Botschaft*, p. 132.

prophecy of Dan. 7 which permitted the formulation of a saying of Jesus threatening the imminent arrival of the Son of Man; there, too, they found the other part of the saying of Jesus, namely Ps. 110.1.

The trial scene as described in Mark 14.61–64 is permeated by Christological reflections which we must attribute to the community at a later stage of history. In this scene a definite correlation of the designations Christ, Son of God and Son of Man is established by placing them as close together as possible. The designation Christ applies to the present; it will be confirmed by the parousia of the Son of Man. The title Son of God is not attested in Judaism as a designation of the Messiah. Hence we must consider the juxtaposition of these designations of sovereignty as un-Jewish. The Q material shows that a deliberate juxtaposition of different Christological titles like the one given in Mark certainly does not belong to an early stage in the synoptic tradition.[1] Thus we reach the conclusion that the Son of Man saying in Mark 14.62 was formulated by the post-Easter community which described Jesus' examination before the Sanhedrin by means of quotations from the Scriptures, showing a special interest in the correlation of the Christological designations of sovereignty. This conclusion is of considerable significance for the detailed exegesis of Mark 14.62: the purport of this scene to the community is that in it Jesus for the first time publicly confesses in the presence of all his adversaries that sovereignty which is expressed by the three titles.

In what manner does the Son of Man appear according to this saying? The second part of the verse speaks of the coming with the clouds

[1] Only the name Son of Man has its roots in Q. Kuhn examines in his essay 'The Two Messiahs of Aaron and Israel' the expectations displayed in the Manual of Discipline, ix.11, of three saviour-figures: the new prophetic lawgiver, the new high-priest out of Levi, and the new king out of Judah. He shows that this juxtaposition of the expected saviours was not continued in the New Testament; we are not told anywhere that in the person of Jesus the expectation of *several* saviours was fulfilled. Hence the current Jewish expectation of *one* Messiah was accepted. It is all the more remarkable that in Mark 14.61 the name Son of Man is placed beside the title of Messiah. Evidence of the absence of this name to designate the Messiah in late Judaism is given in Jeremias, *Parables*, p. 57 n. 39; Schweizer, *Erniedrigung*, p. 87; Kümmel, 'Das Gleichnis von den bösen Weingärtnern' in *Aux Sources de la Tradition Chrétienne, Festschrift für M. Goguel*, Neuchâtel and Paris 1950, p. 129; Dalman, *Words* I, pp. 268–73; Billerbeck III, pp. 19f. Michel in *TWNT* V, p. 211 lines 11f., also shows that the Christian community regarded Jesus' confession before the Sanhedrin as the 'prototype of the forensic confession to which the Christian too is called when following Christ'.

of heaven as stated by Dan. 7.13 without introducing any noteworthy additions or changes. The first part of the verse, however, alluding to Ps. 110.1 causes difficulties if we wish to clarify its relationship with the statement in the second part of the verse. It is announced to the members of the Sanhedrin that they will see the *sessio ad dextram Dei* of the Son of Man as well as his coming with (on) the clouds of heaven—precisely as if both actions could be seen at a glance like a single event.

Few scholars dispute that the arrival on the clouds of heaven signifies the parousia. Amongst them Glasson understands the scene in Mark 14.62 to be strictly parallel to Dan. 7.13. In both cases not the parousia on earth but the arrival at and bestowal of power by the Ancient of Days is signified. By means of this interpretation, Glasson does arrive at the homogeneity of the event announced in Mark 14.62: it is exclusively the exaltation to the position of ruler at God's right hand which is to be demonstrated to the members of the Sanhedrin.[1] Yet this exegesis is untenable. Firstly, our passage cannot be considered completely parallel to Dan. 7, because in the latter passage judgement has already been passed on the old aeon before the Son of Man appears and is installed as ruler of God's kingdom. Next, the succession of the quotations is a serious obstacle; in Dan. 7 the coming with the clouds of heaven provides the presupposition for the enthronement, whilst in Mark 14.62 the coming follows the *sessio ad dextram*.

Lohmeyer made the attempt, with Mark 14.62 especially in mind, to arrange the synoptic sayings concerning the Son of Man in three stages: (1) the stage of exaltation to *Kyrios*, i.e. the Son of Man who was hitherto concealed taking his place at God's right hand, thus being revealed and enthroned as the judge of the last days; (2) the stage of parousia, i.e. the Son of Man coming with the clouds of heaven; (3) the stage of heavenly assize, i.e. the Son of Man acting either as the sole judge or as the spokesman of the tribunal or as the advocate.[2] Lohmeyer postulates a separate stage of the exaltation of the previously hidden Son of Man to God's right hand. This Christological stage is properly designated by the name of *Kyrios*; for the *Kyrios* is the one who is already exalted before the parousia and reigns as the lord of the community, of the underworld, and of the heavenly region.

[1] Cf. Glasson, *Advent*, pp. 64ff.
[2] Lohmeyer, *Gottesknecht*, p. 125.

We must nevertheless draw attention to the following considerations. (a) The Lucan alteration of Mark 14.62 to Luke 22.69 does indeed indicate a stage in which the Son of Man is already exalted to the right hand of God's power before the parousia, and this stage has even acquired such importance that the mention of the parousia is omitted in Luke.[1] But obviously this is a specifically Lucan interpretation. (b) Neither in the Marcan tradition nor in that of Q is there any other Son of Man saying containing that idea of a stage of exaltation (before and apart from the parousia). (c) In a community which knew from the later course of events that Jesus did not become visible to the members of the Sanhedrin in the state (at the stage) of exaltation, that announcement to the Sanhedrin could not be understood as pointing to an intermediate state of exaltation between death and parousia. Accordingly Luke omits the reference to his being seen.[2] (d) Lohmeyer's argument, which is guided by the train of thought in Phil. 2.6–11, is alien to the synoptic sayings concerning the Son of Man. An *itinerary* might be found in the sixth vision of IV Ezra 13 and in Phil. 2.6–11; the synoptic sayings themselves do not furnish adequate criteria to reconstruct a corresponding progression by stages for the Son of Man.

It must be noted as an objection to Lohmeyer's exegesis that in Mark 14.62 there is no intention of exhibiting an apocalyptic picture.[3] What is intended by the community is Jesus' full confession of his Messiahship made publicly at this moment in the presence of all his adversaries. Consequently this scene is to be understood as a proclamation of sovereignty within which the reference to the reign and the coming of the Son of Man assumes an ancillary even if extremely important function. The allusion to the coming Son of Man places the scene before the Sanhedrin in a definite light which illuminates the absurd arrogance of the earthly judges who wish to judge the one who confesses that he is the Christ and the Son of God and will be vindicated as such at the coming of the Son of Man.

If the purport of the scene is a proclamation of sovereignty, then the references to Ps. 110.1 and to Dan. 7 contained in the saying before the Sanhedrin have to be interpreted not as two stages but as two factors equally related to the coming Son of Man. The citation

---

[1] Cf. Conzelmann, *Theology of Luke*, p. 115. Cf. our Excursus II on Acts 7.56, pp. 303ff.
[2] Cf. Kümmel, *Promise*, pp. 64–83.
[3] Cf. Lohmeyer, *Markus*, p. 328.

of Ps. 110.1 signifies that the one who is coming is the one to whom belongs the seat at God's right hand and with it the full authority to act in the place of God. He is to rule at God's side. This is a concept completely familiar to traditional apocalyptic thinking.[1]

Thus we have established the fact that the traits of sovereignty in Mark 14.62 did not have to be conceived differently from the apocalyptic concepts. Certainly the context in which they stand is a new one. They are used in the proclamation of the messianic sovereignty which Jesus already confessed on earth before the Sanhedrin. That Jesus possesses full authority in spite of the external powerlessness in which he stands before his earthly judges will become clearly visible when the Son of Man, ruling at God's side, comes with the clouds of heaven.

(c) **Mark 8.38.** Here we find the only Son of Man logion in Mark which with a certain degree of probability can be traced back to Jesus' preaching. With regard to the history of tradition this saying belongs to a context which differs obviously from the contexts of the sayings in Mark 13.26f. and 14.62. Mark hands it down as one of the sayings grouped in 8.34–9.1. In this section, which we may entitle 'The disciples' way of suffering', Mark refers to a tradition which already arranged a part of these sayings in parallel sequence. A similar combination of sayings existed in Q as well. Matthew presents some of the sayings twice. In Matt. 16.24f. he follows Mark 8.34f.; in Matt. 10.38, 39 he follows Q, as is evident from a comparison with Luke 14.27 and 17.33. Contrasted with Q, the group of sayings in Mark is enlarged by the double proverb in 8.36f. But the next saying (Mark 8.38) on confessing was known to Q, where it likewise stood close to the sayings on bearing one's cross and

---

[1] If it were permissible to take the context of Ps. 110.1 into account (where the session at God's right hand is connected with the fact that the enemies of the one who is enthroned are put under his feet), then the most acute and direct threat against the men judging Jesus would have been uttered. But it is precisely the allusion to the extinction of his enemies which is missing here and everywhere in the Synoptic Gospels in connexion with the name Son of Man. In the discussion about Christ the Son of David (Mark 12.35–37) the whole verse is cited, but the extinction of the enemies has no primary significance for the passage. In Heb. 1.3; 8.1; 12.2 only the first part of Ps. 110.1 is quoted. Both parts appear in Acts 2.34; I Cor. 15.25; Eph. 1.20; Heb. 1.13; 10.12f. An inspection of the use of Ps. 110.1 in these passages shows that we must not interpret the quotation of Ps. 110.1a as an allusion to the Son of Man's negative function as a judge (extinction of his enemies). This quotation primarily signifies the Son of Man's positive function as a ruler at God's side.

surrendering one's life (cf. the proximity of Matt. 10.32f. to 10.38f.)[1] Thus in Mark 8.38 we deal with a Son of Man saying which also occurs in Q and obviously has widespread roots in the tradition; it is found in the New Testament in at least four forms: (1) Mark 8.38 = Luke 9.26, cf. Matt. 16.27. (2) Luke 12.8 = Matt. 10.32; Luke 12.9 = Matt. 10.33. (3) Rev. 3.5. (4) II Tim. 2.12b. We shall limit our present discussion to the form which we meet in Mark.[2]

Mark presents only the negative part of the saying on confessing; the positive quality of the promise which dominates the Q form is lost. Mark emphasizes the danger of *being ashamed* of Jesus and of his words. In Rom. 1.16 the phrase is accentuated: 'I am not ashamed of the gospel.' It is evident from a comparison with II Tim. 1.8 that we are concerned here with an expression current in the terminology of the primitive congregation.[3] In Mark 8.38 the term 'to be ashamed' stands for 'to deny'. The latter term occurs in the Q form of the saying according to Luke 12.9 = Matt. 10.33. The concept of denying is contrasted with that of confessing.

All these terms have in common the connotation of a legally binding obligation in which attachment to a partner is either publicly declared or definitely renounced. G. Bornkamm remarks on Peter's denial according to Mark 14.66ff.: 'Confessing and denying has nothing to do with merely "being acquainted"—even this Peter will not admit to the maid (14.68)—but includes a previous relationship of obedience and loyalty.'[4] In the same way Mark 8.38a presupposes a previous relation of fellowship; Jesus' disciple is warned against giving it up. For the Son of Man will confirm this fellowship only with him who was not ashamed of his fellowship with Jesus before men. The location of Mark 8.38 amidst the sayings on following[5] permits no doubt that attachment to Jesus through following him is what is meant. Whoever renounces this allegiance will be denied any fellowship by the Son of Man when he comes in more than earthly power.

[1] Harnack, *Sayings*, p. 88, has shown that the order of Q is preserved in Matthew in chapter 10 in a more original form than in the parallel passages of Luke.

[2] On the Q form cf. below Chapter II B I 4a, pp. 55ff. Bornkamm, 'Wort Jesu', pp. 109–11, shows the differences between the contexts in which the saying appears in the three synoptic evangelists.

[3] Cf. Bultmann in *TWNT* I, pp. 188f.

[4] Bornkamm, 'Wort Jesu', p. 113. Cf. our Excursus III, pp. 306ff.

[5] Cf. also the context of Matt. 10.32f. and Luke 12.8f. Schlier in *TWNT* I, p. 470 lines 1f., considers 'the absence of any willingness to respond throughout life to Jesus' claim to confession and discipleship' as one of the concrete ways of denial.

The negative statement presupposes the positive promise that whosoever confesses Jesus will be confirmed in that fellowship by the Son of Man at his coming (cf. Luke 12.8 and par.; Matt. 19.28). Jesus and the Son of Man are by no means identified here. Nevertheless the closest connexion is established between the fellowship through following Jesus on earth and the fellowship with the Son of Man. Whosoever abandons his present fellowship with Jesus will thereby lose the future redemptive fellowship with the Son of Man (cf. Matt. 19.28). Thus in this Son of Man saying, whether expressed negatively or affirmatively, we are concerned with a primarily *soteriological* statement: a break in the fellowship on earth will be followed by the loss of the redemptive fellowship in God's reign. This soteriological concept does not as such comprise a Christological statement about Jesus and his person. Jesus' identity with the Son of Man is by no means alleged.[1] The secret of this saying is to be looked for in the correlation between the fellowship with Jesus through following him and the redemptive fellowship with the Son of Man. This correlation is only promised; there is no reason given for it; it is not made intelligible. How Jesus is related to the Son of Man is not taken into consideration. This promise, like promises by Jesus elsewhere, is given with independent authority; freely, without any safeguards, directly, yet with imperious determination.[2] The community which transmitted this saying had arrived at the conviction that it understood that secret of the correlation between the fellowship through following and the future salvation. It had recognized as revealed what remained concealed in Jesus' words, namely that Jesus himself would be the coming Son of Man. Hence the second part of the saying could run in Mark, 'when he comes in the glory of *his* Father'.[3] Q presents the earlier form in which this phrase is lacking (Luke 12.8f.; Matt. 10.32f.).

The two parts which are correlated in this saying will now be examined separately.[4]

[1] Schniewind, *Markus*, p. 120, concludes too early: 'If the Son of Man is "ashamed" of one who denies Jesus, it is presupposed that he knows this human being as one of his own; therefore Jesus and the Son of Man must be treated as identical.' In the saying itself, however, we find only the promise that the Son of Man on his part will treat as legally valid the maintenance or abandonment of the fellowship with Jesus on earth.

[2] Cf. Campenhausen, *Amt*, pp. 4f.

[3] Cf. Klostermann, *Markus*, p. 85.

[4] Bornkamm reckons the saying on confessing amongst those rules which are formed on the pattern of *correspondence*. These sayings—cf. also Matt. 7.1; 6.14f.—

1. The denial on earth occurs 'in this adulterous and sinful generation'. According to the Q form of the saying, it occurs 'before men'
(Luke 12.8f.). This basically expresses the same thing. We have only
to remember that it is not the Son of Man who is confronted with this
generation. The tension exists between belonging to *Jesus* and belonging to this generation. Prerequisite for the tension is that Jesus and
the sinful generation are separated from each other. 'Confessing' the
one side actually involves renouncing the other side.[1] In the course of
our investigation we shall perceive that this tension between Jesus
and this generation, or men, is manifest throughout all the groups of
sayings concerning the Son of Man.[2] Therefore it is of great significance that in the sayings concerning the *coming* Son of Man it is not
the Son of Man but Jesus who bears the tension. The tension comes
into existence here on earth.

What, according to Mark 8.38, are the traits of Jesus in this
tension? He by no means appears as the lowly one, the sufferer, but
demands with supreme authority that allegiance which detaches the
disciple from this generation. In demanding this, Jesus utters an
unsurpassable claim. No prophet in Israel ever claimed that men
should confess him.

At variance with this view Bultmann interprets Mark 8.38 cf.
Luke 12.8f.; Matt. 11.5f. and par.; Luke 6.46 and par. as expressing
the prophetic self-consciousness of Jesus.[3] But the distinguishing mark
of a prophet is the claim of authority not for himself but for the alien
word which he has to deliver. This is just the way in which Bultmann
defines the actual self-consciousness of Jesus. 'If Matt. 11.5f. and
par. does refer to Jesus, it is not necessarily in his messianic role, but

---

coincide in adjusting minutely God's actions at the Last Judgement and men's
actions prior to it. God's sentence is not passed arbitrarily but seals and bestows
on a man what he himself has done. 'The saying on confessing Jesus tells of what
happens both now and at the day of judgement.' Jesus' saying about confessing
him has the quality of a rule. 'We may discern as the distinguishing quality of these
sayings that they are stated in a comprehensive manner. . . . The condition of
the promise is fully stated in the saying, and the reason for the verdict is given
comprehensively. An unexpected third principle will not enter in any case'('Wort
Jesu', p. 112). This quality of a rule attributes to the threat in the saying a harsh
inevitability, but at the same time it comprehends the independent strength of the
promise concealed in the negative form in Mark 8.38.

[1] On ἕν τινι ὁμολογεῖν cf. below p. 55 n. 2.
[2] Cf., e.g., Matt. 11.16 and 19; Mark 9.31.
[3] Bultmann, *Tradition*, p. 151.

much more probably to his preaching, and so it would actually be Jesus' self-consciousness coming to expression in the same way as Luke 12.8f. and par., where the Son of Man will judge a man in the light of his attitude to the teaching of Jesus.'[1] Bultmann fails to demonstrate, however, that Mark 8.38 in quoting the words of Jesus reproduces more correctly than Luke 12.8f. the original form of the saying on confessing. Bultmann obviously locates the different forms of this saying within the history of tradition in this manner because of his assumption that Jesus' claim on his hearers was restricted to the authority of his word as such.

Mark 8.38 alone speaks of confessing Jesus *and* his word. Luke 12.8f. and Matt. 10.32f. present the simple form, 'whosoever will confess to *me*'. There is a fuller wording throughout Mark 8.38; we shall see this more clearly in the second part of the saying. In that part Luke only says that the Son of Man will confess before the angels of God (cf. Matt. 10.32, 'before my Father in heaven') everyone who confesses. Mark describes the arrival of the Son of Man in greater detail: 'of him the Son of Man will be ashamed when he comes in the glory of his Father with the holy angels'. Here the reference to Dan. 7.13f.[2] or to the apocalyptic tradition is obvious. The angels are mentioned, e.g., in Dan. 7.10 and I Enoch 61.10. The editorial introduction to the portrayal of the great world judgement in Matt. 25.31 also speaks of the Son of Man's *doxa* and the angels coming with him.[3] The connotation of the angels in Luke 12.8f. is, however, completely different. In this passage the angels do not accompany the Son of Man in his parousia but are sitting in God's tribunal when the Son of Man appears before it as the guarantor for those who confess Jesus. Originally in Q the phrase 'before the angels' may have been used to paraphrase the name of God.[4] The text in Matthew makes this suggestion probable. It follows that in Mark 8.38c the text of the saying was extended by making use of the same scribal references to Dan. 7 and the apocalyptic traditions as we already found in Mark 13.26f. and 14.62. We shall find additional examples of a parallel use in Matt. 25.31 and 13.41. Since an extension of the text is manifest in Mark 8.38c, it is improbable that the wording in Mark 8.38a, b, which also is fuller than the Q form, should yet be

---

[1] Bultmann, *Tradition*, pp. 128, 112. Cf. Bultmann, *Jesus*, p. 217.
[2] Cf. Klostermann, *Markus*, p. 85.
[3] Cf. below Chapter II C II 1b, p. 77.
[4] Cf. Klostermann, *Lukas*, p. 34, following Dalman and Loisy.

more original than in Luke 12.8.[1] Consequently the phrase 'and of my words' must be regarded as a secondary addition referring to the post-Easter situation. In that situation Jesus could no longer be followed by actually walking in his footsteps; following now meant confessing to Jesus' words.[2]

Because an extension of the text can be recognized throughout Mark 8.38, we arrive at the following conclusion for the first part of the saying. It is a warning that confessing Jesus and his word cannot be reconciled with the claim of this sinful generation. The unsurpassable claim to sovereignty which is expounded in the second part of the saying rests with Jesus himself and with his teaching. Attachment to Jesus is not an ephemeral bond on earth, but a fellowship which will be confirmed at the coming of the Son of Man.

2. In the second part of the saying concrete traits supply us with an insight into the Son of Man concept. In contrast to Luke 12.8f. it is the *arrival* of the Son of Man in more than earthly glory which is described in Mark 8.38. The Son of Man comes in the radiant brightness of the Father. And yet there is no apocalyptic visionary depiction. The parousia is indicated by stereotyped characteristics taken from the stock of tradition. In order to impress upon the one who denies the perversity of his behaviour, supreme sovereignty is assigned to the Son of Man, who will deny everyone who has denied Jesus. The *doxa* of the Father is conferred upon the Son of Man and God's angels become his retinue. The sovereignty of the Son of Man has been increased. He is no longer confronted by the angels; they now accompany him and are subject to him.

We cannot speak of a definite judgement scene in Mark 8.38 any more than in 13.26f. G. Bornkamm, to be sure, infers that 'While Jesus' warning points directly to his office as Judge, his promise to confess marks him out as advocate and intercessor. To intercede for another person is the office of an advocate (a paraclete).'[3] But in its

---

[1] Mark 8.35 and 10.29 provide evidence of Mark's predilection for duplications which correspond to the wording of Mark 8.38a. On this cf. Marxsen, *Markus*, pp. 82–85. Marxsen demonstrates that Mark supplemented within 8.35 and 10.29 an original phrase, 'for my sake', with a duplicating phrase, 'and for the gospel's'. Correspondingly the deviation from Q in the wording of Mark 8.38 must be ascribed to the evangelist. The replacement of the term 'to deny' by the term 'to be ashamed', current in the primitive community, must be accounted for along the same lines.

[2] Cf. Marxsen, *Markus*, p. 85 *et passim*. In Q Jesus' claim generally refers to his person, occasionally to his words.

[3] G. Bornkamm, 'Wort Jesu', pp. 116f.

secondary extension we have rather to interpret the second part of the saying in conformity with Mark 13.26f. In that passage the Son of Man is described not as acting as a judge but as the lord of the angels who sends them out to rescue the elect from the desolation at the end of time. According to Mark 8.38 the Son of Man's being ashamed of those who deny Jesus will consist in not rescuing them from their afflictions. The Son of Man's function as a paraclete is thus no longer seen by Mark, or at any rate it is not expressed. But the transcendent sovereignty of the Son of Man is demonstrated impressively to those who are in danger of denying Jesus and his words before this generation and of thereby losing the future salvation.

Thus Mark 8.38 shares in the stock of apocalyptic concepts which penetrated secondarily into the synoptic tradition. The most striking result of this process might well be the apocalyptic discourse in Mark 13. The wish to gain support from Scripture and tradition undoubtedly played a leading role. But it led conspicuously away from the concepts prevailing in Jesus' eschatological teaching.[1] We shall also observe an increase of apocalyptic concepts when examining the Son of Man sayings in the Gospel of Matthew. We shall, moreover, observe there that a Christian meaning could be attributed to certain apocalyptic elements.

II. Results: The nature of the sayings concerning the coming Son of Man in Mark

1. With regard to the history of tradition the sayings concerning the coming Son of Man in Mark are linked up with two spheres of thought. On the one hand they refer to the use which Jesus made of the Son of Man concept in his teaching. This is evident in Mark 8.38. On the other hand, we perceive a tendency throughout to refer to the Scripture, namely to Dan. 7, and to the concepts of Jewish apocalyptic literature.

In view of this situation it is not possible to determine exactly when the sayings concerning the Son of Man were given the form present in Mark. It is probable that Mark had a considerable share in the final formulation. It is improbable, however, that he formulated them in their basic form. In the case of Mark 8.38, Luke 12.8f. and par. afford reliable evidence that the saying had long been rooted in the synoptic tradition. In the case of Mark 13.26 an earlier form must be presumed, since the section 13.24–27 belongs to those pas-

[1] Cf. Kümmel, *Promise*, pp. 103f.

sages which for cogent reasons scholars are inclined to impute to a
Jewish or Jewish-Christian apocalypse used by Mark.[1] In the case of
Mark 14.62 the saying was hardly pronounced in this form before
the Sanhedrin, but may well have been found by Mark in earlier
narrative tradition.

One thing appears to be clear: The sayings in Mark which we
have discussed are not located at the inlets through which the Son of
Man concept was primarily channelled into the synoptic tradition.

2. With regard to the concepts which are present in the Son of
Man sayings in the Gospel of Mark we have the following comments
to make: The Son of Man always appears as a transcendent figure
coming at the parousia and bringing to an end what happened on
earth. He does not belong to the existing world, but to the new aeon.
The notions about his activity do not differ essentially from Jewish
apocalyptic thinking. The details of the visionary description, however, recede into the background and the depiction of the negative
side of the judgement is omitted. Instead, the traits of sovereignty
attributed to the Son of Man are raised to utmost supremacy. The
doxa of the Father is conferred upon the Son of Man and the angels
are made subject to him. In Mark's view the Son of Man is not the
guarantor or paraclete at the Last Judgement, but the Saviour who
will rescue from the affliction at the end of time.

3. The sovereignty of the Son of Man has a transcendent quality.
It is not confronted with the hostility of this sinful generation, but
is in heaven. The tension on earth exists between Jesus and men. Even
Jesus in this tension does not appear in humility, but claims men's
confession of allegiance with authority and sovereignty, promising that
the Son of Man will confirm this confession. The scene before the
Sanhedrin, though depicting Jesus in the utmost powerlessness, yet
indicates his full authority to announce to his judges the coming of
the Son of Man; and indeed the purport of this scene as a whole is the
proclamation of the messiahship which the words of Jesus declare.

B. THE SAYINGS CONCERNING THE COMING SON OF MAN
ACCORDING TO Q

I. Analysis of the Son of Man sayings from Q

As a rule we can assign a saying to Q when it is present both in
Matthew and Luke in an analogous form. In addition to these there

---

[1] Cf. Kümmel, *Promise*, pp. 103ff.

are sayings about the Son of Man in the material peculiar to Matthew or Luke respectively which were not formulated originally by the authors of the Gospels but represent in part very early material from the Palestinian tradition; examples are Matt. 10.23; Luke 17.28–30. For simplicity's sake we shall put these into the appropriate groups of Q sayings. This procedure will be all the more permissible since a similarity with Q regarding the history of tradition as well as the concepts will become evident.

The form of the Son of Man sayings from Q does not furnish any obstacle which might hinder an incorporation into that section of the tradition which Bultmann named 'prophetic and apocalyptic sayings'.[1] When regarded from our point of view even the saying in Matt. 19.28 with the 'I say' introduction fits into that group.

(1) *The comparisons: Matthew 24.27 and par.; Matthew 24.37–39 and par.; Luke 17.28–30*

If anyone wished to obtain a more precise picture of the coming of the Perfecter at the end of time, he would find himself disappointed by the comparisons concerning the parousia of the Son of Man from Q. The details could hardly be scantier than they are. The striking contrast with Jewish apocalyptic texts catches the eye immediately.

Matthew and Luke differ in their arrangement of the sayings about the coming of the Son of Man. Nevertheless the arrangement previous to theirs, that of Q, can to some extent be reconstructed. We shall have to make this reconstruction the basis of our analysis. Matthew obviously inserted after 24.27f. (Q) material from Mark: 24.29–31; 24.32f.; 24.34–36. This is followed by another saying from Q, 24.37. The sayings which are thus kept apart in Matthew (24.27 and 24.37) are brought close together in Luke (17.24 and 17.26). Only v. 25, probably a Lucan editorial note, stands between them. Luke moved the offensive simile which Matthew (24.28) certainly presents in its original position to the end of the whole section (17.37). Thereby he removed the inconvenient association of the simile with the Son of Man and achieved a cryptic proverb— perhaps because he no longer understood the original meaning. From these considerations the following arrangement of the text in Q results.

Matt. 24.26–28 = Luke 17.23f., 37.

---

[1] Bultmann, *Tradition*, pp. 108f.

Matt. 24.37–39 = Luke 17.26–27 (perhaps 28–30).[1]

Matt. 24.40–41 = Luke 17.34–35.[2]

The transition to this text varies in Mark and in Luke. In 17.20f. Luke states the Pharisees' question, 'When will the Kingdom of God come?' and appends to Jesus' reply (17.21) a connected piece of teaching on the day of the Son of Man, the basic elements of which are those sayings from Q. Matthew on his part takes from the text in Mark (13.22) the prophecy that false Messiahs and false prophets will appear in the affliction at the last days. To him this prophecy obviously links up with the misleading rallying cries at the last days which he takes from Q. There the false watchwords are mentioned, 'the Messiah is in the desert, the Messiah is in a secret place'.[3] These watchwords are bound to cause serious uneasiness to all those who are looking for the coming of the Son of Man; for should they be true, there would be a grave danger of being too late for the involvement in the relationship which the Messiah is going to establish now.[4]

The Son of Man saying which follows is intended to show that there is no reason whatsoever for such fear. It is a word of consolation. 'For as the lightning comes from the east and shines as far as the west' (according to Matthew), 'so will the Son of Man be in his day' (according to Luke). In the part of the saying which contains the simile, the text in Matthew is more concrete and probably therefore more original. In the part of the saying which contains the factual statement, the text in Luke is closer to Q; for here Matthew inserts the term 'parousia', which is a secondary term, as is evident from 24.3; 24.37; 24.39. It is thus said that the coming of the Son of Man will be manifest everywhere on earth so that no one is in danger of missing it. The Son of Man at his coming will attract the attention of everyone like the lightning which no one can fail to see. The

[1] Cf. Bultmann, *Tradition*, p. 117: 'He may have found vv. 28–30 which are parallel to vv. 26f. (= Matt. 24.37–39) at this point in Q; and if that be so, it is then hardly possible that the verses from Matthew are omitted; much rather is it likely that they are a new formulation occasioned by vv. 26f.'

[2] Cf. also Harnack, *Sayings*, p. 145; Manson, *Sayings*, pp. 141ff.

[3] Cf. Arndt and Gingrich, *Lexicon*, p. 811: 'in one of the inner rooms'.

[4] Klostermann, *Matt.*, p. 194, rightly conjectures 'an attack on the concept of the hidden Messiah'. Billerbeck I, p. 955, quotes Justin Martyr, *Dial. c. Tryph.* 8, reporting as a Jewish belief that the Messiah before being anointed by Elijah is unknown, unaware of his task and not yet in possession of his power. 'This tradition is not stated explicitly anywhere in early Jewish literature, yet we cannot object to it merely on those grounds.'

proverb which comes next is to be understood as a commentary on this statement. Matt. 24.28 pronounces it in a more offensive and also a more original manner than Luke 17.37, namely, 'Wherever the carcass is, there the vultures will be gathered together.' The meaning is that as inevitably as a carcass attracts the birds of prey, men will perceive the coming of the Son of Man. This aspect corresponds to the sixth vision in IV Ezra 13; when the Son of Man appears he will irresistibly attract both the hostile and the peaceful multitude.[1]

Another comparison concerning the day of the Son of Man followed in Q, namely Matt. 24.37–39 and par. In the days of Noah the flood took the people unawares; the coming of the Son of Man will find them just as unprepared. In those days before the flood they were eating and drinking, marrying and giving in marriage; *conjugatio periphrastica* underlines that this behaviour was their usual manner of life. This carefree attitude continued right up to the day on which Noah entered the ark and the flood took them all away. Obviously it is not their actions for which Noah's contemporaries are reproached but their unreflecting absorption in these activities. They forgot to watch the signs of time. Thus they were suddenly attacked by the catastrophe—Matthew emphasizes that they suspected nothing—and all perished. Exactly the same will occur at the coming of the Son of Man.

As uttered by Jesus, this saying is apparently not only meant to caution against the coming world-judgement in general; otherwise there would have been no need to mention Noah's behaviour in particular. The meaning is that the present generation, though living before the end, does not watch the signs of the time (cf. Luke 12.54–56 and par.; Mark 13.28f.) in the way Noah did. Hence the same will happen to this generation as happened to mankind in Noah's time: it will perish unsuspectingly. That Noah's activity should not be neglected in the exegesis is evident from the comparison which

[1] The following exegesis has also been attempted to explain this proverb: when the world is ripe for judgement the Son of Man will come as certainly as the vultures come to the place where a carcass is lying. But there are two objections. Firstly, in the Q text the coming Son of Man and the carcass appear to have been intentionally placed into parallel positions. Irritated by this offensive parallel Luke replaced the coarse word 'carcass' by the more refined expression '(dead) body' out of reverence toward the Son of Man. Arndt and Gingrich note (*Lexicon*, p. 735) that in Matt. 14.12 and Mark 15.45 also the v.l. substitutes the more dignified word for the coarser one. Cf. also Klostermann, *Markus*, p. 169. The second objection is the plural number used for the vultures.

follows in Luke (17.28–30). This comparison might be taken from Q, possibly being an imitation of the comparison with Noah which Matthew was not acquainted with.[1] In this comparison Lot's flight is mentioned in particular. Both comparisons, by pointing expressly to Noah's and Lot's responsible action, caution against unmindful behaviour. For the unsuspecting the coming of the Son of Man will mean catastrophe and annihilation.

In Luke 17.22–30 we hear twice of the days of the Son of Man in the plural (vv. 22, 26) and twice of his day in the singular (vv. 24, 30). Which was the form in Q?[2] Verse 22, which has the plural, was formed by Luke.[3] Did Luke introduce the plural into v. 26 as well? This assumption is supported by the following considerations. In v. 24 the Son of Man himself is compared with the lightning which flashes suddenly and cannot be avoided. As the lightning flashes, so the Son of Man will be on his day. Matthew elucidates, 'so will the parousia of the Son of Man be'. He also offers the same phrase in the saying parallel to Luke 17.26. The comparison is not primarily concerned with the established state of affairs in Noah's time, but with the inrush of the destructive flood which was not expected by the heedless population. This inrush corresponds to the coming of the Son of Man, which is conceived of as a sudden act (Luke 17.24). Matt. 24.39 and Luke 17.28–30 are in accord with this in stressing the suddenness of the catastrophe and conceiving of the coming of the Son of Man as something correspondingly sudden. The use of the plural 'days' suggests a different concept; 'days of the Son of Man' implies a state of affairs of some duration rather than the suddenness of an event. Since this concept of a longer duration is in accord with Luke's concept of the Son of Man, we must assume that Luke as editor formulated v. 26.

The threatening announcement of the sudden incursion of the Son of Man falls within that part of the announcements of the imminent entry of God's reign which we classify as Jesus' teaching. The post-Easter congregation understood these sayings as a warning, even a threat, in view of the parousia. They do not depict the event of the Son of Man's coming with a single word; they merely state what this means for men. All interest is directed to this meaning. This is in marked contrast with the visionary depiction of the Son of

---

[1] Compare above note 1, p. 49.
[2] Cf. Vielhauer, 'Gottesreich', pp. 56f.
[3] Cf. below Chapter II D II 3 b, p. 105, and Bultmann, *Tradition*, p. 130.

Man and his activity in apocalyptic literature. Yet in spite of the extreme scantiness of details, there are a few clues elucidating the basic concept of the Son of Man.

When speaking of the parousia of the Son of Man, Matthew[1] replaces the phrase 'the day' or 'the days' of the Son of Man which is preserved in Luke. This phrase brings out clearly a remarkable process. The day of judgement which was formerly understood to be the day of Yahweh has now been transferred from God to the Son of Man. In Luke 17.30 it is likewise the Son of Man who reveals himself. The transcendent sovereignty of the Son of Man has attained so high an importance that prerogatives of God pass over to the figure of the Perfecter.

In Mark 13.24–27 the coming of the Son of Man is one among other stages in the final course of events. This is similar to I Enoch, where also 'that day' is the moment at which the Son of Man appears (45.4). But the day can be conceived of independently, without the arrival of the Son of Man. The Son of Man is, so to speak, fitted into the preconceived framework of 'that day'.[2] But in the synoptic comparisons which we have discussed the coming of the kingdom of God is identified with the day of the Son of Man. This makes it intelligible that no attempt is made to visualize the arrival of the Son of Man. Jesus' 'teaching' does not intend a detailed description of the kingdom of God, but a confrontation with the bare fact *that* it is coming, that it is therefore high time for the hearers to turn round in repentance in order to face it. Thus the coming of the Son of Man is spoken of as something which will be recognized without needing a description in advance. All that matters is for men to be prepared to respond to this coming. The kingdom of God and the parousia of the Son of Man are no longer topics of apocalyptic esoteric knowledge. They are simply announced as the imminent acts of God, thereby summoning men to turn round in repentance in order to face the coming of God's reign.

(2) *The Threat: Luke 11.30*

Luke 11.30 is related to the comparisons discussed above. The saying was present in Q, but has been fundamentally re-interpreted

---

[1] On the introduction of the term parousia in Matthew, see further in Chapter II C II 3, pp. 87f. Cf. Kümmel, *Promise*, p. 32 n. 63.

[2] Cf., e.g., I Enoch 48.8; 50.1; 51.3; 62.3, 8; 60.5; 54.6; cf. Iber, *Überlieferung*, pp. 50f.

by Matthew.[1] Its exegesis is considered extremely uncertain. Are we dealing with a riddle?[2] If we line this saying up with the comparisons which we have discussed, we get the following interpretation.

In Q the Son of Man saying is linked with this generation's seeking a sign. The demand for a sign evinces that this is an evil generation. Their claim is unauthorized. They are not ready to repent unless they are given a sign from heaven. But they will not be given such a sign. The only sign which the evil generation will receive is that of Jonah. This sign consists of Jesus' teaching (Luke 11.32; Matt. 12.41). Evil arises where men do not respond to Jesus' 'teaching' by repenting even though there is indeed 'a greater than Jonah' here. Where men harden their hearts against Jesus' teaching and seek some other sign from heaven, there will only be judgement (Luke 11.32 and par.). This will make the evil generation see and be ready to repent—but there will no longer be any opportunity to do so, as this will be the coming of the Son of Man, which this generation cannot help heeding as the men of Nineveh heeded Jonah—but they did so in time and on earth. 'As Jonah became a sign to the men of Nineveh, so the Son of Man will be to this generation.' The Son of Man who comes in judgement will make this generation repent. His appearance will satisfy their demand for a sign from heaven, but only in the manner described by Matt. 24.30; 'Then the sign of the Son of Man will appear in heaven, and then all the tribes of the earth will mourn, and they will see the Son of Man coming on the clouds of heaven with power and great glory.' This advent of the Son of Man will compel the acknowledgement which the men of Nineveh had given to the teaching long before; but this acknowledgement will come too late.[3] 'The men of Nineveh will arise at the judgement with this generation and will condemn it; for they repented at the preaching of Jonah, and behold, something greater than Jonah is here'[4] (Luke 11.32 and par.).

Luke 11.30 thus contains a threat to those who are unwilling to understand the preaching as a sign of the onset of God's reign. Like

[1] A different view is held by Jeremias in *TWNT* III, pp. 412f. We shall state critical objections to this view below, on Matt. 12.40 in Chapter IV D III e, p. 212.

[2] Cf. Kümmel's attempts at exegesis in *Promise*, pp. 68f.

[3] Cf. Bultmann, *Johannes*, p. 88 and n. 4.

[4] The exegesis which considers that here the Son of Man is the one already acting in the present, and that this generation is demanding a special cosmic sign surpassing his present action, is made impossible by the future tense: so *will* the Son of Man be to this generation.

the contemporaries of Noah and Lot who did not respond to the signs of the times and hence were taken unawares by the catastrophe, this present generation does not respond to Jesus' preaching, although it is an ultimate sign—greater than Jonah. Hence for this generation the coming of the Son of Man will be dismay and judgement.

Here the preaching of Jesus and the appearing of the Son of Man are closely correlated. What the coming of the Son of Man will mean to men depends on their reaction on earth to Jesus' teaching. Whoever confesses Jesus (Luke 12.8), whoever acknowledges his word as a summons to turn in repentance, will see not dismay but salvation at the coming of the Son of Man.

Again there is not primarily a confrontation between the Son of Man and this generation. The tension is initiated by the rejection of Jesus' authority. The coming of the Son of Man will confirm hereafter that the claim which Jesus utters in his preaching is authorized.

(3) *The admonition: Matthew 24.44 = Luke 12.40*

Matthew concludes the comparisons concerning the coming of the Son of Man with an admonition to watch (Matt. 24.42), which is taken from Mark 13.35. Then Q takes over again, evidently inclusive of the connecting link 'but know this'. There follows the parable of the watchful householder, terminated already in Q by the summons, 'Be ready therefore, for the Son of Man will come at an hour you do not imagine.' This admonition was the closing one of a series of sayings concerning the parousia of the Son of Man. It is noteworthy that there is no cogent reason to dispute, in the case of any of these sayings (Matt. 24.27, 39, 44 and par.), their issuing from Jesus' preaching.[1]

The saying in Matt. 24.44 and par. speaks of the coming of the Son of Man as briefly as possible. Attention is directed to the behaviour which will be suitable in view of that well-known fact. It is emphasized that the hour at which the Son of Man will come is unpredictable; hence the admonition to watch: he may be coming at any hour, immediately or later, just like the thief in the night.

The preceding comparisons do not directly express the conclusions which the hearers ought to draw. The implicit exhortation is conveyed appropriately by Matt. 24.44 and par. It is obvious that these sayings belong together.

[1] Cf. Excursus VI, pp. 329ff., for the discussion of the view of Vielhauer, 'Gottesreich'.

(4) *The promises: Luke 12.8f. and par.; Matthew 10.23; 19.28*

(a) **Luke 12.8f. and par.** In the saying parallel to Luke 12.8f., namely in Matt. 10.32f., the name Son of Man is replaced by the 'I' of Jesus. The reasons for which Matthew omitted this name here will be discussed later.[1] Today most scholars agree that the form which discriminates between the 'I' of Jesus and the Son of Man is the more original one. 'No church would have invented at a later time a theology making a distinction so foreign to the feeling of the church, i.e. between the person of Jesus himself, and that of the future judge.'[2]

The structure of the saying is constituted by the direct correspondence between the attitude towards Jesus *on earth* and the attitude of the Son of Man *in the future*. We shall therefore examine the two parts of the saying separately, first the significance of the attitude on earth towards Jesus (a), then the significance of the future attitude of the Son of Man (b); after that we shall investigate the correlation of both parts (c).

(a) Each of the parts of the double saying begins in the form of a fixed general rule: 'Whosoever confesses to me . . .; whosoever denies me. . . .' Thus it does not apply to an isolated occurrence but to the behaviour of everybody. This emphasizes all the more the unequalled claim of the 'I' which confronts everyone in this rule of behaviour. The claim of this 'I' is fully elucidated by the term confession denoting the positive attitude to him, and by the term denial denoting the negative attitude. This does not sound as if anybody at his discretion might either enter into a relationship with this 'I' or keep away from him in unconcerned indifference. The alternative offered is either confessing or denying this 'I'. There is already a relationship established between each one of the hearers and this 'I'. What is left to the hearer is his personal attitude, be it a positive or a negative one, renouncing or denying this relationship.

The positive attitude towards Jesus in the synoptic texts, such as the Son of Man saying in Matt. 19.28, is repeatedly termed 'following'. Following always means attachment to the person of Jesus. The

---

[1] Cf. Chapter II C II 3 c, pp. 89f.

[2] Otto, *Kingdom*, p. 163. Cf. Bultmann, *Tradition*, p. 112. A different view in Bousset, *Kyrios*, p. 7. Linguistic evidence also argues for an early origin of this form of the saying in Q. Instead of the accusative of the person we find ἐν τινι ὁμολογεῖν, an Aramaism. Cf. Arndt and Gingrich, *Lexicon*, p. 571, and the literature given there.

follower cannot attach himself by his own strength; he is called by Jesus to follow him. The one who calls always holds precedence.[1]

Jesus bestows on his own the fellowship with himself on earth.[2] Whoever confesses this fellowship must do so *before men*. They are opposed to a man's belonging to Jesus; their power urges him to deny Jesus. Whoever confesses Jesus has nevertheless to enter into the tension existing between Jesus and this generation. But there is a great promise connected with holding on to the fellowship with Jesus; before God's tribunal the Son of Man will confirm this attachment to be valid. How shall we understand this correlation?

(b) The heavenly scene of confession corresponding to the confessing on earth is scantily sketched, yet can be illuminated by apocalyptic texts.[3] At any rate it takes place before God's judgement seat in both Matthew and Luke.[4] We read from Rev. 3.5, 'He who conquers shall be clad thus in white garments, and I will not blot his name out of the book of life; I will confess his name before my Father and before his angels.' The theme of this scene is the admission into the kingdom of God; the list of its citizens, the 'book of life', is read out. Now it becomes manifest who belongs to the heavenly community. At this moment the one who, according to the context, speaks to the church in Sardis, intercedes for the conquerors. He does not permit their names to be blotted out, but confesses them. Thus he is the advocate, the witness and the guarantor for those who have overcome. This is the same function which in Luke 12.8f. and par. the Son of Man exercises for all who confess Jesus. The Son of Man does not appear as a judge, but as the guarantor for the confessors who affirms in a legally binding manner that those who maintained fellowship with Jesus on earth are attached to him, to the Son of Man.

(c) The relation between the two scenes of confession, the one before men and the one before God, has been interpreted quite differently. Most often attention was directed primarily to the interdependence between Jesus on earth and the coming Son of Man. This

[1] Cf. Schweizer, *Erniedrigung*, pp. 7–19.

[2] For the concept of fellowship with Jesus cf. our Excursus III, pp. 306ff.

[3] Bornkamm, 'Wort Jesu,' p. 117, refers to Rev. 3.5. Compare in addition Dan. 7.10; I Enoch 47.3. Cf. Lohmeyer, *Apokalypse*, p. 34. On Luke 12.8b cf. Luke 10.20.

[4] In Q the phrase 'before the angels' may have been used in order to avoid the name of God, cf. Klostermann, *Lukas*, p. 134. Conzelmann, *Theology of Luke*, p. 173 n. 3, supports this view by his exposition of Luke's angelology. Cf. also Schrenk in *TWNT* V, p. 987 n. 259.

emphasis is not in accordance with the structure of the saying. The saying is not intended to assert the *identity* of Jesus with the coming Son of Man. It rather is concerned with the promise which Jesus gives to the confessors who maintain fellowship with him on earth that the validity of this fellowship will be confirmed by the Son of Man before God's throne. The primary concern of the saying thus is the continuity of the fellowship with Jesus on earth with the fellowship in heaven which bestows salvation. The correlation of the two parts of the saying is a *soteriological* one.

The deduction of a Christological relationship from this soteriological correlation certainly suggests itself—and even the consideration of the Christological relationship as the fundamental one. Then the attention is led from the gift of fellowship to the giver of fellowship who is recognized to be the same both on earth and in heaven. This deduction is not merely a modern view. Undoubtedly the post-Easter community believed from the start that the coming Son of Man would be none other than Jesus. This conviction tended towards recognizing a *Christological* relationship between Jesus and the coming Son of Man in the saying in Luke 12.8f. and par. Taking this into consideration, it is surprising that the community preserved the discrimination between the 'I' of Jesus and the coming Son of Man. The preservation of this discrimination is intelligible only on the assumption that it was handed down in stereotyped Son of Man sayings of Jesus whose authority protected it from being modified.

The sayings in Luke 12.8f. and par.; Mark 8.38 and Matt. 19.28 have given rise to the widespread opinion that Jesus considered himself the *filius hominis designatus*.[1] If this were not the case, how could he have promised that the fellowship with himself would be confirmed and continued (Matt. 19.28) by the Son of Man? But this argument is not cogent. The fellowship of following into which Jesus summons pertains to the coming of the kingdom of God. In Jesus' preaching the coming of the kingdom of God and the coming of the Son of Man appear to have been announced in a parallel manner. In view of this parallel we can realize that Jesus could indeed promise to those who by following him prepare themselves to respond to the coming of the kingdom that they will be attached to the future lord of the kingdom, to the Son of Man. In giving these promises Jesus appears to have pointed away from himself and spoken of the Son of Man as of someone different from himself.

---

[1] Otto, *Kingdom*, p. 219, speaks also of the *filius hominis praedestinatus*.

Jesus' preaching does not convey the meaning that he considered himself to be the Son of Man *designatus*. If he did, why should he have concealed it?[1]

It is precisely to this critical question that the theory of the concealment of the Son of Man seeks to provide an answer. Dibelius among others supported this theory and derived the idea of concealment from those 'conceptions . . . according to which the primal man did not live and die as a man, but as a half-divine being existed in heavenly concealment with God only to be revealed at the end of a whole series of world ages. . . . However the idea of the concealment of the Son of Man provided the first Christians with the key that unlocked for them the earthly life of Jesus. For, finally, the earthly life of Jesus, its ignominious end, and all that was repugnant and humiliating in the historical existence of Jesus, still belonged to this concealment.'[2]

Against this argument we must, however, raise the following objections.

1. The concealment of that *Urmensch* (primal man) is considered to be a concealment in heaven, as Dibelius rightly states. But what right is there to transfer that idea of a concealment in pre-existence to the life of Jesus on earth?[3] We cannot find anywhere in the synoptic Son of Man sayings the idea of a pre-existence of the Son of Man in heaven. But this idea of a heavenly being concealing himself in an alien existence on earth is prerequisite for the theory of the Son of Man's concealment on earth.[4]

2. In the synoptic sayings we do not find a single hint which

[1] Otto, *Kingdom*, p. 220, states: 'But it was not, and according to the logic of Enoch's Messianism it simply could not be, his calling to teach the secret of his person.' We do not dispute the fact that for Jesus' hearers a deep secret shrouded his figure. But since Jesus, as Otto himself states, did not teach this secret, thus never gave expression to it, it is a highly disputable procedure to append to this secret by means of the 'logic of Enoch's Messianism' the reason for which Jesus is supposed to have devised it. It will be more advisable to keep to what is expressed in Jesus' preaching—so much the more as we do not find any authentic Son of Man saying of Jesus which clearly refers to the book of Enoch.

[2] Dibelius, *Jesus*, p. 89.

[3] Iber justly raises this objection in *Überlieferung*, p. 24 n. 127.

[4] For a different view cf. Staerk, *Soter* II, pp. 415f. Mark 14.62 is referred to in order to prove that the primitive community had adopted the apocalyptic idea of pre-existence. But even if the idea of pre-existence were present in Mark 14.62—which in our view (see above) it is not—this saying would not prove that the idea of pre-existence was present in Jesus' preaching; for it can be observed that the Son of Man sayings in Mark were extended secondarily by means of apocalyptic elements.

implies that the Son of Man's activity on earth was an activity in concealment. This idea of activity in concealment is undoubtedly present in that material which belongs to the sphere of the Marcan theory of the Messianic secret, but it has never been admitted into the sayings concerning the Son of Man.[1] Dibelius supposes that the idea of concealment can be found at any rate in *one* of the Son of Man sayings, namely in Matt. 8.20 and par.: 'Thus it was possible for Jesus to speak in such a way as to suggest the contrast between the obscurity of his indigent earthly existence and the glory of the "Man" from heaven, the contrast and at the same time the connexion, for the needy life belongs to the concealment of the Son of Man and points to the future.'[2] But the saying mentioned does not contain a single word about concealment. Even in Q the saying is already addressed to a man who is willing to follow Jesus. It aims at making clear to this man by the example of Jesus what following means: homelessness amongst men, detachment from all earthly ties, even from relatives and friends.[3] Thus the saying is not concerned with the tension between the Son of Man's life on earth (in concealment) and in his future glory, but with the tension between Jesus and men into which each follower must enter; for 'a disciple is not above his teacher' (Luke 6.40, cf. Matt. 10.24).

3. Here that question must be raised which is fundamental for an interpretation of the sayings concerning the Son of Man: may we simply pass over the fact that for all the synoptic sayings on the Son of Man's parousia the heavenly Son of Man belongs entirely to the *future*? May we depend on the image of a divine being's course on earth which offers an intepretation of why this being was not acknowledged on earth, as was his due, in spite of his divine origin? We would be led by this pattern if we interpreted the Son of Man saying in Luke 12.8f. primarily from a *Christological* point of view, pre-supposing in it a statement of the identity (however it might be understood in detail) of Jesus and the coming Son of Man. We have seen that the structure of the saying is constituted not by an identity of persons but by the identity of an attachment both on earth and in the future world which imparts *salvation*. It seemed probable that it

[1] Because of their concept of sovereignty, the Son of Man sayings did not need the idea of concealment; this will be shown below in a summary in Chapter V, cf. also Chapter VI.

[2] Dibelius, *Jesus*, p. 91.

[3] Cf., e.g., Matt. 10.34–39 and par. Our exegesis of Matt. 8.20 and par. is given below in Chapter III A I c, pp. 120ff.

was this soteriological structure which the saying had in Jesus' teaching. Hence we may not interpolate the community's conviction that Jesus was the coming Son of Man into this saying as if it were Jesus' own understanding of his identity. Jesus' promise that the fellowship of his disciples with himself would be confirmed and continued by the Son of Man is clearly evident; that Jesus, however, drew any conclusions from it with regard to the relationship of his person to the coming Son of Man looks natural to our thinking, but cannot be supported by any evidence from the text. The differentiation between the 'I' of Jesus and the Son of Man supports the opposite proposition. All we can say with certainty is that according to Jesus' own understanding the fellowship which he grants to those who follow him pertains to the coming of the kingdom of God and hence will be confirmed by the Son of Man.[1]

The comparisons in Matt. 24.27, 37, 39 and par., the threat in Luke 11.30 as well as the admonition in Matt. 24.44 and par., and the double saying in Luke 12.8f. and par. (cf. Mark 8.38) constitute in Q the group of Son of Man sayings which issue from Jesus' preaching.

(b) **Matthew 10.23.** This saying is located in the Matthaean mission discourse (9.35–10.25). There is no parallel in Luke. Assuming that the mission discourse both as a whole and in its details is historical, i.e. pertains to a situation in Jesus' life, Schweitzer established on the foundation of 10.23b the following hypothesis: Jesus expected this aeon to come to an end before the disciples returned; therefore the experience that Matt. 10.23 was not fulfilled had to be understood as the first postponement of the parousia.[2] Against this hypothesis Kümmel rightly objected that v. 23 is not closely connected with the context and consequently must first of all be interpreted as an isolated saying. We are not convinced by his further arguments concerning the separation of 10.23a from 10.23b; for, though Kümmel disputes it,[3] τελέω may indeed here mean 'reach the end'.[4] Thus

---

[1] From this point of view the combination of the Son of Man and the Servant of Jehovah in the book of Enoch loses its importance for the exegesis of this saying, which does not concern itself with the identification of the person of Jesus with the Son of Man.

[2] Cf. Schweitzer, *Quest*, pp. 357ff.

[3] Kümmel, *Promise*, pp. 61f. For references on the controversy as to whether the saying originated with Jesus himself, see *ibid.*, p. 63 n. 137.

[4] Cf. Arndt and Gingrich, *Lexicon*, p. 818.

we shall expound the whole verse Matt. 10.23 as a single self-contained saying. According to this view the saying is an instruction and a promise to the disciples who meet with persecution while acting as missionaries in Israel. They are told to yield to the persecution and flee into other cities; for both in their missionary activity and in their flight they will not come to the end of the cities of Israel until the Son of Man will have come.

The range of space and time to which this saying addresses itself is strikingly narrow. It restricts its view to the cities of Israel and to only a brief span of time. Although definitely and primarily addressed to Israel, it is not likely that Jesus' word was limited to the region of the cities of Israel in this way;[1] we do not hear from Jesus' teaching that the kingdom of God would come upon these cities alone. This saying apparently speaks from the point of view of a quite early Jewish Christian mission. In a post-Easter missionary situation a prophetic saying may have been uttered which in extreme brevity spoke of the coming of the Son of Man. This prophetic saying was respected by the Christian community as a saying of Jesus. It is a promise to the missionaries which is full of consolation; they will not have to endure the persecution for long because the Son of Man will come soon.

This saying is of considerable importance in so far as it affords a certain insight into the earliest period of the Christian community within Judaism. We perceive a community of Christians in lively expectation of an imminent arrival: they hope for the speedy coming of the Son of Man. The imminent arrival of the Son of Man has become the subject of expectation. We further perceive a community of Christians acting as missionaries precisely because of this expectation. What is the message of the missionaries? According to the early sayings in the mission discourse in Matthew and in Luke they preach, 'The kingdom of heaven is at hand' (Matt. 10.7, cf. Luke 10.9). From the mission discourse in Matthew we cannot be sure whether the connexion between Matt. 10.23 and the sending out of the

---

[1] Manson, Sayings, p. 182: 'It reflects the experience and the expectations of the primitive Palestinian Church.' Taylor, Names, p. 29, does not maintain either that the saying issued from Jesus' teaching in its present version, but holds a different view about an earlier version which may have preceded the present one: 'It may well have been re-interpreted by Matthew in the light of the controversy regarding the Gentile Mission; but it is difficult to think that it was invented for this purpose.' We cannot very well ascribe to Matthew, however, the 're-interpretation' in 10.23, since this saying had become quite inappropriate to the situation of the community in Matthew's day. On the question of the formation of prophetic sayings compare Bornkamm, 'Die Verzögerung der Parusie', pp. 118f.

disciples for missionary activity is *historically* correct; but none the less we cannot doubt that the placing of Matt. 10.23 in this context is based on correct *reasoning*. For the conviction that the Son of Man will come speedily ought to give rise to preaching that 'The kingdom of God has come near to you'. The missionaries in Palestine after Easter appear to have continued to teach the message of Jesus.

It is a significant fact that this prophetic saying addressed to the earliest Christian missionaries formally accords with the Son of Man sayings of Jesus. It is a promise attributed to Jesus on earth and thereby given his authority. The prophet hears the one who is risen in the words of the one who was on earth. The earthly one and the risen one both teach the same thing, the coming of the Son of Man, and teach it in the same way. This will be supported also by the saying in Matt. 19.28.

(c) **Matthew 19.28.** This saying is a promise to the disciples who are following faithfully that they will sit on twelve thrones and judge the twelve tribes of Israel. This statement obviously refers to the concept which we meet in I Enoch 108.12b: ' . . . and I will place each one on the throne of his honour.'[1] The promise is to be fulfilled when the Son of Man sits on the throne of his glory. An analogous concept also occurs at several places in I Enoch.[2] Thus in Matt. 19.28 traditional apocalyptic concepts prevail which were absent in all the Q sayings discussed above. In the three sayings in Mark, however, we observed a similar extension of Son of Man sayings by means of traditional elements. We shall observe it again in the editorial Son of Man sayings in the Gospel of Matthew. This formal similarity discourages us from considering the saying in Matt. 19.28 as an authentic saying of Jesus. Kümmel holds a different view: 'the saying which undoubtedly in this version of Matthew represents the more original form (as compared with Luke 22.28, 30) is in its essence a saying of Jesus, a promise to the group of the twelve, which represent Jesus' claim to win the whole nation.'[3] We agree with the

---

[1] Cf. also Rev. 3.21.

[2] 61.8; 62.2; 69.27; 45.3; cf. 55.4; 51.3.

[3] Kümmel, *Promise*, p. 47, cf. n. 95. The saying in Luke parallel to Matt. 19.28 complements our concept of fellowship through following Jesus by some important statements. Conzelmann in *ZThK*, 1952, p. 29 n. 1, maintains that the phrase 'in my trials' (Luke 22.28) does not denote 'past trials during Jesus' lifetime hitherto, but the present ones'. We agree with Kuhn's objection, cf. 'Temptation', pp. 269f. n. 51, that Luke here inserted a saying which he took from an earlier tradition,

statement that Matt. 19.28 is 'in its essence' a saying of Jesus in so far as the structure of the saying is indeed congruous with the Son of Man sayings in Luke 12.8f. and par. and in Mark 8.38. The disciples who are following Jesus *now* are given the promise that, at their *rebirth* into the fellowship with the Son of Man which means salvation, they will be rulers over Israel. A continuation of fellowship with Jesus in fellowship with the Son of Man is promised. This congruity with the stereotyped form of the authentic Son of Man sayings may, however, have been employed to link this saying up with the utterances of Jesus, and therefore is no proof of its authenticity. Bultmann justly emphasized that there are elements in this saying which pertain to the post-Easter community; the concept of the twelve's representing the community of the last days, the Church as the true Israel, appears to have been developed in the post-Easter situation or, strictly speaking, within the primitive Church of the earliest period.[1]

The concepts present in this saying do not support Kümmel's supposition either. The authentic sayings of Jesus conceive of the Son of Man in his relationship to those who confess Jesus as the guarantor, the witness and the advocate before God's tribunal. Matt. 19.28 no longer conceives of him in a judgement scene but in

---

as is evident from the parallel saying in Matt. 19.28. Kuhn, however, interprets the saying in Luke according to his view of Jesus' temptations to which we cannot assent. Nevertheless, if we accept Kuhn's correct suggestion and interpret the saying as an isolated element from an earlier tradition, we have to consider the temptations in relation to Jesus' lifetime in general. We saw above that belonging to Jesus involves entering into the tension between him and men (Luke 12.8 and par.), or this adulterous and sinful generation (Mark 8.38). Now we see from Luke 22.28 that those who follow Jesus must hold on to him all the way through his trials. The legacy in Luke 22.29 is appointed to those who fully take their share in the fighting. Kuhn illuminates Jesus' fight against temptations by means of the Manual of Discipline: 'It is God's war against Satan in which he (viz. Jesus) is God's warrior.' Cf. *op. cit.*, p. 111. The fellowship through following Jesus involves fighting to the end.

[1] Cf. Bultmann, *Theology*, pp. 48, 37. It can hardly be disputed that Jesus during his earthly activity had already summoned a group of 'the twelve' in particular. The pre-Easter summons 'is supported by the fact that the primitive Christian tradition unanimously calls Jesus' betrayer εἶς τῶν δώδεκα (Matt. 26.14, 47 *et passim*)' and that Paul 'names the δώδεκα beside Peter as the first witnesses of the resurrection (I Cor. 15.5)'; thus Rengstorf in *TWNT* II, p. 326 lines 1ff. Cf. also von Campenhausen, *Amt*, pp. 15–18, and Lichtenstein, 'Die älteste christliche Glaubensformel', pp. 53f. Notwithstanding the pre-Easter origin of the 'twelve', we maintain that the formulation of Matt. 19.28 originated in the primitive community.

that state of everlasting rule which is described in Dan. 7.14. The followers of Jesus now become the Son of Man's fellow rulers. This concept contradicts in a way the rejection of the request of the sons of Zebedee in Mark 10.35–45.[1] It is true that there is a statement in Jesus' preaching, 'yours is the kingdom of God' (Luke 6.20). But this possession of and share in God's kingdom which is simply stated in Jesus' preaching is depicted in Matt. 19.28 with the help of traditional features. The parallel rendering of this saying in Luke appears to have been aware of the contradiction. In Luke 22.30 the fellowship of salvation in God's reign is described as 'to eat and drink at my table', referring to the supper which is eaten; only after this follows the phrase from an earlier tradition about sitting on thrones and ruling the twelve tribes of Israel. Moreover, the promise is not given to the twelve but to all disciples who stayed with him throughout his temptations. Thus in the form of the saying in Luke it is precisely the particular limitation of the promise to the 'twelve thrones' which is missing.

All the considerations which we have mentioned above lead us to the following conclusion. Matt. 19.28 is an early post-Easter prophetic saying which like Matt. 10.23 has been formed in conformity with the authentic Son of Man sayings of Jesus. In the concepts implied in this saying, however, traditional elements of Jewish apocalyptic literature prevail. Thus the saying is out of harmony with Jesus' preaching, which hardly alludes to these elements, and also with the rejection of the request of Zebedee's sons. In the post-Easter logion the group of the twelve appears to have been treated with special distinction; their representing the Israel of the last days is authorized by the promise.

In Matthew the saying 19.28 occurs in a section dealing with the rewards for those who follow. Fellowship through following Jesus demands forsaking everything owned on earth (Matt. 19.27). The disciple exchanges earthly attachments for an attachment which will be confirmed in the world to come in the reign of the Son of Man.

II. Results: *The nature of the sayings concerning the coming Son of Man according to Q*

1. Two groups of Son of Man sayings must be distinguished within Q. The first group consists of authentic utterances of Jesus. The sayings belonging to this group are: the comparisons in Matt.

---

[1] Cf. also Mark 9.33–37. A different view in Kümmel, *Promise*, p. 47 n. 95.

24.27 and par.; 24.37, 39 and par.; the threat in Luke 11.30; the admonition in Matt. 24.44 and par.; the promise in Luke 12.8; and the threat in Luke 12.9.

The second group contains a comparison newly formed within the sphere of the Q tradition. It is the saying in Luke 17.28–30. We add to this group two sayings from the material peculiar to Matthew, namely the consolation in Matt. 10.23 and the promise in Matt. 19.28. Since these sayings both originated very early and move within the range of Palestine, we seem to be justified in adding them to the Son of Man sayings from Q.

The sayings of the second group, which according to our view were formed by the community, conform carefully to the structure of the authentic sayings of Jesus. This conformity is of special importance in the case of Matt. 19.28. This saying differentiates between the 'I' of Jesus and the Son of Man as clearly as Luke 12.8f. and Mark 8.38 do. We conclude from this that although the community had attained by now the Christological insight that Jesus himself would be the coming Son of Man, they retained the differentiating form of the authentic sayings of Jesus when forming a Son of Man saying of their own. Obviously it was because of this insight that the promise which Jesus gave on earth was respected. Thus even charismatic sayings of prophets in the primitive community were placed under Jesus' authority by forming them in conformity with his own utterances. Seeing him as the risen one, the wording and formulation of his teaching on earth were used to bear witness that he who is risen and he who was on earth are one.

2. The Son of Man sayings from Q are obviously close to Jesus' teaching. There are two great themes which belong intimately together, the threat of judgement and the promise of salvation. They are not at all dominated by an apocalyptic visionary strain. What is predominant is the direct claim laid by the teaching upon the hearer. Threat and promise demand of him that he should confess Jesus and his teaching. There is no description of the figure and activity of the Son of Man. By brief indications the hearer is shown what the Son of Man's coming means to him. The Son of Man sayings convey to the hearer both summons and assurance. He is committed to the fellowship of those who in following Jesus are prepared for the coming of the kingdom.

3. The details present in these sayings are scanty with regard to the concept of the Son of Man. His coming or his day is spoken of;

in Luke 17.30 it is the day when the Son of Man is *revealed*. Merely to point to it is sufficient for a threat. For the promise given to the confessor for the world to come, however, it is necessary to elucidate somewhat more distinctly the action of the Son of Man. He will be the guarantor before God's tribunal for those who followed Jesus; to · them he will impart his rule over the heavenly Israel.

It may also be inferred that the appearance of the Son of Man is conceived of as a universal and cosmic event. Everyone will be able to perceive it as they will the inrush of God's reign. Like this inrush the appearance of the Son of Man will terminate the former course of events on earth. The coming of the Son of Man and God's entry upon his reign are the same event.

4. In Jesus' sayings concerning the Son of Man the apocalyptic elaborations are radically cut down. The fanciful features in their glowing colours which powerfully attracted the imagination of the seers of apolcalyptic visions have disappeared. Salvation and perdition are held forth to the hearer, but are never elaborated. As the distance from Jesus' preaching increases, an increasing number of traditional features are channelled secondarily into the Son of Man sayings of Jesus or of the community. This process is evident in Matt. 19.28; Mark 8.38; Mark 13.26f. and Mark 14.62. At the inlet through which the Son of Man concept was primarily channelled into the synoptic tradition, i.e. in Jesus' teaching, this concept shed the features of apocalyptic elaboration and theology. There is not even an allusion to a pre-existence of the Son of Man. In Jesus' teaching all importance is attached to the fact that God's reign stands at the door, that the Son of Man will come. The hearer is to recognize the signs of this imminent event. Threat and promise admonish him to draw his conclusions.

5. In the sayings from Q the sovereignty of the Son of Man is of an altogether heavenly transcendent nature without any limitation. It is impossible to speak of the Son of Man's humility. He is not subject to any of the restrictions of earthly existence. It is not he who endures the tension over against sinful men; they do not oppose him; it is Jesus' claim that they reject. Whoever confesses Jesus must do so before men who wish to enforce their claim upon the confessor. The only possibility left to the disciple is detachment from men who hinder him from following Jesus. On entering into this tension over against men the disciple is given the promise that the Son of Man will take his part before God.

6. In the Son of Man sayings from Q, Jesus does not appear as the lowly one either. In spite of the fact that he is among men when proclaiming his message, he summons with supreme authority and utters the exorbitant claim that he should be confessed. An eternal decision is inherent in this claim. Only the one who follows him will participate in the salvation of the Son of Man. Jesus thus proclaims fellowship with him to be the gateway to salvation.

It is of decisive consequence to recognize the fundamental function of the *soteriological* correlation within the sayings concerning the Son of Man. The promise of attachment to the Son of Man in the future rests on attachment to Jesus on earth (confessing, following). None of the sayings discussed so far expresses a *Christological* relationship, i.e. the identity of Jesus with the coming Son of Man.

The process of recasting sayings concerning the Son of Man or forming them anew can be observed not only in Q but also in Mark. There are traces of the same process in the editorial material and in the material peculiar to Matthew's and Luke's Gospels respectively. We shall now follow these traces in order to find the way in which the Son of Man concept was modified within the synoptic tradition.

C. THE SAYINGS CONCERNING THE COMING SON OF MAN IN THE GOSPEL OF MATTHEW

All the sayings in Mark concerning the coming Son of Man have been taken over into Matthew's Gospel; and all the sayings from Q, so far as we can infer from the comparison with Luke, have been taken over as well.[1] In addition there occur in the material peculiar to Matthew two early sayings, Matt. 10.23 and 19.28, and two sayings which appear to have been formed later, Matt. 13.41 and 25.31. Thus it is certain that Matthew wished to make a link with the sayings which he found ready formed. He did not transmit them unmodified, however. Therefore we shall examine the modification or the new form of the sayings in Matthew in order to find out in which way he conceived of the coming Son of Man.

I. Matthew's relationship to previous Jewish and Christian tradition as the basis for the evaluation of his taking over the Son of Man sayings

It has long been recognized that the Gospel of Matthew must be considered as representative of those circles which maintained a close connexion with Jewish tradition. This connexion also involved the

---

[1] On Luke 17.28–30 cf. above Chapter II, p. 49 n. 1.

apocalyptic traditions. In none of the other Gospels is such an abundance of traditional elements used in reproducing sayings about the Son of Man. Was there, so to speak, a renaissance of the apocalyptic spirit within certain spheres of the synoptic tradition?

The Gospel of Matthew must be considered from a second and equally important point of view. Whilst in the Gospel of Mark not much space is granted to the discourses of Jesus, they occupy a lot of space at prominent points in the Gospel of Matthew. Matthew was determined to link up with the rendering of the teaching of Jesus in Q.

Apocalyptic tradition on the one hand and Jesus' teaching on the other could have become rivals in Matthew's work. Or did he succeed in combining the two spheres of tradition? A similar combination was suggested in the Gospel of Mark, where a Son of Man saying which had issued from Jesus' teaching (Mark 8.38) was extended by means of apocalyptic material and material taken from the Scriptures.

What did Matthew's connexion with Jewish tradition mean for his reception of the Son of Man sayings? This is part of a series of problems pertaining to the theology of Matthew on which a few remarks will be necessary.

Not only in his interpretation of the Son of Man sayings but particularly in his interpretation of the Law, Matthew seeks to link up with the Jewish tradition of the scribes. By linking up with it, however, Matthew modifies this tradition. This has been demonstrated by G. Bornkamm in his essay 'End-Expectation and Church in Matthew'.[1] The traditional understanding of the Law is altered to a more extreme and thorough one. Jesus appears as the exponent of the traditional Law which he expounds with supreme authority both *sub specie principii*, in the light of God's will which shines in his creation, and *sub specie judicii*, in the light of the universal world judgement. Into this framework set up by the tradition Matthew inserts the specifically Christian elements. The outward appearance of the tradition is left untouched, but there is a new spirit within.

In the expectation of the End the concept of judgement which is firmly anchored in the tradition is of far greater importance in Matthew that it is in Mark or Luke. This concept also is modified. Matthew not only stresses the universal significance of the judgement but also its special significance for Christians. The judgement not

[1] Cf. Bornkamm, 'Matthäus als Interpret der Herrenworte'.

only concerns the lawless and the unrighteous but also the Christian community. It is the disciples above all, the Church on earth, who will have to face the judgement. The members of the community are not elect because of their membership; for many are called, but few are chosen. The separation of the disciples one from another at the future judgement becomes the central concept which, as Bornkamm has demonstrated, dominates the Gospel of Matthew throughout.[1]

Thus the question of what will be done with the tares amongst the wheat appears to be of central significance for Matthew's theology. This accounts for his prevailing interest in the judicial function of the coming Son of Man. In order to impress even upon the members of the community that the future separation of those who have stood the test from those who have not will be a dividing within the Church, it is essential to elucidate the criteria of this future judgement. We shall see below how this is achieved by Matthew's depicting in detail the judicial activity of the Son of Man. The modification of the Son of Man concept thus prognosticated needs to be examined in the individual sayings.

II. Analysis of the sayings concerning the coming Son of man in the Gospel of Matthew

(1) Newly formulated sayings: Matthew 13.41 and 25.31

(a) **Matthew 13.41.** In the section Matt. 13.36ff. the parable of the tares amongst the wheat is interpreted allegorically. As convincingly demonstrated by Jeremias, the formulation of this section must be ascribed to Matthew.[2] The first part offers the principles for an interpretation of the parable. A description of the judgement at the end of this world is then evolved from these principles of interpretation whose allegorical nature has practically vanished (vv. 40bff.).

The Son of Man is conceived of in three ways. Firstly, in v. 41 the activity of the Son of Man as the Judge of the world is described in the traditional manner; he sends his angels to execute the verdict. Secondly, the phrase 'basileia of the Son of Man' is introduced in v. 41b. This basileia is not the kingdom over which the Son of Man will rule after the verdict has been executed. It is a provisional institution. The righteous will be gathered out of this temporary basileia into the eternal basileia which according to v. 43 is the kingdom

---

[1] Cf. Matt. 24.40f.; 24.45–51; 25.1–13; 25.14–30; 22.14 et passim.
[2] Cf. Jeremias, Parables, pp. 64ff.

of the Father.[1] According to v. 41b both the righteous and the unrighteous are living together in the *basileia* of the Son of Man, not yet separated. Thus it appears to exist in the period before the end of history. Thirdly, in v. 37 the Son of Man is conceived of as acting on earth, sowing the good seed (cf. Matt. 13.24).

What is the relationship between these variant forms of the concept of the Son of Man? It can hardly be supposed that they were put together incidentally; the careful arrangement and shaping of material throughout the Gospel of Matthew forbid this supposition.[2]

The *parable* of the tares amongst the wheat (Matt. 13.24-30) is intended to restrain human impatience. 'The disciples are to know about this eschatological significance of the present, but they are not to make the separation themselves. . . .'[3] *Matthew's interpretation* (13.36ff.) follows another course. It aims at depicting impressively the coming judgement of the Son of Man. Hence it does not enter into those features of the parable which denote that the lord of the harvest restrains his servants from separating the tares and the wheat prematurely. It merely draws attention to the fact that in the field of this lord both good seed and evil tares are growing together and that both of them will be facing the separation at the harvest. Matthew's interest appears to be concentrated on depicting this separation in lurid apocalyptic colours. The strict interpretation of the parable which is restricted to vv. 37-40 appears designed in order to prepare for the impressive depiction of the final judgement. From v. 41 onwards the interpretation passes over into a prophetic proclamation describing the judgement by means of traditional apocalyptic elements—not without dwelling at some length on the pitiable fate of the 'sons of the evil one' (cf. v. 38).[4] Thus the intense interest of

[1] In another passage the definitely final *basileia* is also called the *basileia* of the Son of Man; this is Matt. 16.28, deviating from the original in Mark. It should be noticed, however, that in Matt. 16.28 it is not a *state* of divine reign that is spoken of but its *coming*. In Matt. 20.21 the kingdom of the eternal rule of Jesus is called 'your *basileia*'. Even though the name Son of Man is not mentioned here, the *basileia* appears to have been attributed to Jesus because of his being the future Son of Man.

[2] By pointing to the careful and systematic work manifest in this Gospel, Bornkamm convincingly demonstrated that Matthew must have been an 'individual figure' in the history of primitive Christian literature. Cf. 'Expectation', pp. 50f. n. 5.

[3] Kümmel, *Promise*, p. 136.

[4] The marked emphasis on the Son of Man's function as a judge also occurs in I Enoch. Thus, e.g., in 61.8 and 62.3ff. the Son of Man's enthronement and his function as the judge are placed together. In chapters 53 and 54, too, the Son of Man's judgement on the unbelievers is strongly stressed.

Matthew in the future separation amongst those who, not yet separated, are found together in the one field predominates over the primary purport of the parable. The elaboration of the contrasting future destinies confronts the hearer with the serious question whether he belongs to the 'sons of the kingdom' or to the 'sons of the evil one' instead (v. 38). This question will be answered at the gathering out of the *basileia* of the Son of Man.

What is meant by this *basileia* of the Son of Man? It is distinguished from the *basileia* of the Father by the fact that only the righteous live in the Father's reign. The *basileia* of the Son of Man is the field which needs to be cleared of the tares at the harvest. By this distinction we are led to conclude that it is the Church on earth which Matthew has in view here. The evidence which Bornkamm adduces showing that the element of the future separation plays a leading role in Matthew's concept of the Church supports this conclusion. According to Matthew even the disciples, even the Church, will be involved in the judgement. Consequently they are confronted with the question whether they are the people bearing the 'fruits of God's reign'.[1] Thus the same Son of Man who will send his angels to execute the verdict is the Lord of the Church (13.41). Indeed, the Church actually appears to be the sphere on which the Son of Man's judging and separating of the good from the evil will be concentrated and to which it will be restricted. The only striking point is that there is no other passage beside this one in which Matthew speaks of the Son of Man in this way.

In v. 37 an action of Jesus on earth is ascribed to the Son of Man. Jesus' teaching is the Son of Man's sowing of the good seed.[2] The seed which the Son of Man sows[3] is personified; the good seed are the sons of the *basileia* (13.38). The difficulties which arise for the interpretation of the sower in the parable obviously do not disturb Matthew. He makes the Son of Man appear as the one who effectively sows the *logos* of the *basileia* and in this way places his own in the *basileia* as the good seed. The distortion of the picture heightens the impression of the Son of Man's effective power: the one who teaches places in the *basileia* with full authority.

---

[1] Cf. Bornkamm, 'Expectation', p. 44.

[2] In Matt. 13.19 the *logos* of the *basileia* is spoken of in deviation from the text in Mark.

[3] As stated by Billerbeck I, pp. 476ff., the children of the *basileia* are related to the *basileia* by way of attachment. According to Matt. 13.37 they are sown, i.e. summoned and effectively planted, into this attachment by the word of the Son of Man. Cf. also I Enoch 62.8; Matt. 8.12.

The mention of the sower in v. 37 refers back to the editorial introduction to the parable of the tares amongst the wheat in Matt. 13.24. During the course of the interpretation the interest shifts from the sowing to the two sorts of seed which exist in the field side by side, good seed and tares. In spite of their growing together in the field, a completely different destiny will come upon each of the two sorts at the harvest. It is this destiny which Matthew wishes to depict with an impressive warning in the extension of the interpretation from 13.41 onwards. All attention now is directed to the field and what is growing in it, to the Christian community. It is seen as a provisional institution on earth, not to be identified with the eternal *basileia* of the Father (13.43) but related to it. For the Church will be confronted by the judgement and therefore does not exist contemporaneously with the Father's reign.[1] Hence every hearer is confronted with the question whether he is but a tare amongst the wheat growing in the field which is the community, and consequently whether he will be burned in the fire at the judgement, or whether he belongs to the sons of the *basileia* and consequently is included in the promise that they will be placed into the future *basileia* of the Father. Quite obviously Matthew steps beyond the sphere of the traditional concepts of the coming Son of Man as well as beyond the sphere of concepts in the teaching of Jesus when conceiving of the Son of Man as the sower on earth. We need not be surprised at his usage, since Matthew knew those sayings concerning the Son of Man's activity on earth in the present and with full authority which we below shall observe in Mark and in the Q tradition.[2] Thus on the one hand Matthew conceives of the Son of Man as the coming Judge of the world, while on the other hand he designates Jesus teaching on earth as the Son of Man.

The concept of the Son of Man being the Lord of the *basileia*, i.e. of the Church on earth, is unique within the whole synoptic tradition. It cannot be doubted in Matt. 13.41;[3] the Son of Man will gather the sons of the evil one out of his kingdom. We shall have to consider

[1] Bornkamm has demonstrated in 'Expectation', p. 44, that the Church is seen in the same way in Matt. 16.17–19.

[2] We shall deal with the connexion between the sayings about the activity on earth of the Son of Man and Matt. 13.37 in Chapter III B I 2 b, p. 135.

[3] Bornkamm, 'Expectation', p. 44, rightly interprets Matt. 13.41 in conformity with Matthew's concept of the Church in this way. Bultmann, at variance, regards the *basileia* of the Son of Man as an entity which will appear at his parousia; cf. Bultmann, *Tradition*, p. 187 n. 3.

carefully, however, the aspect under which the Son of Man is seen as the Lord of the Church. He is the Lord of the Church inasmuch as he sows the good seed, i.e. places the sons of the *basileia* in it. He is the Lord of the Church also inasmuch as he executes the final judgement on it. But he is not seen as the one who rules over the Church during its existence on earth; he is not seen as the exalted one. He is not the Lord acting in the Church. When we speak of the Son of Man under this aspect two periods within the history of salvation become visible, namely the period of Jesus' teaching on earth which is the period of summoning into the *basileia*, and the period of the judgement to come. The intermediate stage which obviously became the pivot of the primitive Christian community's interest very soon, namely the guidance of the Church by the Spirit, is not visible under this aspect.

We should note also the correlation between the variant forms of the concept of *basileia*. The teaching on earth places the good seed in a *basileia*, i.e. in a domain which is under a certain rule and which implies a certain fellowship. This domain will be transferred into the *basileia* of the Father. The correlation here is thus the same as we perceived in the Son of Man saying on confession. As it is promised that attachment to Jesus on earth will be confirmed by the Son of Man, likewise the good seed in the *basileia* are promised that they will be included in the *basileia* of the Father.

(b) **Matthew 25.31.** In the pericope Matt. 25.31ff. we notice a change in the name of the one who is the judge. In v. 31 he is named Son of Man, in vv. 34–41 he is named *basileus* and must be addressed as *Kyrios* by those who answer him.[1] As Jeremias conjectures, we may infer from this change that Matthew himself stylized v. 31 as an introduction. This is supported by the close relationship of v. 31 with Matt. 16.27,[2] and also by the relationship of the last part of the verse with Matt. 19.28. Bultmann's surmise that the description of the world

[1] Johnson in 'Jesus and First Century Galilee', p. 84, says: 'In my opinion, there are a few cases where the evangelists have used Son of Man as a substitute for Messiah—notably in Matt. 25.31, where the introduction has Son of Man but the pericope elsewhere speaks of the king (vv. 34, 40).' In a context like this, however, we have no reason to regard the name Son of Man as a substitute for Messiah, as this name is present in Matt. 13.41ff. and 16.27. Bultmann, *Tradition*, p. 124, conjectures that the name Son of Man has taken the place of the name King which was used to denote God.

[2] Cf. Jeremias, *Parables*, p. 142.

judgement in vv. 32–46 issued from Jewish tradition[1] is rejected on the whole by Jeremias in agreement with Manson, since this pericope contains 'features of such startling originality that it is difficult to credit them to anyone but the Master Himself'.[2] In so far as this point of controversy concerns our investigation it will be elucidated later. At any rate, it should be permissible to assume that the concept of a universal judgement on all nations by the *one* standard of love had already been conceived in Judaism.[3] Bultmann points out that a tension between Christians and non-Christians does not yet exist in Matt. 25.31ff. and that there is nothing specifically Christian about the moral of the pericope.[4] There may be, as Bultmann conjectures, something specifically Christian in relating the good deeds or their omission to the Son of Man. Bornkamm clarifies this conjecture. The concept of a mild and merciful attitude towards the lowly which pervades the Gospel of Matthew attains a pivotal significance in Matt. 25.31ff. The judge maintains that it is he himself who does or does not receive the deeds of mercy done or not done to the least of his brethren.[5] Thus we may state with regard to the Son of Man concept in Matthew that the Son of Man who is also Judge and King enters into a relationship of solidarity with those who are in need of mercy, with the humblest on earth, and will judge according to the standard of this relationship. This statement requires more careful substantiation.

We recall from Mark 8.38 and par. and from Luke 12.8 that the Son of Man will declare his solidarity with those who confessed to Jesus on earth. No such direct confession of Jesus is mentioned in Matt. 25.31ff.; no direct relationship to Jesus is apparently presupposed in this pericope. Any consideration of fellowship with Jesus is avoided, and the immediate attitude toward the least of his brethren in this world seems to have been made the standard for those who will inherit the *basileia* (Matt. 25.34). But are we permitted to assume that the person and the activity of Jesus are of no consequence for the purport of the pericope which seems to confront all mankind immediately with the Son of Man/Judge/King?

The context of this pericope conveys the meaning that it is Jesus himself who describes the judgement, who makes the King speak in

[1] Cf. Bultmann, *Tradition*, p. 124.
[2] Manson, *Sayings*, p. 249; cf. Jeremias, *Parables*, p. 145.
[3] Cf. Billerbeck IV, pp. 199ff.
[4] Bultmann, *Tradition*, p. 124.
[5] Cf. Bornkamm, 'Expectation', pp. 23f.

this way. Moreover the Christian hearer cannot help perceiving that the *criteria* applied by the Son of Man/Judge/King are the reflection of Jesus' messianic activity on earth as it is portrayed by Matthew.

None of the other evangelists conceives of Jesus' confirming the validity of the Law to the same extent as Matthew (5.17–19; 23.1ff.). Jesus does not issue a *nova lex*, but confirms the Law which has been handed down.[1] Yet if Matthew's concepts were confined completely to the traditional Law, he would have been compelled to make the Judge/King of the world use this Law as the basis of his judgement in 25.31ff. In Jewish apocalyptic literature the righteous are indeed measured against the Law and on that basis receive admission into the *basileia*, the fellowship with the Son of Man which means salvation. If in our pericope mercy were considered to be the summary of the purpose of the Law, it would be analogous to the rabbinic concepts of deeds of mercy being the standard for judgement.[2] It would follow from this analogy that in our pericope the Judge of the world would be conceived of as the one who judges all mankind according to the Law which can be summarized as mercy. A description thus confined to the tradition could ignore Jesus altogether.

This interpretation is decisively contradicted, however, by the fact that in Matthew the concept of Law and the Christology are not separated but, as Bornkamm proves,[3] closely correlated. On the one hand Jesus' teaching is supported in every part by references to the Law; his authority is not declared independently. On the other hand it is Jesus alone who fulfils, i.e. interprets with full authority penetrating through the formal legal regulations, the basic and essential will of God. It is Jesus' interpretation which reveals the 'weightier matters of the law, justice, mercy and faith' (Matt. 23.23). To do these three constitutes the righteousness which exceeds the righteousness of the scribes and Pharisees (Matt. 5.20). On these grounds Matthew is able to demonstrate this righteousness which exceeds, as Bornkamm explains in his comment on Matt. 23.23,[4] in both its aspects, namely in its attachment to the law which is fulfilled, i.e. fully interpreted through Jesus, as well as in its attachment to the person and the way of acting of the Messiah. It is no longer

---

[1] On this and on what follows cf. Bornkamm, 'Expectation', pp. 32ff.

[2] Cf. Jeremias, *Parables*, p. 144, and n. 15. Egyptian parallels in Klostermann, *Matt.*, pp. 205f.

[3] Cf. Bornkamm, 'Expectation', pp. 32ff.

[4] Cf. *ibid.*, p. 26.

possible to realize the fulfilment of the Law and the perfection of righteousness in any other way than by following Jesus.

From the triad justice, mercy and faith, mercy can be singled out in order to denote in Jesus' mouth the genuine will of God, the weightiest matter of the Law, its essence (9.13; 12.7). The commandment of Jesus to be observed by the disciples is mercy (5.7; 18.33). This rule made by Jesus will be adopted by the Son of Man/Judge/King for the supreme judgement of the world. In relating to himself what men do or do not do he is, as Bultmann states, conceived of as a more individual personality[1] and moreover reflects features of Jesus' teaching and person.

In this connexion it is necessary to speak of features of Jesus' *person*. According to Matthew, Jesus does not only *teach* mercy but also, calling men in his meekness and lowliness, *is* the one who shows mercy towards the least of his brethren (Matt. 11.28–30). What he himself is determines what following him is like. Following him attaches the disciples to the way of acting and to the person of the one who is meek and lowly, the one who fulfils all righteousness. Thus for Matthew mercy and attachment to Jesus through following him—which pertains to the righteousness which exceeds—are not separate from each other but bound up with each other.

The correlation which we have been considering casts a new light on the Son of Man/Judge/King in Matt. 25.31ff. His declaration of solidarity does not ignore the person of Jesus by universalizing the Law but is analogous to the attachment of the disciples to Jesus through following him. The criteria which are set for following Jesus are the criteria which will be used by the Son of Man/Judge/King at the final judgement.

Hence we cannot with Jeremias[2] look upon this verdict as addressed only to the heathen, the disciples being instead asked at the final judgement whether they overcame 'by open confession of him (Matt. 10.32f. and par.) and obedience (Matt. 7.21, 22f. and par.), by readiness to forgive (Matt. 6.14f.) and merciful love (Matt. 5.7) and by endurance to the end (Mark 13.13 and par.)'. Our pericope does not supplement the criteria for the judgement on the disciples by criteria for the judgement on the heathen. It rather deals with the one judgement which lies ahead for all, inclusive of the disciples, as Matthew emphasizes frequently enough (Matt. 19.30; 20.16; 21.43).

[1] Cf. Bultmann, *Tradition*, p. 123.
[2] Cf. Jeremias, *Parables*, pp. 144f.; similarly Manson, *Sayings*, p. 249.

Thus the standard of mercy is not another one besides those mentioned by Jeremias, but sums them up, according to Matthew. The standard used by the judge of the world to denote the disciples' righteousness applies also to all mankind.

Is this statement of ours contradicted by the surprise of the righteous: Lord, when did we see you hungry . . .? Should the disciple not recognize that it is Jesus who confronts him in the person of one of the least of his brethren? In Matt. 25.40 the Son of Man/Judge/King obviously addresses those whose love of their neighbour was not a looking for a reward, not a side-glance at the lord, not a saying 'Lord, Lord', but doing the Father's will (Matt. 7.21).

From this point of view we now have to consider Matthew's inserting the name Son of Man into the introduction of the whole pericope (25.31). Unquestionably Matthew depicts the coming of the Son of Man by means of traditional features. The Son of Man comes in his *doxa* (cf. Mark 13.26; 8.38); all the angels come with him (cf. Mark 13.27; 8.38); he sits down on the throne of his glory (I Enoch 61.8; Rev. 20.11). Matthew forms this introductory verse thus by the same means and with the same material used for extending the three Son of Man sayings in Mark by reference to Scripture and apocalyptic literature. The reference to the *coming* of the Son of Man common to most of the synoptic sayings concerning the Son of Man is used by Matthew as the introduction to that scene on which his interest is concentrated, namely the scene of enthronement and judgement which conforms to apocalyptic concepts (I Enoch 62.2).

Regardless of how closely Matthew links up with traditional concepts, he does express the close correlation between the Son of Man/Judge/King and Jesus. This is obvious when Matt. 25.31ff. is compared with Matt. 7.21–23. Matt. 7.21 demands that those who are attached to Jesus should *do* the will of his Father in heaven. Matt. 7.22f. predicts that the disciples who in that day before the Lord of the judgement count on the deeds which they have done in Jesus' name out of a supposedly obedient relationship with him will be told that the Lord of the judgement never knew them, never was in fellowship with them. What will then be recognized before the judge of the world as doing God's will? The positive answer may be seen from Matt. 25.31ff.; mercy toward one of the least of his brethren means fellowship with Jesus. At the universal judgement he will profess that he knew those who have done accordingly (Matt. 7.23).

Here the names *Kyrios* and Son of Man are for Matthew located close together. The Lord of the judgement who is *appealed to* is named *Kyrios* (25.37, 44); the Lord of the judgement who is *spoken of* is named the Son of Man. He is *depicted* with the features of the Son of Man concept.

(c) **Summarizing consideration** of the newly formulated Son of Man sayings in the Gospel of Matthew. The two Son of Man sayings newly formulated by Matthew (Matt. 13.41 and 25.31) display new elements of such importance that they deserve a detailed recapitulation. Thereby we shall gain an idea of the main elements of the Son of Man concept in Matthew.[1]

1. In Matt. 13.41 and 25.31 the name Son of Man no longer occurs in brief logia in which it occurred in Q. Both passages in Matthew offer a description of the Son of Man which is suited for use in preaching. The scantiness of details in the Son of Man sayings of Jesus is replaced by the wordiness of an apocalyptic description. There is no longer a mere continuation of Jesus' teaching.

2. Jesus nevertheless is presented as the one who pronounces the descriptions of the world judgement; he is likewise presented speaking of the Son of Man as of a different person—although for Matthew the identity of Jesus with the coming Son of Man is an established fact, as 13.37 proves most clearly.

3. For Matthew the designation Son of Man applies to Jesus under two separate aspects. The coming Son of Man, the universal Judge, is none other than Jesus; but Jesus, teaching on earth, is also designated Son of Man. Under these two aspects Jesus is the Lord of the Church, namely both as the coming Judge of the world who will gather the righteous from his *basileia* into the *basileia* of the Father, and as the teacher who by his word effectively sows the 'sons of the *basileia*'. Matthew does not mix these aspects nor does he combine them in a single statement. For him they are distinctly separate.

4. The correlation between Jesus and the Son of Man who is Judge of the world is expressed in different ways. According to Matt. 13.36ff. the sowing of the sons of the *basileia* by Jesus as the Son of Man acting on earth is done in preparation of the coming *basileia* of the Father. The sons of the evil one who will not be included in the *basileia* of the Father have been sown into the *basileia* of the Son of

---

[1] We shall still exclude Matt. 13.37, cf. Chapter II, p. 72 n. 2, i.e. we shall not yet discuss the connexion of this saying with the sayings concerning the activity on earth.

Man by the evil one himself. They will be weeded out by the angels of the Son of Man who is Judge of the world, whereas the sons of the *basileia* sown by Jesus will stand the judgement of the Judge of the world. Thus the Judge will confirm that Jesus is acting on earth with full authority. Those sown by Jesus' teaching belong to the Kingdom of God. According to Matt. 25.31ff. there is a somewhat different correlation between the Son of Man and the significance of Jesus on earth. The Judge of the world will base his verdict on the same criteria which Jesus imparted to his disciples for their conduct by his true interpretation of the Law. Thus the correlation here connects him who interprets the Law with supreme authority (the second Moses) with the Judge of the world. The joint emphasis on both Jesus' interpreting the Law on earth and the Son of Man's judging the world in the future is the distinguishing mark of Matthew's theology.

5. We can now find an answer to the question raised at the beginning. Does a renaissance of the apocalyptic spirit within the synoptic tradition dominate Matthew's concept of the Son of Man? Do the apocalyptic elements once more win preponderance? Or does Matthew succeed in combining Jesus' teaching on the coming Son of Man with the apocalyptic tradition? We cannot doubt that the apocalyptic tradition has gained *formal* predominance anew and threatens to choke the form of Jesus' teaching concerning the Son of Man. *Conceptually*, however, the apocalyptic material is put to an ancillary use by Matthew. He does not offer apocalyptic descriptions for their own sake. He is rather concerned with the kerygma summoning the disciples; he wishes to demonstrate to them the criteria of the coming judgement on the world so vividly that they will recognize the gravity of the hour by which the Church as well will be met. They are to see that the Judge of the world will pronounce his sentence in conformity with the Law which is in force in the fellowship of following Jesus. The Son of Man/Judge of the world/King in Matthew bears not only the features of transcendent sovereignty but also of Jesus' deeds of mercy: 'as you did to one of the least of these my brethren, you did to me' (Matt. 25.40).

6. How does Jesus appear in these sections in Matthew? Nowhere as the lowly one. When in 13.37 he is named the Son of Man who sows the sons of the kingdom, an act of unique sovereignty is denoted. The *exousia* of Jesus is confirmed in the Son of Man's judgement of the world; the criteria of Jesus' deeds of mercy are in force in the judgement

on the world, the commandment given by Jesus to his own which is to be observed in following him proves to be the ultimate measure. Jesus' merciful attachment to the least of his brethren is indeed an act of supreme authority.

The two sections Matt. 13.36ff. and 25.31ff. imply a clear idea of the creative development of the Son of Man concept in the Gospel of Matthew. In order to see whether this statement of ours holds good or not, we shall confront it now with Matthew's revision of the sayings which he took over from Q and Mark.

(2) *Matthew's revision of the Son of Man sayings received from Mark*

(a) **Matthew 24.30f.** reproduces Mark 13.26f. We have stated above that Mark 13.26f. is the only Son of Man saying in Mark which appears within a genuinely apocalyptic context. Here we have to note the way in which Matthew modifies and supplements this saying.

Matthew inserts 'then', i.e. at a certain stage of the eschatological events, 'the signs of the Son of Man' will appear in heaven. With regard to 24.3 and to what is further said in 24.30, we may presume that the sign in heaven is the Son of Man himself whose appearance will be obvious to all.[1] His appearance which can no longer be over-looked by anyone is the sign of judgement which provokes the mourn-ing of all the tribes of the earth. Thus the purport of Mark 13.26f. is considerably altered. There it is obviously a 'sign of rejoicing' (Wellhausen) which is seen in the Son of Man's coming. Matthew on the contrary induces the opposite impression; in face of the judgement which is about to begin mourning breaks out.

A similar combination of Dan. 7.13 and Zech. 12.10, 12, 14 with a similarly 'inexact rendering of the Zechariah passage' occurs in Rev. 1.7.[2] It is of no consequence here whether Matthew drew from

[1] Cf. Chapter II B I 2, pp. 52ff., on Luke 11.30; also cf. Luke 11.16. Billerbeck I, p. 956, mentions that in PᵉsiqR 36 (162a) the light appears as the sign of the Messiah; similarly in PᵉsiqR 36 (161a). It is not impossible that when speaking of the appearance of the Son of Man in his *doxa* (Matt. 24.31) a phenomenon of light connected with his figure is thought of as being his *sign* in which he *reveals* himself (Luke 17.30). These conjectures are, however, uncertain. Probably this must be considered primarily as a reminiscence of Test. Lev. 18.

[2] Klostermann, *Matt.*, p. 195. The combination of quotations in Matt. 24.30 is discussed by Krister Stendahl in *The School of St Matthew*, Uppsala, 1954, pp. 212–15. His conclusion is as follows: 'However, the combination of Zech. 12 and Dan. 7 makes it necessary for us to assume that very combination to be a common matter, either understood as a *"verbum* Christi" or as belonging to the church's basic teaching in Christology. It is somewhat hazardous however to transform this

a source which he had in common with Rev. 1.7 or whether the
similarity of the passages is founded on a direct dependence of one
on the other. We merely have to note that Matthew, deviating from
Mark, stresses the negative aspect of the Son of Man's appearing,
thus emphasizing the judgement. In comparison with Rev. 1.7 it is
indeed surprising that in Matt. 24.30 no use is made of just that part
of the verse in Zech. 12.10 which could have pointed most precisely
to Jesus, namely, 'him whom they have pierced'. It is intelligible
that Rev. 1.7 does include this part in the quotation. Does Matthew
silently add this phrase, thereby identifying the crucified one with
the Son of Man? In that case the omission is hardly intelligible.
Obviously he does not wish to express the unity of the Son of Man
with the crucified one. He rather wishes to emphasize the judgement
which will be initiated by the appearing of the Son of Man. It is his
special concern to demonstrate what the judgement will mean to the
community and all the world, i.e. to demonstrate that it has a meaning not only for the unrighteous outside the community. By adopting
from Zechariah the allusion to those 'who pierced him' he would have
limited the threat of judgement to enemies and exempted the community from the judgement. This exemption would have conflicted
with his concept of judgement. Hence we suppose that Matthew
intentionally omitted that part of the quotation which alluded to the
one who was pierced. Should this be true, he cannot have wished to
intimate the cross to be the sign of the Son of Man.[1] The evangelist
is interested only in the threat of the Son of Man's judgement on all.
In his modification of Mark 8.38 he likewise expresses this concept

---

rather loose agreement so far as the words are concerned into the basis for a
hypothesis of a collection of testimonies or even of a Book of Testimonies' (p. 214).
If it is thus established that the combination of Zech. 12 and Dan. 7 was a customary one, and if we consider in addition to this that both Rev. 1.7 and John 19.37
adopted the allusion to the one 'whom they have pierced' from Zechariah (according to the text of Theodotion and Aquila as opposed to the LXX), it is all the
more remarkable that Matthew does not reproduce this allusion to him who was
pierced in his combination of quotations. Since as even stated by Stendahl there
is no support for the conjecture that Matthew followed an earlier tradition when
forming this text, we must allow for an arrangement according to the first evangelist's own intentions. For the Jewish interpretation of Zech. 12.10ff. cf. Sjöberg,
Verborgener Menschensohn, p. 267. The Jewish sources testify to an eschatological
interpretation of this passage, though without reference to a suffering Messiah.

[1] The omission of the allusion to him who was pierced corroborates our observation that in the synoptic sayings the coming Son of Man is correlated primarily not
with the crucified Jesus but with Jesus teaching with full authority. There will be
further arguments for this in Chapters III and IV.

of a judgement according to every man's works which applies also and above all to the disciples (Matt. 16.27).

Matthew deviates from Mark by inserting the pronoun 'he will send *his* angels' (24.31). By this tiny addition the sovereignty of the Son of Man is underlined. Matthew does not miss the opportunity of adding a supplementary traditional feature to the mention of angels. Thus in v. 31 in contrast to Mark 13.27 he equips the Son of Man's angels with the apocalyptic trumpet (cf. IV Ezra 6.23; Ps. Sol. 11.1; I Thess. 4.16; I Cor. 15.52).

This demonstrates that Matthew intentionally modifies Mark 13.26f. in conformity with his specific concept of the Son of Man's coming in judgement, and contributes more traditional apocalyptic elements to a further extension.

(b) **Matthew 26.64.** This passage presents us with subtle questions. There are only slight modifications noticeable in the external form, but they may be symptoms of material differences from Mark 14.62. These slight emendations at least indicate that Matthew reflected to some purpose on the connexion between the titles of sovereignty put forward in the examination before the Sanhedrin.

In Mark 14.62 Jesus' confession of his right to the titles of Christ and Son of God ('I am') is followed more or less smoothly by the announcement of the visible coming of the Son of Man as a threat to the members of the Sanhedrin. Matthew instead causes a break by means of the adversative particle πλήν in combination with 'hereafter', distinguishing and differentiating the tenses. Thus Jesus' claim to the titles of Christ and Son is more sharply contrasted with the announcement of the Son of Man's coming. This results in an emphasis on the difference in time: now already Jesus lays claim to the titles of Christ and Son of God; in the future there will be the act of sovereignty of the coming of the Son of Man. The imminence of the future act now already modifies the significance of the scene before the Sanhedrin. The judges' rejection of Jesus in his claim to full authority turns the announcement of the Son of Man's coming into a threat to them.

In what direction does this 'hereafter' deviate from Mark 14.62? There is strikingly enough a parallel 'henceforth' inserted by Luke at the same place. Its purpose in Luke is evident. Luke in conformity with his specific concept of eschatology takes out the statement about the Son of Man's parousia and uses the 'henceforth' to express that what will be in force from now on is the new period of the history of salvation, the period of the Church, the period in which the Son of Man is exalted to God's right hand as the Lord of the community (cf. Acts 7.56). The parousia appears to have withdrawn into remoteness.[1]

Do we have to understand Matt. 26.64 in this way? Is the 'hereafter' used here as well to indicate the beginning of a new period in salvation history? Must we recall here Matt. 13.41 where the Church is called the *basileia* of the *Son of Man*? In solving this problem we shall be aided above all by the other passages in which Matthew uses the 'hereafter' in a somewhat parallel way, namely 23.39 and 26.29.

In Matt. 23.39 there is an emphatic 'hereafter' differing from Luke 13.35, 'undoubtedly an addition of Matthew'.[2] Kümmel propounds the opinion that Matt. 23.37–39 is an independent saying of Jesus from the tradition, which proves 'that Jesus expected a considerable period between his death and the parousia', for 'as this absence is considered in Matt. 23.38 as a punishment, no close temporal connexion between the death and parousia can be assumed'.[3] Bultmann on his part takes Matt. 23.37–39 as being originally a proverbial saying which Jesus is made to utter, v. 39a alone being a Christian addition.[4] Where to locate this saying within the history of tradition is a point of difficult controversy. Here, however, we are only concerned with establishing what Matthew intended when adding 'hereafter'. In the present form of the Gospel of Matthew this added 'hereafter' emphasizes that the occasion for Jerusalem to place herself under Jesus' protection has finally expired; Jesus' death means the end of the city.[5] What remains in the future is but the arrival of him who will come in the name of the Lord. Thus Matthew closely correlates the situation which at this moment is finally terminated, definitely closed, i.e. no longer open to Jesus' saving activity, but solely open to the judgement to come, with the parousia of Jesus. We do not think it possible to say that here an interval between parousia and resurrection was conceived of. Kümmel can assert this only by rather indirect deductions which cannot be proved to be Matthew's views.

[1] Cf. Conzelmann, *Theology of Luke*, p. 84 n. 3.
[2] Kümmel, *Promise*, p. 81 n. 209.
[3] Kümmel, *Promise*, p. 82, cf. 81f.
[4] Cf. Bultmann, *Tradition*, pp. 114f.
[5] In Matthew, v. 39 sounds as though it is giving the reason for v. 38.

Matt. 26.29 should be considered in a similar way. Slightly modifying the text in Mark, Matthew inserts the more precise distinction of the tense that Jesus will not drink 'hereafter' of this fruit of the vine until the day when he will drink it anew with the disciples in the Father's kingdom. The emphasis is placed on the one hand on the fact that the present moment means a definitive termination—and it is precisely this fact that Matthew wishes to stress by his insertion—on the other hand on the promising prospect of a new fellowship in the *basileia* of the Father. The interval is not spoken of here in such a way that we need to consider it a direct presupposition.

Thus we can see from the way in which the 'hereafter' is used in Matt. 23.39 and 26.29 that Matthew connects with it a meaning which considerably differs from what is meant in Luke 22.69. Luke is concerned with the beginning of the period of the Church which has been opened by Jesus' condemnation, execution, and resurrection; hence he does not point to the coming of the Son of Man. Matthew is concerned with the irrevocable, conclusively final ending which was fixed by the attitude of the members of the Sanhedrin in this episode; hence he points to the coming of the Son of Man to whom the seat at God's right hand is due, i.e. who in view of this attitude cannot be expected to come otherwise than in judgement. In this orientation on the parousia the real nature of the scene is revealed.

Jesus' 'hereafter' separates his present claim to the title of Christ and Son of God from the future sovereignty of the Son of Man in his parousia. By this 'hereafter' Matthew terminates the time of Jesus' activity as the King meek and lowly[1] and as the Son of God obediently identifying himself with the least of his brethren. In the first words of Matt. 24.64 Jesus openly acknowledges the titles of Christ and Son of God which according to Matthew's concept accompanied him on this road of humility. This now is the end of the road: 'But I tell you, hereafter you will see the Son of Man seated at the right hand of power and coming on the clouds of heaven.' Here the lowliness of Jesus who is rejected by his judges is correlated with the manifest sovereignty of the Son of Man which will be visible to the eyes of all. It is, however, the future sovereignty becoming effective at the parousia.

(c) **Matthew 16.27.** This passage depends loosely on the last part of the double saying on confession reproduced in Mark 8.38 (cf. Luke

---

[1] Cf. the pericope of the entry into Jerusalem in Matt. 21.1ff.

12.8f.; Matt. 10.32f.); however, it omits the first part of the saying and completely recasts the second. Matthew was free to proceed thus, since he had already offered the saying on confession in 10.32.

We notice at first that Matthew transformed the structure of the saying into a sweeping announcement of the Son of Man's coming: 'For the Son of Man will come . . .' In its context, however, this is a weighty announcement which serves as conclusive support at the end of a long passage.[1] It is preceded by the sayings on following through suffering (16.24–26) which on their part are preceded by a section which Matthew arranged differently from Mark, namely Peter's confession, which in Matthew is followed by the promise to Peter that this will be the foundation of the Church (16.18f.). This in turn is followed by the announcement of suffering with the subsequent rebuke to Peter which in spite of its severity does not cancel the promise. Matthew gives this passage an eschatological emphasis by pointing to the coming of the Son of Man who will judge each man according to what he has done. By this connexion with the purport of the preceding passage the concept of the Son of Man is also affected. The Son of Man's judgement according to works is announced in reference to the members of the Church. The Church which has been given the full promise in 16.18f. is as an immediate consequence placed under the law of suffering while following Jesus as the one who goes before (16.21).[2] While Peter at Caesarea Philippi, rebuking Jesus for his readiness to suffer, relinquishes his place amongst his followers,[3] the faithful disciple holds on to Jesus when following him through suffering. Terminology which expresses this following is concentrated in 16.24–26. But it is announced to those who follow that this course of following is also destined to be submitted to the Son of Man's judgement according to works. This judgement will finally

---

[1] Matt. 16.27 is formulated in a way which makes this verse the reason for the preceding summons of the disciples to follow Jesus.

[2] It is worth noting that Matthew in 16.21 alters the text of Mark. According to Mark 8.31 Jesus speaks of the coming suffering of the *Son of Man*; according to Matthew *Jesus the Christ* shows to his disciples that he must suffer. Thus Matthew does not attribute the *suffering* of Jesus in particular to the name Son of Man. Yet he uses the name Son of Man quite pointedly and again at variance with Mark in the formulation of Jesus' question in 16.13, 'Who do men say that I the Son of Man am?' We shall see in a detailed discussion of Matt. 16.21 and 16.13 in Chapter IV B 3, pp. 150f., that in this passage Matthew perceives in the name Son of Man the *sovereignty* of him who immediately afterwards will proclaim the period of his Church.

[3] Is there a play on words intended in the double ὀπίσω μου in Matt. 16.23–24?

bring to light whether the disciple belongs to the good seed or to the tares amongst the wheat.[1]

Thus Matthew here uses the stereotyped reference to the Son of Man in the manner which we already observed in the Son of Man sayings from Q, namely in order to elucidate an actual situation on earth. The concept of the Son of Man, however, appears to have been valuably developed. The Son of Man's function as judge is emphasized and made fundamental; 'then he will repay every man according to what he has done.' This is an element which occurs in Ps. 62.13; Prov. 24.12; Ecclus. 32.24; and also, clearly referring to the Son of Man, in I Enoch.[2] It does not occur anywhere else in the synoptic Son of Man sayings. Matthew joins this traditional element with his concept of the Church, thus giving it a special significance; the coming of the Son of Man to judge every man according to what he has done applies in particular to the disciples and *what they have done*.[3] Another useful development of the concept is the stress on the Son of Man's independence. This appears most clearly in Matt. 16.28, where the *basileia* of God (Mark 9.1) is declared the *basileia* of the Son of Man. Matt. 16.27, 'with *his* angels', accords with this stress on the independence.

The correlation between Jesus' lowly course through suffering (16.21) and the Son of Man's coming in sovereignty and power to judge (16.27) and to bring the *basileia* of God (16.28) which is established in the text in Matthew is more clearly distinguishable here than in Mark. Mark, to be sure, does lead the section up to the double saying on confession, thereby pointing to the Son of Man. But Matthew detaches the reference to the Son of Man from the narrower context of the saying on confession and makes it apply to the wider context. Thus the eschatological prospect of the Son of Man at the end of the section serves as a strong emphasis on the preceding statements and is brought into relation with the announcement of Jesus' suffering. Yet this relationship is not an immediate one; it is mediated by the concept of the disciples' following through suffering. They follow Jesus' path of suffering, a path which will end up at the judgement of the Son of Man where the promise will be fulfilled. Hence the correlation is a soteriological, not a Christological

[1] Cf. Matt. 13.36ff.
[2] Cf. in I Enoch 45.3 and chapter 46; cf. also Volz, *Eschatologie*, p. 303; Billerbeck I, p. 751.
[3] Cf. Matt. 7.21ff.

one.[1] It accords with this that Matthew, contrary to Mark and Luke, removed the name Son of Man from the first prediction of suffering in 16.21.

(3) *Matthew's revision of the Son of Man sayings received from Q*

There are further clues for Matthew's specific concept of the coming Son of Man in his revision of the Son of Man sayings from Q.

(a) In **Matthew 24.27, 37, 39** the threefold use of the phrase 'parousia of the Son of Man' stands out. Parousia is a Hellenistic term. It does not occur in Acts, and the primitive community 'probably did not possess a noun equivalent to it'.[2] But the term parousia 'in the technical sense of designating the *arrival* of Christ in messianic glory can be proved to have penetrated into primitive Christianity from Paul on'.[3] Within the Synoptic Gospels the term occurs exclusively in the above-mentioned passages in Matthew. Hence it must be assumed that Matthew here inserted a primitive Christian technical term.[4] This assumption is supported by the fact that Luke in the parallel passage uses the phrase 'day of the Son of Man'; here he appears to be closer to the wording of Q. Our assumption is also supported by the conclusive example of a secondary introduction of the term parousia by Matthew in 24.3. It is finally supported by the observation that the comparisons taken over in

[1] Contrasting with this, a Christological interest appears to have determined the placing of Luke 17.25 within the nexus of 17.24 and 17.26.
[2] Oepke in *TWNT* V, p. 865.
[3] Oepke, *ibid.*, p. 863.
[4] Thus also Kümmel, *Promise*, p. 38 n. 63. A. Feuillet in his essay 'Le sens du mot parousie dans l'évangile de Matthieu', in *The Background of the New Testament and its Eschatology*, Cambridge, 1956, pp. 261–80, advocated the following opinion: 'Matt. 24 and James 5.1–11 understand the Lord's parousia in the sense of the judgement on the Jewish people within history; in this they differ from the other New Testament writings, which apply the term parousia to the supreme manifestation of Christ at the end of the history of the world' (p. 278). According to this an *archaic* expression occurs in Matt. 24 which is not yet the Pauline and primitive Christian technical term for the concept of parousia (p. 279). This thesis is based on Feuillet's presupposition that our text of the Gospel of Matthew is a translation of an older Aramaic text (cf. Papias!). In this text an expression is supposed to have occurred bearing that archaic meaning (p. 279). Even from Matt. 24.3, however, it is evident that this thesis cannot be verified. We see from a comparison of the textual forms in Mark, Luke and Matthew that the editor Matthew used the term parousia in 24.3 to express that End which Mark in 13.5ff. described as the universal cosmic End; Matthew faithfully followed Mark.

Matt. 24.37 and 24.39 would be consistent if both in the simile and in the factual statement the 'days' were spoken of.

What motives impelled Matthew to introduce the phrase 'parousia of the Son of Man'? In the language of the primitive Christian community obviously the actual expectation of the coming of the Christ, the *Kyrios*, had been bound up with the term parousia. The term is prominently used in the exhortations pointing to the End, as can be seen from, e.g., I Thess. 2.19; 3.13; 5.23; II Thess. 2.1. The Son of Man sayings had already been hortatory in Q. Thus when he introduced the term parousia into the sayings from Q, Matthew confirmed that also according to his own view the reference to the coming Son of Man serves the purpose of an exhortation which understands eschatology as a direct summons and assurance, not as a wide-open space for apocalyptic imagination.

(b) In **Matthew 24.44** there are no noteworthy traces of revision; we have to note, however, its location in the context. Pointing in warning to the uncertainty of the hour in which the Son of Man will come, this verse concludes the short parable of the thief at night. This termination is an obvious parallel to v. 39b, which concludes the simile of the comparison in vv. 38 and 39a by a factual statement, simply repeating what has already been stated in the brief comparison in v. 37 which serves as a heading. Between the two sections, vv. 37–39 and vv. 43–44, is another short sequence of sayings which Matthew adopted from Q in a manner partly different from Luke; the conclusion, however (v. 42), was received from Mark 13.35. That according to the editorial method in Matthew this verse (24.42) is intended as a termination can be gathered from the parallel closing verse of the parable of the ten virgins (25.13).

Thus three parallel concluding verses occur in Matt. 24.39, 42, 44, their location at this place being essentially due to Matthew's editing. Twice the coming of the Son of Man and once the coming of the *Kyrios* is spoken of. The name *Kyrios* in 24.42 is obviously not determined by its use in the simile of the succeeding parable. The master of the house in the parable, who watches for the hour of the breaking in, is to be compared with the watchful disciple. The *Kyrios* in 24.42, however, is not a person in a parable but a name by which without a simile the fact is stated that he will come at an hour not yet determined. Hence the prospect of his coming admonishes to constant watchfulness. Used thus in an exhortation, the designation *Kyrios* becomes directly associated with the reference to the coming Son of Man. The meanings of the designations Son of Man and *Kyrios* converge when serving to designate the coming Judge of the world.[1] Bornkamm rightly noted that in the parables in Matt. 24 and 25 the term *the Kyrios* which at first designates the master of the household on earth immediately passes over from the simile into the factual statement; it then designates what can be considered the equivalent of what is designated by the title of the coming Son of Man.[2] The names Son of Man and *Kyrios* converge not only in the meaning of his coming at the parousia as judge of the world; there is another convergence of the two in Matthew. The name *Kyrios* is already attributed to Jesus on earth in so far as he acts miraculously as the merciful Saviour.[3] This is analogous to the two-fold attribution of the name Son of Man both to the one who is coming and to the one who is active in the present. Is this structural convergence due to the fact that the name *Kyrios* took this structure over from the name Son of Man which was rooted earlier in the synoptic tradition?

(c) In **Matthew 10.32f.** it is noteworthy that the name Son of Man which occurs in the parallel passage in Luke 12.8 is replaced by the 'I' of Jesus here speaking of himself. Bousset takes this passage as evidence of the secondary infusion of the title Son of Man into a saying of Jesus about himself.[4] Against this Kümmel in agreement with numerous exegetes[5] rightly maintains that Luke 12.8f. is to be regarded as original whilst Matt. 10.32f. is a Christian interpretation. It is surprising, however, that Matthew, who inserted the name Son of Man at several other places,[6] here omitted it. What caused this omission?

We have noticed that Matthew is particularly intent on depicting

---

[1] For the following cf. Bornkamm, 'Expectation', pp. 42f.

[2] Cf. also Matt. 7.21ff.; 25.11; 25.37, 44. Also in the parable of the faithful and wise servant and his opposite (24.45–51) Matthew insinuates by an addition (v. 51b) that he considers the *Kyrios* of the parable the Judge of the world. By the phrase 'there men will weep and gnash their teeth' (occurring six times in Matthew, once in Luke, namely in 13.28, which is parallel to Matt. 8.12 and hence from Q; but nowhere else in the Synoptic Gospels), Matthew implies clearly enough that in his view the punishment of the bad servant means that rejection which is the negative answering to admittance into the *basileia* (Matt. 8.11f.).

[3] Matt. 8.2; 8.6; 9.28; 15.22; 15.25 and elsewhere.

[4] Bousset, *Kyrios*, p. 7.

[5] Kümmel, *Promise*, p. 44. For the literature cf. also note 86.

[6] Cf. 16.28; 25.31; 13.36–43.

the Son of Man's function as the Judge. He is further intent on emphasizing that the *basileia* belongs to *him*, the Son of Man. Contrary to this intention the saying from Q on which Luke 12.8f. and Matt. 10.32f. are based obviously implies a situation in which the Son of Man is acting not as the independent Judge but as an intercessor or guarantor before the assize. Was this incongruity with his specific concept of the Son of Man Matthew's motive in replacing the name Son of Man by the 'I' of Jesus?

The formulation of Matt. 19.28 supports this. Matthew did not as a general principle (as we might be induced to think when combining Matt. 10.32f. and 16.27) abandon the differentiation between the 'I' of Jesus and his speaking of the Son of Man in the third person; he retained it in Matt. 19.28. The only conclusion which therefore remains probable is that the situation implied in 10.32f., in which the Son of Man is not acting as the Judge of the world, prompted Matthew to omit the name Son of Man and introduce the 'I' of Jesus instead. Matthew was all the more inclined to omit this name since he had already given a saying on the coming of the Son of Man in 10.23. That he likes to avoid repetition can be seen from another passage containing Son of Man sayings. The name Son of Man anticipated in 16.13 is not repeated in 16.21 in the first prediction of the passion taken over from Mark 8.31.

(d) In **Matthew 10.23** we cannot ascertain any traces of a specific revision by Matthew. We can deduce from Matthew's location of this early logion within the mission discourse certain elements pertaining to his concept of the Son of Man.

It must first be noted that Matthew reproduces the content of the mission discourse to the disciples in a very early form. They are to say nothing but 'The Kingdom of heaven is at hand'.[1] There are no directly Christological elements in this summary of the mission teaching. In emphasizing the imminence of the kingdom of God, it corresponds with the saying 'You will not have gone through all the town of Israel before the Son of Man comes' (10.23). The expectation of the End in the very near future and limited to the orbit of Israel appears to be in tension with Matthew's views elsewhere, since he knows the summons of the Risen One to make disciples of all nations (28.19f.). But for Matthew all emphasis obviously rests on the assur-

[1] Matt. 10.7; cf. Luke 10.9 and Mark 1.15 compared with Matt. 4.17.

ance, full of promise, that the Son of Man will come soon. This assurance is given in Matthew explicitly to the post-Easter community; the last part of the mission discourse from 10.17 onwards is no longer instruction for missionaries in particular but instruction for the Church as a whole.[1] Here we are told what the Church as a whole must be ready to endure. Corresponding to this, Matthew also incorporates logia from the apocalyptic stock of sayings of Mark 13 and from Q into the section 10.17–22.[2] These logia suggest the situation after Easter in general.

At the end of this last section Matthew now places the saying which has been transmitted to him. The announcement of the imminent parousia of the Son of Man is used to put the situation of the disciples in the right light. The saying conveys a great promise to one who is delivered up to the Sanhedrin, the synagogue, the heathen authorities (vv. 17f.); to one who has to give an answer at a trial (vv. 19f.); to him who in these things already experiences the tribulations of the End (v. 21); to one who has to bear the hatred of the Last Days for his confession of Jesus' name; to one who strives in order to endure to the end (22).

(e) In **Matthew 19.28** the moment of the Son of Man's sitting in the throne of his glory is denoted by the phrase 'in the regeneration'. This is a technical term also used by Josephus and Philo[3] which expresses the Jewish belief in the rebirth of the dead and the regeneration of the world.[4] This regeneration of the world is conceived of as taking place at the time of the Messiah, that is to say, it is a concept pertaining to the traditional Jewish eschatology. We cannot decide with certainty whether it was Matthew who inserted this technical term, since the saying may have been formed by the primitive community (see above). But comparison with Luke 22.28–30 suggests that we owe the interpolation to Matthew. The Son of Man is depicted here not as the judge but as the ruler in the sense of Dan. 7.13f. We may conclude from this passage that Matthew related his concept of the Son of Man to other comprehensive eschatological concepts. The 'regeneration' appears to be a universal event.

[1] Cf. Bornkamm, 'Wort Jesu', p. 110, especially 'Expectation', pp. 18f.
[2] Cf., e.g., Mark 13.9ff.; Luke 21.12ff.
[3] Cf. Arndt and Gingrich, Lexicon, p. 611. Professor Kuhn has called my attention to a corresponding phrase also in the Manual of Discipline iv.25.
[4] Cf. also Büchsel in TWNT I, p. 687; Bousset, Religion, pp. 280ff.

III. Main elements of Matthew's concept of the Son of Man

In Matthew's Gospel the form of the sayings about the coming Son of Man exhibits traces of a preceding process of assimilation. Matthew did not merely take over sayings transmitted to him in Q and in Mark (or an earlier original text of Mark?), but reached back independently to apocalyptic concepts which were either present already within the Christian community or drawn by him directly from Jewish sources. It is noticeable that Matthew did not, as was done in Mark 13.26f. and 14.62, formulate the sayings in correspondence with Dan. 7.13f.; the elements in the Son of Man sayings which are peculiar to him refer repeatedly to I Enoch.[1]

We observed the following specific features of the Son of Man concept in the sayings from this Gospel which we have discussed.

1. In making the reference to the Son of Man's coming serve the purpose of exhortation, Matthew follows Q. Matthew will, however, transfer the Son of Man sayings and their hortatory meaning from the narrower framework of an isolated logion into the wider context of carefully composed groups. Several times he endeavours to append to the concluding sections of long passages an eschatological emphasis. He prefers to achieve this by means of Son of Man sayings.[2] The eschatological prospect of the Son of Man elucidates the preceding text.

2. The strengthened link with apocalyptic tradition which we observed in Matthew apparently does not fetter him to an unmodified apocalyptic spirit. Matthew's descriptions of scenes concerning the Son of Man (25.31ff.; 13.40ff.) may, to be sure, conform formally to apocalyptic descriptions, but his prevailing interest is a specifically Christian one. To the members of the Christian community Matthew wishes to depict impressively and on a large scale the judgement by the Lord of the Church[3] which will face all disciples (16.27). The vivid depiction serves to display the criteria of the judgement. For Matthew these correspond exactly with Jesus' revelation of his Father's will (25.31ff.; 7.21ff.).

3. The same interest in confronting the community with the judgement by which it will be faced leads Matthew to emphasize in particular, in contrast to Mark and Q, the Son of Man's activity as

---

[1] We recognized this in Matt. 19.28; 16.27; 25.31; 13.41.
[2] On this compare the location of the following sayings in their contexts: Matt. 10.23; 16.27, 28; 19.28; 15.31ff.
[3] Matt. 13.41.

the Judge. In Matthew's view the Son of Man is the sovereign Judge and King who in his sovereignty declares by free mercy that the least of men are his brothers.

4. Because the Son of Man (who is also Judge and King) proclaims the same criteria of mercy towards the least of his brethren which Jesus taught as his own criteria, we perceive an insertion of Jesus' features into the concept of the Son of Man. It is striking that despite this insertion Matthew nowhere simply identifies Jesus with the coming Son of Man.[1] He always speaks of the Son of Man's parousia, nowhere of his return. In the parable of the faithful and wise servant and his opposite (24.45–51), which emphasizes the delay in the lord's return and to which an allusion to the judgement on the world is added, Matthew speaks of the *Kyrios* throughout, but nowhere of the Son of Man. At any rate the Son of Man is not identified with Jesus by expressly stating that the Son of Man's coming would be Jesus's return.

5. In one passage (Matt. 13.37 and 41) the Son of Man appears as the Lord of the Church. But even here, in contrast with the parable of the tares amongst the wheat with which it is connected, all interest is concentrated on the Son of Man's future activity as the Judge separating the tares from the seed. The stress is on his impending judgement which alone is authorized to dispose of the *corpus permixtum* nature of the Church. Thus the concept appearing here is immediately linked to the concept of the Son of Man as the coming Judge of the world. On the one hand the Son of Man, who alone is the Judge, is the Lord of the Church. On the other hand the Son of Man, who is the sower of the good seed, i.e. he who teaches on earth, is attached to the Church in a way which is related again to the coming judgement; for at the harvest the seed sown by Jesus as by the Son of Man acting on earth will be gathered from the field into the *basileia* of the Father by the Son of Man.

6. Matt. 24.42 and 24.44 demonstrate that the name *Kyrios* is used

---

[1] I.e. Matthew nowhere makes Jesus say, I am the coming Son of Man. Matt. 10.32f. certainly contains Jesus' promise that he will confess before his Father in heaven those who confessed him. We saw, however, that in Matthew's view this statement differs from a declaration by Jesus that he is the coming Son of Man/King/ Judge of the world. Of course, this is not to deny that Matthew did attribute to Jesus the rank of Son of Man. We only want to stress that even in the Gospel of Matthew the name Son of Man appears exclusive in Jesus' own pronouncements and that Jesus is nowhere made to pronounce that he would be the coming Son of Man. Thus the evangelist maintains the distinction between his post-Easter recognition and the utterances of Jesus.

with the same meaning as the name Son of Man for him who will come at the parousia. In addition to this the name *Kyrios* can be used to designate Jesus' works of mercy on earth in the same way as the name Son of Man can be used to designate Jesus' teaching on earth with full and effectual authority (13.37). If we take into account that in the Hellenistic community the title *Kyrios* chiefly denoted the Lord ruling the Church *at present* (i.e. in the interval between resurrection and parousia),[1] it is all the more conspicuous that there appears to have been no development toward that concept in Matthew's use of the names Son of Man and *Kyrios*.

7. It is evident that Matthew revised the sayings which he received from Mark and from Q from that point of view which we found in 13.36ff. and 25.31ff. The Son of Man's function as the Judge of the world is emphasized, his independence is stressed; the angels are called *his* angels (16.27), the coming reign of God is called *his basileia* (16.28). As compared with Mark and Luke, Matthew on the one hand intensifies the transcendent sovereignty and power of the Son of Man. On the other hand he intimates that the supreme Judge of the world will use the standards which Jesus teaches on earth as the fully authorized exponent of the Law. The correlation between attachment to Jesus on earth and attachment to the Son of Man before God which is stated in Luke 12.8f. and Mark 8.38 is modified in Matthew. Here the correlation is stated between the criteria which hold good before Jesus and those which hold good before the Judge of the world. Whoever by following Jesus is led to the righteousness that exceeds will find himself acknowledged by the Judge of the world.

D. THE SAYINGS CONCERNING THE COMING SON OF MAN IN THE GOSPEL OF LUKE

I. Luke's concept of eschatology as the basis for the evaluation of his taking over the Son of Man sayings

It has long been observed that in Luke, the evangelist of the Hellenists, 'the Jewish thought-world from which the New Testament arose fades away'.[2] The retreat of this specifically Jewish understanding can be seen from various points of view. For our study the comparison with Matthew is of particular importance. Luke does not

---

[1] Bousset, *Kyrios*, pp. 88f.
[2] Hauck, *Lukas*, p. 10.

emphasize the eschatological material as much as Matthew does. When comparing Matt. 24 and 25 with the parallel passages in Luke this is evident. But he does not dismiss the eschatological tradition; he takes over material from it and transforms this material. Conzelmann has demonstrated that Luke used material which had originally been shaped by a concept of imminent eschatology to express a new concept of eschatology. The nature and course of the events at the End is now determined by the concept of God's order of succession in time. This treatment of the traditional material rests on the following presuppositions. In Jewish apocalyptic the expectation of an imminent coming was a looking for a speedy deliverance. As time ran on this expectation necessarily turned to apocalyptic descriptions. The same thing happened in the primitive community. The postponement of the parousia extends the time and allows the old apocalyptic tendencies to intrude. This intrusion inevitably results in a tension between the eschatological starting-point and the spread of apocalyptic descriptions. Standing within this tension Luke offers instead of the concept of imminent eschatology his concept of God's ordered plan in the continuity of the history of salvation. The kingdom of God now becomes an entirely transcendent reign. What is actual in the present period of the Church is but an image of the reign by means of which the Christian way of life is perseveringly adjusted to the distant kingdom.[1]

This alteration of the concept of eschatology must be of consequence for Luke's concept of the Son of Man. Conzelmann rightly states that Luke's use of the name Son of Man largely depends on the original use in Mark. We have to question, however, whether Luke is still aware of the original meaning of the title or whether he conceives of the Son of Man according to his own ideas. Conzelmann maintains that there are neither positive nor negative clues for a specific Son of Man Christology in Luke.[2] We shall scrutinize this view as we proceed to examine the Son of Man sayings in detail. In the Gospel of Matthew we clearly recognized an intention to develop the Son of Man concept to some purpose. Did Luke in contrast to Matthew simply adopt the title Son of Man from the tradition? In that case there would be no useful development of the Son of Man concept specific to Luke. Or did Luke, conforming to his altered concept of eschatology, conceive of the Son of Man in an entirely new

[1] Cf. Conzelmann, *Theology of Luke*, pp. 95ff.; 131f.; 120f.
[2] *Ibid.*, pp. 170f.

way without knowing of the original purport of this title? In that case there would be no connexion with the preceding tradition in those passages where Luke, independent of sayings transmitted to him, speaks of the Son of Man in a way of his own.

II. Analysis of the sayings concerning the coming Son of Man in the Gospel of Luke

(1) Sayings dominated by Luke's formulation

(a) **Luke 21.36.** In Matthew the eschatological discourse of chapters 24 and 25 concludes with the description of the judgement on the world of the Son of Man/Judge/King. In Luke, too, the apocalyptic material of chapter 21 culminates in the summons to watch at all times with prayer 'that you may have strength to escape all these things that will take place, and to stand before the Son of Man' (21.36). It was not the original text in Mark that constrained Luke to conclude the discourse thus. In Mark the synoptic apocalypse ends not with a reference to the coming Son of Man but with a repeated summons to watch instead of falling asleep, since the final time is uncertain (13.33f.; 13.35); for the absent master of the house will come back suddenly (13.36). Expanding this summons beyond the more intimate circle of the disciples to apply to all, the discourse ends with the repeated rallying cry 'Watch!' (13.37). Luke when deviating from this termination of the discourse obviously referred to the Son of Man of his own accord. He replaced the whole final section Mark 13.33–36 by the section Luke 21.34–36. A kind of link with and reproduction of the text in Mark can be found, if anywhere, in the first words of v. 34, 'Take heed to yourselves . . .',[1] and in v. 36, 'Watch at all times . . .'[2] Yet it appears from the very summons to watch *at all times* that Luke understood in a different way even the words he linked up with.

There is a widespread consensus that Luke 21.34–36 is a late composition.[3] According to Jeremias the section is a late composition, though a revision of old material.[4] According to Bultmann it is 'a quite late Hellenistic composition with so characteristic a terminology, related to that of Paul, that it might almost be conjectured

---

[1] Cf. Mark 13.33, 'Take heed, watch . . .'
[2] Cf. Mark 13.33: 'Watch, for you do not know when the time will come . . .'
[3] Cf. Bousset, *Kyrios*, p. 6. Conzelmann, *Theology of Luke*, p. 134.
[4] Jeremias, *Parables*, p. 62 n. 76.

that Luke had used a passage from a lost letter of Paul or his followers'.[1] The accumulation of peculiarities of style in Luke 21.34–36,
however, forces upon us the conclusion that we owe the formulation
of this section mainly to Luke himself.[2] He used his specific terminology to express elements from various traditions. It is noteworthy
that he used the name Son of Man although he was not prompted
to do so by the elements of the tradition which he received. We
might infer from this association of the designation Son of Man with
a Hellenistic presentation of hortatory material that the meaning
of this designation had not completely disappeared in the area
dominated by Hellenistic language. Obviously Luke meant the
Hellenistic terms which he accumulated in v. 34 to express what in
the comparisons in Q concerning the coming Son of Man had been
expressed in the simile. Here as there the saying cautions against an
absorption in mundane activities; for to this absorption the Son of
Man's appearance will be an unwelcome shock. Correspondingly the
Q phrase of 'that day' (cf. Luke 17.22–30) occurs again in Luke 21.34.

Whilst 21.35 largely depends on Old Testament concepts,[3] 21.36
is a summary formulated by Luke. This assumption may be supported by the following arguments in addition to what has already
been adduced. (a) 'At all times' is an expression specific to Luke. It
accords with the 'always' in the editorial introduction Luke 18.1.
This expression intimates the concept of eschatology which takes into
account the long stretch of time between resurrection and parousia.
(b) Luke 21.36 displays the same technique in composition as 18.8b.
In both cases the same intention prompted the placing of the looking
forward towards the Son of Man at the end of the passage.[4]

In the reference to the Son of Man's coming in 21.36 we can
clearly recognize the tendency which caused the concept of imminent eschatology to be altered.[5] It is no longer that coming of the
Son of Man which may happen at the very next moment on which the
summons to watch is grounded. It is no longer the attitude in view
of the imminent End which is reflected. Now the emphasis is on watching and praying continually at all times, and on a manner of life
which may enable the believer to escape during the period of the
signs of tribulation which according to Luke's concept of eschatology

---

[1] Bultmann, *Tradition*, p. 119.
[2] Kümmel, *Promise*, p. 36 n. 56, collects the words and phrases in question.
[3] Cf. Klostermann, *Lukas*, pp. 204f.
[4] That the author himself is speaking in Luke 18.8b will be demonstrated below.
[5] Cf. Conzelmann, *Theology of Luke*, pp. 125–32.

do not yet indicate the End itself but only announce its approach.[1] In that period of the approaching End other men will perish in senseless terror and apprehension of future evil. But the Christians will then be enabled to raise their heads to recognize that the *basileia* is approaching and their deliverance is drawing near. They need to be prepared, however, by praying and watching at all times; otherwise they will not be able to endure all this and stand before the Son of Man.[2] Thus even in Luke, in spite of the altered concept of eschatology, the Son of Man is seen as the supreme figure at the ultimate End. Even according to Luke's view the believer will be faced by the Son of Man at the coming of God's reign.

Does Luke agree with Matthew in regarding the Son of Man chiefly as the Judge? Luke rather regards him as the intercessor and advocate. He obviously refuses to subordinate the angels to the Son of Man in 12.8f. and in 9.26. He suppresses in 21.27f. the statement in Mark 13.27 according to which the Son of Man sends out the angels. The angels are traditionally the court officials.[3] Since they are deliberately not placed at the disposal of the Son of Man, we may conclude that in Luke's view the Son of Man is not felt to be as the Judge and the one who executes the judgement, but rather as the advocate and intercessor of the Christians before God. The Son of Man thus is seen particularly in his relationship with believers. In his coming he will look for *faith* on earth (18.8b). In none of the sayings in Luke is the Son of Man mentioned as judging or acquitting.

We hinted above at the time-sequence into which Luke fits the Son of Man concept. The Son of Man belongs to God's transcendent reign which will come with certainty in the future and which already exists now in heaven (Acts 7.56). Luke does not depict the coming of the reign in chapter 21; he stresses the preceding signs and tribulations. In a similar way, deviating from the text which he received, he does not depict the coming of the Son of Man either (21.25–28; 21.36). He rather wishes to stress the connexion between the Son of Man in that transcendent reign and the believer on earth for purposes of exhortation. The Son of Man will be the advocate and guarantor of salvation only to those Christians who have continued in watching and prayer at all times.

---

[1] Cf. Luke 21.28 and 21.31.
[2] Cf. Luke 18.1 and 21.36.
[3] Cf. Volz, *Eschatologie*, pp. 276f.

(b) **Luke 18.8b.** This passage is considered by the majority of critical scholars to be a secondary addition.[1] Jeremias rightly notes the distinctively Lucan language and the use of the concept 'faith' reminiscent of Paul.[2] Luke 18.8b is an explanatory supplement added to the interpretation of the parable of the unjust judge. When we compare this verse 8b with Luke's introduction to the parable (18.1) on the one hand and with 21.36 on the other, the tendency which lies behind this supplement becomes visible. In both of the passages we are comparing there is the summons to continue in constant prayer. But while in 21.36 this summons is linked directly to the reference to the Son of Man, the parable of the unjust judge is set between the summons and the reference to the Son of Man. These two statements provide the frame which is Luke's own interpretation of the parable.

As rightly stated by Jeremias, the parable makes the hearer draw the conclusion *a minore ad maius* which is explicitly drawn in the interpretation in vv. 7–8a. Since even the unjust judge helps the widow in order to get rid of her troubling him, how much more will God speedily vindicate those who cry to him day and night, though he may 'delay long over them'.[3]

Unexpectedly the Lucan supplement to the interpretation in v. 8b directs the attention away from the vindication by God and focuses it on men. Instead of being assured that God will vindicate them speedily (v. 8a), they are now questioned; 'However—will the Son of Man find faith on earth when he comes?' Here again the altered concept of the Son of Man is brought out by Luke. The phrase about the Son of Man's coming does refer to earlier Son of Man sayings, but this coming is no longer conceived of in general as the coming of the judgement or of God's reign. Now the Son of Man's coming is in particular brought into an intimate logical relation with individual faith on earth.

What kind of faith will the Son of Man be looking for? The answer may be found in Luke's introduction to the parable of the unjust judge. To keep on praying and not to lose heart is a distinguishing mark of faith. The Son of Man will look for this behaviour on earth. We have here the only passage within the synoptic tradition in which the concepts of the coming Son of Man and of the Christian's faith are immediately linked to each other. We cannot say that a faith in the

---

[1] E.g. Bultmann, *Tradition*, p. 175.
[2] Jeremias, *Parables*, p. 84.
[3] Jeremias, *Parables*, p. 115.

coming Son of Man is spoken of. It is a faith in Jesus, in his person and his authority.[1] The coming Son of Man will look for that particular kind of behaviour which is distinguished by constant prayer on earth. 'What matters is to remain faithful, "to stand firm" in faith during all trials, above all during persecution.'[2]

(2) *Luke's revision of the Son of Man sayings from the Gospel of Mark*

The main statements in the Son of Man sayings in Luke 21.36 and in 18.8b accord with each other. Do these specific elements recur in the revision of the Son of Man sayings from Mark?

(a) **Luke 21.27** is formed in analogy to Mark 13.26. The following verse, however, Mark 13.27, which is part of the Son of Man saying, is replaced in Luke by a newly formed saying, 21.28. What was the motive for this alteration?

In chapter 21 Luke in general conforms quite carefully to the material provided by the apocalyptic discourse in Mark. But the small insertions, modifications and omissions which we can observe suggest a plan according to Luke's altered interpretation of the material. If Luke did revise 'according to a definite plan' here,[3] he must have altered Mark 13.26f. with a definite intention. In Luke 21.27 he adopts the announcement that the Son of Man will *then* be seen coming on (in) a cloud with power and great glory. But he understands this *then* differently from Mark, conceiving of eschatological time differently. In Mark's description in 13.24f. the cosmic catastrophe which leads to the end of the world coincides with the Son of Man's coming in heavenly power. Luke in 21.25f. avoids speaking of cosmic events that would bring about the end of the world. He rather speaks of signs in the celestial bodies and of men's senseless apprehension of what is impending. The events exciting their anxiety are not yet the End. They occur at that future moment after which the Christians are to raise their heads to recognize that their deliverance is near.[4] In Luke's view the incidents of 21.25f., 21.28 and 21.31 will take place contemporaneously and will mean but the announcement of the approaching kingdom and the coming of the Son of Man (21.27). The ultimate end will indeed be brought about

[1] Cf., e.g., Luke 7.1–10.
[2] Bultmann in *TWNT* VI, p. 217 lines 19ff.
[3] Conzelmann, *Theology of Luke*, p. 125.
[4] Conzelmann, *Theology of Luke*, p. 114: 'For the most part it is a time *in the future*, from the point of view of which the Kingdom is near.'

by the visible coming of the Son of Man; any depiction of it, however, is avoided by Luke (cf. 21.27; 21.36; 18.8b).

According to Luke 17.20b the coming of God's reign cannot be observed. What cannot be observed cannot be described either. Unlike Matthew, Luke does not describe any activity of the Son of Man; he simply omits Mark 13.27.[1] He does not depict what the angels do but in 21.28 brings out the hortatory implications of the prospect of the Son of Man's coming which brings salvation.

A small alteration remains to be discussed: in 21.27 Luke puts the singular in place of the plural 'in (or on) the clouds of heaven' as rendered in Mark and Matthew referring to Dan. 7.13. This alteration is often connected with Acts 1.9 (cf. 1.11).[2] Conzelmann conjectures that the number was altered in order to stress the parallel between the descriptions of ascension and parousia.[3] If so, this would be a passage in which a stereotyped element of the traditional concept of the coming of the Son of Man was modified by a specific element of the tradition concerning Jesus. Luke would have had the ascension in mind while reproducing the saying about the parousia of the Son of Man which had been influenced by Dan. 7.13.

(b) **Luke 22.69** when compared with Mark 14.62 exhibits some trenchant and intentional alterations. These show that Luke had a different conception of the Christological titles mentioned by Mark in the trial before the Sanhedrin. In Luke's account the Sanhedrin at first only asks whether Jesus is the Messiah; it does not ask whether he is the Son of God until later (v. 70). Jesus' answer to the Messiah question reveals his lowliness; the judges' disbelief covers up the validity of his claim to be the Messiah (v. 67b). That is why Jesus can neither tell them anything they would accept nor ask them any significant questions. Whilst Jesus cannot demonstrate his claim to be the Messiah, his announcement about the Son of Man goes far beyond the barriers erected by disbelief. 'From now on the Son of Man will be seated at the right hand of the power of God.' According to Ps. 110.1 the one who is seated at God's right hand will have his enemies put under his feet. Thus the complete reversal of the lowliness

---

[1] The omission of Mark 13.27 may also have had as its motive the fact that Luke maintains a specific angelology. The angels are immediately under the power of God, not under that of the Son of Man. Cf. Luke 12.8f. and Luke 4.13 with Mark 1.13.

[2] Cf. Klostermann, *Lukas*, p. 203.

[3] Conzelmann, *Theology of Luke*, p. 183 n. 1.

in which Jesus stands defenceless before disbelief is announced. From now on, from the stage of utmost humiliation onwards, the heavenly sovereignty of the one who is seated at God's right hand is in force. This is an irrefutable fact which, unlike the messianic claim, is raised above belief or disbelief. Luke consequently strikes out the prediction 'you will see' in favour of the direct statement 'he will be'. The distinction of the tense 'from now on' shows that the hour in which darkness was in force is now over (Luke 22.53). The period of Jesus' *peirasmos* and suffering gives way to the period in which he is installed at God's right hand in power and glory.

How exclusively the emphasis rests on the *sessio ad dextram dei* is indicated by the deletion of Mark 14.62c. The coming in power (with the clouds of heaven), the essential element of the synoptic sayings concerning the Son of Man's parousia, simply drops out. Luke does know this element, as 21.27 shows. In 18.8b he even speaks of the coming of the Son of Man in a formulation of his own. For Luke, too, the day of the Son of Man (17.24, 26, 30) is the day of his parousia. But Luke obviously does not wish the members of the Sanhedrin to hear the menacing announcement of the impending day of the Son of Man. What he sets store by is what is said to the community through this saying of Jesus before the Sanhedrin, namely that from now on the Son of Man is sitting at God's right hand. To behold this *sessio ad dextram dei* strengthens the Church in its present afflictions; the commission given in Acts 1.8 is unthinkable without it. Thus Luke from his point of view does not see an immediate correlation between lowly suffering on earth and future parousia. Differing from Matthew and Mark, he sees Jesus passing through suffering into an intermediate stage of exaltation. 'Was it not necessary for the Christ to suffer these things and enter into his glory?' (24.26) According to Acts 7.56 Stephen in his martyrdom beholds the Son of Man standing at God's right hand in this state of *doxa*. Whilst in Mark 14.62 and Matt. 26.64 the chief emphasis of the Son of Man saying falls on the quotation from Dan. 7.13, Luke retains nothing but the name Son of Man from Dan. 7 and combines it with the quotation from Ps. 110.1 He thereby produces for the first and only time a Son of Man saying in which the main content is the *sessio ad dextram dei*.

How do we have to understand Luke's placing beside the concept of the Son of Man's coming the *sessio ad dextram dei* as an independent Christological element which can be stated even without mentioning the Son of Man's parousia? Regarded as a mere matter of formal alteration, Luke separated that quotation from Ps. 110.1, which in Mark 14.62 indicates the Son of Man's sovereignty and supremacy, from the concept of parousia and gave it an independence of its own. But this procedure appears to be prompted by the community's recognition that the parousia does not immediately follow Jesus' suffering. The Son of Man remains indispensably the ruling figure in God's transcendent world; he will, however, not only come in the future but exists in reality already with God.[1]

The name of the one who will bring the world of God at the End is thus already during the period of the persecuted Church ascribed to the Lord of this transcendent kingdom. Because the concept of the kingdom of God was expanded, the concept of the Son of Man can also be expanded, the *sessio ad dextram dei* can become an independent Christological element. At the trial before the Sanhedrin *all* draw the conclusion from Jesus' announcement of the exaltation of the Son of Man, 'Are you therefore the Son of God?' This immediate conclusion presupposes that the *sessio ad dextram dei* is the position which distinguishes the Son of God. Considering the unanimous response of the members of the Sanhedrin, Jesus' rejoinder to the question whether he is the Son of God (v. 70) must be understood not as an evasion but as a confession.[2]

The altered arrangement of the titles of sovereignty in Luke 22.67–71 exhibits specific reflections upon the meaning and correlation of the Christological designations. Conzelmann justly comments that Luke makes the trial into a compendium of Christology for his readers. We must question Conzelmann's opinion, however, that Luke 22.67–70 is intended 'to set out explicitly the fundamental identity of the current Christological titles'.[3] Luke arranges the trial so as to come to a climax. As the trial takes this course, the titles of sovereignty which are employed successively—*the Christ, Son of Man, Son of God*—attain varying importance. Thus we cannot speak of a fundamental identity.[4] In our view the titles rather complement each other. This complementary relationship is established by Luke's attributing all the designations to the one Jesus, but each with a meaning of its own.

[1] Cf. Conzelmann, *Theology of Luke*, pp. 113–20.
[2] Cf. Conzelmann, *Theology of Luke*, p. 84 n. 3.
[3] Conzelmann, *Theology of Luke*, p. 84. So also Schrenk, *TWNT* V, p. 989 n. 278.
[4] In case of a fundamental identity the titles would have to be interchangeable; this is impossible in Luke 22.67–70.

(c) **Luke 9.26** on the whole reproduces Mark 8.38. Yet a few small changes show the revision. Firstly, the phrase 'in this adulterous and sinful generation' is deleted. Next, the Son of Man does not come *with* the holy angels but *in* his own glory and that of the Father and that of the holy angels. By means of the glory which pertains to all three, the Son of Man, the Father and the angels are arranged together as a triad. Thus the expression that the Son of Man is the 'Son of the Father' which is intimated in Mark 8.38 disappears. The *doxa* pertains to the Son of Man as well, but he is further removed from that nearness to the Father in Mark. This accords with Luke's inclination to make the angels subject to God alone. Thus in Luke 9.26c the Son of Man comes without the angels, but has been given their *doxa*. Here, too, the Son of Man is therefore understood as a heavenly being.

It is, moreover, worth noting that Luke does not relinquish the ifferentiation between Jesus and the Son of Man which he here dopts from Mark 8.38, just as he keeps the differentiation in 12.8f. hich he takes over from Q.

3) *Luke's revision of the Son of Man sayings from Q*

Some of the Son of Man sayings from Q which Matthew reproduces at the end of the material from the apocalyptic discourse in Mark 13 (Matt. 24) are given by Luke at an earlier place, namely within the account of the journey in 17.22ff. This section follows the Pharisees' question, 'When will the Kingdom of God come?' (17.20). It is meant as eschatological teaching for the disciples in particular (cf. v. 22a), but the material which it contains is clearly parallel to the public eschatological teaching in chapter 21.

(a) The section **Luke 17.22-37** with 18.1–8 affixed to it is composed in a way which demonstrates quite distinctly the importance which Luke attaches to the designation Son of Man. This well-planned accumulation of Son of Man sayings supports our view that for Luke this name is neither antiquated nor devoid of meaning. Luke considers the name to be appropriate for the heading of the eschatological teaching for the disciples. He uses it throughout—apart from 17.25—in its traditional meaning, i.e. in general conformity with the synoptic tradition. Luke three times reproduces sayings from Q with hardly any alteration (17.24, 26, 30) and twice employs the name in formulations of his own (17.22; 18.8b). In Luke's own formulations we have to look for a Son of Man concept specific to him.

(b) In **Luke 17.22** Jesus speaks to his disciples of the coming days in which they will eagerly desire to see but 'one of the days of the Son of Man' and will not see it. Thus Jesus here predicts a future situation of the disciples unlike the situation implied in Luke 21.28 and 21.31; they will *not* be able to recognize at that time the nearness of God's reign. They will watch in vain for the parousia, for participation in the messianic reign. How does this prediction accord with the statement in Luke 17.21, 'Behold, the kingdom of God is (already) in the midst of you'?

In Jesus' presence the kingdom is in the midst of the disciples. After his departure the time will come which is not characterized by a joyful expectation of nearness but by a yearning for that which is remote. Thus the kingdom does not remain with the disciples (in the period of the Church).[1] Luke chooses the designation 'days of the Son of Man' (17.22, 26) for the coming kingdom for which the disciples are on the watch. The plural number is noteworthy.[2] Mention of the days of the Son of Man does not suggest the single event of his sudden arrival but a situation which lasts for some time. In 22.69 Luke omitted the statement about the Son of Man's coming which was present in Mark. Obviously Luke takes into account in 22.69, 17.22 and 17.26 alike that the Son of Man is already seated at God's right hand when the disciples are on the watch for his days during the period of the Church. During this period the kingdom is not visible. Accordingly the disciples are strengthened not only by looking forward to what they expect in the remote future but even more by looking to the kingdom which in Jesus' person was in the midst of them. Luke's new concept of eschatology is at work here in the understanding of the dimensions of time, enabling him to take over earlier concepts without alteration and yet to expound them anew.

(c) In **Luke 17.25** we have particularly important evidence of Luke's method of composition. Here a combination is explicitly established which does not find expression in any of the other Synoptic Gospels, namely the combination of sayings which elsewhere occur separately

---

[1] Cf. Conzelmann, *Theology of Luke*, pp. 125f.
[2] Cf. above Chapter II B I 1, p. 51.

about the Son of Man's parousia and his passion. Of course, we can also occasionally surmise from the arrangement of the text in Mark and Matthew (e.g. running on from Mark 8.31 to 8.38f.) that the groups of sayings concerning the parousia and the passion which are separated in the history of tradition are not unconnected in the evangelists' view. But only Luke, and he alone in this passage, expresses this combination explicitly. 'But first he must suffer many things and be rejected by this generation.' Luke fixes his view on the *course* of the Son of Man with its different stages. This view reveals a direct Christological interest.

The vocabulary of 17.25 permits no doubt that this saying was formulated in intentional analogy with the stereotyped announcements of the Son of Man's suffering. By means of the temporal particle 'first', Luke links this announcement of the passion with the context of the statements concerning the parousia. In 17.24 attention was focused on the Son of Man's parousia, which is still remote but will burst in suddenly. Now it is directed to the Son of Man's passion (which from the point of view of the gospel-reader has happened already), which Jesus announces here as a future necessity. According to Luke 17.21 the kingdom of God is in the midst of the disciples; likewise the Son of Man's suffering happens in the midst of this generation.

The phrase 'must first' occurs also in Luke 21.9 where the 'first' is interpolated in contrast with Mark 13.7. Luke thereby fits the coming tribulations more precisely into the eschatological sequence according to his specific concept of eschatology. A similar temporal connexion occurs in Mark 13.10, an isolated saying which must be considered as a secondary interpolation between vv. 9 and 11.[1] Mark 13.10 is a prophetic saying from the post-Easter community; the teaching of Jesus is not yet aimed at world mission (Matt. 10.5ff.). This prophetic saying declares that Christian missionary preaching must precede the tribulations and catastrophes. This preaching itself counts as the first event of the eschatological sequence. Thus the traditional sphere of apocalyptic events is expanded by an event which takes place within the general course of events in the world and yet is distinguished as the prerequisite of the final cosmic events. A similar joining of events by means of 'must first' occurs in Mark 9.11f. The coming of Elijah, which is said to precede the ultimate End, already bears the weight of the eschatological 'must' and is

[1] Kümmel, *Promise*, p. 84.

fitted into the history of past events by interpreting it as the appearance of the Baptist. Matthew continues this train of thought in 17.12b by the analogy between what was done to the Baptist and the suffering of the Son of Man; in both cases these events are thus recognized as eschatologically necessary.

So when Luke in 17.25 makes the Son of Man's suffering precede the parousia in *time* by referring to its eschatological necessity, he does not do anything novel. He does, however, do something novel and unique here by directly joining the *sayings* on the Son of Man's suffering and parousia which are kept separate from each other everywhere else.

Kümmel wants to dispel the objections raised against the assumption that Luke 17.25 is 'a reliable early tradition' and indeed 'a detached saying'.[1] But in addition to the arguments which he endeavours to refute, the following fact speaks decisively against his view. Luke 17.24 is taken over from Q. Matt. 24.27, the parallel passage to Luke 17.24, is not followed by a reference to the suffering Son of Man. Since no sayings on the suffering Son of Man occur in Q, we may be sure that Luke did not find 17.25 in Q. Luke 17.26f. and 17.28f., however, are again taken over from Q. Thus 17.25 appears to be an interpolation into sayings which had been taken over. In view of the conformity of this interpolation with Luke's specific theology, we have no need to assume a special tradition to account for its origin. To be sure, we do not consider this saying to be an isolated *vaticinium ex eventu*. In our view Luke, reflecting on the history of salvation, formulated this saying with the help of references to the stereotyped announcements of the Son of Man's passion. To point to Jesus' resurrection would be neither necessary nor appropriate at this place.[2] The verse calls the disciples' attention to the Son of Man's passion and rejection by this generation. The suffering is recognized to be a necessity which pertains to the period of life on earth and exists in correlation with the Son of Man's parousia. It is of primary importance that the attention is no longer solely directed toward the future parousia of the Son of Man as is done in the other sayings concerning the Son of Man's coming, but is complementarily directed to an historical event which must happen *first*. Thus correlated with

[1] Kümmel, *Promise*, pp. 70ff.
[2] Against Kümmel, *Promise*, p. 71. In 9.44 also the resurrection is omitted by Luke. It is the suffering proper which bears the weight of the divine 'must'. This view also appears in the formulation of Luke 24.26. Thus the omission of the resurrection proves 17.25 as well to have been formulated by Luke.

the parousia, that preceding event attains an eschatological meaning. We shall consider later when examining the announcements of suffering what the name Son of Man means for the statement in Luke 17.25.

(d) In **Luke 12.8f**, there appears to be but one alteration by Luke, namely the addition 'before the angels of God' in both v. 8 and v. 9. Klostermann conjectures with Dalman and Loisy, 'Probably Q did not contain the $\tau o\hat{v}$ $\vartheta\epsilon o\hat{v}$ which counteracts the purpose of the phrase "before the angels", namely avoidance of the name of God.'[1] Luke's formulation of the saying stresses the prominence of the angels which here act as an assize before which the Son of Man appears as the guarantor.[2] Luke, contrary to Matthew, is inclined to restrict the competence of the Son of Man in favour of the pre-eminence of God.

(e) In **Luke 12.40** we cannot see any traces of revision when comparing it with Matt. 24.44.

III. Main elements of Luke's concept of the Son of Man

We are now able to give a distinct answer to the questions raised at the beginning of this section. Luke conceives of the Son of Man in a specific way. The evidence for this is a well-planned use of this designation within longer compositions (cf. 17.22–18.8b) and the emphatic termination of the apocalyptic discourse by a Son of Man saying (21.36). From the re-formulated or newly formed Son of Man sayings (21.36; 18.8b; 17.22, cf. also 17.25 within the context) it is evident that in Luke's view considerable importance is attached to the designation Son of Man; Luke not only takes over the name but also develops the concept usefully according to his theological understanding.

In this development we are able to perceive a characteristic difference from Matthew. The first evangelist often reaches back behind the Son of Man sayings from Q and Mark to elements of the concept in Jewish apocalyptic tradition which he employs independently to modify and expand the concept of the Son of Man. Luke does not reach back to the Jewish tradition. He obviously refers only to the Son of Man sayings transmitted to him by Christian traditions. It is

[1] Klostermann, *Lukas*, p. 134.
[2] Conzelmann, *Theology of Luke*, p. 173 n. 3.

the concept in these sayings which Luke develops by associating it with Christian Hellenistic terms and by fitting it into his specific concept of eschatology.

The main elements of this altered concept of the Son of Man held by Luke are the following.

1. In the Gospel of Luke more distinctly than in other synoptic texts the reference to the Son of Man serves to emphasize the primitive Church's *exhortation* (cf. 21.36; 18.1 and 8b; 21.27 and 28 *et passim*). Correspondingly not only the apocalyptic depiction but also the stereotyped features with which other sayings from the synoptic tradition describe the coming of the Son of Man are reduced to the utmost minimum. On the other hand the exhortation in support of which Luke uses the Son of Man concept is amplified by Christian Hellenistic terms.

2. In none of the sayings in the Gospel of Luke is the Son of Man's function as the Judge or the one who executes judgement on the world expressly stated, quite contrary to the Gospel of Matthew. According to Luke 12.8f. the Son of Man appears before God's tribunal as the intercessor, the advocate, the guarantor for the Christians. The sayings formed by Luke, 18.8b and 21.36, do not conflict with this concept of the Son of Man; still they intimate that the Christians have to stand before the Son of Man at his appearance. Thus undoubtedly the Son of Man is thought of as in some way passing sentence or being in a position of authority. Not everyone belonging to the community may be assured of his intercession, of his advocacy before God's tribunal—only those who kept on watching and praying at all times. The Son of Man's coming seems to concern the Christians exclusively; he will come to look for faith on earth. Correspondingly this faith must be understood in relation to the Son of Man's coming; it is a 'praying always' which awaits that day in faithful watchfulness.

3. For Luke also the Son of Man is the traditional agent of God's reign which will come some day. Luke, however, does not only conceive of God's reign as a future quantity; he also presupposes it as already in existence in the transcendent world above at present during the period of the *ecclesia pressa*. Correspondingly he can conceive of the Son of Man not only as the coming agent of this reign but also as already seated at God's right hand now (Luke 22.69). The expansion of the concept of the coming Son of Man coincides with the expansion of the concept of the kingdom of God.

4. According to Luke the Son of Man is no longer in any respect the object of imminent expectation. The right relationship to him consists in praying and watching *at all times* on earth. According to 21.25–31, however, there will nevertheless come a period of eschatological signs by which Christians may recognize with a sigh of relief that their deliverance, the kingdom of God, is near and that the Son of Man will therefore come soon. That future period will be, so to speak, the time of the legitimate expectation of the Son of Man's imminence.

5. Luke in reflecting on the history of salvation combines the reference to the Son of Man's parousia *in the days to come* with the reference to the Son of Man's suffering *at first* (cf. 17.25). This suffering is subordinate to the *must* of God's order and is the eschatological prerequisite of what is to come. The concept of the Son of Man is not really expanded in 17.25 in a way comparable to its expansion in 22.69. Luke rather sets in an explicit relationship the groups of sayings on the coming and on the suffering of the Son of Man, which elsewhere in the synoptic texts stand disconnected alongside each other and differ both in concept and history of tradition. Now the suffering and the coming of the Son of Man appear as the consecutive and necessary stages of a single course. This arrangement corresponds with Luke's tendency to distinguish the successive periods of salvation history which are ordered by God's will and to characterize their relation to each other. On the one hand the synoptic tradition of the Son of Man's *coming*, formed while the expectation of his imminence radiated, and on the other hand the primitive Christian kerygma proclaiming the Son of Man's *suffering* on earth, though they remain incompatible, are joined by reflection. Here the endeavour is made to join the incompatible elements within a continuous succession of stages.[1] Does this concept of the succession of periods in salvation history have to lead in the direction of the Son of Man vision in IV Ezra 13, namely toward the structure of an itinerary of a gnostic type? At any rate there seems to be an inclination to statements resembling Phil. 2.6ff.

6. In Luke's view the sovereignty of the Son of Man pertains to the transcendent world. Luke restricts this sovereignty carefully, for example by assigning the angels to the sphere of God's competence only. Luke avoids emphasizing the Son of Man's independence.

7. In Luke's view there is a sovereignty of the Son of Man existing even now. It is expressed in his being seated at God's right hand and

---

[1] Conforming to this, Luke in 24.26 co-ordinates the Christ's suffering and entry into the *doxa*.

can be perceived by a specially distinguished martyr already in the period of the Church (Acts 7.56). At the Son of Man's coming it will be revealed to all the world (Luke 17.30).

8. In Matt. 25.31ff. we observed that certain features of Jesus on earth and his attachment to the least of his brethren were inserted into the picture of the Son of Man's sovereignty. Matthew thus Christianized the figure of the Perfecter. There is no parallel to this procedure in Luke. By explicitly joining the coming with the suffering Son of Man (17.25) he rather stresses the Christological correlation in salvation history.

9. It is a remarkable fact that the material of Jesus' teaching is given space and emphasis in the Gospel of Luke. Not much of this material was admitted into the Gospel of Mark. This difference may not only be explained by different source material but apparently also by different theological concepts peculiar to each of them. Mark organized his presentation of the material with the passion narrative always in view; to him, what Jesus means for salvation can be understood above all from his passion, from his giving his life as a ransom for many (Mark 10.45). Luke has a different understanding of the passion and consequently of what Jesus means. Conzelmann has rightly maintained 'that there is no trace of any Passion mysticism nor is any direct soteriological significance drawn from Jesus' suffering or death. There is no suggestion of a connexion with the forgiveness of sins.'[1] We can understand why the passion was less emphasized by Luke when we take into account that in his view salvation already appears on earth in Jesus' actual presence. Jesus is the centre of the history of salvation not as the one who is dying but as the one who is active. 'The centre of the story of salvation is a period described by Luke 4.13 and 22.3 as one free from the activity of Satan.'[2] In this period of Jesus' saving activity, his message, his teaching, is of momentous significance. Luke does not give Jesus' teaching that dominance which is granted to it by Matthew, but he regards it as an inseparable part of Jesus' activity. Since Luke sees salvation present in Jesus' presence, he is intent on incorporating into his Gospel the material of Jesus' teaching as it was transmitted to him mainly in Q. Together with the other material from Q, Luke took over the sayings concerning the coming Son of Man without essentially altering them. He did not extend the Son of Man sayings transmitted to him by referring to Dan. 7 or to

[1] In the presentation of the passion; Conzelmann, *Theology of Luke*, p. 201.
[2] *Ibid.*, p. 170.

apocalyptic traditions in the manner of the scribes. Even in the sayings which he formulated anew he closely conformed to the meaning of the authentic sayings of Jesus (18.8b; 21.36). There are, to be sure, alterations in formation and wording. But for Luke, Jesus remains unalterably the one who speaks exclusively of the Son of Man's coming and speaks of the Son of Man as of someone different from himself. Luke retained this peculiarity of the Son of Man sayings which had issued from Jesus' teaching.

It might seem appropriate to give a provisional summary of the reception, modification and development of the concept of the coming Son of Man within the synoptic tradition at this point of our study. We prefer, however, to postpone it to a later section[1] in order to examine first the two other groups of Son of Man sayings, those concerning his present activity and those concerning his suffering. The real significance of the Son of Man concept within the synoptic tradition will become clear only from the relationship between the different groups of sayings.

[1] Cf. Chapter V, pp. 222ff.

IIII

THE SAYINGS CONCERNING THE SON OF MAN'S ACTIVITY ON EARTH

WITHIN THE SYNOPTIC tradition there are, besides the sayings on the Son of Man's parousia, other sayings designating certain ways of Jesus' activity on earth as activity of the Son of Man. These sayings no longer link up with Jewish apocalyptic traditions. The Son of Man no longer appears as the heavenly being who—even according to some synoptic parousia sayings—by his appearance terminates the course of the world. His activity rather enters into the course of events on earth and is identical with that of Jesus.

The question of how the name Son of Man came to be used in this new way has troubled scholars for a long time. Are there perhaps after all forerunners of this usage in the sphere of Jewish eschatology? Scholars who favour this conjecture appeal to the fact that already in I Enoch the *transcendent* figure of the Son of Man had been combined with the figure of God's Servant *on earth*. In their view this combination provided the foundation for Jesus' consciousness of his mission.[1] Other scholars assume that Jesus uttered the sayings on the Son of Man's activity on earth out of the depths of his understanding of himself without referring to prototypes.[2] Others again object to both suppositions, thinking that the origin of this group of synoptic Son of Man sayings is merely due to an error in their translation into Greek. In Aramaic the 'son of man' in these sayings was not a messianic title at all but meant "man" or "I" '.[3] According to these scholars this group of sayings is not supposed to have come into being before their passing from Aramaic into Hellenistic Greek. Hence this use of the

---

[1] Recently again Jeremias, *Servant*, pp. 61f.
[2] Cf. W. Manson, *Jesus the Messiah*, p. 117.
[3] Bultmann, *Theology* I, p. 30; cf. T. W. Manson, *Teaching*, pp. 217f.; Taylor, *Names*, p. 32.

name Son of Man would have been alien not only to Jesus himself but also to the primitive Aramaic-speaking community.

Bultmann's supposition that the sayings concerning the present activity of the Son of Man originated relatively late on account of a linguistic error solves many difficulties with a single stroke. How else would it be comprehensible that on the one hand in the parousia sayings Jesus spoke of the Son of Man as of someone different from himself, someone in the future, while on the other hand in the sayings on his present activity he expressly identified himself with the Son of Man? How else would it have been possible that the tradition maintained the differentiation between the 'I' of Jesus and the figure of the Son of Man right up to the late imitative formulations (cf., e.g., Matt. 19.28), while Jesus himself frankly abandoned the differentiation by designating his present 'I' to be the Son of Man? According to Bultmann the two groups of sayings are separate in the history of their traditions, since the latter group originated in an error. There is no sense in co-ordinating them. If we want to challenge Bultmann's view we shall have to establish a meaningful relationship both for the history of the tradition of the two groups and for the concepts present in the synoptic texts.

A. THE SAYINGS FROM Q CONCERNING THE SON OF MAN'S
ACTIVITY ON EARTH

I. Analysis of the individual sayings

(a) **Matthew 11.19; Luke 7.34.** This Son of Man saying concludes a section of Q which is often called Jesus' testimony to the Baptist. This section Matt. 11.16–19 = Luke 7.31–35 is more or less complete in itself.[1] It deals with this generation's rejection of the Baptist as well as of Jesus. The comparison of the Baptist with Jesus is not the point of interest. The characterization of this generation and the unreasonable pretexts with which they evade the message is the central concern. They reproach the Baptist with having a demon by reason of his abstention from eating and drinking. They reproach the Son of Man, who did eat and drink, 'Behold, a glutton and drunkard, a friend of tax collectors and sinners.'

---

[1] According to Dibelius, *Tradition*, p. 252, Matt. 11.16f. = Luke 7.31f. is a parable which contains a story or fable with typical motifs. Cf. on the section Matt. 11.16–19 and par. Manson, *Sayings*, pp. 67–71.

This generation's objection to the Son of Man's mode of behaviour[1] is the dominant point in this section. It is the same point which dominates the so-called controversial discourses. We can infer from this saying what feature of the Son of Man's behaviour his opponents object to in particular. We shall begin with the second part of the reproach, 'a friend of tax collectors and sinners'. The words tax collector and sinner are often combined in a quasi-stereotyped manner.[2] In Mark 2.15–17 it is stated that Jesus sits at table in the house of Levi with many tax collectors and sinners and is therefore reproached by the Pharisees and scribes; he answers this reproach by asserting that he is come to call sinners. Matt. 11.19 and par. is to be interpreted exactly in the same sense. The Son of Man in fact wishes to be a friend of the tax collectors and sinners. He gives them fellowship which is expressed in the common meal. This establishing of a fellowship with sinners which to a Jew who faithfully observes the Law means a most serious defilement, is designated by Jesus in Mark 2.17 as his most particular task. Jesus is come to summon the tax collectors and sinners to the kingdom of God, or as Zahn no doubt rightly comments, to the supper of God's reign.[3]

Now if the Son of Man is reproached for being a glutton and a drunkard, this reproach is caused by the fact that Jesus expresses his friendship for tax collectors and sinners by bestowing on them the table-fellowship which means a place at the bridegroom's supper. To eat and drink with the bridegroom is in Mark 2.18ff. sharply contrasted with the fasting practised by the Pharisees and John's disciples. This contrast might have been the reason for the reproach that he was a glutton and a drunkard. The action of the Son of Man here appears in a certain light; he acts with supreme authority when bestowing table-fellowship on tax collectors and sinners, when bestowing his fellowship on those with whom the religious man is not allowed to have anything in common; this is what he is come to do. We have to consider this when answering the question whether the name Son of Man is here used as a synonym for the pronoun in the first person singular[4] in Jesus' discourse or whether it implies a

---

[1] 'He is come' is a phrase which denotes the Son of Man's activity as a whole.

[2] Cf. Matt. 9.10; cf. also, in Q, Matt. 5.46 and Luke 6.32f.

[3] Quoted in Klostermann, *Markus*, p. 27. For the following cf. Campenhausen, *Askese*, p. 21: 'The absence of an ascetic strain in Jesus' behaviour aroused . . . attention and gave offence; his enemies call him a glutton and a drunkard.'

[4] Manson, *Sayings*, pp. 70f.: 'It is probable that the phrase here, both in Matthew and Luke, rests on a misunderstanding of an Aramaic idiom in which the

designation of sovereignty. Obviously that action of the Son of Man for which this generation reproaches him here is a specific act of sovereignty superior to the restraints of the Law by virtue of the authority of a direct mission. It is action which befits only an authorized person. It is this distinctive action which is emphasized by the name Son of Man.

The section Matt. 11.16–19 and par. is concerned with this generation which refuses both the Baptist and the Son of Man. In the sayings on the Son of Man's coming there also appeared a refusal by this generation, by men; that tension, however—and this is a fundamental difference—did not exist between the (transcendent) Son of Man and men but between Jesus and men. This generation refused to recognize Jesus' message;[1] it urges those who followed Jesus to be ashamed of him, to deny him.[2] The tension recurs in Matt. 11.16ff. and par. This generation turns against the Son of Man in the manner of naughty children. The place which Jesus' claim assumed in the sayings of the coming Son of Man is designated by the name Son of Man in the sayings on his present activity. This designation applies to Jesus acting in his sovereignty. It does replace the 'I' of Jesus, but does so in a specific way, expressing the sovereignty of the Son of Man's mission as a whole which is denoted by the phrase 'he is come'. It must be realized that the sovereignty pertaining to the transcendent Son of Man is thereby *not* brought down to the level of Jesus on earth. The heavenly Son of Man at his coming will be restricted by nothing which exists on earth; when he appears, then 'all the tribes of the earth will mourn'.[3]

But what does the designation Son of Man in Matt. 11.19 and par. still have in common with the traditional name, since the attributes of the transcendent Son of Man are no longer designated by it? How could the name shed its earlier meaning in being transferred to Jesus?

It is not enough here to point to Jesus' understanding of himself, i.e. to assume that Jesus understood his activity as that of the Son of Man. To this assumption Bultmann rightly objects: 'In that case he

phrase "that son of man" = "that man" is used as a periphrasis for the first personal pronoun.'

[1] Luke 11.30.
[2] Mark 8.38; Luke 12.8f.
[3] Matt. 24.30.

would not have understood himself according to Daniel's Son of Man but would have understood the latter according to himself— only there seems no reason why he should have done so.'[1] And if it was not Jesus but the community that understood Daniel's Son of Man according to Jesus, abandoning all traditional meaning of that name, there would also have to be a reason why they should have done so. We shall try to solve this problem at a later point of our investigation.[2] At this point we wish to discover where the Son of Man saying Matt. 11.19 and par. is situated within the history of tradition.

Klostermann summarizes the opinion of Bultmann and Dibelius as follows: Verses 18f. are 'supposed to have been formed later and to be an allegorical interpretation, which might be inferred from the backward look towards Jesus' whole appearance in history, and from the hardly justifiable use of the title Son of Man'.[3] Yet Bultmann himself feels some scruples about simply alleging that Matt. 11.18 and par. is a late formation. 'Here some older source might have provided the text in which the Son of Man was not an apocalyptic figure, but as in Mark 2.10, 28; Matt. 8.20 and par. simply meant "man".' The only criterion which occasions the assumption of its having been formed later is that the apocalyptic title Son of Man is applied to Jesus on earth, which proves Matt. 11.18f. and par. to be 'a Hellenistic product'.[4] We saw above that the meaning connected with the name Son of Man here is neither that of the apocalyptic figure nor that of man as Bultmann maintained with the support of Mark 2.10, 28; Matt. 8.20 and par. The name rather designates Jesus in his specific sovereign activity by reason of his mission, that is to say, Jesus in his specific supreme authority. There is no proof whatsoever that this use of the name Son of Man originated in the Hellenistic sphere. Why should the Hellenistic community have been interested in transferring an Aramaic name to Jesus?[5] We learn from the New Testament texts that the name Son of Man was not current within the Hellenistic community, but was replaced by other names, especially by the titles *Kyrios* and *Christos*. Hence we may with more probability assign the use of the name Son of Man in the case of the Q saying Matt. 11.19 and par. also to the Palestinian community to whom this designation was

[1] Bultmann, 'Matt. 16.17–19', p. 278.
[2] Cf. Chapter V D 3, pp. 271ff.
[3] Klostermann, *Matt.*, p. 99.
[4] Bultmann, *Tradition*, p. 155.
[5] Lohse, *Märtyrer*, p. 118.

familiar. In our view, as will be stated below, Mark 2.10, 28 and the Q saying Matt. 8.20 and par. can on no account be employed to support any other meaning of this name. On the contrary, the fact that the name Son of Man occurs in the Q sayings Matt. 11.19 and par.; 8.20 and par. and (perhaps on the basis of the Q text) in Luke 6.22 makes it probable that this use of the designation originated in the Palestinian community.

(b) **Matthew 12.32; Luke 12.10.** There is a different form of this saying in Q and yet another in Mark. In the context in Mark the saying on blaspheming the Holy Spirit (Mark 3.28f.) follows as Jesus' reply to the reproach of being possessed by demons. Manson asserts that the form in Mark was original as compared with the form in Q, since no blasphemy against the Son of Man is mentioned in Mark, but blasphemies which men utter against each other.[1] Of these blasphemies it was said that they can be forgiven, whilst only blasphemy against the Holy Spirit cannot be forgiven. But what are these blasphemies of men against each other supposed to mean here? In Manson's view they mean blasphemies against the disciples which cannot be forgiven from the moment that the Holy Spirit who worked in Jesus works also in those who follow him. According to Manson the interpretation of the saying in its form in Q is quite difficult; he sees more sense in the saying in its form in Mark which he consequently regards as more original. We want to object to this conclusion, if only for reasons of method; for Manson removes the saying from its original context in Q and attempts to interpret it in connexion or rather by contrast with Luke 12.8f. The juxtaposition of the sayings 12.8f. and 12.10 in Luke appears to be a secondary one on account of the catchword Son of Man. The saying on blaspheming pertains to Jesus' defence against the reproach of being in league with demons. This is evident not only from the context in Mark but also from a comparison of the texts Matt. 12.25–30 and Luke 11.17–23. These texts deal with blasphemies against Jesus, who casts out demons not by Beelzebul but by the Spirit, with the finger of God. When in the context the reproaches of opponents are the point of concern, the connexion with the saying on whether blas-

[1] Manson, *Sayings*, p. 110. In Manson's view blasphemies against the Son of Man would establish an unthinkable situation, whilst the difficulties would disappear on the assumption that 'Son of Man' in Luke 12.10 is to be read simply as 'a man'.

phemies can be forgiven follows quite logically.[1] Thus the saying
states that opposition to the Son of Man can be forgiven, but opposition to the Holy Spirit cannot. Here, too, the name Son of Man does
not designate the figure of a transcendent Perfecter, but in accordance
with Matt. 11.19 and par. it designates Jesus acting on earth and
being attacked by his opponents.[2] The point of interest here is not
how Jesus may be defended but how his opponents may be forgiven.
They can be forgiven in so far as they turned against the Son of Man
merely in his activity on earth. But there is no forgiveness—in the
post-Easter situation—for the one who sets himself in opposition to
the manifest activity of the Holy Spirit. Two periods in the history of
salvation are distinguished here in the saying from Q, the period of
Jesus' activity on earth as the Son of Man and the subsequent period
of the activity of the Holy Spirit.[3] The meaning of this distinction is
quite intelligible. In the Spirit the exalted Lord reveals himself.[4] He
who did not follow the earthly Jesus may nevertheless find forgiveness
when following the exalted Lord, i.e. if he does not blaspheme
against the Spirit.[5]

The text in Mark obscures this distinction and with it the meaning
of the saying.[6] The Spirit is here considered to be active already in
the time of Jesus' activity on earth. Consequently the following
meaning is expressed: all blasphemies can be forgiven except the
blasphemy against the Holy Spirit, whose activity is manifest in

---

[1] To connect this saying with Luke 12.8f. is not equally satisfactory. In Luke
12.8f. the Son of Man appears as the guarantor before God's tribunal, thus in
transcendent sovereignty. How could there be blasphemy against him in that
situation? Manson justly notes the dissonance between the two sayings Luke
12.8f. and Luke 12.10. In our view, however, that does not make it appropriate to
re-interpret the meaning of one of the two sayings. Each one should be fitted into
its proper context in Q. The saying on whether blasphemy can be forgiven belongs
to the Beelzebul pericope. This is also evident from the way in which Matthew
connects the form in Mark (Matt. 12.31) and the form in Q (Matt. 12.32) in spite
of their competing content.

[2] For this reason Manson, in *Sayings*, rightly places this saying under the heading of 'Jesus and his Opponents'.

[3] Bornkamm, 'Expectation', supports this view on p. 34.

[4] It also appears from this saying that no explicit relationship between the Son
of Man and the Holy Spirit was in view. The Son of Man was regarded either as
coming at the parousia or as active on earth. The Spirit, however, was regarded as
pertaining to the exalted one acting after Easter but before the parousia.

[5] For the statement that opposition to Jesus' claim to full authority can be
forgiven, compare, e.g., Acts 3.17ff.; 13.27ff.; Luke 23.34.

[6] Cf. Lohmeyer, *Markus*, p. 79. Lohmeyer speaks of the text in Mark here as
being quite 'loose' and 'inexact'.

Jesus' victory over the demons.[1] This statement conforms to Mark's concept of Jesus as the Son of God, the Lord over the demons; hence Mark's form of the saying appears to be later than the form in Q.[2] It is not improbable that Mark or a predecessor knew the Q form of the saying, but considered it to be offensive since to him it seemed unthinkable that a blasphemy against the holy transcendent figure of the Son of Man, the Judge of the world, should be forgivable. So the saying was altered and given a less precise and more general conception by association with the expression Son of Man: the sons of men will be forgiven all sins and blasphemies.[3] This conception does not, however, accord with the context; for the pericope deals with reproaches against Jesus and is consistently continued in Q by a saying which deals with reproaches against the Son of Man and states whether these reproaches can be forgiven.

Both in the saying Matt. 12.32 = Luke 12.10 and in the saying Matt. 11.19 = Luke 7.34 the designation Son of Man does not indicate the transcendent sovereignty of the heavenly Perfecter but means the claim to full authority uttered by Jesus on earth which the opponents resist.

(c) **Matthew 8.20; Luke 9.58.** Martin Dibelius attached great significance to this saying. All other sayings on the Son of Man's

---

[1] Thus Bornkamm, 'Expectation', p. 34, in my opinion rightly; a different view in Lohmeyer, *Markus*, p. 80.

[2] For a discussion of Wellhausen's exegesis of the saying cf. Excursus IV below, pp. 312ff.

[3] If this is true, Mark (or his predecessor) no longer understood the use of the name Son of Man as a designation for Jesus acting on earth with full authority. The use of the Son of Man sayings in the composition of the Gospel of Mark supports our conjecture. The sayings in Mark 2.10, 28 are taken over from pre-Marcan material. In the other sayings in this Gospel the designation Son of Man is used in a way which makes it obvious that Mark was intent on two aspects of it, namely on the one hand the transcendent coming Son of Man and on the other hand the suffering Son of Man, but not on the Son of Man as acting on earth with full authority. When Mark regards the Son of Man on earth, he sees him as the suffering and rising Lord. In Mark's view it is indeed impossible to consider blasphemy against the Son of Man as forgivable; blasphemy against the suffering and rising Lord is as unforgivable as blasphemy against the heavenly Son of Man who will come on the clouds of heaven. Since Mark fails to understand the third way in which the name Son of Man is used (to designate the one who acts on earth with full authority), he makes alterations. Lohmeyer, *Markus*, p. 80, comments on the meaning which the saying was given by the formulation in the Gospel of Mark, 'All blasphemies not only can be forgiven but will be forgiven—a monstrous saying from which it would follow that all discernment of sin and all final judgement would be eliminated.'

existence on earth appeared to him as Christian interpretations, explanations by the evangelists. In the case of this saying, however, he reaches the conclusion that it might have issued from Jesus' own life. 'Thus it was possible for Jesus to speak in such a manner as to suggest the contrast between the obscurity of his indigent earthly existence and the glory of the "Man" from heaven—the contrast and at the same time the connexion—for the needy life belongs to the concealment of the Son of Man and points to the future.'[1] This conclusion is complemented by the following consideration: 'The idea of the concealment of the Son of Man provided the first Christians with the key which unlocked for them the earthly life of Jesus. For, finally, this earthly life and its ignominious end, and all that was repugnant and humiliating in the historical existence of Jesus still belonged to this concealment.'[2] We cannot assent to this conclusion. There is neither a direct nor an indirect clue to the Son of Man's 'concealment' given in Matt. 8.20 and par. or in any other saying concerning the present activity of the Son of Man. Matt. 8.20 and par. speaks of homelessness. The idea of concealment which Dibelius inserts—incorrectly—into the synoptic Son of Man sayings is taken from Jewish apocalyptic literature; for the book of Enoch to which Dibelius refers[3] merely says that the Primal Man 'had existed with God as a semi-divine being in heavenly concealment only to be revealed at the end of a whole series of world ages'.[4] It does not support a transference of this idea of a heavenly pre-existent concealment to Jesus' existence on earth.

We saw from the sayings already discussed concerning the present activity that the designation Son of Man does not transfer the nature and sovereignty of the transcendent Perfecter to the historical Son of Man. For the latter is none other than Jesus acting in full authority, even though this activity is not acknowledged by his opponents, by this generation. The idea of the pre-existent Son of Man's concealment does not apply to this activity on earth; especially since neither a pre-existence nor a concealment is intimated in any of the synoptic Son of Man sayings.

Manson thinks that 'foxes' are a symbol for the Ammonites and 'birds' for the Gentile nations; considered thus the saying might mean

---

[1] Dibelius, *Jesus*, p. 91.
[2] *Ibid.*, p. 89.
[3] *Ibid.*, pp. 89f.
[4] *Ibid.*, p. 89.

'everybody is at home in Israel's land except the true Israel'.[1] This interpretation in which the Son of Man becomes a collective concept looks rather far-fetched to us. It may certainly be possible that the form of this saying in Q referred to an older version of a proverb.[2] We do not think it possible, however, that previous versions contained the name Son of Man. Our exegesis must keep to the clearly discernible meaning of the Q form.

According to Matt. 8.19b and Luke 9.57, and therefore according to the text from Q, Jesus' saying about the Son of Man's homelessness is addressed to a man who promises to follow Jesus. Jesus draws that man's attention to what following him means. To follow Jesus requires the acceptance of the same homelessness amongst men which the Son of Man takes upon himself. Elsewhere, too, Jesus' sayings declare that following him means a radical separation from all attachments; this same meaning appears, for example, in the saying immediately adjoining in Q, 'Follow me, and leave the dead to bury their own dead' (Matt. 8.21f.).[3]

The saying is not primarily intended to speak only of the Son of Man's existence on earth, of his homelessness as such, but primarily to expound what following is like. It is understood here that the same will happen to the one who follows as to the one who leads the way. Following means matching up with the one who goes before. And the one who leads the way, the Son of Man, lives amongst men without having a home. We are reminded of the tension with this generation, or men, which we perceived both in the sayings about the coming of the Son of Man and in those about his present activity.[4] This tension recurs in the saying about the Son of Man's homelessness. The very one who summons men to follow with full authority is the same whom this generation refuses to receive, thus depriving him of a home. Again it is men's hostility to Jesus' claim to full authority which refuses a home to the Son of Man as well as to Jesus' followers; it is that hostility which presses the disciple to deny Jesus (Luke 12.9). The Son of Man here is not conceived of as the transcendent Perfecter; the latter cannot be thought of as suffering on earth from having no home. The name Son of Man here designates Jesus in his homelessness. What does this name signify for Jesus?

[1] Manson, *Sayings*, pp. 72f.
[2] Cf. Bultmann, *Tradition*, p. 97.
[3] Cf. also Mark 10.28 and par.; Matt. 10.37 and par.
[4] Cf. Mark 8.38; Luke 12.8f.; Luke 11.30 and Matt. 11.16, 19 and par.

Why is it used? Why does it not simply say, '*I* have nowhere to lay my head'? The answer appears distinctly from the context. Jesus is acting as the one who with full authority summons men to follow him. The name Son of Man is thus used to designate his sovereignty, his supreme authority. This factor of sovereignty, of Jesus' claim, is common to all three Q sayings on the Son of Man's present activity discussed so far. Jesus' claim arouses his opponents' opposition. They reproach him for bestowing his table-fellowship on tax collectors and sinners; they blaspheme against him; they refuse a home to him and to his followers—in the same way as, according to Mark 8.38, they urge the disciple to deny Jesus.

(d) **Luke 6.22.** It may be conjectured but cannot be proved that the phrase 'for the Son of Man's sake' in Luke 6.22 already occurred in the text in Q.[1] At any rate, it seems probable when comparing Luke 6.22 with Matt. 11.19; 12.32 and 8.20 and par. that this formulation did not originate with Luke.

Luke 6.22f. appears to be, as convincingly demonstrated by Bultmann by means of the comparison with Matt. 5.10–12, a 'new piece of tradition' composed by the community.[2] What is the significance of the name Son of Man here? Why did the community use it for this formulation of its own?

We must notice that the point is not a persecution on account of the coming Son of Man. Even the parousia sayings always speak of the disciples' confessing Jesus—or of their denying or being ashamed of him. In the same way here a persecution is spoken of which occurs on account of the Son of Man's activity on earth. He alone exists in the tension over against this generation. Attachment to him exposes his follower to men's hostility. Thus here, too, the name Son of Man is used to designate Jesus' acting in a certain way. For his sake the disciples are subject to persecution. This sovereignty and this uncompromising claim are emphasized by the name Son of Man. In this way the name is here a title designating the specific unique authority of the one who bears the title.

The disciples who endure men's hostility 'for the Son of Man's sake' are given an eschatological promise. They are *blessed.* Verse 23 shows that this is a promise of joy and reward on that day in heaven.

---

[1] Vielhauer, 'Gottesreich' p. 52, maintains emphatically that Luke in 6.22 took over the name Son of Man from Q.

[2] Bultmann, *Tradition*, p. 110.

In the sayings Mark 8.38; Luke 12.8f. and par.; Matt. 19.28, those who confess Jesus are similarly promised a future reward.

II. *Results: The nature of the use of the name Son of Man in the sayings from Q concerning the Son of Man's activity on earth*

1. In Q there are sayings on the coming Son of Man and on the Son of Man in his present activity side by side, neither confused nor combined with each other. In the first group of sayings Jesus speaks of the Son of Man as of another in the future. In the second group Jesus speaks of the Son of Man when speaking of his own present activity on earth. In the former group the sovereignty of the Son of Man is unrestrictedly transcendent; in the latter, the sovereignty of the Son of Man is not that of a transcendent being.

2. The same tension over against men or this generation which we perceived in the parousia sayings prevails also in the sayings on the activity on earth. In the parousia sayings the tension did not exist between the transcendent Son of Man and men, but existed between Jesus and men. In the sayings on the activity on earth the Son of Man enters into this tension and occupies the place where according to the parousia sayings Jesus stood claiming full authority. Thus the function of the name Son of Man in these sayings concerning the activity on earth is to designate Jesus' *exousia*. It is not merely a substitute for 'I'.

3. By the name Son of Man a unique sovereignty is ascribed to Jesus. It may be called a Christological dignity in a wider sense. What this dignity conveys is not determined by the traditional concepts of the transcendent Son of Man.

4. Did Jesus speak of himself as of the Son of Man acting on earth? It is certain that he spoke of the coming Son of Man as of another. He pointed away from himself to another one in the future and did not declare his identity with this other one, the coming Son of Man. Since this manner of speaking is established without exception for all sayings concerning the coming Son of Man, we must not assume that in another group of sayings Jesus spoke frankly of his own activity as that of the Son of Man. We do not see why he should have rigorously avoided the identification of his 'I' with the Son of Man in the one group whilst he expressed it quite openly in the other group. We do not see, moreover, why that differentiation should have been distinctly preserved in the tradition of the

post-Easter community.[1] An interpretation which assumed that Jesus in the *parousia* sayings spoke of the Son of Man as of a transcendent figure, whilst he formulated other sayings in which the Son of Man was devoid of all traditional attributes and conceived according to Jesus' own activity on earth, would face an unsurmountable difficulty.

5. What are we to think about the authenticity of the sayings dealt with so far? The comparison with Matt. 5.10–12 proves Luke 6.22 to have been formed by the community. The distinction made between the period of the Son of Man's activity on earth and that of the Holy Spirit betrays the post-Easter formulation of Matt. 12.32 and par. There remain Matt. 8.20 and par. and Matt. 11.19 and par. We are inclined to see their authenticity disproved by their dissimilarity from the authentic parousia sayings of the Son of Man, which has been dealt with above, and by their analogy to the sayings in Mark and Luke about the Son of Man's present activity which are about to be discussed.

B. THE SAYINGS CONCERNING THE SON OF MAN'S EARTHLY ACTIVITY IN THE GOSPELS OF MARK, MATTHEW AND LUKE

I. Analysis of the individual sayings

(1) *Sayings concerning the Son of Man's present activity in the controversy dialogues in Mark*

The sayings from Q about the Son of Man's activity on earth demonstrate that the opponents direct their attack upon Jesus' claim to full authority. It is the Son of Man who is opposed; he is reproached for his fellowship with tax collectors and sinners; to him and to his followers no home is granted on earth; for his sake the disciples are rebuked and turned out. Mark 2.10 and 2.28 accord with this. Both passages occur in controversies which are received from pre-Marcan material (Mark 2.1–3.6).[2]

---

[1] There is no foundation for the opinion frequently expressed that Jesus spoke in public of the Son of Man as of another, but to the initiated of himself as of the Son of Man. (This supposition became widespread through Albert Schweitzer, cf. *Quest*, pp. 385–9.) The sayings concerning the Son of Man's activity on earth consistently do not, as the sayings concerning the passion do, belong to the esoteric teaching to the disciples after Peter's confession.

[2] Cf. M. Albertz, *Botschaft*, p. 142; E. Fascher, *Die formgeschichtliche Methode*, 1921, pp. 146ff.

(a) **Mark 2.10.** 'But that you may know that the Son of Man has authority on earth to forgive sins . . .' It has been noted again and again that this is the only passage within the synoptic tradition where the name Son of Man is associated with forgiving sins. From this association a variety of conclusions have been drawn. Lohmeyer, for instance, declares, 'Here we meet for the first time Jesus' self-designation "Son of Man"; that it is interpolated here can easily be shown. For here alone and never again is the function of forgiving sins connected with this name.'[1] We are not satisfied by this conclusion; for it remains incomprehensible how the name Son of Man came to be connected with the authority to forgive sins.

The account of the healing of the paralytic has been vigorously debated in recent exegesis and in form-criticism as well. Dibelius objects to the labelling of this account by Bultmann and Albertz as a 'controversy dialogue'.[2] He attempts to demonstrate that the narrator, that is to say the preacher who used this pericope as a paradigm, inserted an imaginary conversation, vv. 6–10, proclaiming Jesus' authority to forgive sins. The intention of this interpolation is the proclamation of Jesus' *dignity*;[3] thus it has a Christological meaning. Bultmann however attempts to demonstrate that the middle portion, 5b–10, resulted from the controversy on the authority to forgive sins. This authority is confirmed by the power of miraculous healing. Verse 10, according to Bultmann, originally spoke of the *exousia* of Jesus; the designation Son of Man is a periphrasis of 'I' due to a misunderstanding.[4]

For our purpose it is enough to note that there is a near consensus that the Son of Man saying belongs to a portion which is an interpolation formed by the post-Easter community. This is not even disputed by W. Manson in his critical discussion of Bultmann's analysis.[5]

Wellhausen holds the view that the designation Son of Man in Mark 2.10 originally asserted in general the authority of man to forgive sins. This view is untenable; for even in Matt. 9.8 the authority of men is a special one received by the community from Jesus;[6] and the context in Mark 2.5b–10 clearly shows that the

[1] Cf. Lohmeyer, *Markus*, p. 54.
[2] Dibelius, *Formgeschichte*, p. 64 n. 1 (*Tradition* omits).
[3] Dibelius, *Tradition*, pp. 66ff.
[4] Cf. Bultmann, *Tradition*, p. 15; *Theology* I, p. 31. Counter-arguments by Dibelius in *ThR*, 1929, p. 211.
[5] Cf. W. Manson, *Jesus the Messiah*, p. 42.
[6] Cf. Matt. 16.17–19; 18.18 *et passim*.

special authority of Jesus is the issue at stake. It is Jesus as the one to whom the community traces back its authority who is reproached for presumptuous blasphemy in v. 7. Verse 10 is intended to emphasize that the *exousia* which Jesus claims and exercises does pertain to him.[1] The introduction of the name Son of Man here does not, in fact, mean a colourless substitution of 'I', but aims at emphasizing Jesus' full authority. Thus the name Son of Man is to be understood as a title of dignity.

While we assent to Bultmann's exegesis of Mark 2.10, we cannot assent to his location of the saying in the history of tradition. Bultmann considers in general that 'application of the apocalyptic title Son of Man to the earthly Jesus' is a criterion proving a saying to be a Hellenistic product.[2] In our view this is disproved by the fact that the name Son of Man is used in this way several times in sayings from Q. Already in the Palestinian tradition the name Son of Man was used in two ways, denoting on the one hand the 'apocalyptic' future Son of Man, on the other hand the 'earthly Jesus'. Bousset realized the difficulty created by this fact. 'And above all, if the Son of Man, according to what appears to be commonly accepted now, can denote only the supra-terrestrial transcendent Messiah, it is inexplicable how Jesus could already in the present claim for himself the designation and the rights of the Son of Man.'[3] We must carry Bousset's question further. The synoptic tradition on the one hand scrupulously preserves in all the sayings concerning the coming Son of Man that structure of differentiation in which Jesus speaks of the Son of Man as of someone different from himself.[4] On the other hand there are sayings in which the designation Son of Man is already applied to Jesus when acting in full authority, any differentiation between the 'I' of Jesus and the Son of Man being abolished. At variance from Bousset we want to note that it is not the designation and rights of the *transcendent* Son of Man which are claimed in the sayings concerning the activity on earth. In these sayings the name Son of Man is used in a new way. What is conveyed by it is Jesus' *exousia*. This concept of the Son of Man meaning Jesus' *exousia* appears to have been the reason for the introduction of this name into the controversy dialogues.

[1] Cf. Bultmann, *Tradition*, pp. 15f., on Mark 2.10: 'In any case it was originally the exousia of Jesus that was the subject of discussion.'

[2] Bultmann, *Tradition*, p. 155.

[3] Bousset, *Kyrios*, p. 9.

[4] Cf. Mark 8.38 and par.; Luke 12.8f. and par.; Matt. 19.28.

Albertz rightly stresses that all the individual points of controversy in the dialogues refer to one question, that of the new teacher's authority.[1] The early community had to deal with this question in particular. 'Mark 2.5b–10 has manifestly been given its place because the Church wanted to trace back to Jesus its own right to forgive sins.' The members of the community know that they do not have any authority except that which has been given to them by Jesus' authority.[2] Hence in all controversy dialogues they must have recourse to Jesus' *exousia*. Since they want to build on the foundation of their Master and his fundamental authority, they designate his activity on earth with the title of dignity 'Son of Man'.

It is of no consequence for this supposition whether the sayings Mark 2.10 and Mark 2.28 belonged to the earliest stock of the material within which they occur. If originally both of them were independent sayings and were interpolated or secondarily added into that narrative material as interpretations, the meaning of the designation Son of Man would stand out all the more clearly. In that case, moreover, these two sayings would approach all the more closely the Q sayings concerning the Son of Man's activity on earth. It is rightly maintained that there is hardly any real narrative or discourse material in Q.[3] If the sayings Mark 2.10 and 2.28 did belong to the controversy dialogues, they would be distinct from the Q sayings concerning the Son of Man's activity on earth. If the two sayings were primarily independent and only later interpolated or added, that difference from Q would disappear. We may, however, not overlook another difference. The comparable Q sayings do not speak directly of the Son of Man's authority but only imply it indirectly; the central issue is the opponents. The two sayings in Mark, on the contrary, express the fact of the *exousia* directly and positively.

The Son of Man sayings Mark 2.10 and 2.28 belong in fact and perhaps also in the history of tradition to the sphere of transition from sayings transmitted without a context *via* sayings within a context (*apophthegmata*) to the narratives. To establish this is of less help in judging their age within the synoptic tradition than is their proximity to the Son of Man sayings from Q and to the situation presupposed in them, namely the discussion with opponents.

---

[1] Cf. Albertz, *Botschaft*, p. 56. The following quotation from Bultmann, *Tradition*, pp. 15f.
[2] Cf., e.g., Luke 10.16 and par. (Q); Matt. 16.17–19; 18.181.
[3] Cf. Harnack, *Sayings*, p. 181.

How is the *exousia* of the Son of Man conceived in Mark 2.10? According to Mark 2.5b–10 Jesus by granting to an individual person the forgiveness of his sins utters a claim which must seem blasphemous to his opponents (v. 7). 'For by forgiving sins Jesus not only places himself at variance with the existing Law which demands the punishment of the sinner but also assumes that very place at which according to Jewish belief and knowledge God alone can stand.'[1] Seeing Jesus standing at this place, the community calls him Son of Man. This is unparalleled and unprecedented; neither in the synoptic nor in the Jewish apocalyptic tradition is there any other indication that the Son of Man forgives sins. The ascription to Jesus of the power of forgiving sins is thus not inspired by attributes of the transcendent Son of Man. Rather is the reverse process recognizable; by calling Jesus in his unique authority Son of Man and conceiving of Jesus' authority as including the forgiveness of sins, the community can formulate the saying that the Son of Man has the *exousia* to forgive sins on earth.[2]

The forgiveness of sins, which Jesus according to Mark 2.10 claims as part of his activity on earth, is part of his way of acting with a mission, part of his authority. How are the *exousia* in general and the authority to forgive sins in particular correlated? Jesus' preaching of the coming of God's reign not only summoned men to turn round in repentance in face of this coming but also included the assurance of God's forgiveness. How else could entry into God's kingdom be possible?[3] It is not the assurance that sin may be forgiven at the Last Judgement which gives offence. The Christian community realizes that offence lies in the fact that already here on earth a man grants forgiveness of sin. Offence is also taken because it is after all the rejected and depraved, the violators of good order, the sinners, who receive forgiveness from Jesus. 'Thus in view of the coming reign of God not only the individual barriers and precepts of the Law, but all basic moral and religious gradations and distinctions of men become immaterial. Not only the power of demons but sin, too, is deprived of its importance and significance. And again it is in Jesus' own activity that this deprivation first happens and becomes visible. Jesus has table-fellowship with tax collectors and prostitutes and dares to announce explicitly to individuals the forgiveness of their

---

[1] Campenhausen, *Amt*, pp. 8f.
[2] Cf. on this Bultmann's supposition above, pp. 116f. of our Chapter III.
[3] Cf. Luke 18.9–14; 15.1–10; 15.11-32.

sins. Here the pivotal point is reached where the right both of the "gospel" and of Jesus' authority stands to be acknowledged.'[1] The one who is standing at this pivotal point the community speaks of as the Son of Man.

That the community associates the name Son of Man with Jesus' particular authority to forgive sins is suggested by a further consideration. In the sayings on the Son of Man's parousia, Jesus is already recognized as the one who makes his fellowship with the confessor the basis for the promise that none other than the Son of Man will guarantee this fellowship before God. Thus Jesus has the authority to summon into a fellowship which guarantees entry into God's kingdom. But entry into God's reign is open only to those who turn round in repentance.[2] Turning round implies turning away from all that is opposed to God, being detached from all earthly ties. When Jesus promises to his own with legal validity fellowship with the coming Son of Man,[3] he frees them already on earth from the bondage of sin.

Is Mark 2.10 to be regarded as an authentic saying of Jesus? Taylor maintains that it is.[4] But the present form of the controversy dialogues in Mark can only be understood as having issued from the situation of the community.[5] The manner in which the name Son of Man is used in Mark 2.10, which contrasts with the authentic parousia sayings, supports our assumption that the saying was formed by the community.

(b) **Mark 2.28.** 'So the Son of Man is lord even of the sabbath.' It is not difficult to discern that Mark 2.28 is an addition; 'the typical connecting formula καὶ ἔλεγεν αὐτοῖς shows clearly that the saying which was originally isolated has been added in Mark 2.27f.'[6] But we cannot consider even 2.27 and 2.28 to have originally been intended as a unit. The Son of Man saying is rather 'an early comment on the saying, "The sabbath was made for man, and not man for the sabbath".'[7] With the disciples' behaviour in view, the con-

---

[1] Campenhausen, *Amt*, p. 8.
[2] Cf., e.g., Mark 1.15 and par.; Matt. 18.3; 11.20ff.
[3] Cf. Matt. 19.28.
[4] Taylor, *Names*, p. 27.
[5] Cf. Bultmann, *Tradition*, pp. 14ff.
[6] Bultmann, *Tradition*, p. 17.
[7] Taylor, *Names*, p. 28.

troversy dialogue Mark 2.23–26 elucidates with support from Scripture the problem of keeping the sabbath holy.

Matthew and Luke agree in omitting v. 27.[1] Are they here following the text of an earlier version of Mark?[2] Lohmeyer notes the considerable difference between what is stated in v. 27 and in v. 28. The first saying states a particular relationship between man and sabbath. The objective validity of the sabbath is affirmed, but its purpose is directed to man. The second saying, however, states that the Son of Man is lord over the sabbath.[3] In the first saying there is no hint at any particular relationship between Jesus and the sabbath. The general purpose of the sabbath, with which it is vested since its origin, serves to justify the disciples' behaviour (v. 23). According to the appended second saying the reason for the disciples' behaviour is the Son of Man's lordship over the sabbath. There is reason enough for their action in Jesus' full authority. As the lord over the sabbath Jesus is called Son of Man by the community. These decisive differences between v. 27 and v. 28 oblige us to expound Mark 2.28 as an independent saying whose meaning is closely related to 2.10.[4]

In the traditional Jewish view the sabbath is God's holy institution. There are, to be sure, also mitigations of the strict view of the sabbath which approximate to Mark 2.27. 'The sabbath is delivered to you, and you are not delivered to the sabbath.'[5] What is enunciated in Mark 2.28, however, is a fundamental lordship of the Son of Man over God's holy institution of the sabbath.

Matthew makes an important contribution to the exegesis of

---

[1] On this and on the variants of the text cf. Lohmeyer, *Markus*, p. 65 and n. 4.

[2] Bussmann, *Synoptische Studien*, p. 92, includes Mark 2.27 amongst the many 'small extensions and explanations' added mostly in the manner of glosses which are to be imputed to the last reviser of G = the synoptic *Grundschrift* (basic document) which was used by Matthew and Luke; cf. p. 70. It may, anyhow, be noted that Mark in 3.28 gives the saying on blasphemy in the form which only speaks of the blasphemies of the 'sons of men' in general. Mark in 2.27, again unparalleled in the other Gospels, gives a statement on how 'man' is related to the sabbath. Is it perhaps a specific interest of Mark's to speak of 'man' or 'men' in general? Bussmann demonstrates, however, that a reviser of G played a part in the formulation both of Mark 3.28 (as for Bussmann it becomes evident from the *figura etymologica*) and of Mark 2.27; cf. pp. 83 and 99. Is it, then, an interest of the reviser?

[3] Lohmeyer, *Markus*, pp. 65f.

[4] Campenhausen, *Amt*, p. 9, places the two sayings immediately next to each other.

[5] Mechilta on Ex. 31.14; cf. Lohmeyer, *Markus*, p. 63.

Mark 2.28. To the justification by referring to David's behaviour, Matthew in 12.5 adds a further argument. The priests in the temple must actually profane the sabbath in order to carry out the prescribed rituals. This argument reaches its real point in 12.6, 'But I tell you, here is more than the temple.' The comparison with Matt. 12.41 demonstrates that Jesus himself is that which is more than the temple. G. Bornkamm notes that Matthew wishes to say: greater than the *temple*, but no more than the *Law*. For the section vv. 3–7 appeals to the Law itself as a witness for Jesus. Accordingly v. 8 states that the Law legitimizes the Son of Man as the lord of the sabbath.[1] Thus it is by no means intended to proclaim man, i.e. the disciples, the community, as being lords of the sabbath;[2] their behaviour is rather traced back to Jesus' *exousia*, to Jesus' lordship. In this, too, 2.28 agrees fully with 2.10. Mark 2.28 is a product of the community, a fragment of the primitive Christian preaching.[3] The post-Easter community makes Jesus in his supreme authority utter the name Son of Man as his designation of himself.[4]

(c) **Summing-up on Mark 2.10 and 2.28.** Mark 2.10 and 2.28 are the only Son of Man sayings which occur in the controversy dialogues. They are likewise the only Son of Man sayings which are employed before Mark 8.31. There can be no doubt that the evangelist Mark intented the scene at Caesarea Philippi as the first and crucial preparation for the secret of the Son of Man. It does not fit in with this intention that Jesus in 2.10 and 2.28 frankly speaks of his supreme authority as of the Son of Man's. It may be best to assume that Mark felt obliged to retain the Son of Man sayings 2.10 and 2.28 in spite of their awkward position in the general arrangement of the Gospel —because they were transmitted to him in the context of the controversy dialogues.

We have noted above the close relationship between Mark 2.10; 2.28 and the Q sayings about the Son of Man's activity on earth, and have established the reasons for supposing that these sayings did not originate with Jesus himself but from a community who by means of the designation Son of Man acknowledged a specific sovereignty, authority and mission in the 'I' of Jesus on earth. In the sayings from

[1] Cf. Bornkamm, 'Expectation'.
[2] Klostermann, *Markus*, p. 31.
[3] Manson, *Jesus the Messiah*, p. 116.
[4] See above on Mark 2.10.

Q attention was paid to the arguments, reproaches and blasphemies of Jesus' opponents. In these sayings in Mark, however, in the dispute with the opponents the emphasis is laid positively on the mode of activity of the Son of Man. This difference does not abrogate the association of the sayings from Q and in Mark. In both cases Jesus appears as the one having full authority at whom his opponents take offence. Jesus' activity on earth is in no way regarded as an existence in humility or in concealment. It is with full authority that Jesus summons men to follow him. Even in Matt. 8.20 and par. homelessness is not mentioned in order to illustrate the humiliation of the Son of Man, but in order to demonstrate that the summons to follow him involves an all-embracing claim on the disciples. The aspect of suffering, of humility and of concealment does not appear in the sayings about the activity on earth. This is of the greatest significance for the further course of this investigation.

(2) *Sayings concerning the mission of the Son of Man*

Three sayings are to be discussed here, namely Luke 19.10; Matt. 13.37 and Mark 10.45. They all refer to the Son of Man acting on earth with full authority.

(a) **Luke 19.10.** 'The Son of Man is come to seek and to save that which was lost.' This is the saying which concludes the narrative about the chief tax collector Zacchaeus, which is peculiar to Luke. Scholars usually refer to the parallelism with the narrative about Levi's feast which also concludes with a saying summarizing Jesus' mission, 'I am not come to call the righteous, but sinners to repentance', in Luke 5.32. Bultmann ascribes to Luke the appending of 19.10 to the original point of the narrative in 19.9.[1] Klostermann holds that v. 10 'in spite of its late form' may belong to the basic text.[2] This latter assumption is supported by the parallel case Luke 5.32; there only 'to repentance' has been added by Luke.[3] Since we cannot find anywhere else sayings concerning the Son of Man's activity on earth which were produced by Luke, it seems probable to us that he also received the saying 19.10 from traditional material peculiar to him. As regards its meaning, the saying stands very close to Mark 2.10 and 2.28. The phrase 'is come' need not indicate a late origin;

---

[1] Cf. Bultmann, *Tradition*, p. 34.
[2] Cf. Klostermann, *Lukas*, p. 184.
[3] Cf. Bultmann, *Tradition*, pp. 92, 327.

it occurs already in Q, namely in Matt. 11.19 in connexion with the name Son of Man. Nevertheless by analogy with the other sayings about the present activity of the Son of Man it is not to be assumed that we have here an authentic saying of Jesus.

In Luke 19.10 Jesus' mission is formulated as a general obligation by means of the designation Son of Man; the Son of Man turns to the lost to save them, just as according to Mark 2.28 he has the authority to forgive sins. There can be no doubt that this designation in Luke 19.10 is a name of sovereignty which emphasizes the legitimacy and *exousia* of Jesus' mission. The preceding narrative tells of the opposition aroused by his activity; 'when they saw it, they all murmured, "He has gone to be a guest of a man who is a sinner" ' (Luke 19.7). This recalls immediately the reproach, 'friend of tax collectors and sinners'.[1] It is no accident that the name Son of Man is used on each occasion.

Additional sayings about the Son of Man's activity on earth occur in several manuscripts as variant readings. Luke 9.56: 'For the Son of Man has not come to destroy men's lives, but to save them.'[2] Matt. 18.11: 'For the Son of Man is come to save the lost.'[3] In both cases the manuscripts prove that these are secondary variants, which may be dependent on Luke 19.10. The variant Luke 9.56 gives the reason for Jesus' rebuking James and John for their wishing to call down fire from heaven on a Samaritan village which would not receive Jesus. According to the original text Jesus rejects their proposal without giving any reason. Apparently, however, the need for such reason existed. This need led to the interpolation of the variant in 9.56 which expresses Jesus' mission both negatively and affirmatively by reference to the designation Son of Man. The association with the meaning of the sayings concerning the Son of Man's acting on earth discussed hitherto is evident. The variant Matt. 18.11 appears secondarily, as regards the history of the text, in the discourse dealing with the life of the community. The section 18.10–14 concerns the 'saving of the lost', appealing to the hearers to pay respect to the little ones because they are near to God's heart.[4] Matt. 18.10 gives a *theological* reason for the respect to the little ones; their angels in heaven always behold the face of the

---

[1] Matt. 11.19 and par.
[2] FKΘ it^var syr^c Marcion.
[3] D it^var syr^c against S B it^var syr^s.
[4] Cf. on Matt. 18.10, Otto, *Kingdom*, p. 181; Bousset, *Religion*, p. 324.

heavenly Father. Matt. 18.11 gives a *Christological* reason; the Son of Man is come to save the 'lost'. A modification of terminology from the 'little ones' to the 'lost' has taken place.

(b) **Matthew 13.37.** 'He that sows the good seed is the Son of Man.' We already discussed this statement in Chapter II. It refers clearly to Jesus' activity on earth as the teacher. He is sowing the good seed, namely the sons of the *basileia*. The teacher thus acting with full authority is designated by the name Son of Man. This would have to be considered an astonishing innovation on Matthew's part if no other sayings about the Son of Man's activity on earth were known to us.[1] What Matthew does, in fact, is to adopt the twofold use of the name Son of Man in the sayings concerning the parousia and concerning the activity on earth and to present them *side by side* in the interpretation of the parable of the tares among the wheat. This juxtaposition demonstrates how closely in Matthew the two aspects under which the Son of Man is seen are conjoined in the one figure of Jesus, who is designated by the name Son of Man used in both ways. This one figure involves, so to speak, several dimensions in the history of salvation. Jesus is the Son of Man both as the one who teaches on earth with full authority and as the one who will judge the world according to 'the weightier matters' of this teaching (cf. Matt. 23.23; Matt. 25.31ff.).

(c) **Mark 10.45.** 'The Son of Man is come not to be served but to serve, and to give his life as a ransom for many.' This is one of those sayings which have aroused particularly vigorous debates in the recent history of exegesis. Holtzmann still found in this saying a 'reminiscence of the Pauline doctrine of redemption'.[2] Bousset can even demonstrate the 'operation' by means of which the wording transmitted in Luke was transformed into the 'dogmatic saying Mark 10.45'.[3] Bultmann refers to Bousset and concludes that Mark 10.45 'has formed its conception of Jesus from the redemptive

---

[1] Matthew has already cited sayings about the Son of Man acting on earth in 9.6 and 12.8 as well as 12.32. So the reader of 13.37 has become familiar with the use of this name for the one who is active on earth.

[2] Holtzmann, *Synoptiker*, p. 52.

[3] Bousset, *Kyrios*, p. 8 n. 1. The stages of this 'operation' are: '(1) Interpolation of the title Son of Man; (2) interpolation of the current formula ἦλθεν; (3) introduction of the antithesis οὐ διακονηθῆναι ἀλλά; (4) adding a gloss on διακονῆσαι by alluding to the sacrificial death.'

theories of Hellenistic Christianity';[1] it is a 'secondary formulation of a later stage'.[2]

A. Schweitzer maintained the historical authenticity of Mark 10.45.[3] Jeremias strongly affirmed the authenticity and great age of Mark 10.45; he did so most recently in the article on the Servant of Jehovah in Kittel's *Theologisches Wörterbuch*. Mark 10.45 belongs to the pre-synoptic stock of traditions and formulae;[4] it must be interpreted in relation to the Christological formulae which refer to Isa. 53.[5] The saying shows that Jesus knew himself to be the Servant of Jehovah.[6] But he revealed this secret only to his disciples.[7] Many of our contemporary commentators are inclined to agree with Jeremias' view; thus they regard Mark 10.45 as an authentic saying of Jesus, fundamental for conclusions concerning his knowledge of himself. It follows from this that the scholar's judgement on Mark 10.45 decisively helps determine his view of Jesus himself, of his teaching and of the community's witness to Jesus and his message.

According to Klostermann there is a correct consensus amongst most recent exegetes that v. 45b is a secondary addition by Mark in which he glosses the earlier saying about serving.[8] This statement will at any rate be correct is so far as it expresses that there obviously is a possibility of interpreting Mark 10.45 as a complete saying even without the comment about giving his life. Making use of this possibility, we shall first examine Mark 10.45a as if it were an independent saying. We cannot, of course, arrive at a final judgement on

[1] Bultmann, *Tradition*, p. 144.

[2] Bultmann, *Tradition*, p. 155.

[3] Cf. Schweitzer, *Mystery*; the 'historical saying' in Mark 10.45 (p. 2) does not show Pauline influences. In Schweitzer's view 'Jesus' own notion of the Passion contained this bold conception of atonement' (p. 6). 'Service is the fundamental law of the *interim-ethics*' (p. 10). 'In the case of the disciples it is merely a question of unselfish subjection, in the case of Jesus it meant the bitter suffering of death. Both count as serving, inasmuch as they establish a claim to a position of rule in the Kingdom' (p. 9). Otto, *Kingdom*, p. 252, perceives in Mark 10.45 a synthesis between Son of Man and Servant of Jehovah in Deutero-Isaiah. He considers this passage to belong to the 'genuine *Urworte*' (original sayings) in which Jesus taught his new *didache* of the necessity of suffering (*ibid.*, p. 250). W. Manson, *Jesus the Messiah*, would like to trace back the 'doctrine' of Mark 10.45 to Jesus himself and to his great intuition which arose out of his experience of suffering (cf. pp. 68, 111f., 131ff., 163).

[4] Jeremias, *Servant*, pp. 89f.; cf. also Jeremias, 'Lösegeld', pp. 258-64.

[5] *Servant*, p. 95.

[6] *Ibid.*, pp. 98ff.; cf. Wolff, *Jes.* 53.

[7] Jeremias, *op. cit.*, p. 104. For Lohse's view in *Märtyrer*, cf. below Chapter IV D III d, pp. 203ff.

[8] Klostermann, *Markus*, p. 109. May we really say 'most' recent exegetes?

the nature of the whole saying in Mark 10.45 until after we have interpreted the comment about giving his life, in Chapter IV.

If the first part of the saying had been transmitted alone, then it could be fitted into the context in the following manner. Whoever wishes to be great among you must be your servant (v. 43); and whoever wishes to be first among you must be slave of all (v. 44); for the Son of Man also came not to be served but to serve (v. 45a). Considered thus, the statement in Mark 10.45 would to some extent accord with Luke 22.27, apart from the fact that the name Son of Man is not mentioned in Luke.

Within this context Mark 10.45a conforms quite well to the sayings about the Son of Man's activity on earth discussed up to now. It regards the mission as a whole: he is come. This corresponds with Matt. 11.19 and par.; Luke 19.10; and a comprehensive view of the Son of Man's authority is also taken in Mark 2.10 and 2.28. Admittedly, Mark 10.45 does not suggest a dispute with opponents about Jesus' authority. For the purpose of teaching the disciples, it contains nothing but the positive statement that the Son of Man came to serve.

There is also a close correspondence with the Son of Man saying Matt. 8.20 and par. In this saying it is made clear to a man who sets out to follow Jesus that he who follows must take upon himself that homelessness which is borne by the Son of Man. In Mark 10.45a it is made clear to the disciple who wishes to be great that he must look for his greatness in analogy to the Son of Man, namely by serving. In both cases a rule as to how the disciples should follow is based on the example set by the Son of Man.

Nevertheless Mark 10.45 deviates from all the sayings about the Son of Man's activity on earth discussed hitherto in one essential respect. Here we find expressed the deliberate humility of the Son of Man, who fulfils his mission by serving. This is a different conception from the one expressed by the Son of Man's homelessness in Matt. 8.20 and par. The homelessness of the Son of Man as well as of his followers is brought about essentially *from without*, namely by the opposition of 'this adulterous and sinful generation' which denies them a home. It is different also from what is expressed in Luke 19.10 and in Matt. 11.19 and par. The Son of Man does attach himself to the lost, to the tax collectors and sinners; yet he does not do so by making himself equal to them, but by summoning them with authority into the fellowship that results from following him. The

s.m.–e*

saying on serving now implies that the one who serves subordinates himself, that he subjects his sovereignty to those whom he serves. Thus here for the first time in our study of the Son of Man sayings we meet the great paradox that he who has full authority makes himself the lowly one. We can understand why this particular Son of Man saying was extended by an allusion to his giving his life for many; for in the structure of this saying alone we see that paradox which is dominant in the sayings about the suffering Son of Man and in the passion narrative. In this way Mark 10.45 is a real bridge between the kerygma of the passion and the sayings about the Son of Man's acting on earth with full authority.

II. Results: The nature of the use of the name Son of Man in the sayings concerning the Son of Man's activity on earth in the Gospels of Mark, Matthew and Luke

1. We perceived a congruity of the concept present in the sayings about the Son of Man as active on earth in the controversy dialogues in Mark, in Matt. 13.37, in Luke 19.10 and in Mark 10.45a with the concept present in this group of sayings in Q. In both cases the name Son of Man is used in the same way. Hence it is impossible that some of these sayings should have arisen from a linguistic misunderstanding. In all the sayings of this group the name Son of Man characterizes Jesus in the *exousia* of his activity on earth. Consequently most of these sayings reveal the opposition of his adversaries who turn against Jesus' claim to full authority.

2. Since sayings concerning the Son of Man acting on earth occur in Q and in the pre-Marcan controversial discourses as well as in Mark 10.45 and in material peculiar to Matthew and to Luke, we can affirm that their roots must have been widespread in the history of tradition. The fact that they appear also in Q excludes the assumption that it was the Hellenistic community which first produced these sayings. Of course, it does not exclude the possibility that corresponding sayings also appeared in the Hellenistic sphere.

3. The fundamental problem is that in the tradition, even in Q, strictly separated sayings concerning the parousia and sayings concerning the activity of the Son of Man on earth appear side by side. Both groups of sayings have in common the fact that the name Son of Man is used, but they differ in the way in which it is used. In the one group Jesus speaks of the Son of Man as of another, a future

being, differentiating between his 'I' and the person of the Son of Man. In the other group Jesus, expressly identifying the Son of Man with himself, speaks of the Son of Man as of a being who is active at present. We found authentic sayings of Jesus amongst the parousia sayings; among those about the Son of Man's activity on earth, however, sayings which have certainly been formed by the community predominate. Therefore we may conclude that the different ways of using the name Son of Man begin at different points within the history of tradition. The community, even when forming sayings concerning the coming Son of Man on their own, retained the stereo-typed structure of the authentic sayings; when expressing their post-Easter recognition, however, in the sayings concerning the activity on earth they designated Jesus as the Son of Man even in this activity. We shall endeavour to elucidate in Chapter V why these different groups of sayings were not intermingled within the tradition.

4. Notwithstanding the difference between the two groups, we yet perceived concordant elements appearing both in the parousia sayings and in the sayings about the earthly activity of the Son of Man.

(a) Both have in common the emphasis on the tension over against men, against this generation. This tension is mentioned so often that we cannot assume its having been associated by chance. It is rather an intrinsic element. This will be evident from the following point of agreement.

(b) In both groups of sayings Jesus is regarded as claiming with supreme authority men's confession of himself; as summoning men to follow him; as bestowing on those who follow him a fellowship which radically confronts them with the opposition of those who will not recognize Jesus' *exousia*. According to both groups of sayings, it is Jesus' claim to sovereignty that stimulates men's opposition to it; consequently, to follow Jesus means to hold on to him and not to be held by men.

(c) Both groups of sayings have a third element in common. Jesus always appears in his sovereignty, i.e. as the one who with supreme authority summons men to follow him. His own homelessness and subsequently the sufferings of those who follow him are caused by the opposition of men who shut themselves up against God's will. Only according to Mark 10.45 does Jesus, the Son of Man, volun-tarily make himself the lowly one. No other sayings express either the motif of concealment or the paradoxical unity of being both divinely authorized and given over to the humility of human existence. Hence there is no need for the concept of willing obedience in the sayings concerning the Son of Man.

5. In addition to the concepts of concealment and of willing obedience, or self-abasement, something else is missing in the sayings about the Son of Man's activity on earth. The transcendent attributes, rights, functions and limitlessness of the heavenly Son of Man are not at all transferred to Jesus on earth.[1] It may be said that in spite of the identical designation 'Son of Man' the *material* identification is absent. The transcendent subject is not incorporated into the subject who exists on earth. Why Jesus was not identified with the transcendent Son of Man is comprehensible if it is realized what the person of Jesus meant according to these sayings. In the attitude towards this person an eternal decision takes place in the realm of history. The attitude towards Jesus, the acknowledgement or rejection of Jesus' claim, is decisive. Men oppose the Son of Man on earth; when the transcendent Son of Man appears, 'then all the tribes of the earth will mourn',[2] for his transcendent sovereignty will be irresistible.

[1] If that were the case, the Son of Man acting on earth would have to be associated with material of the kind found in the narrative of the transfiguration, Mark 9.2–8.

[2] Matt. 24.30.

IV

THE SAYINGS CONCERNING THE
SUFFERING AND RISING OF
THE SON OF MAN

I N THE ANNOUNCEMENTS of the Son of Man's suffering, of his
being rejected and delivered up, of his being killed and of his
rising, this name is used in a way which differs both from that in
the parousia sayings and that in the sayings about the activity on
earth. Ever since critical scholars attempted to prove these announcements to be *vaticinia ex eventu*,[1] assumptions have hardened which
violently contradict each other. The fundamental question is: What
do these sayings have to do with the sayings about the Son of Man's
parousia? What do these two groups have in common? Of course,
the name Son of Man; but this name has a different meaning in the
two groups.

According to Bousset, the passion sayings issued from the primitive
community's or the disciples' dogmatic teaching concerning the
Son of Man; the sayings were formed by systematizing and dogmatiz-
ing.[2] In this view announcements of suffering and parousia prophecies already appeared in juxtaposition in the Palestinian community.
Bultmann takes a different view. He emphasizes that without any
doubt the prophecies of rising are *vaticinia ex eventu*. The two types of
prophecies—of rising and of the parousia—appeared in juxtaposition
rather late; for the prophecies of rising were formed by the Hellenistic community. They appeared only after the original meaning of
the designation Son of Man was no longer understood. Bultmann is
so sure of this assumption that he uses it as a basis for differentiation

[1] Cf., e.g., Wrede, *Messiasgeheimnis*, pp. 82–92; Wellhausen, *Einleitung*, pp.
79–82.
[2] Boussset, *Kyrios*, p. 9, cf. p. 8; p. 16 with n. 2. For the following compare also
our preliminary remarks to Chapter III, pp. 113f., and the Introduction, pp. 17f.

in the history of tradition. Thus to him a saying is a Hellenistic product as soon as the name Son of Man is applied to Jesus on earth,[1] and the relationship to Daniel's Son of Man has been lost in such a saying.[2]

Bultmann's view provoked violent controversy. It was argued that the different groups of Son of Man sayings could not have been juxtaposed without having been connected, since the concept of a period of suffering through which the eschatological Perfecter passes is already present in Judaism. Thus the coming and the suffering Son of Man had been connected before Jesus used these concepts.[3] The discussion has, however, shown that this assumption lacks sufficient evidence. Therefore it was argued that in I Enoch the suffering Servant of Jehovah had been connected with the coming Son of Man; this combination served as the foundation of Jesus' consciousness of his mission.[4] In W. Manson's view it was Jesus himself who recognized the consequences arising from the synthesis of the lowly Servant of Jehovah and the glorious Son of Man in the figure of the Messiah.[5]

A. Schweitzer solves the problem in a different way. ' "Son of Man" is accordingly the adequate expression of his messiahship, so long as he, in this earthly aeon as Jesus of Nazareth, has occasion to refer to his future dignity. Hence when he speaks to the disciples about himself as Son of Man he assumes this duality of consciousness. "The Son of Man must suffer and will then rise from the dead": that is to say, "As the one who is to be the Son of Man at the

---

[1] Bultmann, *Theology*, pp. 29f., 82f.; *Tradition*, p. 155 *et passim*.

[2] Bultmann, 'Matt. 16.17–19', pp. 278f.

[3] Jeremias argues thus in 'Erlösung', pp. 106ff. Cf. also Staerk, *Soter* II, pp. 406ff.

[4] Jeremias, *Servant*, pp. 61f. Jeremias' proposition that already in I Enoch and IV Ezra the Son of Man had been a suffering figure (cf. Jeremias, 'Erlösung', pp. 106ff.; and *Servant*, pp. 59f.) is convincingly refuted by Sjöberg. The larger the number of individual connexions found by Jeremias between the *Ebed* Songs and the Son of Man, the greater is the importance of the fact that no traits of the *Ebed's* humility or suffering were used to describe the Son of Man. Cf. Sjöberg, *Verborgener Menschensohn*, pp. 70f.; and *Menschensohn*, pp. 116–39. This statement accords with the fact that the traits of suffering were omitted when Jesus' activity was interpreted by reference to Isaiah 53 in Matt. 8.17, cf. also Matt. 12.18–21.

[5] Cf. W. Manson, *Jesus the Messiah*, p. 117. Manson follows Goguel in assuming that the definite expectation of the path of suffering and rejection led Jesus finally to regard the path of the Messiah and his own path as one and the same. Thus Jesus' consciousness of himself is raised above the stage of a merely prophetic vocation to the anticipation that he himself after his rejection will appear as the glorious Son of Man. Cf. Manson, *Jesus the Messiah*, pp. 126f., and Taylor, *Origin*, pp. 159–69.

resurrection of the dead, I must suffer." In the same way we must understand the word about serving: as the one who in the appointed character of the Son of Man is destined to the highest rule in the Messianic aeon, I must now humble myself to the lowliest service (Mark 10.45). Therefore when they come to arrest him he says, The hour is come in which he who is to be the Son of Man must be delivered up into the hands of sinners (Mark 14.21 and 41). The problem about the Son of Man is herewith clarified. It was not an expression which Jesus commonly used to describe himself, but a solemn title which he adopted when in the great moments of his life he spoke about himself to the initiated as the future Messiah, while before others he spoke of the Son of Man as a person distinct from himself.'[1] M. Werner adopted Schweitzer's view. To him the prophecies of suffering are the solution supplied by Jesus himself to the difficulties resulting from the postponement of the coming of the kingdom.[2] R. Otto argues similarly. Jesus regarded himself as the claimant for the title Son of Man. He thought in 'post-existential' terms, i.e. referring to his future existence which in this reference is anticipated.[3] This concept was already at hand in the Enoch Apocalypse.[4] Correspondingly Jesus knows himself to be the *filius hominis designatus*,[5] the one who is designated to be the Son of Man. The prophecies of the passion are original passages (*Urstellen*) in which the tradition is 'as hard as diamonds' (*diamanten fest*).[6] In Mark 10.45 the connexion with Isa. 53 has been achieved.[7]

In contrast to Bultmann the other exegetes mentioned are united in the conviction that the name Son of Man is a homogeneous designation of sovereignty conceiving of an identical subject in all groups of sayings. Consequently they are convinced that this

[1] Schweitzer, *Mystery*, pp. 192f. This solution of the Son of Man problem is of seductive simplicity and clarity, but it already suffers shipwreck on the fact that in Q not a single saying concerning the suffering and rising of the Son of Man occurs. Schweitzer allows himself to ignore what has been established in the history of tradition in favour of a speculative reconstruction of Jesus' acting according to the so-called logic of *consequent eschatology*. For theological criticism of Schweitzer cf. Schniewind, *Messiasgeheimnis*, pp. 1ff.

[2] Martin Werner, *Die Entstehung des christlichen Dogmas*, 2nd ed., 1953, pp. 73f.

[3] Otto, *Kingdom*, p. 175.

[4] *Ibid.*, pp. 176–201.

[5] *Ibid.*, p. 219.

[6] *Ibid.*, p. 235.

[7] *Ibid.*, p. 252. Staerk, *Soter* II, pp. 93f., regards Jesus' consciousness of being Son and Saviour as the clasp binding together the sayings about the glory and those about the passion; he does not, however, see a reference to Isa. 53.

designation embraces both the transcendent sphere which will break in at the parousia superseding the sphere of the earth, and the sphere of human history in which Jesus acts and suffers. But can this view be supported from the synoptic texts? Are the attributes and functions of the transcendent Son of Man really implicated in the sphere of Jesus' history? In the sayings concerning the activity on earth we recognized that the sovereignty attributed to Jesus by means of the name Son of Man is not the transcendent sovereignty. This is confirmed by the relationships in the history of tradition which have been thoroughly worked out by Bultmann. If the sayings both in the group concerning the coming and in the group concerning the suffering Son of Man had issued from Jesus himself, or if the spheres of concepts expressed in the two groups had been connected already in Judaism, why these groups stayed strictly separate within the synoptic tradition is and remains incomprehensible. It would be incomprehensible as well why Jesus in the parousia sayings spoke of the Son of Man as of another whilst in the other groups of sayings he spoke of his lot and his person unambiguously using the designation Son of Man. This difference might be disregarded only if the tradition had not, contrary to what is the case, separately retained the structure of the sayings in the two different groups with such invariable strictness. The following examination of the individual sayings concerning the Son of Man's suffering and rising should contribute to a clarification of these problems.

A. THE SAYINGS CONCERNING THE SUFFERING AND RISING SON OF MAN WITHIN THE STRUCTURE OF THE GOSPEL OF MARK

Within the synoptic tradition the sayings concerning the suffering Son of Man occur first in the Gospel of Mark. Q does not know them. We might suppose that this group of sayings issued from the surroundings of that community in which the Gospel of Mark was composed; this is at any rate not the Palestinian community.

The sayings concerning the Son of Man's suffering are not primarily connected with the *material* transmitted in Mark; they are of great significance, however, for its *composition*. Therefore we shall start with examining this composition.

It should be noted that sayings concerning the suffering Son of Man occur only in the second part of the Gospel of Mark, i.e. after

Peter's confession at Caesarea Philippi in 8.27ff.; and here they occur only in the two sections 8.27–10.52 and 14.1–42. These sections have the parallel function in the composition of the Gospel of leading up to the passion narrative. Within these sections the announcements that the Son of Man must needs be delivered up according to the Scriptures function as preparatory interpretations of the event of the passion. It seems all the more strange, then, that the series of Son of Man sayings breaks off at 14.41 immediately before the beginning of the account of what really happened in connexion with the passion. The early material pertaining to this account could dispense with using the designation Son of Man.[1] This observation requires elucidation in greater detail.

1. The particular nature of the section *Mark 8.27–10.52* has long been recognized. Bultmann states, 'Here Christian *kerygma* has attained its point of greatest influence on the presentation.'[2] Lohmeyer concludes, 'The section is held together by the three announcements of the passion which are carefully allotted to the three stages of the journey. The theme of suffering is also alluded to in other passages (8.34ff.; 10.35ff.); thus here for the first time a logical perspective of arrangement is expressed.'[3] According to Wellhausen's telling comment this section presents the evangelist's '*theologia crucis*'.[4]

The systematic arrangement by means of the three announcements of the passion is obvious. The announcements are also allotted geographically. Mark 8.31 belongs in the north to Caesarea Philippi, Mark 9.31 to Galilee, Mark 10.33f. to the road to Jerusalem. We must regard the whole section as teaching for the disciples.[5] The theme of Jesus' suffering and of what this means for those following him determines the context. To denote the theme of the teaching for the disciples and the community[6] about suffering and following through suffering, Mark consciously uses the key-word Son of Man. This way of using the designation Son of Man in composing the Gospels is something new as contrasted with the sayings about the

---

[1] Mark 14.62 does not belong to the account of what happened in the passion, since this saying tells of the future glory of the coming Son of Man.

[2] Bultmann, *Tradition*, p. 350.

[3] Lohmeyer, *Markus*, pp. 160f.

[4] Cf. on this Ebeling, *Messiasgeheimnis*, pp. 57f.

[5] Cf., e.g., 8.27; 9.2; 9.28; 9.31; 9.33; 9.38; 10.28; 10.32; 10.35.

[6] That Mark is thinking of the community appears, e.g., from the phrase 'and for the gospel's (sake)' which stresses the relevance of the pronouncement in 8.35 for the post-Easter situation.

parousia and the activity on earth which were not used in any fundamental way in the composition.

Apart from the announcements of the Son of Man's suffering, the section also contains a saying about his parousia in 8.38. According to Bultmann's view the sayings 8.31 and 8.38 were placed side by side without being adjusted to each other. Bultmann uses his statement as an important argument that the juxtaposition of the two types of Son of Man sayings is an unconnected juxtaposition.[1] The two types of sayings are, in fact, separate, both with respect to the history of their tradition and with respect to their content. But did Mark himself regard these sayings as unconnected?

We must first of all take into account that Mark in the section 8.27–10.52 repeatedly makes sayings to the disciples follow after the announcements of the suffering, and these sayings repeatedly allude to the coming *basileia* which is the promised prize in store for those who follow.[2] Thus for Mark there is a fixed connexion between the disciples' following and their entering into the *basileia*. In this way the evangelist leads the reader from Mark 8.31 to 8.38 and 9.1. He first guides the view towards the Son of Man's suffering, then to the disciples' following through suffering, and finally to the future participation in the glory of the transcendent Son of Man. To be sure, the sayings on the suffering of the Son of Man on earth and those on the glory of the transcendent Son of Man to come are not immediately and directly joined here as they are in Luke 17.24, 25, 26. They are not connected in a primarily Christological way; there is no direct connexion of the Son of Man's state of humility with his state of glory. Mark rather directs the reader's attention from the Son of Man's suffering on earth towards the community's following through suffering; this he subordinates to the promise of participation in the future glory of the transcendent Son of Man. Thus Mark 8.31 and 8.38 are not juxtaposed unconnectedly; they are connected by way of the disciples' following. Thereby a *soteriological* correlation of the two types of sayings is effected. This procedure corresponds with the structure of the Son of Man sayings on confessing and denying. We stated above in Chapter II[3] that what is intended in these sayings is not a Christological correlation of Jesus with the Son of Man but the promise of a soteriological continuity between the fellowship with

---

[1] Bultmann, 'Matt. 16.17–19', p. 279.
[2] Mark 9.1; 10.15, 17; cf. Mark 10.28–31 with Matt. 19.28; also Mark 10.37.
[3] B I 4 a, p. 57.

Jesus on earth and fellowship with the Son of Man in the kingdom of God.[1] Mark deliberately inserts the saying about the coming Son of Man into a text whose arrangement is determined by the theme of announcing the Son of Man's suffering and rising; 8.38 is indeed the only Son of Man saying in Mark with a structure appropriate for this association.

The section 8.27–10.52 contains the narrative of the transfiguration and the subsequent conversation in 9.9–13 during the descent. Bultmann maintains that the narrative of the transfiguration contained the concept of the rising, whereas Mark 9.1 and 9.11–13 merely presupposed the parousia; Mark 9.12b is according to Bultmann a secondary interpretation founded on Matt. 17.12b. We shall discuss this view below in the detailed analysis of Mark 9.9–13.[2] Even when Mark 9.12b is excluded, one statement which belongs to the group of sayings concerning the Son of Man's suffering and rising (9.9b) is left in the section 9.9–13 whose connexion with the parousia motif in Mark 9.1 must be understood.

There is no saying on the Son of Man's suffering in the section Mark 11–13, which follows after the section Mark 8.27–10.52. Evidently this is not the right place for such a saying. The teaching for the disciples about suffering and following has been concluded. The entry into Jerusalem has completely changed the situation. Now the holy city, the kingship of David, the temple, ultimate points of controversy, and the deadly enmity of the Jewish leaders are the predominant concerns. Chapter 13 then turns to eschatological themes, to the destruction of the temple, to the last tribulations, to the definitive end which is brought about with the saving coming of the Son of Man.

2. In the section *Mark 14.1–42* account is given of the activities of the opponents (14.1f.; 14.10f.) as well as of words and deeds of Jesus that are the immediate presuppositions for the passion event which is about to occur. Jesus twice announces the Son of Man's being 'delivered'. He does not speak of it any longer as of something in the future, but as of something which happens now. 'The hour is come, behold, the Son of Man is delivered into the hands of the sinners' (14.41; cf. 14.21). These sayings do not mention the rising. They lead up to the entry into the event of the passion—and hereafter not even the suffering Son of Man is mentioned again. Why not?

---

[1] Matt. 19.28; Luke 12.8f. and par.; Mark 8.38 and par.
[2] Cf. Bultmann, *Theology* I, p. 30, and 'Matt. 16.17–19', p. 279.

Mark 14.42 marks an important caesura within the passion account. Jeremias arrives at the conclusion that 'at a very early stage the account of the passion started with Jesus' arrest'.[1] Bultmann thinks 'that there was a primitive narrative which told very briefly of the arrest, the condemnation by the Sanhedrin and Pilate, the journey to the cross, the crucifixion and death'.[2] According to these statements therefore a ready-formed narrative sequence was taken over by Mark into his Gospel after 14.42. Thus there was no possibility for him to introduce secondarily into this section any sayings on the suffering Son of Man. This was different before the caesura. The analyses by Jeremias and Bultmann which we quoted above clearly demonstrate that the section 14.1–42 had been put together relatively late by loosely relating various independent pieces.[3] Thus there was a possibility for the editor to shape the material more freely; Mark even had to arrange the pieces himself in order to lead up to the event of the passion and its commencement with the arrest. This was a problem of the same kind as that which he had already solved in the section 8.27–10.52. In both cases he achieved the solution by means of the sayings on the Son of Man's suffering and being delivered up.

3. *Results*. Obviously a relationship exists between the Marcan understanding of the material from the synoptic tradition and the sayings on the Son of Man's suffering, because these sayings are used by Mark in his composition to lead up to the heart of his Gospel, the passion narrative. Mark uses the Son of Man sayings as preparatory interpretations of the event of the passion.

The 'genuine' text of Mark which we have ends rather abruptly at 16.8 The women flee from the grave and keep silent about the young man's great news, 'He is risen' (16.6). Why does Mark not speak of the fundamental fact of his rising with a fuller emphasis? Why does he not stress the resurrection story in such a way as would bring the narrative of the Gospel to a climax? Evidently he did not feel this to be necessary, since he had made *Jesus himself* solemnly announce his rising in the weighty sayings on the Son of Man's suffering in

---

[1] Jeremias, *Eucharistic Words*, p. 66.

[2] Bultmann, *Tradition*, p. 279, cf. 276. Schille rightly questioned Bultmann, 'What need was there for the community to draw up the earliest (historical) report?'; cf. *Leiden*, pp. 161ff. This problem, however, does not concern our investigation, since the early narrative sequence, which is amply attested by the agreement of all the synoptists with John, is located on the other side of that caesura Mark 14.42.

[3] Cf. 14.3–9; 14.12–16; 14.17–21. Jeremias, *Eucharistic Words*, p. 64. Bultmann, *Tradition*, pp. 264ff.

8.31; 9.31; 10.33f.; 9.9.[1] Thus in the composition of the earliest Gospel the sayings concerning the Son of Man are indispensable conveyers of the message of the Lord's rising. Did Mark himself form these weighty sayings?

Before we clarify this question we shall consider the function of the sayings concerning the Son of Man's suffering in the other two Synoptic Gospels.

B. THE USE OF THE SAYINGS CONCERNING THE SUFFERING AND RISING SON OF MAN IN THE GOSPEL OF MATTHEW

1. *The composition of the Gospel of Matthew* deviates in essential points from Mark's composition. Matthew allots considerable space to Jesus' teaching; Mark led up swiftly to the passion narrative. Thus Matthew not only extends Mark's work but also modifies Mark's theme. Do the sayings on the suffering Son of Man have the same leading function in Matthew's composition as they had in Mark's?

Matthew took over most of Mark's sayings concerning the suffering Son of Man and did not detach them from their context. He reproduces the second and the third announcement of suffering, Mark 9.9 and 9.12 and Mark 14.21 and 14.41, without appreciably altering them. He proceeds independently only in two places.

2. *Matt. 26.2b* is inserted by Matthew into the two verses with which Mark introduces the passion narrative. The insertion shows that as much weight is attached in Matthew to the announcement of the Son of Man's 'being delivered' as in Mark. The saying of Jesus announces in advance the theme of the account of the passion which follows.

Did Matthew formulate this saying himself? None of the Son of Man sayings in Mark employs the word 'crucify'; they only employ the phrase that the Son of Man will be killed. Matthew replaces this phrase as early as the third announcement of the passion by the word 'crucify'. Moreover, Matt. 26.2b is smoothly adjusted to Mark's context. Hence it may well be a formulation of Matthew. The phrase of the Son of Man's 'being delivered' corresponds to Mark 14.21, 41. In general Matthew has largely taken over the section Mark 14.1–42 and left it intact.

---

[1] In Luke 24.7 there appears a late reminiscence that may be compared with Mark of this function of Son of Man sayings which Jesus is made to utter.

3. *Matt. 16.21* is formed in conformity with the first passion announcement in Mark, except that the designation Son of Man is omitted and the saying is modified according to this omission. This omission has given rise to various conjectures. Does the comparison of Matt. 16.21 with Mark 8.31, i.e. the substitution of the personal pronoun 'he' for 'Son of Man', prove that in Matthew's understanding no difference exists between the simple 'I' of Jesus and the designation Son of Man in so far as it applies to him who is suffering? Is the name Son of Man anything more than a neutral designation of Jesus' 'I'?

In our view the omission of the designation Son of Man in Matt. 16.21 is due to Matthew's technique of composition. The context predisposed Matthew to omit the name. As recognized already by Holtzmann, Matthew had moved the name Son of Man forward from 16.21 to 16.13.[1] In Matt. 16.13 the use of the designation Son of Man seems hardly suitable to us. 'The expression here in Matthew can after all hardly be a messianic title; for if it were the answer to the question would have been given beforehand. It can only be a commonplace self-designation.'[2] But obviously Matthew does not wish to put a *genuine* question at the beginning. He understands the section about Peter's confession in 16.13-20 differently from Mark. In Mark's Gospel Peter answers the question by openly declaring the *fact* of Jesus' messiahship. In spite of this declaration the disciple tries to obstruct the way leading to the Master's future suffering—he has misunderstood the *meaning* of the messiahship[3] which must needs remain in concealment here (Mark 9.9). In the Gospel of Matthew it is different. Peter's confession initiates the period of the Church; this is proclaimed by Jesus himself (Matt. 16.16ff.). Thus the section 16.13-20 is given a new function. The sovereignty of the one who announces the period of his Church is solemnly enunciated at the beginning of the section. This is done by using the name Son of Man as an emphatic heading.[4]

This supposition is decisively substantiated by 26.2. Here Matthew sets the name Son of Man at the head of the passion account. We cannot take this name in 16.13 for a neutral self-designation by Jesus. In both cases Matthew places the name Son of Man at the

---

[1] Cf. Holtzmann, *Synoptiker*, p. 259. Cf. on Matt. 16.21 and 16.13, also Chapter II C 2 c, pp. 85f. and n. 2 as well as 3 c, p. 90.
[2] Klostermann, *Matt.*, p. 138.
[3] Exegesis according to Bornkamm, summer term of 1955.
[4] Cf. Iber, *Überlieferung*, p. 31.

commencement of sections which in Mark were determined by sayings about the Son of Man suffering and being delivered up (Mark
14.1–42 and Mark 8.27–10.52), and which are taken over without
essential modifications. Thus Matthew understands this name to be a
title of dignity.

4. Matthew places marked stress on the sayings concerning the
Son of Man's suffering and rising. If they nevertheless do not carry
as much weight in the composition of his Gospel as they did in
Mark's, this is due to a variation of the general theme of what Jesus
means. This variation is perceptible also in the emphasis on the
Easter and post-Easter events which was lacking in Mark apart from
Jesus' predictions.

C. THE USE OF THE SAYINGS CONCERNING THE SUFFERING AND RISING SON OF MAN IN THE GOSPEL OF LUKE

Luke takes over most of the sayings concerning the suffering Son
of Man from Mark, but does not give them the same function. He
breaks up the theme of Mark's composition in general as well as the
section Mark 8.27–10.52 in particular; the section Mark 14.1–42 is
also rearranged.

The first announcement of the passion, the transfiguration, and
the second announcement appear almost at the end of the material
concerning the Galilean period of Jesus' life; then the great account
of the journey begins and separates the last announcement of the
passion from the two preceding ones. This last one, however, occurs
in the same geographical situation as it did in Mark, namely on the
road to Jerusalem. 'The feeding, the confession, the announcement
of the passion, the transfiguration' form 'a complete cycle to which
Luke assigns a prominent function in his whole structure (*Aufbau*)'.[1]
Regarding Luke's use of the transfiguration scene Conzelmann says,
'The purpose behind the heavenly manifestation is the announcement of the passion.'[2] By this modification Luke closely connects the
transfiguration event with the announcements of the Son of Man's
suffering. Thus the conversation during the descent which in Mark
presents reflections on suffering and rising may drop out in Luke.

In spite of major alterations of Mark's composition Luke does take

---

[1] Conzelmann, *Theology of Luke*, p. 56.
[2] *Ibid.*, p. 57; cf. Luke 9.31.

over the announcements of suffering. He recognizes their importance. This is also demonstrated by the way he reproduces Mark 14.1–42. Obviously Luke cannot give the sayings concerning the Son of Man's being delivered up in a position parallel to Mark's. But he does not drop them, as is evident from Luke 22.48. Luke offers a substitute for Mark 14.41 which uses the name Son of Man, though detached from the earlier context and within an altered formulation.

Luke attaches great value to the concept of the suffering Son of Man as is also evident from the fact that on his own account he inserts 17.25 between the two sayings concerning the Son of Man's parousia. This is confirmed by 24.7. Luke here formulates a Galilean announcement by Jesus of the Son of Man's being delivered up and crucified, and of his rising. The two 'men' at the grave (24.4) remind the women of this announcement. The term 'crucified' shows the lateness of the formulation.[1] But except for this, the wording conforms to the other sayings about the Son of Man's being delivered up; it stresses, however, as befits the situation, the rising on the third day.

D. THE MEANING OF THE SAYINGS CONCERNING THE SUFFERING AND RISING SON OF MAN AND THEIR LOCATION IN THE HISTORY OF TRADITION

In the preceding survey a consistent picture became visible. Most of the sayings concerning the suffering and rising Son of Man were first used by Mark for his Gospel in which he gave them leading positions in significant sections. Matthew and Luke follow Mark. They use in significant places the sayings which they receive, and they make the sayings which they form on their own account conform to the sayings in Mark. The three gospel-writers agree in the concepts expressed in these sayings. Hence we do not see anything which would hinder us from starting the analysis mainly with Mark.

I. The problem of the three announcements of suffering
Mark 8.31; 9.31; 10.33f.

Whoever reads the three passion predictions one after the other will notice their similarity. It is natural to assume that 'the fact that there are three of them is obviously due to the editorial procedure of the second evangelist. . . . He trebled the prophecy of the passion

---

[1] Cf. above on Matt. 26.2.

which was transmitted to him by the tradition within the community.'[1] This assumption meets, however, with difficulties. When we compare the three announcements we quickly see how widely the terms which are employed vary and how differentiated the concepts are.

All three announcements have in common the following: (1) the name *Son of Man*, (2) the phrase *rise after three days* (cf. Mark 9.9), (3) the term *kill*.

Features shared by two announcements are: (4) the expression *to deliver* (9.31; 10.33f.; cf. 14.21; 14.41), (5) the naming of *chief priests and scribes* (8.31; 10.33); 8.31 also names the *elders*, 9.31 speaks of his being delivered into the hands of *men*, 14.41 into the hands of *sinners*.

Peculiar to a single announcement are the following: (6) the phrase, the Son of Man *must* (8.31; cf. *it is written* in 9.12; 14.21), (7) the expression *suffer many things* (8.31; cf. 9.12), (8) the term *to be rejected* (8.31; cf. *to be treated with contempt* in 9.12), (9) the string of predictions which occurs solely in 10.33f., 'and they will condemn him to death—and will deliver him to the Gentiles—and they will mock him—and spit upon him—and scourge him. . . .' These predictions may be considered as a self-contained passage from a summary; they must be dealt with together, but do not have to be taken into account here. Allowing ourselves this device, we are able to reduce the announcements to a basic type with the following elements:

    I. The name Son of Man.
    II. To be 'delivered'/rejected (Nos. 4 and 8).
    III. The authorities who take part in the 'delivering' (No. 5).
    IV. The killing (No. 3).
    V. The rising after three days (No. 2).

Hence the basic structure of the announcements could be set forth by means of those expressions which most frequently occur as follows: The Son of Man will be delivered to the chief priests and scribes and killed and will rise in three days.

What do we gain by extracting this minimum structure? First a most compact statement of the facts of the passion *kerygma*.[2] Then a base from which the variety of meanings implicit in the terms employed for the passion announcements stands out. We cannot arrive

---

[1] Thus recently Iber, *Überlieferung*, pp. 61f.
[2] Cf. Bultmann, *Tradition*, pp. 275f.

at a judgement on whether the threefold formulation of the announcement issued from Mark until after an analysis of the various phrases.

Lohmeyer thinks it possible to deduce from Mark 8.31 as the primary form the sentence, 'The Son of Man must suffer many things and be rejected'; everything else should be regarded as a secondary accretion.[1] Michaelis accordingly considers 'to suffer many things and be rejected' to be an early two-membered expression.[2] Even the mention of the killing means to him an extension of the 'formula'.[3] There is a corresponding two-membered expression in Mark 9.12. In Jeremias' and Michaelis' view this is the preliminary stage of the developed announcement of the passion in Mark 8.31 and par., closely dependent on Isa. 53.[4]

Have the other announcements of suffering been elaborated from this preliminary stage? It looks fairly certain that Mark gave the announcements of suffering that pragmatic function which they have in the composition of his Gospel. But it looks improbable that Mark is responsible for their formulation and triplication. Passages such as 3.6; 11.18; 12.12 which also have pragmatic functions show that Mark did not allow himself much liberty in developing such expressions or forming new ones. This conjecture will be substantiated more precisely in the course of our enquiry. But where did the formation of the three passion announcements originate? Is the Hellenistic community, as Bultmann maintains, their seed-bed? If so, this would have to be distinguishable in the terms employed and in the meaning denoted by them. Or are the announcements to be traced back to authentic sayings of Jesus which may depend on Isa. 53?

Our decision is made more difficult by the fact that the announcements of suffering pertain to that section in which Mark used the greatest freedom in exposition and composition. Mark distributed the announcements according to his plan; consequently we may interpret them as isolated from any definite situation. In doing so we find ourselves guided by the conspicuous similarity of the different passion announcements. When we look at their language we notice at once that it is narrowly limited. The total vocabulary associated with the name Son of Man in the announcements of suffering and rising will be called by us its *train of terms*. One may speak of a *train of terms* in

[1] Lohmeyer, *Markus*, pp. 164f.
[2] Michaelis in *TWNT* V, p. 914 lines 1f.
[3] *Ibid.*, p. 914 n. 80.
[4] Jeremias, *Servant*, p. 90 and n. 406; Michaelis, *op. cit.*, pp. 914f.

cases where a distinguished leading concept attracts somewhat exclusively a group of terms pertaining to a range of related concepts within relatively distinct limits. The above survey of the terms commonly used in the three passion announcements and the related sayings demonstrates that the concept of the suffering and rising Son of Man is thus distinguished. It is exclusively associated with specific concepts. If we can demonstrate that the train of terms issued from a definite sphere within the history of tradition, we shall thereby gain instructive perspectives. For this purpose we have to analyse the individual elements of the train of terms.

II. The train of terms of the concept of the suffering and rising Son of Man in the three announcements and in the related Son of Man sayings

The train of terms in the passion announcements contains a limited number of significant elements. Even when the four other statements in Mark concerning the Son of Man's 'being delivered' or rising, and the newly formulated sayings in Matthew and Luke (Matt. 26.2; cf. 16.13; Luke 24.7; 17.25) are included, there is hardly any addition to the number of typical terms. This supports our speaking of a train of terms. We are thus immediately encouraged to extend our investigation to all synoptic sayings concerning the Son of Man who is 'delivered'.

We shall analyse the train of terms in the following order.

1. Terms denoting the Son of Man's 'being delivered' and suffering.
    (a) To be 'delivered'.
    (b) To suffer many things and be rejected, or treated with contempt.
2. Terms denoting the authorities who take part in the 'delivering'. Terms denoting their activity.
    (a) Elders, chief priests, scribes.
        (a) Mention of them in the early tradition of the primitive community.
        (b) Their activity according to the summary in Mark 10.33f.
        (c) The killing of the Son of Man.
    (b) Men.
        (a) The meaning of this term in the groups of sayings on the parousia, the activity on earth and the 'being delivered' of the Son of Man.

(b) The distinction of this term from elders, chief priests and scribes.
3. Terms denoting the rising after three days.
4. Related phrases from the context.
    (a) 'The hour is come', Mark 14.41.
    (b) 'The Son of Man goes', Mark 14.21.
5. Phrases interpreting the passion announcements as a whole.
    (a) The Son of Man 'must'.
    (b) 'It is written' of the Son of Man.

In analysing the train of terms we must pay attention to details, because we are looking for clues which might help to decide the controversial question whether the sayings concerning the suffering Son of Man are to be regarded as formed by the Hellenistic community, and in fact as *vaticinia ex eventu*, or whether they are to be regarded as a Christological interpretation of the Servant of Jehovah in Deutero-Isaiah, and in fact as an interpretation which issued from 'the Palestinian pre-Hellenistic stage of the early Church'.[1]

(1) *Terms denoting the Son of Man's 'being delivered' and suffering*

(a) **To be delivered.** The strikingly frequent use of this term in the passion announcements and in kerygmatic formulae of the primitive Christian community easily induces the mistaken assumption that the word 'to be delivered' is in itself a formula. With regard to the passage which will be investigated here, Jeremias speaks of a 'frequent παραδιδόναι formula'.[2] Yet we must realize how widely this word is used both in secular and in New Testament literature. In the one as well as in the other the word signifies the transfer of a person, especially in the language of the police and the legal authorities. Usually it is supplemented by expressions signifying the way or the purpose of this transfer. In Matt. 5.25, 'lest the adversary deliver you to the judge, and the judge deliver you to the guard, and you be cast into prison'. In Mark 13.9, 'they will deliver you up to the councils'.[3] The use of the word as a technical term in the Jewish records of lawsuits and of martyrs is closely associated with its use in legal language.[4]

[1] Jeremias, *Servant*, p. 94.
[2] Jeremias, *Servant*, p. 90.
[3] Cf. Matt. 10.17; Acts 12.4. Examples in Arndt and Gingrich, *Lexicon*, pp. 793f.
[4] Cf. Schelkle, *Passion*, pp. 70f.

Correspondingly we can discern a range of meaning within which the word is varyingly used in the passion account. Its application ranges from the mere execution of a legal action[1] to the summing-up of the passion announcements in the one phrase in Luke 9.44, 'to be delivered into the hands of men'. Within this range of application the word is not used as an unvarying formula, even though certain associations are connected with it. Its definite meaning depends on the words with which it is combined. Firstly, 'to be delivered' occurs in the combination with Judas. Judas appears as the one who delivers Jesus.[2] The designation ὁ παραδούς sticks to him throughout the synoptic tradition. The particular shade of meaning 'to betray' is here suggested by Judas' belonging to the circle of the twelve. Next, 'to be delivered' occurs combined with the Jewish authorities. In Mark 15.1 and par. they deliver Jesus to Pilate. Luke in the parallel passage 23.1 uses the expression 'they led him to Pilate'; it is evident from this that Luke did not here regard the word 'to deliver' as an irreplaceable term. Yet the fact of Jesus' having been been delivered by the Jewish authorities to the Gentiles was highly significant to Luke, as the formulation in Acts 3.13, for instance, demonstrates. Luke 24.20 speaks of Jesus' being delivered by the chief priests and rulers to be condemned to death. In all these passages the word receives its precise meaning from the context. Michel states on Rom. 4.25, 'παρεδόθη (passive) is a fixed passion formula and is explained by I Cor. 11.23; Rom. 8.32; Gal. 2.20; Eph. 5.2'.[3] But in none of these passages is 'he was delivered' used absolutely. It is rather used in combination: delivered for our offences; the night in which he was betrayed;[4] delivered for us all; who gave himself for me; who has given himself for us. Again it is the context which here makes the word 'to be delivered' approximate to a formula.

It appears from the passages just cited (Rom. 4.25; 8.32; I Cor. 11.23) and their agreement with Acts 3.13 that *already before Paul* the concept of being delivered had settled into comprehensive phrases denoting Jesus' passion. On the other hand this concept is intimately connected with the concept of the suffering Son of Man within the synoptic tradition, as can be seen from the passion announcements. What can we conclude from this?

[1] Cf. Mark 15.15, to be delivered to the soldiers; cf. Klostermann, *Markus*, pp. 160f.
[2] Cf. Mark 3.19; 14.11; Matt. 26.15; 27.3 *et passim*.
[3] Michel, *Römer*, p. 111.
[4] Cf. on this also Büchsel in *TWNT* II, p. 172 n. 1.

A further observation may be helpful. Even in the Hellenistic community before Paul the name 'Christos' was often used when speaking of the passion. Thus in the fundamental formula in I Cor. 15.3 we meet that combination which often recurs in Paul, 'Christ died'.[1] Another usual combination is Christ's suffering, in Acts 3.18; 17.3; 26.23; cf. Luke 24.26. But nowhere is the expression found that Christ is 'delivered'. The word 'to be delivered' is reserved for the Son of Man. Not until the Epistle to the Ephesians is Christ's giving himself spoken of, cf. Eph. 5.2, 25. But the concept of giving himself is a novel one compared with what was expressed by the earlier formulations. And again nowhere in the New Testament is it said that the Son of Man delivers himself up. In most cases men are brought in as the subordinate agents of the delivering up; but above all God is thought of as the one who actually 'delivers'. In apocalyptic literature, in conformity with the Judaism of that period, an action is indirectly referred to God by using the passive mood.[2] The invariability of the usage proves that the linking of 'Christ' with 'to die' and 'Son of Man' with 'to be delivered' are not haphazard; they are not interchangeable combinations. If in the pre-Pauline Hellenistic community the stereotyped phrase 'Christ died' was in general use, it is improbable that this same community would have formed the other connexion between 'Son of Man' and 'to be delivered' without at least occasionally interchanging these four terms.

This conclusion is supported also by the following observation. The term 'to be delivered' also appears in the pre-Pauline formulae. The one who is delivered here, however, is neither the Christ nor the Son of Man but the *Kyrios Jesus* or God's own Son.[3] This usage had been transmitted to Paul; 'he evidently recast it in speaking of the Son's self-surrender'.[4] We have already seen that the Son of Man formulae differ from the Pauline view in that they do not speak of

---

[1] It is evident also from Paul's usage of the titles of dignity for Jesus how carefully certain titles were connected with certain phrases concerning the passion. In the formulae which Paul adopted we find the statement, 'Christ died for our sins', I Cor. 15.3; Rom. 4.25. The reference to Isa. 53 is obvious; Mark 14.24; 10.45; I Peter 3.18 may be compared. Wherever Paul is not restricted by a ready-formed text transmitted to him, he prefers the phrases 'died for us', 'died for the brother', thus in Rom. 14.15; I Cor. 8.11, etc. A transition between the two kinds of phrase mentioned occurs in Rom. 5.6 and 5.8, namely, 'whilst we were yet sinners, ungodly, Christ died for us'.

[2] Cf. Volz, *Eschatologie*, p. 6.

[3] Cf. I Cor. 11.23; Rom. 4.24f.; Rom. 8.32.

[4] Cf. Bultmann, *Theology* II, p. 12; cf. Gal. 1.4; 2.20.

the Son of Man's giving of himself. The formulae in Rom. 4.25;
8.32; I Cor. 11.23f. always state explicitly the 'for you', 'for us all',
'for our trespasses'; the announcements of suffering never state it.[1]
We do not see how this distinction would be intelligible if both groups
of sayings had issued from the Hellenistic community.

A further question must be included in our discussion. The term
'to be delivered' is used by Jeremias to prove that the Christological
interpretations in the New Testament are dependent on the statements about the Servant of Jehovah in Deutero-Isaiah.[2] The 'for-
mula-like use of $\pi\alpha\rho\alpha\delta\iota\delta\delta\nu\alpha\iota$ in the passive voice (replacing the
divine name) for the purpose of indicating the passion of Jesus is
probably connected with Isa. 53'.[3] Jeremias cites Mark 9.31 and
par.; 10.33 and par.; 14.41 and par.; Matt. 26.2; Luke 24.7; Rom.
4.25 and I Cor. 11.23 in order to support his assumption. Jeremias
further points out that the $\pi\alpha\rho\alpha\delta\iota\delta\delta\nu\alpha\iota$ formula is often connected
with the $\dot{\upsilon}\pi\acute{\epsilon}\rho$ formula and related forms, as in Luke 22.19; Rom.
4.25; 8.32; Gal. 1.4; 2.20; Eph. 5.2, 25; I Tim. 2.6; Titus 2.14.[4] In
his view the frequent $\pi\alpha\rho\alpha\delta\iota\delta\delta\nu\alpha\iota$ formula makes it evident 'that the
numerous general references to scripture which are met with in all
three synoptics in connexion with Jesus' words about his passion are
also—probably even primarily—allusions to Isa 53.[5]

With these far-reaching assumptions in mind, we shall first try to
decide whether we can perceive a reference to Isa. 53 in the way the
term 'to be delivered' is used in the announcements of the Son of
Man's suffering.

We cannot speak of a '$\pi\alpha\rho\alpha\delta\iota\delta\delta\nu\alpha\iota$ formula'[6] as Jeremias does,
because in our view this is not appropriate. We stated above that the
term $\pi\alpha\rho\alpha\delta\iota\delta\delta\nu\alpha\iota$ is used within the synoptic tradition in a variety
of ways throughout the range from police and legal language to the
comprehensive expression for the whole of the Son of Man's suffering; the precise meaning of the term is defined by the context, or by
the phrases connected with it. We would understand by a formula
an order of words of a somewhat stereotyped uniform structure and
content as well as a concept which is comparatively self-contained,
not needing completion by other phrases. Thus we have had to

---

[1] On Mark 10.45 see below, Chapter IV D III d, pp. 202ff.
[2] Cf. Jeremias, *Servant*, pp. 88f., 96.
[3] *Ibid.*, p. 96.
[4] *Loc. cit.*
[5] *Ibid.*, p. 90.
[6] *Ibid.*, pp. 90, 96.

conclude that the word παραδίδοσθαι in itself is not a formula, and that
the phrases connected with it are too varied to allow us to ascribe
to it a formula-like nature. It might be permissible to speak of a
παραδιδόναι formula, but only on the assumption that all the New
Testament passages to which Jeremias refers can be traced back to
Isa. 53. But this is just what must first be proved. So we assume that
the term 'to be delivered' does not contain in itself a definite meaning
like a comprehensive formula.

The case is different with the phrase 'to be delivered into the hands
of someone'. We find it in Mark 9.31 and par. and abbreviated in
Luke 9.44. Luke, having left out the announcements of being killed
and rising which occur in Mark, employs the 'to be delivered into
the hands of men' to express comprehensively the passion as a whole.
We further find the phrase in Mark 14.41 and par. and in Luke 24.7,
where 'into the hands of men' from Mark 9.31 and 'into the hands of
sinners' from Mark 14.41 have been conspicuously combined within
the phrase 'The Son of Man must be delivered into the hands of
sinful men and crucified'. The formula παραδίδοσθαι εἰς χεῖράς τινος
pertains to the Palestinian sphere of language as the citations
collected by Schlatter unmistakably demonstrate; in pure Greek
usage this formula is not attested.[1] For our argument it is decisive
that this formula-like phrase 'to be delivered into the hands of someone' does not occur in Isa. 53. There the concept of delivering is
combined with other important phrases. The following combinations
appear in the LXX:

53.4, οὗτος τὰς ἁμαρτίας ἡμῶν φέρει καὶ περὶ ἡμῶν ὀδυνᾶται

53.6, καὶ κύριος παρέδωκεν αὐτὸν ταῖς ἁμαρτίαις ἡμῶν

53.12, ἀνθ' ὧν παρεδόθη εἰς θάνατον ἡ ψυχὴ αὐτοῦ . . .

    καὶ διὰ τὰς ἁμαρτίας αὐτῶν παρεδόθη.

There is a free quotation from Isa. 53 in Rom. 4.25,[2] similarly
in Rom. 8.32.[3] The word 'to deliver' here is joined by further expressions from Isa. 53 (53.12, 4, 5). Hence we see the corroboration of our
separation of Rom. 4.25 and 8.32 on the one hand from the announcements concerning the Son of Man's suffering on the other hand.
The pre-Pauline passages in the Epistle to the Romans are dependent on Isa. 53, the predictions of suffering are not.[4] For if we

---

[1] Schlatter, *Matt.*, pp. 537f. Cf. also Büchsel in *TWNT* II, p. 172 lines 8ff.
[2] Cf. Jeremias, *Servant*, p. 89 n. 397; Michel, *Römer*, p. 111.
[3] Cf. Michel, *op. cit.*, pp. 184f.; Jeremias, *op. cit.*, p. 89.
[4] Cf. Bultmann, *Theology* I, p. 31.

look for passages in the Old Testament to which the formula-like phrase 'to deliver into the hands of men' might refer, we do not meet them in Isa. 53, but, e.g., in Jer. 33.24.

Here it becomes fully evident that we cannot speak of the isolated word as of a παραδιδόναι formula. The term 'to be delivered' provides conclusive evidence for the dependence of a synoptic text upon Isa. 53 only if this term is combined in the synoptic text with a phrase similar to one in Isa. 53. None of the announcements of the Son of Man's 'being delivered' satisfies this condition.[1]

We shall have to take into consideration a further step. If in a community the term 'to be delivered' was stressed within the statements concerning Jesus' suffering as much as it in fact was in the synoptic announcements of the suffering, this community would be obliged to refer back to Isa. 53—as soon as a prophecy of that messianic passion was discovered in this text; for undoubtedly the term 'to be delivered', occurring three times in Isa. 53.6–12 (LXX), occupies a marked position there. Christians who were eagerly looking for interpretative phrases were obliged to combine those from Isa. 53 with the concept of delivering—as soon as Isaiah was read by Christians with Jesus' passion in mind. Early evidence for this can be found in Rom. 4.25; 8.32; I Cor. 11.23. But since this combination of 'to be delivered' with the interpretative phrases from Isa. 53 had not yet happened in the synoptic announcements of the suffering we have to conclude that these issued from a sphere, or pertain to a stratum, in which Isaiah had not yet been discovered as a prophecy of the messianic passion of Jesus. The formulae in Rom. 4.25; 8.32; I Cor. 11.23 in which the combination with the interpretative phrases from Isa. 53 has already been established pertain to the pre-Pauline community; hence we have no occasion to regard the predictions of the passion as products of the early Hellenistic community—at any rate not in so far as can be judged from the term 'to be delivered'. Will this conclusion be confirmed also by other elements of the train of terms?

(b) To suffer many things and be rejected, or treated with contempt. In the announcements of suffering in Mark the word 'to

---

[1] Maurer, *Knecht Gottes*, pp. 1ff., also employs without hesitation the fact that the concept of 'delivering' appears in Mark 14.21 and in Isa. 53.12 to prove by it the dependence of the text in Mark upon Isa. 53 and attaches weighty considerations to this conclusion; thus he can speak of Mark's 'precise and deliberate

be rejected' occurs only once, namely, in Mark 8.31. It is omitted in
Matthew's parallel formulation in 16.21; it is adopted by Luke in
9.22 and 17.25. Michaelis convincingly demonstrates that 'to be
rejected' and 'to be treated with contempt' are synonymous expressions, being alternatively employed to render in the New Testament
that scriptural passage from Ps. 118.22 which concerns the rejection
of the corner-stone.[1] Consequently we have to consider the following
Son of Man sayings in Mark to be parallel phrases: the Son of Man
must suffer many things and be rejected, in Mark 8.31; and, it is
written of the Son of Man that he will suffer many things and be
treated with contempt, in Mark 9.12. We might almost consider
9.12 to be an excerpt from 8.31 or 8.31 to be an expansion of 9.12.
At any rate, it is advisable for us to treat the phrase 'to suffer many
things and be rejected, or treated with contempt' as a whole; it is
also transmitted thus in Luke 9.22 and 17.25.

Lohmeyer regards the announcement in Mark 8.31 as the result
of several extensions. In his view the primary form ran approxi-
mately as follows: 'The Son of Man must suffer many things and be
rejected.'[2] He supposes that Luke 17.25 preserved this form almost
unaltered. In reconstructing the primary form out of Mark 8.31
Lohmeyer starts with the assumption that 'to suffer many things and
be rejected' already denotes comprehensively the 'meaning and law
of all impending events', as Luke 17.25; cf. 24.26; Acts 1.3; 3.18;
17.3 show. The comprehensive terms 'to suffer many things and be
rejected' convey the apocalyptic 'must' of the passion.[3] Michaelis,
following Lohmeyer, arrives at similar conclusions. In his view 'to
suffer many things and be rejected' is 'an early two-membered expression', 'a preliminary stage of the elaborate announcement of
suffering in Mark 8.31 and par.'.[4] 'This is proved firstly by Luke
17.25. . . . Even if the present context of this saying were a secondary

---

procedure' regarding the scriptural testimony from Isa. 53 (p. 9). In his view the
influence of the Hebrew Bible on the passion account prevailed in the very earliest
stage of the tradition; even Mark gives the references already in a less distinct form.
If this were so, it would be far from supporting the assumption that Mark 14.21
could be traced back to Isa. 53.12. Maurer himself adds the note: this time, the
Septuagint; cf. pp. 9 and 10.

[1] Michaelis in *TWNT* V, p. 913 line 29 and n. 79.
[2] Lohmeyer, *Markus*, p. 165.
[3] Lohmeyer, *Markus*, p. 165; a different view in Campenhausen, *Martyrium*,
p. 62.
[4] Michaelis in *TWNT* V, p. 914 line 2; p. 913 lines 23f.

one, the saying itself, at least as regards the combination of πολλὰ παθεῖν and ἀποδοκιμασθῆναι, may yet be of early origin. Moreover, in Mark 9.12 as well πολλὰ παθεῖν and ἐξουδενηθῆναι (without any further addition) which is synonymous with ἀποδοκιμασθῆναι are combined.'[1]

This proof obviously lacks consistency; it might convince only after Luke 17.25 and Mark 9.12 were proved to have been formulated earlier than and independent of Mark 8.31. To be sure, Michaelis does refer to statements on Luke 17.25 by Kümmel.[2] Kümmel is certainly partly right in challenging Bultmann's sweeping argument against an early origin of Luke 17.25. But his own arguments for 'the assumption that Luke 17.25 is a reliable early tradition' are none the less sweeping, namely 'Luke 17.25 contains no mention of Jesus' resurrection, though such a mention is characteristic of the later prophecies of suffering. It is on the contrary so indefinite that it can scarcely be explained as a *vaticinium ex eventu.*'[3] Rising and parousia might well have been mentioned jointly in the saying.

Indeed, Luke 17.25 is hardly comprehensible as an independent *vaticinium ex eventu*. From our point of view, however, it can be readily seen as an interpolation by Luke between two sayings concerning the coming Son of Man. The allusion to the rising may well be missing, then, because of the statements concerning the Son of Man's parousia which form the context already. Considered thus, what Kümmel wonders at is quite natural. It is evident from the connexion which the sayings enclosing Luke 17.25 had in Q that this verse was interpolated by Luke. Nearly at the same place at which Luke interpolated, Matthew interrupted the sequence of sayings in Q by inserting material from Mark (Matt. 24.29–31; 24.32f.; 24.34–36). Luke in addition transfers the proverb in Matt. 24.28—obviously on account of the offensive simile—to the end of the section, thereby eliminating its immediate connexion with the Son of Man.[4] Taking the rearrangements or insertions by Matthew and Luke into account, we have to conclude that the sayings which are merely separated in Luke by 17.25 followed each other in Q. Whence did Luke receive this saying about the Son of Man's passion? As it appears in complete isolation, we cannot assume another source in addition to Q. In Q

[1] Michaelis, *ibid.*, p. 913 lines 24ff.
[2] Kümmel, *Promise*, pp. 70f.
[3] *Ibid.*, p. 71.
[4] Cf. above Chapter II B I 1, p. 48, and D II 3 c, pp. 105ff.

itself, however, we do not find a single saying about the suffering of the Son of Man. Nevertheless, the essential concepts are already present in Luke 9.22 (a formulation parallel to Mark 8.31) and are reproduced in 17.25 without alterations. The phrase 'first he must' is to be understood as the introduction to a reflection on the temporal order of events, as is evident from Mark 9.11. Thus nothing supports the assumption that Luke here received an early saying from a special tradition, whilst it can very well be understood, considering Luke's intention to distinguish periods in salvation history which has been demonstrated by Conzelmann,[1] that Luke 17.25 was a new formulation.

Lohmeyer and Michaelis consider the phrase 'to suffer many things and be rejected, or treated with contempt' as it occurs in Luke 17.25 to be the primary minimum form of the passion announcement. In order to substantiate our refutation of their assumption we still have to elucidate the fact that, in so far as Mark 8.31 is regarded as the earlier form, there is drastic abbreviation in Luke 17.25. We therefore refer to the second announcement of suffering. Here Luke as editor abbreviates the text from Mark in a parallel way. Here also the form in Luke does not mention the rising. Kümmel's argument, which rests on the absence of a mention of the rising and on the vagueness of the announcement,[2] is thus refuted by Luke's editorial procedure in 9.44. The briefer and more indefinite form appears to be of later origin than the more elaborate sayings.

The second passage for which Jeremias with reference to Otto and Michaelis also maintains an early origin is Mark 9.12. We do not, however, see any evidence for its archaic origin. We have already established that neither the indefinite wording nor the concise form of Luke 17.25 could be regarded as primary.[3] We shall discuss Mark 9.12 in detail later on.

How do we have to understand the terms 'to be rejected' in Mark 8.31 and 'to be treated with contempt' in Mark 9.12? In Mark 12.10 the term 'to reject' occurs as part of a scriptural proof. It is here used (implying the whole of the passion) in contrast to the statement about becoming the corner-stone. Jeremias convincingly demonstrated that the scriptural evidence adduced in Mark 12.10f. already

---

[1] Conzelmann, *Theology of Luke*, p. 120 *et passim*.
[2] Kümmel, *Promise*, pp. 70f.
[3] Cf. Jeremias, *Servant*, p. 90 n. 406.

belongs to the 'Christological colouring of the parable'.[1] The interpretation of the parable by means of this scriptural evidence, however,
is of pre-Marcan origin;[2] it was adopted from an earlier tradition and secondarily applied to the parable.[3] The scriptural evidence
thus used is Ps. 118.22f. It is stated there that the very stone which
the builders rejected was made the head of the corner by God. The
parable of the wicked husbandmen in Mark 12.1–11 contains a
severe accusation. 'The vineyard is clearly Israel, the tenants are
Israel's rulers and leaders, the owner of the vineyard is God, the
messengers are the prophets, the son is Christ.'[4] The simile of the
rejected stone is unambiguously aimed against the Jewish authorities.
They rejected the stone. Yet God made it the head of the corner.
This acute antithesis of the forcible rejection by the Jews and the
exaltation by God himself also occurs in Acts 2.22–24; 3.13, 14, 15;
4.10f.; 5.30 *et passim*. In Acts 4.9–11 as well as in Mark 12.10f. the
term 'to reject' refers to Ps. 118.22f. It is always the Jewish authorities
to whom the responsibility for the rejection is imputed. Hence Mark
does not arbitrarily name the three Jewish groups of elders, chief
priests and scribes explicitly in connexion with the rejection of the
Son of Man in 8.31. In doing so he rather conforms to the pre-
Marcan use of the scriptural evidence from Ps. 118.22f. Hence we,
unlike Lohmeyer and Michaelis, cannot assume a minimum form of
Mark 8.31 which would have contained the term 'to be rejected'
without the Jewish authorities who were responsible being named.[5]

In Mark 8.31 and 9.12 the terms 'to be rejected' and 'to be treated
with contempt' are used alternately. This alternation is congruous
with that in Mark 12.10 and Acts 4.11. Since the first announcement
of suffering conforms to the wording of the scriptural evidence in
Mark 12.10f., which as we stated above is of pre-Marcan origin, and
since the same scriptural passage in Ps. 118 is referred to by the alternative term 'to be treated with contempt' in Mark 9.12, we have to
conclude that the wording of the first announcement of suffering is
pre-Marcan.

[1] Jeremias, *Parables*, p. 58.
[2] *Ibid.*, p. 58 n. 44.
[3] *Ibid.*, p. 81. Ps 118.22 is also cited in I Peter 2.7 with regard to the fate of those
who do not believe.
[4] *Ibid.*, p. 55.
[5] Cf. Acts 4.11 with 4.9. The connexion of the term 'to be rejected' with the
naming of the elders, etc., must not be broken, because Acts 4.11; I Peter 2.7;
Mark 12.10; 8.31 all agree in identifying the Jews clearly with the guilty builders.
Ps. 118.22 is cited for that very purpose.

How do we have to understand the phrase 'to suffer many things' in the context of the predictions of passion?[1] It is conspicuous that this phrase is fixedly combined with the terms 'to be rejected' or 'to be treated with contempt' (Mark 8.31 and par.; 9.12; Luke 17.25). This combination is only broken up in Luke 24.46. There are quite a number of other alterations in this passage; the suffering of the Christ is spoken of instead of that of the Son of Man, and the suffering—comprehensive of the entire passion, the meaning of the word having been thus newly coined in the manner of a new Christian development[2]—is immediately connected with the rising from the dead. According to Bultmann Luke 24.44–49 is 'a quite late achievement of Hellenistic Christianity (if not also in part of Hellenistic Jewish Christianity)'.[3] Thus we may disregard this passage here and assume for our present purposes that in the sayings concerning the suffering Son of Man the phrase 'to suffer many things' occurs exclusively in combination with 'to be rejected' or 'to be treated with contempt'.

We saw above that both Mark 8.31 and Mark 9.12 even if in variant wordings allude to the scriptural evidence from Ps. 118.22. Consequently 'to be rejected' or 'treated with contempt' must already have been combined with 'to suffer many things' in the tradition before Mark and with regard to Jesus' rejection by the Jewish authorities. This is not improbable; for it can be demonstrated that the term 'to suffer' which in its new Christian meaning comprises the entire passion may have been 'formed within the context of evidence adduced from scriptural prophecies', as is done in Acts.[4] As Michaelis has shown, this term is always used absolutely in the context of the Acts formulae in so far as they mention the suffering and is therefore employed to sum up the passion in the concept of dying.[5] This fact, however, suggests the assumption that before the acceptance of the term 'to suffer' as comprising the entire passion a number of concrete terms were used to express Jesus' destiny inflicted on him 'by the definite plan and foreknowledge of God' (Acts 14.23) through chief priests and scribes. This is indeed obvious in the kerygmatic formulae in Acts (cf., e.g., Acts 3.18 with 3.13ff.). Hence we may assume that the phrase 'to suffer many

[1] Cf. for Michaelis' view *ThLZ* 75, 1950, p. 35.
[2] Campenhausen, *Martyrium*, p. 62.
[3] Bultmann, *Tradition*, p. 289.
[4] Campenhausen, *Martyrium*, p. 62 n. 5.
[5] Michaelis in *TWNT* V, pp. 911f.

things' originated in that stratum in which evidence from scriptural prophecies was adduced in order to reckon up the Jews' offences against Jesus, confronting them with what God had done to him, and that this phrase was firmly combined with the term 'to be rejected' or 'treated with contempt' before being received into the announcements of suffering.[1]

Lohmeyer based his supposition of a primary minimum form of the passion announcements which we discussed above mainly on the assumption that in the sentence 'The Son of Man must suffer many things and be rejected'[2] 'the original focal point of interest', namely 'the apocalyptic "must" of the passion', maintained predominance. This reference to the 'apocalyptic law of suffering' has gained much approval.[3] Now, the distant allusion to Dan. 2.28 (LXX) would hardly suffice[4] to prove that in Mark 8.31, too, the 'must' has an apocalyptic meaning. For here again the meaning of the term is not imparted by the term in itself, but by the nexus within which it occurs in different passages. The meaning of the 'must' depends on the nexus of necessity, which may be of an apocalyptic nature, or may be provided by the pattern of promise and fulfilment, or may be prescribed by still other laws.

Since the term 'to be rejected' or 'treated with contempt' was introduced with the scriptural evidence from Ps. 118.22, and since the phrase 'to suffer many things' probably was formed within the context of evidence adduced from scriptural prophecies,[5] that nexus of necessity by which the 'must' in Mark 8.31 is determined is none

[1] Michaelis, *op. cit.*, p. 914 lines 13–28 (cf. also Michaelis, *Leiden*), endeavours to prove that 'to suffer many things' might refer to Isa. 53. 'Isa. 53 is in particular the source of the active attitude which distinguishes Jesus' pronouncements about suffering' (*TWNT* V, p. 915 lines 3f.). To us a reference to a phrase like Ps. 34.20, where the many sufferings of the righteous are mentioned, rather suggests itself. It should also be noted that in the LXX πάσχω is never used with the meaning of 'to die'. Cf. Michaelis, *ibid.*, pp. 906–8. With Josephus the phrase πολλὰ παθών occurs in *Ant.* 13.268 'obviously referring to tortures preceding death' (*ibid.*, p. 909 lines 2f.). We shall also have to understand the phrase 'to suffer many things' in Mark 8.31 and 9.12 in this latter sense.

[2] The following quotations are from Lohmeyer, *Markus*, p. 165. Cf. Michaelis, who to a large extent follows Lohmeyer, in *TWNT* V, p. 914 lines 7ff. and n. 81.

[3] Cf. Schelkle, *Passion*, p. 110. Fascher in 'Theologische Beobachtungen zu δεῖ', pp. 251f., justly objects to the perplexing vagueness with which Lohmeyer when expounding Mark 8.31 speaks of the δεῖ sometimes as of an apocalyptic 'must' and at other times as of an eschatological 'must' without reaching any clear distinction.

[4] Cf. Lohmeyer, *Markus*, p. 165 n. 7; Schelkle, *Passion*, p. 110.

[5] Cf. Campenhausen, *Martyrium*, p. 62 n. 5.

other than the necessity according to the Scriptures. This assumption of ours is directly supported by Mark 9.12, where the same phrase 'to suffer many things and be rejected' or 'treated with contempt' appears under the simple heading of 'it is written'. Thus we cannot see how it might be permissible to read an apocalyptic meaning into the 'must' unless this concept be understood in a considerably altered manner which will be dealt with below in greater detail.[1]

We have stated in the previous section that in our view the term 'to be delivered' as it is used in the synoptic announcements of the Son of Man's suffering does not contain a reference to Isa. 53, but rather refers back to other Old Testament passages. We noted in particular that any combination of this term with interpretative phrases from Deutero-Isaiah is missing in the passion announcements.[2] Jeremias in his investigations about the connexion between synoptic passages and Isa. 53 uses Mark 9.12 as important evidence. 'That the numerous general references to Scripture which are met with in all three synoptics in connexion with Jesus' words about his passion are also—probably even primarily—allusions to Isa. 53 is evident from the ancient character of Mark 9.12 (ἐξουδενηθῇ cf. ἐξουδενωμένος Isa. 53.3 'A, Σ, Θ = נִבְזֶה), also by the frequent παραδιδόναι formula and Luke 22.37.'[3] The unfitness of the so-called παραδιδόναι formula as evidence of this connexion appeared to us above; we do not have to deal with Luke 22.37 within the scope of this enquiry; but we have to consider here Mark 9.12.

According to Jeremias the connexion between Mark 9.12 and Isa. 53 is to be proved by the fact that the term 'to be treated with contempt' occurs in 'AΣΘ, whereas in the principal text of the LXX a different term occurs. But we have already seen above that Acts 4.11 also speaks of the stone's being treated with contempt by the builders, thus using the same term as used in Mark 9.12. But this coincidence alone would not be sufficient to demonstrate a correlation. There are, however, two more conformities to be taken into account, namely, (a) that Mark 8.31 and Mark 9.12 are formed alike except for the apparently interchangeable synonymous terms 'to be rejected' and 'to be treated with contempt'; and (b) that both Mark 8.31a and Mark 12.10 speak of being rejected, and both Mark 9.12 and Acts 4.11 speak of being treated with contempt, while Mark 12.10 as well

[1] Cf. Chapter IV D II 5 a, pp. 188ff.
[2] On Mark 10.45 cf. Chapter IV D III d, pp. 202ff.
[3] Jeremias, *Servant*, p. 90.

as Acts 4.11 refer to Ps. 118.22. Consequently we may not have any doubt that Mark 9.12 also refers to the Psalm passage which we have mentioned; hence we do not see a reference to Isa. 53 in it.[1] We cannot, then, accept Jeremias' supposition that the general references to Scripture in the synoptic announcements of suffering refer to Isa. 53.

Our conclusions so far enable us also to contrast our view with that of Bultmann. Bultmann considers the passion prophecies to be products of the Hellenistic community; 'Verse 12b [of Mark 9] is an interpolation modelled after Matt. 17.12b.'[2] How can this interpolating have been done? A comparison with Matt. 17.12b instantly exposes deviations. Or could the interpolator rather have had Mark 8.31a in mind? In this case it would be incomprehensible why he exchanged the striking term 'to be rejected' (Matt. 17.12b: 'to suffer') for 'to be treated with contempt', thus in fact conforming to the scriptural evidence in Acts 4.11. From our point of view we cannot regard Mark 9.12b as produced by an interpolator, but as belonging to the original text of Mark.

Did the evangelist himself form the pronouncement about the Son of Man in Mark 9.12b? This assumption is supported by the similarity to Mark 8.31; it is contradicted by the striking dissimilarity of the verbs used, namely 'to be rejected' over against 'to be treated with contempt'; because the term 'to be rejected' in combination with 'to suffer many things' already occurs in Mark 8.31 and recurs as a quotation from Ps. 118.22 in Mark 12.10f. Thus the change to the verb 'to be treated with contempt' in 9.12 is intelligible only if it was caused by a previously formed text. Acts 4.11, deviating from Mark 12.10, Mark 8.31, and I Peter 2.7, demonstrates that the scriptural evidence from Ps. 118.22 might equally well have been rendered by means of the verb 'to be treated with contempt'. Consequently we conjecture that Mark in 9.12b used a ready-formed pronouncement about the Son of Man.

Did the phrase 'to suffer many things and be rejected' or 'treated

---

[1] We may further note that the term ἐξουδένημα, cf. עָם וּבְזוּי, occurs at a characteristic place in Ps. 21.7 (LXX). As it may be shown that this Psalm was of great significance for the description of the passion, we would prefer to conjecture an influence of that passage on Mark 9.12b—if only we might subscribe to the method of using the consonance of isolated words for establishing proofs of origin. Cf. on Mark 9.12b the quotations brought together in Huck-Lietzmann's *Synopsis* (10th edition).

[2] Bultmann, *Theology* I, p. 30.

with contempt' issue from the Palestinian or the Hellenistic community? The expression 'to suffer many things' does not comprise all the passion events, but denotes one particular aspect. We can understand this only on condition that the individual term 'to suffer' did not yet signify the passion as a whole. However, we have to take into account that there is no fixed term in the Semitic language which corresponds with the word πάσχειν. Hence we cannot decide whether the phrase 'to suffer many things' issued from the Palestinian sphere of language. The reference of the term 'to be rejected, or treated with contempt' to Ps. 118.22 cannot contribute to a decision on this question either. We must leave it undecided.

(2) *Terms denoting the authorities who take part in the 'delivering'. Terms denoting their activity*

The different predictions of the passion, although seemingly resembling each other, yet display a great variety of distinctions in detail. This also becomes manifest when we consider the authorities who take part in the 'delivering'.

The predominance of the passive voice in the verbs denoting delivering leaves no doubt that the one who delivers is God himself. Only on the surface, though nevertheless inexcusably, does Judas take part in the delivering according to Mark 14.21. In the same way, according to Mark 10.33f., the chief priests and scribes make themselves guilty of delivering the Son of Man to the Gentiles; but again they are the agents only on the surface.

Two groups to whom the Son of Man is delivered are spoken of, namely the Jewish authorities on the one hand—thus also in Acts 2.23—and men, or sinners, on the other hand. It might be suggested that historically seen the two groups were but one and the same. But this entity was then at any rate regarded under two different aspects which were denoted by two different terms. We shall have to illustrate this in the next two sections.

(a) Elders, chief priests, scribes

(a) Their mention in the early tradition of the primitive community.

Though Mark 10.33f. only names the chief priests and scribes, this passage fundamentally means the religious authorities as such.[1] In other passages of the Gospels it is repeatedly stated that the deadly enmity against Jesus came from the religious, cultic and political

[1] Schrenk in *TWNT* III, p. 271 lines 42f.

authorities of Jewry.[1] The scriptural evidence in Acts 4.11 is directed particularly against those who are at the head, i.e. chief priests[2] and elders and—according to 4.5—also scribes. They are immediately addressed with the words from Ps. 118.22, 'This is the stone which was treated with contempt by you builders (but) which has become the head of the corner'. Here the legitimate officials, faced by the Scriptures, are impeached with regard to their liability; they are the lawful builders, but they have rejected the head of the corner. We have already demonstrated above the relationship of this passage to Mark 9.12 and Mark 8.31a.

In the Emmaus story, which 'in its form is like the oldest of the synoptic resurrection stories',[3] the two disciples report in archaic phrases what recently happened in Jerusalem 'concerning Jesus of Nazareth who was a prophet mighty in deed and word before God and all the people, and how our chief priests and rulers delivered him to be condemned to death'.[4]

Without doubt the naming of the Jewish authorities in the announcements of the Son of Man's suffering is related to the kerygmatic pronouncements about Jesus' dying and the Jewish officials' guilt which we have cited.[5] The necessity according to the Scriptures which is presupposed by the phrase in the passion announcements 'it is written' that the Son of Man must suffer many things and be treated with contempt is, for example, expounded in Acts 2.23.[6] Faith in the risen one as well as the dispute with the Jewish authorities[7] prompted the interpretation of the passion events by means of scriptural evidence.

(*b*) The activity of the Jewish authorities according to the summary in Mark 10.33f.

In Mark 8.31 the Jewish authorities are charged with rejecting the Son of Man. This is a comprehensive pronouncement the particular meaning of which is implied in the scriptural evidence from

---

[1] Cf. Schürer, *Jewish People*, Dir. II, Vol. I, p. 206. Schrenk, *op. cit.*, pp. 270–2.
[2] Cf. Schrenk, *ibid.*, p. 271 lines 42f.　　[3] Bultmann, *Tradition*, p. 289.
[4] In Luke 24.20 we read παρέδωκαν αὐτὸν οἱ ἀρχιερεῖς καὶ οἱ ἄρχοντες ἡμῶν εἰς κρίμα θανάτου; in Mark 10.33f., παραδοθήσεται τοῖς ἀρχιερεῦσιν καὶ τοῖς γραμματεῦσιν καὶ κατακρινοῦσιν αὐτὸν θανάτῳ.
[5] This will be supplemented in our discussion of the term 'to kill' in Chapter IV D II 2 a c, pp. 175f.
[6] On this compare Luke 22.22 with Acts 2.23.
[7] In Acts 4.11, the legitimacy of the Jewish officials is recognized and thus becomes the reason for the reproach.

Ps. 118.22. In Mark 10.33f., the chief priests' and scribes' guilt is especially emphasized. To them the Son of Man will be delivered. This statement is followed by the above-mentioned summary, (1) they will condemn him to death, (2) and deliver him to the Gentiles, (3) and mock him, (4) and spit upon him, (5) and scourge him. The performance of the acts in question is delegated to the Gentiles, but the Gentiles merely continue what is in effect the deed of the Jews.

The details stated in the summary merit a comparison with the synoptic passion accounts. This summary begins precisely at the point where the synoptic tradition of the passion started at an early stage, namely at Jesus' arrest.[1] Nevertheless a number of differences from Mark's account of the passion can easily be demonstrated. Lohmeyer has done this in particular with regard to Mark 15.16–20.[2] We have to consider first of all what, according to the summary in Mark 10.33f., is the capital reason for the reproach. It is not the *skandalon* of the curse connected with the cross (Gal. 3.13; I Cor. 1.23) —although in Mark's passion account the term 'to crucify' is heavily stressed. In the summary the reproach pertains indeed to the death sentence, but above all to the delivery to the Gentiles and the outrage connected with this. It is not surprising that the same reproach appears in Acts 2.23—also without pointing to the cross, although the crucifixion is alluded to; the Israelites who are addressed (v. 22) are above all reproached for having made lawless hands crucify[3] and do away with Jesus. The denial in the presence of Pilate appears in the same sense in Acts 3.13.[4] The absence of the kerygmatic term 'cross' and the disparity over against the Gentiles indicate to us an early stage in which the views of the Hellenistic community did not yet prevail.

The announcement 'they will condemn him to death' accords with the synoptic account of the passion (Mark 14.64; Matt. 27.3). The condemnation is also mentioned elsewhere in the primitive Christian kerygma. In Acts 13.27 we read, 'those who live in Jerusalem and their rulers, because they did not recognize him nor understand the utterances of the prophets which are read every sabbath, fulfilled these by condemning him. Though they would charge him with nothing deserving death, yet they asked Pilate to have him killed.'

[1] Cf. Chapter IV A 2, p. 148.
[2] Cf. Lohmeyer, *Markus*, p. 220.
[3] Translator's note: The RSV has the word 'to crucify', though the literal meaning of the Greek word is 'to affix'.
[4] Cf. Acts 7.52.

Here the condemnation is spoken of as an unconscious fulfilment of what is written in the Scriptures. 'Paul is proving that Jesus in spite of his having been rejected by the Jews of Jerusalem is the Messiah foretold by the prophets.'[1] Thus the condemnation is mentioned here, as in Luke 24.20, in connexion with scriptural evidence.

In the summary three verbs now follow, 'to mock', 'to spit upon' and 'to scourge'. Amongst these 'to mock' is the most comprehensive term; in accordance with Luke 22.63 (23.11) and Mark 15.20a it may be understood as comprising the acts of scorn inflicted upon Jesus as a whole. Even in Jewish religious history in the Old Testament, martyrdom is conceived of as a mocking; in the brutal act of violence the sinful attitude of the mocker against the bringer of the revelation comes to light.[2] In the synoptic account of the passion the theme of mocking occurs in addition to Mark 10.33f. and par. three more times.

Immediately after the death sentence by the Sanhedrin we read in *Mark 14.65*, 'Some began to spit on him, and to cover his face, and to strike him, saying to him, "prophesy!", and the guards received him with blows.' The term 'to mock' is absent in the immediate context; what is meant, however, is not only cruel deeds but obviously mocking words also. It is not this scene, though, which is alluded to in Mark 10.33f., but the ill-treatment by the Romans. Bultmann considers Mark 14.65 to be a displaced fragment of an earlier account transmitted to Mark which he fitted into an especially unfortunate place.[3] This observation that the comparable summary enumeration

[1] Haenchen, *Apostelgeschichte*, p. 358 n. 2.
[2] Cf. Bertram in *TWNT* V, p. 635 lines 3ff.
[3] Bultmann, *Tradition*, p. 271. Lohmeyer, *Markus*, p. 330, and Dibelius, *Formgeschichte*, p. 193 n. 1, wish to show that Mark 14.65 was formulated with Isa. 50.5f. in view, and hence with regard to the fulfilment of what is written in the Scriptures. Maurer in his essay 'Knecht Gottes und Sohn Gottes im Passionsbericht des Markusevangeliums', following Lohmeyer (*Markus*, p. 330), places Mark 14.65 with its 'literary connexion with Isa. 50.5ff.' at the head of his argument. He complements and supplements the evidence adduced by Jeremias for the dependence of the synoptic passion accounts upon Deutero-Isaiah (pp. 2 and 7). 'Jeremias' assertion (in *TWNT* V, p. 688 lines 1ff. [= *Servant*, p. 62]) that the messianic interpretation of the sayings concerning the Servant of Jehovah in the New Testament is limited only to the passages Isa. 42.1ff.; 49.6 and 52.13ff., is also to be supplemented with the third of the four Servant Songs' (p. 8 n. 1). By this supplement he does not strengthen Jeremias' chain of evidence, but breaks off an indispensable link. Jeremias emphasizes that the messianic interpretation of the Servant of Jehovah of Deutero-Isaiah in Palestinian Judaism (which was limited to the above-mentioned passages) accords with the interpretation in the New Testament. To him it is evident from this agreement as regards the messianic

of injuries after the death sentence in Mark 14.65 probably was not formed by Mark himself but originated earlier is of importance for conclusions concerning Mark 10.33f.

In *Mark 15.29–32* a mocking is reported again. 'So also the chief priests mocked him to one another with the scribes.' In this passage the report of the mocking unambiguously refers to Ps. 21.8 (LXX), so not to Deutero-Isaiah. This is supported also by Matt. 27.43.[1] Mark 10.33f. does not allude to this scorning of Jesus by the chief priests and scribes; for in the third passion announcement the mocking is delegated to the Gentiles. In consequence of this the scourging according to Roman law is mentioned at the end of the individual reviling—at variance with the course of events recounted in Mark 15.15bff.

In *Mark 15.16–20* Jesus' being mocked in the Pretorium is reported. It is obvious that there is a relationship with Mark 10.33f. Bultmann considers those verses to be an interpolation developing the theme of the *verberatio* given in 15.15b into a short narrative which is dominated by a dogmatic point of view.[2] The vv. 17–20 summarize concisely what the soldiers do, employing terms similar to those in Mark 14.65 and 10.33f. All three passages speak of spitting on him. The disdainful blows are spoken of in 14.65 and 15.19; not in 10.33f., where only the official *verberatio* is mentioned.

We have considered the three scenes of mocking, Mark 14.65;

---

interpretation that passages from Deutero-Isaiah were not used atomistically in the synoptic texts, i.e. that these passages did not merely furnish unconnected individual traits to fill in the details of the passion accounts, but that they were adopted with a messianic *figure* of the Servant of Jehovah in mind. From this agreement Jeremias further concludes 'that the christological interpretation of these passages originated in the Palestinian pre-Hellenistic stage of the early Church' (*Servant*, pp. 93f., 77). Maurer by abandoning this agreed limitation of the messianic interpretation to those three passages deprives his argument on Mark 14.65 of its force; for even granted that Lohmeyer's above-mentioned proof be conclusive, i.e. that a literary connexion of this verse with Isa. 50.5ff. would have been established, it is still by no means established that the narrator not only used a suitable saying from the Scriptures to formulate this scene but that he also had the messianic figure of the Servant of Jehovah in mind when referring to Isa. 50.5ff. Obviously this is presupposed by Maurer. But proof of it is lacking. Cf. also the following footnote.

[1] This might have been the proper place within the passion account to refer to Isa. 50.5ff. if the figure of a messianic Servant of Jehovah had been seen in that text from Isaiah; for the one who is mocked here is the Christ, the King of Israel (Mark 15.32). But the report is content with the Psalm which represents an individual lament in cultic form and metre.

[2] Bultmann, *Tradition*, pp. 277, 306, 284.

15.29–32, and 15.16–20, intending to find an answer to the question whether the evangelist formed the third passion announcement himself. The conclusion was that both 14.65 and 15.29–32 refer to scriptural passages, whilst 15.16–20 contains an enumeration appended to 15.15b in form of a short narrative. Mark 10.33f. records most briefly the Son of Man's whole passion up to his rising; only what is done by the Gentiles is described in the summary in 10.34 which gives details. This summary, however, does not conform well with 15.16–20. Firstly, in 10.34 the mocking is spoken of at the beginning and on a par with other injuries—in 15.20 the term 'to mock' comprises all that was done before. Secondly, in 10.34 the *verberatio* concludes the mocking—in 15.15b it precedes the scene of the mocking. These discrepancies support the assumption that Mark did not form the third announcement of suffering independently with the subsequent passion account in mind. When in Mark 10.33f. the being delivered *to the Gentiles* is regarded with harsh one-sidedness as the essential ignominy,[1] this is seen from within the Jewish point of view. The evangelist Mark on his part stresses by his narrative twice, namely in 14.65 and in 15.29–32, that the chief priests and scribes themselves scorn Jesus and let him be reviled and injured before their eyes *by Jews*. The Jewish point of view which can be perceived in Mark 10.33f. also appears in the Acts in several kerygmatic pronouncements in which the Jews are reproached for having done away with Jesus through the hands of lawless men.[2]

To be sure, the considerations mentioned merely support the assumption that Mark 10.34 may be traced back to an earlier form transmitted to Mark. It still remains possible that the third passion announcement as a whole was formulated by Mark on the basis of material which he received.

(c) The killing of the Son of Man.

The three announcements in Mark agree in speaking of the Son of Man being killed, not of his crucifixion. The term 'to kill' appears to have been frequently employed in the polemic of primitive Christianity against the Jews.[3] It is particularly evident from I Thess. 2.15 how

---

[1] Cf. Lohmeyer, *Markus*, p. 220.

[2] Acts 2.22ff.; 3.13ff.; cf. Haenchen, *Apostelgeschichte*, p. 148.

[3] Matt. 23.34 and par., from Q. Matt. 23.37, a threat from Q. Acts 7.52; 3.15; Mark 12.8 and par., cf. also Matt. 22.6; I Thess. 2.15 *et passim*. Cf. on this I Kings 19.10; Rom. 11.3.

in the primitive community in connexion with the killing of Jesus the killing of the prophets (looked for in the Scriptures) was now also thrown into the controversy as a proof of the Jews' permanent rebellion against God's will. Here 'to kill' seems to be almost a technical term. It surely is a technical term in the announcements of suffering where, contrasting with the variants in the formulation of all other statements, it invariably recurs. Obviously this term pertains to the sphere of the controversial discourses (in the broadest sense) between the primitive community and the legitimate Jewish authorities.

In view of the wide range within which the word 'to kill' can be used we have, however, to test the validity of our assertion by a counter-check. Is this word really chosen with a definite purpose in the announcements of suffering, related to the Son of Man concept and thus one from its train of terms? Firstly it is conspicuous that throughout the New Testament this term is *not* combined with the title of *Christ*. Secondly, we have to note that in several passages in Paul the title of Christ is combined with the word 'to crucify'.[1] Thirdly we observe in Matthew's and Luke's formation of the passion announcements the tendency also to replace the statement about the killing of the Son of Man by the kerygmatic term 'to crucify' with its richer meaning, in Matt. 26.2; 20.19; Luke 24.7.

In the early controversies with the Jews for which evidence from the Scriptures was highly important[2] we find the term 'to kill' drawn from the Scriptures; it is in some measure replaced by the kerygmatic term 'to crucify', obviously in the Hellenistic community. This is of consequence for locating the three announcements of suffering in Mark within the history of tradition. We clearly see from the passion account how much Mark values the term 'to crucify'. Nevertheless in the three announcements of the Son of Man's suffering only the earlier term 'to kill' occurs, denoting a biblical concept which can be traced back to I Kings 19.10 (cf. Rom. 11.3). In view of Matt. 23.34 and par. and Matt. 23.37 and par. we have to conclude that the stereotyped use of this term helps to prove the pre-Marcan origin of the announcements of suffering.

(b) **Men as taking part in the 'delivering'.** In Mark 9.31; Matt. 17.22; Luke 9.44; 24.7; Mark 14.41 we read that the Son of Man will

[1] E.g. I Cor. 1.23; 2.2; Gal. 3.1; 6.14.
[2] Cf. in Mark 12.8, 10f.; and in Q Matt. 23.34f. and par.

be delivered into the hands of men, or sinners. The unvarying combination of the term 'to be delivered' with the phrase 'into the hands'
indicates a formula-like nature, as we stated above.[1] According to
Schlatter, the formula issued from the Palestinian language area.[2]

(*a*) Who are the men, or sinners, named in the announcements of
suffering? In Mark 9.31 men appear—to judge by the wording—as a
species.[3] But in Mark 14.41 and Luke 24.7 they appear distinctly as
sinners. Accordingly the Son of Man will be delivered into the hands
of sinful men. A rigid tension exists between the one and the many.
We met this tension first in the sayings concerning the Son of Man's
parousia; whoever holds on to Jesus must resist the claim of men.
We next met the same tension over against this generation in the
sayings concerning the Son of Man's activity on earth. Now we meet it
also in the announcements of suffering.[4] But in this third group of
sayings a new element is added. In the other two groups Jesus'
authority faced the claims of men, and he who wished to follow Jesus
was made to realize that he had to make up his mind whether to be
attached to Jesus or to side with this generation. Now the tension
over against men is strained to the uttermost. The Son of Man himself is delivered into the hands of men. At first sight this delivering
looks as if men had won a victory over Jesus' claim to sovereignty;
'this is your hour, and the power of darkness' (Luke 22.53). God
himself seems to admit the legitimacy of this sinful generation's claim.
It is fundamentally paradoxical that God delivers the one to whom
he has given authority over all men into the hands of sinners.

This paradox was perceived very early. Mark 9.31 presents an
Aramaic play upon words, בַּר נָשָׁא/בְּנֵי נָשָׁא.[5] Here the name Son
of Man is set in direct contrast to men. The formula-like phrase
discussed above, 'to deliver into the hands of', confirms that
Aramaic roots underlie the formulation of Mark 9.31a.[6] In the
sphere of Greek language the meaningful contrast of Son of Man and
men was certainly still perceived; this is supported by Mark 14.21,
that 'obscure announcement which sets the Son of Man and "that
man" in such sharp opposition yet such close relationship'.[7]

---

[1] Chapter IV D II 1 a, p. 160.
[2] Cf. Schlatter, *Matt.*, pp. 537f.; cf. above, Chapter IV, p. 160 n. 1.
[3] Cf. Arndt and Gingrich, *Lexicon*, p. 67.
[4] For Lohmeyer's view cf. *Gottesknecht*, pp. 127, 57ff.; *Markus*, p. 6.
[5] Jeremias, *Servant*, p. 102.
[6] Büchsel in *TWNT* II, p. 172 lines 8f.
[7] Lohmeyer, *Markus*, p. 301.

There is a trend in recent exegesis to paraphrase the pronouncement of Mark 9.31a as follows: the Son of Man, the Judge of the
world, will be delivered into the hands of men. Thus the Son of
Man's transcendent glory and his powerlessness on earth willed by
God are contrasted. The paradox then would be that a heavenly
being is submitted to the most extreme restrictions on earth. Hence
the question must arise how this heavenly being might be humbled in
powerlessness below men. The answer had to be that the Man from
heaven *conceals* his transcendent attributes for the time of his indigent
existence on earth,[1] or that he *parts* with them because of his obedience, as we read in Phil. 2.6–8.

But Bultmann is right in stressing that we cannot interpret these
Son of Man sayings by means of the *Danielic* concept of the Son of
Man.[2] We stated above that in the sayings discussed so far the poles
of the tension were not the transcendent Son of Man and men, but
Jesus and this generation, and that the designation Son of Man did
not bring the transcendent attributes down to the activity on earth,
but emphasized Jesus' *exousia*.[3] Hence we expect the name Son of
Man to have been similarly used in the sayings concerning the
suffering, i.e. to designate Jesus' *exousia*. God seems to side not with
the one whom he authorized but with those men who are opposed to
God. For the disciples this is the enigma of the passion.

In which of the strata within the history of tradition is this concept
rooted? Jesus and men are contrasted already in a parousia saying
from Q, in Luke 12.8f. and par. The phrase 'to confess before men'
is based on an Aramaism.[4] Already in sayings from Q also, Jesus
as the Son of Man in his present activity is contrasted with this
generation. The term 'this generation' which occurs, e.g., in Matt.
11.16 (cf. 11.19) and in Luke 11.30 is a 'rendering of the rabbinic
הַדּוֹר הַזֶּה, as is evident from the unvarying suffix αὔτη.'[5] But
there are no sayings from Q which contain the paradox that the Son
of Man is delivered to men. Yet these sayings were framed already
in the Palestinian community, as the Aramaic play upon words in
Mark 9.31 proves.[6] Thus the sayings concerning the Son of Man's

---

[1] Dibelius, *Jesus*, pp. 89ff.
[2] Bultmann, 'Matt. 16.17–19', pp. 278f.; cf. above p. 142, n. 2.
[3] Cf. also below, Chapter V D 3, p. 272, and E, pp. 274f.
[4] Cf. the evidence cited in Arndt and Gingrich, *Lexicon*, p. 571; Nestle in
ZNW 7, 1906, pp. 279f., and Bl.-Debr. *Grammatik* §214.6; also Schlatter, *Matt.*, p. 348.
[5] Büchsel in *TWNT* I, p. 661 lines 25f.
[6] Cf. Jeremias, *Servant*, p. 102.

suffering have at least *one* pre-Hellenistic root. We have been prepared for this result by the conclusions from the part of the train of
terms pertaining to the concept of the suffering Son of Man which
we have already considered.[1]

How do we have to understand this tension between the Son of
Man and this generation? A comparison with some synoptic sayings
will be helpful. Regarding Mark 9.19 Windisch, Dibelius, Bultmann
and others are largely agreed, judging from parallels in the history
of religion, that this is a saying with a mythical background; in it
'the God of an epiphany' is speaking 'who appears in human form
only for a time and will soon return to heaven'.[2] Yet we nevertheless
are reminded of Old Testament passages here.[3] Elsewhere, too, Jesus
rebukes and deplores, as in Mark 4.40; 6.4; 8.33; 10.38. Still, in
Mark 9.19 a wider range is within sight. Jesus as the one with unique
authority faces all others; all the others merge without differentiation
into that disbelieving generation whom the one blesses by his
presence, bearing them as Yahweh bears Israel according to Isa. 40.11
and 46.4.[4]

The range of Jesus' authority is similarly widened in the lament
over Jerusalem, taken from Q, in Matt. 23.37–39 and par. Here
'Jesus himself appears as God's presence bestowing protection from
the judgement'.[5]

We single out the following aspects from the passages mentioned.
The first aspect: both Jerusalem, the holy city, and this present
generation merge into a homogeneous entity of a specific quality
when confronted with Jesus' authority. The second aspect: as homogeneous entities both appear in opposition against Jesus' authorized
way of acting, and thus in sin.

Now, this is not at all different from how men appear in the three
groups of sayings concerning the Son of Man. It is this generation in
their sinful opposition against God into whose hands the Son of Man
is delivered. The two marks distinguishing this paradoxical statement are the *full authority* of the Son of Man acting on earth and the

---

[1] The terms 'to be delivered', 'to suffer many things and be rejected, or treated
with contempt' and 'to be killed' already indicate a predominantly pre-Hellenistic
sphere.

[2] Cf. Bultmann, *Tradition*, p. 157 and n. 1; Dibelius, *Tradition*, p. 95.

[3] Cf., e.g., Deut. 32.5; Isa. 6.11; 65.2, etc. Cf. Klostermann, *Markus*, p. 91;
Lohmeyer, *Markus*, p. 187.

[4] This exegesis is dependent on G. Bornkamm, summer term of 1955.

[5] Thus Bornkamm, summer term of 1955.

sinfulness of this generation. That God 'delivers' the one whom he authorized into the hands of men who are opposed to God is what constitutes the paradox. The pronouncements in Acts 2.22–24 as well speak very similarly of the 'delivering' of the one attested by God whose *exousia* has become manifest in his activity on earth; even while he is thus authorized, he is 'delivered according to the definite plan and foreknowledge of God'. The same paradox is stated.

(*b*) In Mark 8.31; 10.33f. the Jewish legal authorities were named in particular, whereas in 9.31; 14.41 men were spoken of in general. These variant forms correspond with different concepts.

Where the Jewish legal authorities are named, the association of scriptural evidence adduced from Ps. 118.22 and also from Ps. 21.8 (LXX) against the Jewish rulers is suggested. Details of the passion become visible, cf. Mark 10.33f. The capital reproach is the delivering to the Gentiles.[1] These parts of the announcements of suffering stem from a time and from a sphere concerned with controversial discussions with the legitimate Jewish officials for which scriptural evidence was employed.

Where the being delivered to men is spoken of, however, differentiations between Jews and Gentiles do not become visible at all. Here the one who is fully authorized by God faces men and by his claim confronts this generation as a whole with the inevitability of decision.

This difference in the concepts evokes the question: should the announcements of suffering be divided into two separate groups, the one represented by Mark 8.31; 10.33f., the other by Mark 9.31; 14.41?

(3) *Terms denoting the rising after three days*

In each of the three announcements of suffering in Mark this phrase occurs in a similar form.[2] This is conspicuous for several reasons. First: Matthew alters the phrase in all three cases, and therefore on purpose, into 'to be raised, or rise, *on* the third day'.[3] ἐγείρειν is 'a favourite term of Matthew';[4] he uses it also in 17.9 as he did in the three announcements of suffering. Secondly: Luke omits the

---

[1] Cf. Mark 10.33f.; Acts 2.22f.; 3.13.
[2] I.e. employing the expressions μετὰ τρεῖς ἡμέρας and ἀναστῆναι.
[3] Cf. Matt. 16.21; 17.23; 20.19.
[4] Oepke in *TWNT* II, p. 334 line 9.

statement about rising in the second passion announcement, and he alters the corresponding phrase in Mark 8.31 and 10.33f. into '*on the third day*'. In the first instance he conforms to Matthew's using the term for 'to be raised'; in the second instance he follows the text in Mark, and uses the term for 'to rise' also in 24.7 and 24.46, that is to say, in verses which he helped form. Luke 24.6 conforms again to Matthew's usage. Thirdly: In Jesus' announcement in 14.28 that after being raised he will go before them to Galilee,[1] Mark does not use the term which he used in the announcements of the Son of Man's rising. Nor does he use it in the statement of the young man at the empty grave (Mark 16.6), ἠγέρθη, οὐκ ἔστιν ὧδε. Thus in Mark a clear differentiation of terms is to be noted. In the sayings concerning the Son of Man the term 'to rise' is used; in the sayings concerning Jesus of Nazareth the term 'to be raised, or rise'.

On this observation E. Lichtenstein in his enquiry 'Die älteste christliche Glaubensformel' established extensive conclusions. He arrives at the view that ἐγείρειν is used where thought in relation to the resurrection is directed towards the fixed condition of being dead as contrasted with being alive, where the essence of God's deed of salvation is consequently understood as redemption from the law of death; here the third day is seen as that eschatological day on which the first bodily resurrection happens as the start of the raising of the dead at the end of time according to Jewish orthodox teaching.[2] The set of concepts operating here is called by Lichtenstein a Christology of resurrection.[3] In the formula it can usually be recognized from the combination of 'to be raised' and 'on the third day'.[4] The Christology of resurrection is contrasted by Lichtenstein with a Christology of exaltation. This can be recognized from the alteration of 'on the third day' into 'after three days'. The latter phrase is invariably combined with the verb ἀνίστημι, cf. Mark 8.31; 9.31; 10.34. Here it is the raising of *Jesus* that is in view, not resurrection in general.[5] This Christology is founded on the experience of Christ's appearing; therefore here the exaltation of the one who was crucified is always associated, too, with reflection on the rising. This Christology issued from the 'Petrine circle'; it is closely connected with the

---

[1] ἀλλὰ μετὰ τό ἐγερθῆναί με προάξω ὑμᾶς εἰς τὴν Γαλιλαίαν.
[2] Cf. Lichtenstein in *ZKG* 63, pp. 29, 31, 35, 41f.
[3] *Ibid.*, p. 29 *et passim.*
[4] The moment, not the span of time, is thought of.
[5] Lichtenstein, *ibid.*, pp. 38f.

Christology of the Servant of Jehovah,[1] which must be understood in its correlation with the concept of the Son of Man.[2]

We cannot discuss here Lichtenstein's far-reaching combinations which, on the basis of ideas from R. Otto and Lohmeyer, he connects with the differentiation between ἐγείρω and ἀνίστημι. As regards the announcements of suffering, however, we have to challenge his argument.

Firstly, at least the supposition that Mark would sedulously avoid rendering Jesus' certainty of his resurrection with ἐγείρω cannot be maintained.

(a) In order to maintain his case, Lichtenstein needs to declare Mark 14.28, because of its use of the word ἐγείρω, to be a post-Marcan interpolation. He finds vague support in the absence of Mark 14.28 in the Fayum papyrus. But this is a rather unreliable foundation. According to Bultmann it is probable that Mark himself inserted 14.28.[3] According to Dibelius, in the earliest account Mark 14.29–31 was already attached to 14.28.[4] Lohmeyer bases on Mark 14.28 and 16.7 the theory that in Mark Galilee is still considered to be the place of the Lord's future imminent parousia.[5] Thus the conclusions concerning Mark 14.28 are somewhat incongruous.

(b) In Lichtenstein's view Mark is supposed to have retained the word ἐγείρω in 16.6 because he received it with early material transmitted to him in which it was used as a formula. Outside of Mark 14.28 and 16.6 statements about the rising only occur in the three announcements of suffering. In these the word ἀνίστημι is used throughout. Now, Lichtenstein obviously assumes that Mark formed the announcements; consequently in his view the word ἀνίστημι signifies Marcan usage, and Mark's Christology of exaltation, as the use of this same word in Mark 9.9 is a sign of this same Christology.[6]

(c) The literary interdependence of the rendering of the three passion announcements in the Synoptic Gospels is thus seen as follows: It was Mark who altered the phrases 'on the third day' and 'to be raised';[7] the earlier form is to be found in Matthew and Luke.[8] We cannot assent to this train of thought; for in our view, as already

---

[1] Lichtenstein, op. cit., p. 29.   [2] Ibid., pp. 37, 39.
[3] Bultmann, Tradition, p. 267.
[4] Dibelius, Tradition, p. 183; cf. pp. 181, 189, 192.
[5] Lohmeyer, Galiläa, p. 14.
[6] Lichtenstein, op. cit., pp. 28f.
[7] Lichtenstein, ibid., pp. 27f., 38.
[8] Ibid., pp. 43 and 38, on 'the glorification of the Son of Man on the third day'.

stated, Matthew and Luke are dependent on the text in Mark when reproducing the announcements.

(*d*) The decisive objection to Lichtenstein's view is provided by the pre-Marcan origin of the announcements of suffering. Since we have seen that Mark did not formulate them independently, we assume that he also received the statements about the rising. This is supported by the words Mark uses in 14.28 and 16.6; here Mark was independent of formula-like material transmitted to him and was free to choose the wording.

Secondly, Lichtenstein's supposition cannot be maintained that with the phrase ἀνίστημι μετὰ τρεῖς ἡμέρας a distinct concept of rising, of sojourn in the grave and of exaltation is associated. Luke at any rate was not aware of such an association, as is obvious from the varying usage mentioned above. The phrase 'on the third day' is supposed to mark the moment, the point of time at which the resurrection happens, as the eschatological day initiating the messianic time at the End[1] and therewith the general admittance to the salvation which the resurrection of the dead means. The phrase 'after three days', denoting a span of time, an interval, is supposed to imply the idea of a sojourn in the grave, of the Son of Man's descent into the lower regions, according to the concept of the Son of Man's concealment as mythically depicted in the book of Enoch. Lichtenstein here refers to R. Otto.[2]

Apart from all other objections it is to be noted here that the announcements of suffering do not refer to the concept of the *transcendence* of the Son of Man in the book of Enoch. Nor can the concept of concealment be employed as a bridge. In I Enoch it is tied up with that of pre-existence; but the concept of pre-existence does not occur in any of the groups of synoptic sayings concerning the Son of Man, least of all in the sayings about his suffering. Thus we do not see a reason which might make it permissible to employ that concealment of the heavenly Son of Man from I Enoch in interpreting the three days as the interval of the sojourn in the grave. This is, moreover, supported by our earlier observation that the attributes of the transcendent Son of Man are not introduced into the sayings concerning his activity on earth and his suffering.[3]

---

[1] *Op. cit.*, pp. 39f.

[2] *Ibid.*, p. 39; cf. Otto, *Kingdom*, pp. 194f., and Gressmann, *Messias*, pp. 370f.

[3] On Matt. 12.40 cf. below Chapter IV D III e, pp. 213f., and above, Chapter II B I 2, pp. 53f.

Jeremias concludes that Matthew and Luke quite independently of each other altered the formula concerning the rising after three days *ex eventu*. We assent to the literary relationship between Mark on the one hand and Matthew and Luke on the other hand assumed here. What Jeremias hints at, however, is that the two announcements Mark 8.31 and 9.31 on their part were not formed *ex eventu* throughout.[1] The 'predictions of the passion, especially, reveal on comparison a secondary tendency to assume concrete features and to become assimilated to the actual course of history'.[2] But these considerations can by no means arrive with any certainty at authenticated announcements by Jesus; for the tendency towards the concrete is also perceivable within the post-Easter tradition and does not at all oblige us to presuppose sayings that had authentically issued from Jesus. We should rather assent to Schelkle's supposition that Matthew and Luke when making changes independently of each other and yet in agreement were both 'bound by the credal formula which was in process of formation'.[3] The very early formula in I Cor. 15.3f. already speaks of the resurrection on the third day; hence there might have been a still earlier stage at which the phrase 'after three days' was in use, as in the form of the passion announcements in Mark. For if in Matthew and Luke the earlier form was superseded by the more precise phrase 'on the third day', this would correspond with the replacement of the word 'to kill' used in the passion announcements by the kerygmatic term 'to crucify' (cf. Matt. 20.19; 26.2; Luke 24.7).

How do we have to understand what is expressed in Matt. 27.63 and 64? Here the phrases 'after three days' and 'until the third day' are used in rapid succession, and so with the same meaning. In this late legend of the guards at the tomb, however, it is not possible to distinguish where the evangelist is speaking and where he is simply adopting the text transmitted to him. Moreover, this section is not intended to be a kerygmatic formula-like epitome, but is a narrative which according to its nature may be less precise; so there is a slight possibility that Matthew when reproducing this legend did not feel obliged to insert those phrases which were consistent with his own

[1] Jeremias, *Servant*, p. 100.
[2] *Ibid.*, pp. 99f.
[3] Schelkle, *Passion*, p. 66. We must take into account here that the term ἐγείρειν is used to denote Jesus' being raised many times in the Pauline writings, never in the Acts except in 10.40.

understanding here with as much precision as he inserted them in the weightier announcements of suffering.

The fact that the phrase 'raised on the third day' was a predominant formula is also supported by Acts 10.40. This is the only passage in the Acts where a pronouncement about the resurrection is combined with a statement about the third day. And here, too, the verb ἐγείρειν is used in combination with the phrase 'on the third day'.

It has long been asserted that the formula of being raised on the third day was formed under the influence of scriptural evidence. In I Cor. 15.4 we read: raised on the third day according to the Scriptures. The passion announcements as well corroborate this supposition. Mark 9.12; 14.21 speak of the Son of Man's suffering as it is written of him. Mark 8.31 and Luke 17.25; 24.7 emphasize the necessity of the suffering, and the reason for this necessity is that what is written in the Scriptures must be fulfilled, as can be seen from the dependence of Mark 8.31a and 9.12b on Ps. 118.22.[1] In Matt. 12.40 the Son of Man's spending three days and three nights in the heart of the earth is related to Jonah 1.17; the passage is formulated in exact conformity to the text in the LXX. But the scriptural text which is fundamental for announcements of the resurrection is Hosea 6.2; the LXX furnishes a text which includes both a span of time—after two days—and a point of time—on the third day—and also the word ἀνίστημι, thus providing the elements which recur in the phrases about the resurrection within the announcements of suffering in Mark. In view also of the terms used to denote the resurrection in Hosea 6.2 we would prefer the assumption that the earlier ἀνίστημι was superseded by the later ἐγείρω. In the discussion of these details we move on precarious ground. It appears probable, however, that here too scriptural evidence used in pre-Marcan times furnished the material which reappears in the announcements of resurrection.

We arrive at the following conclusion. The earliest, namely the Marcan form of the announcements of suffering denotes the resurrection of the Son of Man by the word ἀναστῆναι. This word pertains to the biblical foundation supplied by the text in Hosea 6.2. Thus in the announcements of suffering it is not said that God raised the Son of Man but rather that the Son of Man rose himself. 'A comparison with the formulae concerning the *Christos* can take us still a step further. In these we read "to die—to be raised"; in the announcement of suffering in Mark 9.31 the emphasis rests on "to be

[1] Cf. above Chapter IV D II 1 b, pp. 162, 167.

killed—to rise". The use of the active and passive voices respectively is reversed. This means that in Mark 9.31 a degree of sovereignty is preserved for the suffering and rising one which is not attempted in the *Christos* tradition.'[1]

(4) *Related phrases from the context*

(a) **The hour is come** (Mark 14.41). Here Jesus proclaims before he is arrested that the hour has come. This statement is the termination and the response to the struggle in prayer at Gethsemane. The proclamation shows the sovereignty of Jesus' free acceptance of suffering.

Hour in a specialized sense means in Judaism the dawn of the apocalyptic day on which God will consummate the destinies of the world and of the nation.[2] With this meaning the word also occurs in the synoptic apocalypse, in Mark 13.32 and par., and in a saying concerning the Son of Man's *parousia*, in Matt. 24.44 = Luke 12.40. In apocalyptic speculation the *hour* is fitted into an ordered sequence in time at a definite point. This point may indeed be a preferred one, but it is nevertheless fixed by a plan. The due time of the *hour* is the consummation at the end of the old aeon,[3] that is to say, the moment toward which the course of the old aeon is directed. It is presupposed here that he who can speak of this *hour* has a special insight into the secret plan and will of God.

This apocalyptic concept may still be perceived in Mark 14.41; yet a profound transmutation has taken place. It is Jesus himself who directly states that the hour has come, thus acting in sovereignty. He needs no special instruction about God's plan to know that this is the hour; he understands when struggling in prayer at Gethsemane that the hour is now approaching him, and he is free to pray to the Father that if it were possible it might pass by (14.35). So the *hour* no longer marks a point at which a fixed sequence aims but a moment which specially and meaningfully aims at Jesus. That the hour has arrived is not realized out of the necessity of the time sequence, but out of the actuality of God's will which reveals itself here and now in Jesus and wins his assent. His accepting the cup is thus seen as a free act (14.36).

---

[1] Quoted from a letter from Ferdinand Hahn, Heidelberg. I owe to him some important suggestions and corrections for Chapter IV.

[2] Cf. Schelkle, *Passion*, p. 75; Dan. 11.40, 45 LXX.

[3] Cf. Dan. 11.40, 45; Matt. 13.39, 40, 49; 24.3.

On the surface men whose will is opposed to God achieve their end. 'But this is your hour and the power of darkness' (Luke 22.53). The hour is thus distinguished by that tension which we perceived in all three groups of the Son of Man sayings where this generation and Jesus or the Son of Man were set over against each other. But there is also a particular distinction besides. The Son of Man whose claim is opposed to the claim of this generation is delivered to men. He seemingly loses his *exousia*, and the power of darkness prevails. According to the traditional eschatological plan the one commissioned by God will triumph over the sinful powers. According to Mark 14.41, however, the counter-movement seems to have arrived at its final goal, the Son of Man being delivered into the hands of sinners. The disciples are unable to follow here; they are asleep when the hour is come.

Considered thus, *hour* in this context should not be called as is often done in recent exegesis an apocalyptic eschatological term; for its traditional characteristics have vanished. The Son of Man's being delivered distinguishes this expression in a new way.

(b) **The Son of Man goes as it is written of him** (Mark 14.21). In his parallel formulation Luke uses the word πορεύομαι which he had already employed in Jesus' prediction of his inevitable course 'today and tomorrow and the day following' (13.33). The word ὑπάγω (Mark 14.21) is used in the Gospel of John as an expressive term denoting Jesus' departure to the Father. According to Bauer, 'in Matt. 26.24; Mark 14.21 it places less emphasis on going to God; it is rather a euphemism for death; the Son of Man goes = he must die.'[1] Probably the full Johannine meaning of the phrase is not yet implied in the text in Mark; nevertheless in our view it means more than a mere euphemism. Throughout the other phrases the delivering of the Son of Man is spoken of in the passive voice. In Mark 14.21, however, the Son of Man acts as the one who goes of himself. This corresponds with what is said in 14.41f.: 'The hour is come . . . Rise, let us go; see, my betrayer is at hand.' Jesus here actively initiates the course of ensuing events. Accordingly it is said in 14.21, 'The Son of Man goes.' He resolves to act sovereignly himself. This is affirmed by the parallel passage in Luke which may be interpreted in the light of the section Luke 13.31-33. In Luke 13.33 as well, with the passion in Jerusalem in view, the saying refers to a *walking* on the

[1] Cf. Arndt and Gingrich, *Lexicon*, p. 844.

day following the next. This statement is formed in analogy to that in Luke 13.32, 'Behold, I cast out demons and perform cures today and tomorrow, and on the third day I shall finish.' Thus here, too, we have to understand the going in an active sense.

These considerations help to answer the question of what significance the use of the name Son of Man has for that which is conceived in the sayings in Mark 14.21 and 14.41. This name, implying the *exousia* of the one who is delivered up, brings out the stark paradox in the course of events. The Son of Man is he who goes his way, miraculously aware of what lies ahead; he himself announces that the hour has come, he himself summons the disciples to set out on the road. Thus the two expressions *hour* and *he goes* suggest Jesus' *exousia*. In the Gospel of John both expressions have been developed in that direction to become terms denoting significant concepts.[1]

(5) *Phrases interpreting the passion announcements as a whole*

(a) **The Son of Man must . . .** Within the synoptic announcements of suffering the term δεῖ undoubtedly contains a rich theological content; it is difficult, however, to define this concept precisely. Investigations of this problem usually start from the basic passage in the LXX, Dan. 2.28, where the translator rendered what in the original text was simply stated in the future tense, מָה דִּי לֶהֱוֵא בְּאַחֲרִית יוֹמַיָּא, by ἃ δεῖ γενέσθαι ἐπ' ἐσχάτων τῶν ἡμερῶν. In this translation the *must* no doubt signifies conformity with an apocalyptic eschatological regularity. But it should be noted that Dan. 2.28 is the *only* passage in Jewish apocalyptic literature in which the δεῖ is used strictly with this meaning.[2]

The term we are discussing occurs several times in the synoptic apocalypse; in Mark 13.7 and par. we read δεῖ γενέσθαι. It is noteworthy that in this passage the events which must happen are not yet those of the conclusive cosmic catastrophe connected with the activity of the one who will judge the world. Here the subject is rather the necessary coming of messianic deceivers, of wars, earthquakes and famines which are only preliminary signs and begin the

---

[1] John 7.33; 16.5, 9; 13.3; 8.14a, and 2.4; 12.23; 17.1; 7.30; 8.20; 13.11.

[2] The phrase 'these things must be fulfilled in their season' does occur in Test. Napht. 7.1. But the necessity here is that of a dream coming true. The event of fulfilment thus is determined by a necessity the primary reason of which is the dream's power to reveal the truth. The nature of this necessity is not the subject of reflection.

travail of bringing forth the End, but are not yet the End itself. Accordingly speaking of that which needs must happen implies an element of exhortation here. The community is assured that they need not be struck with terror, since these things do not happen without a necessity of which one may be aware beforehand. The necessity for their happening has its basic reason in God's will. But in this passage the attention is primarily directed to the exhortation not to be caught unawares by these events. They happen of necessity, but the community may endure them with confidence.

Rev. 1.1[1] obviously alludes to Dan. 2.28f. Here events are men-tioned which must shortly come to pass. 'This δεῖ denotes a pro-phetic necessity, the absolute certainty that God's plan will be fulfilled.'[2] What is that which must happen soon? It is what may be found in the book of Revelation, according to the statement in 22.6. This book itself gives an account of what must come to pass. Here it is noteworthy above all that the necessity of this 'must' is grounded in the authority of him who reveals these visions, i.e. in Jesus Christ as the guarantor for their truth. The 'must' is thus established on this unassailable foundation (cf. 22.6f.).

In Mark 13.10 the necessity denoted by the 'must' is of a nature essentially different from that in the passage in Daniel. 'The gospel must *first* be preached to all nations.' By this isolated saying[3] the task of missionary teaching is conceived in its relation to eschatological events. Thereby an essential significance is assigned to an element which had not been emphasized in the traditional Jewish apocalyptic literature. The 'must' which originally pertained to the narrower sphere of the catastrophe at the End is here anticipated in the sphere of historical events *before* the End.[4] The shifting of the 'must' from the one period into the other is clearly indicated by the 'first'. The 'must' now pertains to the sphere of *salvation history* within which missionary activity takes place. This implicates two more shifts of emphasis among the elements which constitute the nature of the 'must'.

[1] Cf. Rev. 4.1; 22.6; also 1.19. For the following compare also the treatise by Fascher, 'Theologische Beobachtungen zu δεῖ', already mentioned above in note 3 on p. 167.

[2] Lohmeyer, *Rev.*, p. 8.

[3] Cf. Kümmel, *Promise*, pp. 54f.

[4] This is even clearer in Matt. 24.14, cf. Mark 13.7 and par. The reason for the anticipation is that the Christian community understood itself as the true Israel of the Last Days, as the eschatological community, consequently understanding their missionary acting as in its essence no longer pertaining to the course of historical events.

1. Neither the inevitability which can be observed in the course of historical events that happened in the past[1] nor the authority of a visionary or prophetic 'must' which is directed toward the future without any point of reference on earth, are advanced as the reason for this necessity. Instead, the reason is the Christ-event which initiates the mission as the teaching of the Gospel to all nations.

2. The 'must' does not refer to Jesus' coming as the Son of Man. This is not in view here. The necessity is rather stated for that which precedes this coming, namely for the history of salvation founded in Jesus Christ, the course of which naturally leads toward the End. That there is something new preceding the cosmic End is shown in the 'first' in Mark 13.10 and Luke 21.9.

The shifts of emphasis mentioned are all the more noteworthy since the basic passage in Dan. 2 ought to have suggested a combination of the apocalyptic 'must' with the sayings concerning the Son of Man's coming at the definitive End of the world. For according to Dan. 2.34f. the stone which destroys the image and then becomes a great mountain and fills the whole earth unequivocally means the final cosmic catastrophe. Seeing this we are cautioned against the conclusion which has been drawn by a number of scholars that the 'must' in the announcements concerning the suffering Son of Man is pervaded by an eschatological apocalyptic meaning.[2] We should rather enquire more precisely about the *power* which effects and distinguishes the necessity in each respective case. It is self-evident that within the Scriptures this power is always God. But we have to understand in which way God effects the necessity. Obviously there are several possible ways. This becomes evident especially with Luke, who chooses to use that 'must' in his writings no less than forty-one times. Grundmann names some of the ways implicit in the Gospel of Luke of giving the reason for the necessity.[3] (a) The reason for the 'must' is God's will as revealed in the *Law* (11.42; 13.14, *et passim*). (b) God's will is fundamental as expressed in a general Christian maxim or rule for life (15.32; 18.1). (c) The 'must' is effected by God's specific will as regards Jesus (2.49; 4.43; 13.33; 19.5). (d) The 'must' which issues from God's will also reigns over disciples, apostles and communities. According to Luke 12.12 it is mediated by the Spirit.

We did not mention the 'must' of the passion announcements in

---

[1] Cf. contrasting with this Dan. 2.
[2] Cf., e.g., Schelkle, *Passion*, p. 110.
[3] Grundmann in *TWNT* II, p. 23.

the above list. Now the question has to be discussed: What is the nature of God's will as effectual in the necessity of the Son of Man's suffering, and where do we see it revealed?

That 'must' appears but once in the announcements of suffering in Mark, namely in 8.31. This is astonishing in view of its frequent occurrence in the passion announcements in Luke (9.22; 17.25; 24.7). Thus the text in Mark does not suggest the conjecture that it was based on an earlier δεῖ-formula. It must further be noted that twice in the announcements of the Son of Man's suffering in Mark, namely in 9.12 and 14.21, the Scripture is named as giving the reason for what will happen. Thence the conjecture is suggested that in 8.31, too, the reason for the necessity in the 'must' is that what is written in the Scripture must be fulfilled. This is corroborated by what we established above, namely that both Mark 8.31a and 9.12b—parallel formulations—refer to scriptural evidence adduced from Ps. 118.22. The 'must' in Mark 8.31 thus has the same meaning as the phrase in Mark 9.12b, 'it is written'.

Consequently we cannot speak of an apocalyptic eschatological 'must'-formula in the announcements of suffering. The reason for the 'must' of the Son of Man's suffering is rather God's will as revealed in *Scripture*. This is also evident from other passages, Matt. 26.54; Luke 24.25, 26, 27, 44 *et passim*.

This conclusion hinders us from sharing Bultmann's view of the nature of the synoptic tradition concerning the passion. He sees the passion 'narrated as a gruesome and enigmatic event', as an event which 'seemed to be due to a divine δεῖ that at first was incomprehensible, that was difficult for the community to understand.'[1] Bultmann refers to Mark 8.31; Matt. 26.54; Luke 17.25; 22.37; 24.7, etc. Regarding the announcements of suffering from our point of view, however, we can hardly assent to speaking of an incomprehensible divine 'must' and in consequence of this of a gruesome and enigmatic event. From the beginning the reason for that 'must' is given by way of scriptural prophecy and is thus rendered comprehensible. The announcements of suffering are not concerned with the enigma of God's will as seen apart from the Scriptures.

It is significant for the way in which the term δεῖ is used that within the synoptic tradition it is combined several times with the word 'first'. The latter expression, too, may well be used in connexion with evidence adduced from the Scriptures as shown in Mark 9.11. Here

[1] Bultmann, *Johannes*, p. 489; also n. 4.

the controversy of the primitive community with the Jews appears to have been further developed. The Jews now wish to demonstrate by means of their argument, 'Elijah must first come', that what the Christians assert cannot be true, namely that the suffering of Jesus as the Messiah corresponds with the Scriptures. But the Christians confirm that Elijah did, in fact, come first, in the person of the Baptist (Matt. 17.13), and that moreover according to the Scriptures, I Kings 19.2, 10, violence was done to him.

We have here to consider the statement in Luke 17.25, 'first he must suffer many things and be rejected by this generation'. Conzelmann justly objects against Grundmann[1] that we cannot simply speak of an eschatological nature of this 'must'. The 'first . . . must' distinguishes the statement in 17.25 as not denoting an eschatological event in the strict sense, but as pertaining to a certain situation within salvation history. And this situation in the history of salvation is separated from the onset of the eschatological events by the long-lasting period of the *ecclesia pressa*. Here a reason is provided for the 'must' by Luke's division of history into periods. His procedure thus shows a formal similarity to Jewish apocalyptic thinking in which the orderly succession of events in time provides the basis on which the 'must' is established (Dan. 2.28 LXX). Instead of the immediacy of the 'must' which comes into existence in Jesus by virtue of his unobstructed openness toward God and has its reason in God's openness toward Jesus (Mark 14.36; 14.41), the 'must' is here mediated by the order of events in salvation history. Luke's thinking in terms of a sequence of periods in salvation history may have contributed to the frequency of his using that expression 'it must'. Yet there are deep-rooted differences between Luke's view and apocalyptic thinking. According to the latter, the nexus of events will be exclusively established in the future. Luke, however, accepts as his starting-point the fact that what will be the foundation of the future salvation has already happened in Jesus' presence.

The result of our enquiry about the 'must' in the announcements of suffering may be summed up briefly. In Mark 8.31 the 'must' is to be understood as equivalent to the 'it is written' in Mark 9.12, both passages referring to Scripture (Ps. 118.22). Where Luke uses the term 'must' with regard to the Son of Man's suffering (17.25; 24.7), he no longer deduces the necessity from a particular passage in Scripture; he sees the reason for the necessity of the occurrence of

[1] Conzelmann, *Theology of Luke*, p. 153 n. 3.

suffering in its determined and predetermined situation at the end of
that period of salvation history which was constituted by Jesus' presence on earth. Neither with Mark nor with Matthew and Luke has
the 'must' an apocalyptic eschatological meaning in the strict sense.
Its meaning is understood and the reason for it is given from a
Christian point of view.

(b) **It is written of the Son of Man.** Present-day critical scholars
declare that only one passage in the Old Testament speaks of the Son
of Man, namely Dan. 7.13f., and that there it only speaks of him
as the ruler of God's reign to come. But the first Christians found in
Scripture evidence for their experience that Jesus as the Son of Man
delivered into the hands of men must suffer. This scruptural evidence
was of greatest importance to them in the controversies with the
Jews. Only by putting Scripture to this new use were they able to
vindicate their special position in Israel, indeed their claim to be
the true Israel as against official Judaism. And at the same time
they were effectually joined with the old Israel by referring to
Scripture. Had the Christians referred exclusively to the spiritual
experience of the resurrection, they would have departed from the
synagogue congregation at once. However, they established material
parts of their message on scriptural foundation. It is this fact which
is reflected by the phrase 'it is written'. It was on ground which they
had in common with the Jews that their controversy with the Jewish
authorities could take place.[1] Yet right here in the reference to
Scripture it becomes evident that a new authority has appeared.
Jesus himself announces according to Mark 14.21 what is written.
He is aware beforehand of the necessity of the Son of Man's being
delivered up. So wherever scriptural evidence was adduced regarding
Jesus' course, an attempt to elucidate the relationship of these two
authorities, to correlate them positively, had to be made. In the
Gospel of Matthew we perceive one of these attempts.

There is one element of the announcements of suffering, however,
which apparently does not refer to a scriptural foundation in the
narrower sense. It is the element of the Son of Man's being delivered
into the hands of *men*. Here the view is extended beyond the nearer
tension of being confronted with the Jewish authorities to *men* who as
this generation in their sinfulness confront the one Son of Man standing
on the other side.

[1] Cf. Mark 9.11–12; 8.31; 14.21.

S.M.–G

The results of our analysis of the train of terms need not be summed up expressly at this place. They will become clear and be employed in the appropriate place in the following discussion of the individual sayings concerning the Son of Man's suffering and rising.

III. Analysis of the individual sayings concerning the suffering and rising of the Son of Man

(a) **Mark 9.9–13.** Since Wrede's revolutionary theses about the concept of a Messianic secret the section Mark 9.9–13 has become the battlefield of heated discussions. Wrede had propounded that this section be used to interpret the Messianic secret, which is connected with the material constituted by narratives of possession by demons, theories about the parables, and statements of the disciples' lack of understanding, and which is expressed in Jesus' command to tell no man. It may be indirectly inferred from Mark 9.9 that the concept of a messianic secret was infused into this material in retrospect. Bultmann, further developing Wrede's basic theses, analysed the section Mark 9.9–13 in order to locate it within the history of tradition, with the following results.

1. In a pre-Marcan source Mark 9.1 was immediately followed by 9.11. 9.2–10 is an interpolation by Mark. Within this interpolation vv. 9 and 10 are due to Marcan editing.[1] The wording in 9.9b, 'until the Son of Man should have risen from the dead', is a 'deposit' from the three passion prophecies which on their part were formed secondarily by the community.[2] Bultmann considers the isolated and intrusive sentence about the Son of Man in v. 12b to be a post-Marcan interpolation from Matt. 17.12.[3]

2. The train of thought in the pre-Marcan source ran as follows. In Mark 9.1 the coming of God's reign was announced for a time which some of those present at this scene will live to see. This was directly continued by the disciples' question in v. 11 dealing with a Jewish objection, namely that Elijah must come first.[4] 'The early saying in verse 1, which is incompatible with the Jewish theory of a forerunner of God's reign, has to be reconciled with it by stating that the forerunner has already come. Undoubtedly Mark saw the Baptist

---

[1] Bultmann, *Tradition*, p. 332.
[2] *Ibid.*, p. 152.
[3] *Ibid.*, p. 125.
[4] Cf. Kümmel, *Promise*, p. 64 n. 139.

in that role, as Matt. 17.13 adds explicitly.'[1] So the passage Mark 9.12–13 states 'the fulfilment of an apocalyptic prophecy'.[2]

3. Bultmann draws the conclusion that only the parousia is presupposed by Mark 9.1, 11–13, and only the resurrection is contained in the interpolated narrative of the transfiguration in 9.2–10.[3]

From our point of view we have to object to this conclusion. Bultmann wishes to exclude the sayings on the suffering and rising Son of Man from the original context of the source, and even from the context of the Marcan text. He supposes the section to be determined merely by the concept of parousia. But even if originally in this section the Christians had indeed only intended to reconcile the parousia saying in 9.1 with the Jewish theory of a forerunner of God's reign, the solution offered by them was probably from the beginning the identification of that forerunner with the Baptist. Otherwise it would not have been possible to state that Elijah had come already and thereby to answer the Jewish objection. But the Baptist could hardly have been seen in the traditional manner as the forerunner of the coming transcendent Perfecter of the End, as the direct forerunner of God's reign. Since the actual fate of the Baptist was known, the theory of Elijah's coming as the forerunner, accepted in the main, needs to be revised: 'Also Elijah has come (already), and they did to him whatever they pleased, as it is written of him' (Mark 9.13). Now, the Christians certainly identified the Baptist as the forerunner of the judge of the Last Days, as Matt. 3.12 and par. (Q) proves. But precisely because of that he was seen as the forerunner of Jesus; for Jesus was not only acknowledged as the authorized proclaimer of God's final judgement, but he was also expected from the primitive community as the coming executor of that judgement. Moreover, the Baptist was seen in the tradition as the forerunner of Jesus' messianic activity on earth (Mark 1.7f. and par.). Hence it was natural enough to regard the Baptist's fate and Jesus' suffering as near parallels without losing sight of their connexion with the coming of God's reign. The reason for the Baptist's not having restored all things, as he should have done according to the Jewish theory of the forerunner, is given in Mark 9.13 as the Jews' opposition. The same opposition is encountered by the Son of Man (Matt. 17.12b). His sovereignty is not acknowledged; consequently he must suffer. Yet

[1] Bultmann, *Tradition*, p. 125.
[2] *Ibid.*, p. 124.
[3] Bultmann, *Theology* I, p. 30.

the coming of God's reign is as near at hand as Jesus promises in Mark 9.1. It appears from this that in Mark 9.11–13 the concept of parousia is connected with the sayings about the Son of Man's suffering. This is achieved as soon as the Baptist is on the one hand identified with Elijah in order to refute the Jewish objection stated in Mark 9.11, and on the other hand seen as the forerunner on Jesus' course of suffering. Notwithstanding the incongruous wording of the text in Mark we cannot say that the mention of the Son of Man's suffering would rupture the train of thought. Matthew explicitly states what Mark had in mind. Hence to us it looks improbable that the original context here should have spoken only of the parousia. The suffering of the Baptist is the decisive argument against the scribes' objection. And the mention of his fate inevitably reminds the Christians of the suffering of the 'greater one' prophesied in Scripture.

We find our conclusion corroborated on discerning that there is no support for Bultmann's supposing Mark 9.12b to be a post-Marcan interpolation from Matt. 17.12b.[1] We have already established the fact that Mark 9.12b cannot possibly be an interpolation from Matt. 17.12b.[2] For 9.12b conforms with Mark 8.31a, both passages being formulated in dependence on Ps. 118.22 and employing variant wordings of the evidence adduced from Scripture; 'to be treated with contempt' (Mark 9.12b and Acts 4.11) and 'to be rejected' (Mark 8.31a and Mark 12.10) are synonymous expressions, as is obvious when Acts 4.11 and Mark 12.10 are compared. Consequently Mark 9.12b is not dependent on Mark 8.31a either, but is to be considered as an independent statement which issued from the debates of the Christians with the Jews on the fulfilment of scriptural prophecies. The mention of the Son of Man's suffering according to the Scriptures is indispensable in a section concerned with refuting Jewish objections that are supported by the traditional theory of a forerunner. In Mark's view 9.9b[3] is an appropriate transition to the

---

[1] Lohmeyer, too, takes into account the possibility that the sentence about the Son of Man was not part of the original text. He states in *Markus*, p. 183 n. 1, 'It interrupts the train of thought which is concerned with Elijah, not with the Son of Man; therefore it is probably a marginal gloss which slipped into the text. Cf. Couchoud, *JTS* 34, 1933, p. 123.' But it is just this assumption that the sentence would interrupt the train of thought which we wish to question. In our view the text appears to be concerned with the messianic nature of Jesus' suffering; for this is just what might well have been disputed by the Jews with the help of the traditional theory of the forerunner.

[2] Cf. above Chapter IV D II 1b, p. 169, and Chapter IV D II 5a, p. 191.

[3] Cf. above in this section under (1), p. 194.

discourse which follows, the naming of the Son of Man introducing the topic. This key-word is combined by Mark with an abbreviated version of the announcements concerning the *rising* of the Son of Man which in 9.12b is joined by the mention of the *suffering* of the Son of Man, both statements, so to speak, completing each other to conform to a passion announcement with all its parts.

What does the link between the narrative of the transfiguration and 9.9–13 signify in Mark's view? Do we have to understand it as a key-word association based on the word Elijah? At any rate, v. 9 links up clearly with the preceding scene; when descending from the mount of transfiguration, Jesus utters the command to tell no one. The disciples are not allowed to talk about what they have seen to those who have not, until the Son of Man will have risen from the dead. Apparently it is presupposed here that Jesus' glory as it shone at the transfiguration cannot be recognized and proclaimed before the rising. The phrase 'to rise from the dead' becomes the subject of a discussion amongst the disciples; what was said is not reported. But Mark makes this discussion lead up to the disciples' asking Jesus, 'Why do the scribes say that first Elijah must come?' The 'first' here obviously refers to Mark 9.1. Consequently we have to consider the narrative of the transfiguration as an interpolation and 9.9f. as the juncture at which the interpolated narrative of the transfiguration is linked up with the main problem in the following section which is in correlation with Mark 9.1.

We have to consider correspondingly the use of the name Son of Man in the transition Mark 9.9f. The way in which Mark uses the name Son of Man here is the same as in the three announcements of suffering and in the section 14.1–42, namely, he uses it in its function as the leading thematic concept as he forms his composition. By 9.9 the narrative of the transfiguration is related to the event of the resurrection. The resurrection is the only key that opens an understanding of the revelation of Jesus' supra-terrestrial glory to the community. The statement concerning the Son of Man's rising thus serves to interpret the scene of transfiguration as announcing the glory of resurrection. The name Son of Man points to the sovereignty of the one who descends from the mount of transfiguration and goes forward to be met by his death; it signifies that the course through suffering is the course of the one who will show forth his glory at his rising.

We cannot but understand the name Son of Man in Mark 9.12b

in the same way. This passage is concerned with discussing objections by Jewish scribes which are refuted by referring to Scripture. Scriptural evidence is adduced against scriptural evidence. Thereby the community wants to prove that Jesus, who promised that God's reign is at hand (9.1), who nevertheless must suffer many things and be treated with contempt (9.12b), is really speaking and acting with *exousia*. As the one who has *exousia* he is to be called the Son of Man (cf. Mark 2.10).

(b) **Mark 14.21 and 14.41.** The saying in *Mark 14.21* is fitted so snugly into the context that it is difficult to consider it by itself. Even Luke who, rearranging the sections, makes the prediction of the betrayal follow after the institution of the Lord's Supper, did not detach the designation of the betrayer from the saying concerning the Son of Man's being delivered. Bultmann conjectures that the Son of Man saying in Luke 22.22 was formed by the author conforming to Mark 14.21.[1]

Mark 14.17–21 is a prophetic saying together with the narrative context in which it is presented. Its main point is Jesus' sovereign foreknowledge. He knows the intention of the Scripture (Ps. 41.10) which is to be fulfilled by the betrayer (Mark 14.18b). In John 13.18, too, Jesus' prediction is combined with the same quotation from Ps. 41.10. It was a grievous offence to the community that one of the twelve betrayed Jesus. They overcame this offence by acknowledging that Jesus sovereignly foreknew the betrayal and that evidence of God's ordering this event himself was furnished by the Scriptures. So in Mark 14.21, too, the authority of Jesus is combined with the authority of Scripture. We did not find this combination in the sayings concerning the coming and the present activity of the Son of Man. There the immediate authority of Jesus or of the Son of Man was in view. In several of the sayings concerning the suffering of the Son of Man, however, the reference to Scripture is added (Mark 14.21; 8.31; 9.12). The adducing of scriptural evidence pertains to those strata of the tradition in which the passion account and certain groups of the controversial discourses were transmitted. Hence we have to presuppose for the sayings cited a connexion between the tradition of the Son of Man sayings and the tradition about the passion. Since Mark 14.21 issued from the Palestinian sphere of language we must assume that there the connexion of the

[1] Bultmann, *Tradition*, p. 264.

tradition concerning the Son of Man with the tradition concerning the passion was already established.

Mark 14.21 expresses that the delivering up of the Son of Man is a shameful deed for the man who does it. This is evident from the cry of woe about that man. The play upon the words *that man* and *Son of Man* recalls Mark 9.31 and Luke 9.44, where the opposition between sinful men and the Son of Man is in view. *That man* in Mark 14.21 may probably be regarded as an exponent and representative of *men*.

What view is taken here of the one who is 'delivered'? He goes, freely determining his own way. What happens does not take him by surprise nor against his will. In this is manifested his authority which is superior to the world, and is expressed by the name Son of Man. But what is in view is not the irresistible sovereignty of the Judge of the world who brings to an end all power on earth and pronounces his verdict on it. The sovereignty of the one who is 'delivered' is of a different kind. It is the *exousia* of the one who on earth forgives sins. By this *exousia* the opposition of this generation is endured, not eliminated in the way in which the coming Son of Man enforces the prompt recognition of his sovereignty (Matt. 24.30). Therefore this *exousia* is exposed to being spoken and blasphemed against (Matt. 11.19 and par.; 12.32 and par.).

Thus here it is the sovereignty that enters into the restrictions of an existence on earth which is denoted by the name Son of Man. It corresponds to the authority exercised by Jesus according to Luke 12.8f. and par.; Mark 8.38; Matt. 19.28; Luke 11.29f. This authority is on the one hand differentiated from that of the transcendent Son of Man, but on the other hand related to it.

Mark 14.41 marks the end of the account of Jesus' struggle in prayer at Gethsemane in 14.32–42, which is 'originally an individual story of a thoroughgoing legendary nature which has not survived intact in Mark'.[1] Bultmann considers v. 41b, i.e. the Son of Man saying, and v. 42 to be secondary additions inserted by Mark. We cannot assent to this view, but would prefer the results of the literary analysis of Mark 14.32–42 presented by Kuhn in his essay, 'Jesus in Gethsemane'.[2] According to these, a version of the

---

[1] Bultmann, *Tradition*, pp. 267f.

[2] In *EvTh*, 1952, pp. 260–85. On the basis of his literary analysis of the narrative about Gethsemane, Kuhn is able to assign to the postulated pre-Marcan source the following verses: Mark 14.32, 35, 40, 41. This results in a self-contained account

Gethsemane narrative, the point of which was Jesus' concluding pronouncement about the hour of the Son of Man in Mark 14.41, was already present in a source transmitted to Mark. Mark combined this source with another one and, fitting in additions of his own, composed the narrative as we have it now. At any rate, Mark used the saying about the Son of Man in his context as an interpretative saying which like 14.21 leads up to the passion.

It has recurrently been emphasized that Jesus' bitter cry reveals his human nature which fully shares the fear and trembling of mortal men. Yet this must not make us overlook the other aspect of what we are told, namely, that Jesus is contrasted with his disciples and distinguished in his sovereignty in a unique manner. The Master separates himself from the larger circle of his disciples, at first together with the three intimately attached to him; then he leaves these three behind as well and is alone. They can only stand and watch from a distance; but even that is beyond their capability. Significantly enough, they fall asleep. In impressive repetition the Master's readiness to respond to God is contrasted with the three faithful disciples' falling asleep. They are overwhelmed by the temptation (14.38), they are not capable of withstanding the power of darkness. All initiative lies with Jesus. He alone stands his ground in the struggle. With that freedom which is constituted by the correspondence of his will with the will of the Father he initiates the ensuing course of events (14.41f.).

Thus Jesus' sovereignty in contrast to men's failure is strongly emphasized in the narrative. The use of the name Son of Man in the interpretative saying accords with this. The one who subordinates his will to the Father's will is *in so doing* delivered into the hands of sinners. The one who is not overwhelmed by the power of darkness is delivered up by God. Here again we see that by using the name Son of Man Jesus' *exousia* is expressed.

(c) **Mark 8.31; 9.31; 10.33f.** The use of the name Son of Man in Mark 9.11–13; 14.21 and 14.41 accords with that in the three announcements of suffering. In these as well the paradox prevails that the one on whom the *exousia* rests is delivered to men.

Jesus' authority and sovereignty, expressed by the name Son of

---

'the meaning and purpose of which is exclusively the Christological pronouncement about the hour of the Son of Man' (p. 274). Thus already in pre-Marcan material the Son of Man was spoken of as being delivered.

Man, provide the shining background against which the dark deeds of rejection, mocking, delivering and killing are set off. But the suffering is not only contrasted with the *exousia* with which Jesus acts on earth but also with his rising. While his being rejected and suffering might give the impression that the Son of Man is deprived of any authority, his rising vindicates and enforces his authority. The announcements of suffering are obviously content with having expressed this; in none of them are the exaltation and the parousia of the Son of Man referred to. They all end with the mention of the rising.

There is a second element which is of great significance. In none of the sayings discussed up to now concerning the Son of Man's suffering and being delivered up is the soteriological meaning of this event mentioned. They make it clear that the suffering is not an unforeseen catastrophe but must happen according to the Scriptures, but they do not make clear what his suffering means for the many. This observation accords with the result of our enquiry into the train of terms. We have established the fact that the terms 'to suffer many things and be rejected, or treated with contempt' and 'to be delivered' cannot be traced back to Isa. 53. It is surprising that the soteriological interpretation of suffering which is anticipated in Isa. 53 and alluded to in Rom. 4.25; 8.32; I Cor. 11.23; Mark 14.24; 10.45 was not admitted into the passion announcements.

As regards the location of the three announcements of suffering within the history of tradition, we may conclude the following. The second announcement, Mark 9.31, originated without doubt in the Palestinian language area.[1] It is related to the sayings about the Son of Man's activity on earth, yet clearly differs from them, inasmuch as it contains the paradox that the one who is authorized is delivered up by God himself, whilst the sayings about the activity on earth only point to the Son of Man's sovereignty and men's opposition without referring to Jesus' passion. Consequently the combination of the traditions concerning the Son of Man and concerning the passion appears to have been brought about already in the Palestinian community.

The first announcement, Mark 8.31, is at least in its first part not dependent on Mark 9.31. It is undoubtedly of pre-Marcan origin and refers to the scriptural evidence which had early been adduced from Ps. 118.22. However, we cannot find unequivocal criteria

[1] Cf. Chapter IV, p. 160 n. 1, and p. 177 and nn. 5 and 6.

which might prove that it belonged to the Palestinian language area. The introductory δεῖ in Mark 8.31 refers to the necessity of the fulfilment of what is written in the Scriptures, whilst Mark 9.31 refers to God's activity and the Son of Man's sovereignty without linking up with the Scriptures. Mark 8.31 conforms to the tradition concerning the passion which is concerned with adducing scriptural evidence. No scriptural evidence is adduced in the sayings about the Son of Man's activity on earth. In agreement with this difference, in Mark 9.31 men are named in a comprehensive sense, while in Mark 8.31 those who reject the Son of Man are named specifically. The builders mentioned in Ps. 118.22 are specified as elders, chief priests and scribes.

The third announcement, Mark 10.33f., conforms to Mark 9.31 merely in the name Son of Man and in the word denoting the delivering. Those to whom the Son of Man is delivered are not denoted as men, as they are in 9.31, but as chief priests and scribes. There are considerable deviations from Mark 8.31. Mark 10.33f. is unique amongst the passion announcements in regarding the deliverance to the Gentiles as the capital reproach against the specifically named Jewish authorities. This announcement is thus oriented on a purely Jewish point of view. This orientation accords as little with Mark's passion account as the summary of the mockings by the Gentiles in 10.34.[1] Consequently the third announcement of suffering was not formed by Mark either. We cannot decide, however, whether it originated in the Palestinian or in the Hellenistic language area. At any rate, it uses the terms pertaining to the tradition of the passion, thereby presupposing the combination of this tradition with that of the Son of Man.

(d) **Mark 10.45.** A brief review of the judgements in recent exegesis was given in our provisional discussion of this saying in Chapter III. It was Jeremias who took into consideration particularly important aspects of Mark 10.45.[2] In his view the sayings belong to the material of esoteric instruction for the disciples.[3] Since Luke 22.24–27 shows strong Hellenistic influence, it cannot be regarded as primary over against Mark 10.42–45 with its use of Palestinian expressions.

[1] Cf. on this Chapter IV D II 2 a b, p. 175.
[2] Jeremias' latest publication on this subject available to us is *The Servant of God*, pp. 98–104.
[3] *Ibid.*, p. 104.

E. Lohse relies on Jeremias' view of many details, in particular as regards linguistic arguments, but he does not understand Mark 10.45 to be an authentic saying of Jesus.[1] He emphasizes together with M. Werner that Pauline concepts cannot be used to interpret Mark 10.45. It is the stage of tradition at which Mark stands which accounts for the 'Pauline' way of speaking about Jesus' death.[2] He stresses further that there is a history of tradition leading to Mark 10.41–45 and another one leading to Luke 22.24–27, and that the respective histories of tradition are not interdependent. Neither of the two versions can be derived directly from the other one. Hence their relative ages may only be judged by their language and their concepts.[3] The decision is easily made; the Lucan tradition uses a great number of definitely Hellenistic words, whilst Mark 10.45b has its linguistic roots definitely in the Palestinian sphere, containing allusions to Isa. 53 which presuppose the Hebrew text and not the LXX.[4] Thus also according to Lohse the Marcan version is the earlier one.

But however incontestable the Palestinian origin of Mark 10.45b may be, this does not elucidate the nature of the saying as a whole. Could 10.45b not be a Palestinian gloss on the Son of Man's serving? Has the combination—the *unique* combination—of the name Son of Man with the pronouncement about giving his life as a ransom for many already been proved to be original? According to Lohse, Isa. 53 is referred to in a parallel way both in Mark 10.45b and in 14.24. 'The original meaning of the saying in Mark 14.24 is that Jesus' death is interpreted to be the death of atonement of the Servant of Jehovah who gives his life for many.'[5] This exegesis presupposes that 'the version in Mark is to be considered as the earliest form of the cup-word'.[6] Should this presupposition not hold good, Mark 14.24 will have to be understood in a different manner. We cannot, infact, share Lohse's view. 'In what is probably the oldest version of the cup-word, I Cor. 11.25, there is no reminiscence of

[1] Lohse, *Märtyrer*, p. 117.
[2] *Ibid.*, p. 118.
[3] *Ibid.*, p. 118.
[4] *Ibid.*, p. 119.
[5] *Ibid.*, p. 126. Jeremias arrives at the conclusion that 'we cannot even exclude the possibility that the λύτρον-saying is a secondary reflection on Mark 10.45a. (The association of the concepts present in the λύτρον-saying with those in the eucharistic sayings however apparently does not encourage this assumption.)' ('Lösegeld', p. 262).
[6] Lohse, *Märtyrer*, p. 123.

Isa. 53.'[1] The assumption thus stated by Kümmel that the Pauline version of the cup-word is based on the earliest tradition available to us is supported also by Dibelius and recently by Marxsen as well as E. Schweizer with substantial arguments.[2] G. Bornkamm, too, adduces the following arguments to support the assumption that the Pauline text in spite of some Hellenistic re-formulations is based on the earlier tradition. In the text in Paul the phrase 'after the meal' has been preserved, which shows that this version still presupposes the separation of the bread-word and the cup-word by the whole meal, whilst in the text in Mark this separation has been abandoned.[3] Notwithstanding the re-formulations according to Hellenistic usage—traces of which are not completely missing in the text in Mark either—the text in Paul appears to express the earliest type of tradition which conveyed the meaning, 'In analogy with the manner in which the Mosaic covenant was instituted (Ex. 24.8), God's "new covenant" with his people prophesied in Jeremiah (31.31) has been instituted by Jesus' offering his blood.'[4] In the text in Mark the reference to Jer. 31 has dropped out; what is retained is the reference to Ex. 24.8 where the subject is the blood of the covenant at the institution of the Sinai covenant.

The question now arises whether by the phrase 'poured out for many' Mark 14.24 refers to Isaiah. If so, the concept of the blood of the covenant would have been interpreted by means of Isa. 53 and with regard to its power of bestowal: for many, for all. Lohse supposes the phrase about pouring out the blood to be a free reference to Isa. 53.12, 'Because he poured out his soul to death.'[5] But it is still possible that it might be a reference to something else, namely, that the expression 'to pour out' was suggested by the terminology used for the sphere of concepts connected with sacrifice.[6] Nor is the possibility excluded by the observation that the phrase 'my blood of the covenant' (Mark 14.24) is fixed to the Greek language and cannot

[1] Kümmel, *Promise*, pp. 73f. n. 181. Kuhn holds a different view in *EvTh*, 1950/51, pp. 508–27.
[2] Cf. *EvTh*, 1952/53, pp. 296ff., and *ThLZ*, 1954, pp. 579ff.
[3] Bornkamm, *ZThK*, 1956, pp. 327f.
[4] Lietzmann's *An die Korinther I/II*, 4th edition supplemented by Kümmel, p. 57.
[5] According to the Hebrew text. Lohse, *Märtyrer*, p. 124 and n. 3.
[6] Cf. Lohse, *Märtyrer*, p. 125 n. 1. Arguments that this expression is not dependent on a certain text but original may also be found in Jeremias, *Eucharistic Words*, pp. 118 and 122f. On pp. 122f. Jeremias advances as an argument the conformity with linguistic characteristics of the *ipsissima vox* of Jesus; we are unable to endorse this procedure.

be translated back into Aramaic; for the reference to the institution of the covenant appears already in the Pauline version and is therefore not dependent on this phrase in the text in Mark.

Also the phrase 'for many' is far from proving with certainty that there is a reference to Isa. 53, this phrase being a current Semitism, as Jeremias has demonstrated. But the clearer reference to Isa. 53 in Mark 10.45b permits the conjecture that Mark 14.24b refers to this text as well.[1]

Even if the reference to Isa. 53 is probable and the Palestinian usage of the language in Mark 10.45b is certain, Bousset's supposition that Mark 10.45b is a gloss on the preceding phrase about the Son of Man's serving still is not refuted.[2] Lohse points out that the name Son of Man and the '*καί* = }' in the epexegetical sense'[3] help to establish the Palestinian origin of the saying. This does not take us any further, since it is of no consequence for the original relationship between the first part of the verse (together with the title Son of Man) and the second part; for a gloss referring to Isa. 53 (in the Hebrew text) on the first part of the verse may have already been added in the Palestinian language area as well. Moreover, Lohse establishes by his own arguments that the connexion of the title Son of Man with the saying about the ransom cannot be considered as a genuine connexion. 'In Mark 14.24 the title Son of Man is absent. Hence it is established beyond doubt that we must understand the λύτρον-saying as having a messianic meaning even without the designation of Jesus as the Son of Man.'[4]

We must examine still more thoroughly the relationship of the first part of Mark 10.45 with the second. As already stated, we see in Mark 10.45b and 14.24b a parallel way of referring to Isa. 53, the reference presupposing in both cases not the LXX but the Hebrew text.[5] Granting I Cor. 11.24f. to have been based on an earlier tradition which did not refer to Isa. 53, the appending to the cup-word of

---

[1] Cf. Jeremias, *Eucharistic Words*, pp. 123f. The parallel way of speaking in 10.45b and 14.24b which we consider to be the decisive argument for the latter passage's referring to Isa. 53 has been investigated and recognized several times; cf. H. W. Wolff, *Isa. 53 im Urchristentum*, 1950, pp. 58ff.; also Käsemann's critical review in *Verkündigung und Forschung*, 1952, p. 202. Käsemann underlines Wolff's assertion that there is a reference to Isa. 53 in Mark 14.24. A different view in Bultmann, *Tradition*, p. 93 *et passim*.

[2] Bousset, *Kyrios*, p. 8 n. 1.

[3] Lohse, *Märtyrer*, p. 118.

[4] Lohse, *Märtyrer*, p. 121.

[5] Cf. Lohse, *Märtyrer*, p. 119 n. 2; p. 124 n. 3.

an interpretative phrase that does refer to Isa. 53 must have happened rather early. In this phrase the bestowal on many is expounded. In a comparable way we are told in Mark 10.45 what the Son of Man's serving means for the many. This parallel way of speaking suggests that in both cases we have to do with a similar procedure which is located in a certain situation within the history of tradition; that is, as soon as the community had discovered in Isa. 53, the text which delineates suffering more sharply than any other text in the Old Testament, its association to Jesus' suffering, they used this text as scriptural evidence when interpreting the Last Supper and the Son of Man's mission as a whole. Thus they epitomized this mission (Mark 10.45) in the words which were also used to expound the meaning of the Last Supper, i.e. in that interpretative phrase from Isa. 53.

But can we in fact demonstrate that in Mark 10.45, as similarly in 14.24, an earlier saying already formed was supplemented by another phrase? The following observations corroborate our assumption.

1. In none of the synoptic Son of Man sayings is the implication of dying for our salvation expressed. We read of the necessity of the death according to the Scripture, nothing more. Thus a new concept is introduced when we read that serving means giving his life for many. This concept is not connected with the name Son of Man anywhere except in Mark 10.45. Now, it is highly improbable that a connexion as distinct and meaningful as this, if it had issued from Jesus himself or from a very early stage of using the name Son of Man, would have left no impression on the rest of the Son of Man sayings.

2. The concept of serving is evident in itself without reference to Isa. 53. Luke 22.27 proves this. The concept of ransom and even that of giving his life introduce divergent and supplementary elements into the Son of Man sayings.

3. Moreover the concept of serving is to be understood in precise connexion with the train of thought in the preceding text and therefore stands in a certain tension with 10.45b. The train of thought can be outlined as follows. Mark 10.42: the rulers of the Gentiles lord it over them (by force) (= Luke 22.25); Mark 10.43f.: this shall not be the practice amongst the disciples; the greatest among them shall be (= Luke 22.26) the servant; Mark 10.45: for even the Son of Man is come to serve . . . ; = Luke 22.27: I (Jesus) am amongst

you as he who serves. In both cases, in Mark as well as in Luke, at first customary practice in the world is mentioned, and then comes the summons for the disciples to reverse this practice in their conduct. The summons is stated as a rule for the disciples to follow, the reason for this rule being given by pointing to Jesus', or the Son of Man's, mode of behaviour. The disciples' behaviour is to correspond to that of Jesus, or the Son of Man. They are not merely summoned to follow an example. The behaviour of Jesus, or the Son of Man, rather provides the possibility of thus reversing the customary practice. Throughout the train of thought outlined there appears a strict correspondence between the behaviour of the disciples and that of the Son of Man. But this correspondence disappears when the sentence 10.45b is included in the interpretation. The disciples cannot be summoned to give their lives as a ransom for many, or all. In the view of the New Testament this giving of the life has happened once for all, a repetition being neither needed nor appropriate. Clearly Mark 10.45b is not consistent with the theme of correspondence.

This gives great significance to Lohse's affirmation that a separate history of tradition lies behind Mark 10.42-45 and Luke 22.24-27 respectively.[1] For in both forms of the tradition strict correspondence prevails. Both texts proceed step by step in so similar a manner that we cannot doubt their being dependent on the same material. And this material obviously contained the theme of strict correspondence which is common to both texts and which cannot include in its meaning the statement in Mark 10.45b. Thus we have here, in fact, an extension which, intended to expound the Son of Man's serving, no longer conforms to the original structure of the rule of humility for the disciples, but now develops on its own account what that serving of the Son of Man which happened once for all means, namely, giving his life as a ransom for many. Thus this extension is a Christological-soteriological interpretation. It relies on Isa. 53 as Mark 14.24 also does for the interpretation of the cup-word.

We have so far avoided considering the use of the name Son of Man. Did it originally pertain to the material transmitted or was it perhaps inserted together with the interpretative phrase from Isa. 53?

We have to take into account that from our point of view we did not see any evidence proving that there is any authentic saying of Jesus which speaks of the Son of Man's activity on earth. But the post-Easter community does, in fact, speak of Jesus' acting with full

[1] Lohse, *Märtyrer*, p. 118.

authority as of the activity of the Son of Man. Only in these elements of the synoptic tradition which cannot be traced back to Jesus himself does the tendency appear which places Jesus' earthly activity under the meaningful heading of the designation Son of Man. An inclination to strike out the name Son of Man in this connexion cannot, however, be proved in any passage of the synoptic tradition, which is intelligible enough. Consequently, considering the absence of the designation Son of Man in Luke 22.24ff., it appears to be probable that the material to which the separate lines of tradition behind Mark 10.42ff. and Luke 22.24ff. both lead back did not contain the name Son of Man.

On the other hand it is unlikely that the name Son of Man was introduced at such a late stage in the tradition as that at which the interpretative phrase from Isa. 53 was appended, no longer taking into consideration the theme of correspondence. For it is evident from Matt. 8.20 = Luke 9.57 (Q) that the name Son of Man is indeed appropriate within that pattern of correspondence; the disciples' following is here described in its correspondence to the Son of Man's existence on earth. Thus going their way, the disciples still follow the one who has full authority; in this correspondence the Son of Man's precedence is none the less preserved.

There remain two questions. (1) What is the meaning of the saying concerning the Son of Man's serving, apart from its being connected with the statement on giving his life? (2) What motives incited the appending of the phrase dependent on Deutero-Isaiah about the ransom for many?

1. We have already analysed above the meaning of Mark 10.45a detached from the second part of the verse and have understood it as follows. The saying belongs to that group in which the designation Son of Man is introduced in order to emphasize that Jesus acted on earth with full authority. Whilst in Luke 22.27 it is simply said, 'I am amongst you as he who serves', the designation Son of Man reveals the specific distinction of this 'I'. It is the 'I' to whom full authority has been given (Mark 2.10; 2.28). The paradox of the reversal that he who has full authority serves and does not rule by force—as he well might do—is the reason why the disciples are to act with humility.

Now, we must clearly recognize that in this saying on serving more is expressed than in the other sayings about the Son of Man's activity on earth. These speak of the Son of Man's possessing authority;

they characterize him as the one who is free to associate with tax collectors and sinners. And this association lays all the more stress on his authority, which is not lessened by the opposition which arises against his acting in sovereignty (Matt. 11.19 = Luke 7.34). One saying, namely Matt. 8.20 and par., does go farther. The Son of Man here becomes the living admonition to his followers. The thoroughness of the summons to follow is revealed in and based on his being without a home himself. This statement is primarily oriented on the opposition which the Son of Man's claim meets; this generation does not take him in, does not grant him a home. He is denied what is given to animals. This is a humiliation, a rejection, which is inflicted upon the Son of Man *from without*; it is not conceived as primarily inherent within himself but as coming into existence by way of the tension between this sinful generation and himself. The disciple as well, meeting treatment fully corresponding to that meted out to the Son of Man, is not exempt from the hostility but fully exposed to it. In Mark 10.45, however, for the first and only time within the group of sayings concerning the activity on earth, to become lowly, or to serve, is seen as the Son of Man's *mission*, as a mode of action which—highly paradoxically—is inherent in his sovereignty itself. The lords of this world possess the power to impose claims; and the disciples deduce claims from their attachment to Jesus (Mark 10.35ff.)—not mistakenly; for they have received a promise (Matt. 19.28). Is there anyone better authorized to lay claims than the Son of Man? But he is not come to enforce these claims but to serve.

The significance of his serving stands out in all clarity only against the background of his authority. Hence it is appropriate when Mark 10.45, going beyond Luke 22.27, designates the 'I' of the one who serves by the name Son of Man. In this sovereign 'I', however, is inherent the will to humble himself. Nowhere else in the sayings concerning the Son of Man in his present activity is it said that his own will seeks the humility of serving. It is the distinction of the saying in Mark 10.45 that offers the possibility of appending a Christological-soteriological interpretation as given in that phrase from Isa. 53.

2. Why is it just Isa. 53 that can be brought into play for that extending Christological interpretation? The bridge by means of which the association is achieved is provided by the word 'to serve'. It is noteworthy that Luke, in contrast to the arrangement in Mark incorporates the saying on serving into the conversation at table

during the Last Supper. This was certainly not done by chance.[1] We must realize that in the New Testament 'διακονέω primarily and originally means "to wait at table" '.[2] Thus the situation at table is already associated with this word. We find support for this also in the Gospel of John, where 'the saying of the Lord in Luke 22.27 or a variant of it'[3] underlies the narrative of the foot-washing which forms part of the account of Jesus' last meal with his disciples (John 13.1–30). The situation at table is expressly referred to in Luke 22.27: 'For who is the greater, one who sits at table, or one who serves? Is it not the one who sits at table? But I am among you as the one who serves.' A few verses later a table-fellowship is spoken of again, namely in Luke 22.30a, where Jesus bequeathes to his disciples that they 'may eat and drink at my table in my kingdom'. A reference to the situation at Jesus' last meal with his disciples is also implied in the saying, 'Truly, I say to you, I shall not drink again of the fruit of the vine until that day when I drink it new in the kingdom of God' (Mark 14.25).

It is therefore not surprising when the occurrence of the term διακονέω in Mark 10.45 calls to memory Jesus' meal with the disciples. And where the mission of the Son of Man is summed up in the one term 'to serve', this suggests the association with that meal in which Jesus communicated to his own the entirely unique service, namely the giving of the blood of the covenant for many. Hence the same interpretative phrase which occurs in Mark 14.24 is appended in 10.45. In the former it is said that he gives his blood for many, in the latter that the Son of Man is come to give his life as a ransom for many.

The result of the analysis of Mark 10.45. The saying about the Son of Man serving, which in its form and content is closely connected with the preceding verses, appears to have been extended already in the Palestinian language area by an interpretative phrase containing a reference to Isa. 53. The formation of this phrase probably took place when the bestowal of the gift of the Lord's Supper on many was first interpreted by means of the Scripture (Mark 14.24). The bestowal of the given life on many, once recognized with regard to the Lord's Supper, could then also be understood, owing to the central significance of the Lord's Supper in the life of the community, as comprising the specific meaning of Jesus' mission, of his serving.

---

[1] Dibelius, *Tradition*, pp. 200f., cf. Kuhn in *ThLZ*, 1950, col. 399ff.
[2] Beyer in *TWNT* II, p. 83 lines 34f.
[3] Bultmann, *Johannes*, p. 352 n. 2.

In the material to which the separate traditions lying behind the texts in Mark and in Luke may be traced back the name Son of Man was probably absent. This might be expected especially if this material was indeed based on a saying which had issued from Jesus. This saying could have been formed in a manner rather like Luke 22.27.[1] The name Son of Man was probably introduced very early; for it is fitted into that pattern of correspondence by which the context is distingushed, whilst the interpretative phrase in 10.45b does not conform to it.[2]

Hence we may conclude that the saying in Mark 10.45a is not to be grouped with those concerning the Son of Man's suffering and dying, but belongs to the group of sayings concerning his activity in the present. Jesus' giving his life for many, expressed in that interpretative phrase, was only secondarily associated with it. Unlike the announcements of suffering and rising this Son of Man saying was not connected with the passion kerygma in the stricter sense, but with the tradition about the Lord's Supper to which Mark 10.45 refers. This connexion appears to have been brought about already in the sphere of the Palestinian community.

(e) **Matthew 12.40.** 'Although it has been asserted again and again that the form of this saying in Matthew is the original one, it can hardly be doubted that Matt. 12.40 offers an artificial parallel between Jonah and Jesus foreign to Jesus' original saying.'[3] Kümmel would like to ascertain that the form of the saying in Luke 11.29 = Matt. 12.39, as compared with Mark 8.12, was the earliest since the enigmatic addition 'except the sign of the prophet Jonah' was hardly inserted subsequently.[4] There must therefore have occurred in Q a saying in which Jesus rejected the demand for a sign, and said that only the sign of Jonah would be given. This must have been followed, then, by a saying stating some kind of analogy between the Son of Man and Jonah (cf. Luke 11.30; Matt. 12.40). In view of the divergences between the formulations in Matthew and in Luke it cannot be established with certainty which analogy was intended. Probably the form in Luke 11.30 was the original one. In that case, however, exegetes are faced with an enigmatic saying the interpretation of which is a rather difficult task.

[1] Cf. Bultmann, *Johannes*, p. 352 n. 2.
[2] Cf. pp. 206f. above.
[3] Kümmel, *Promise*, p. 68.
[4] *Loc. cit.*

Now, the figure of Jonah appears to have been spoken of in different sayings in Q. In the text in Luke the threatening prediction that the men of Niniveh will arise at the judgement with this generation does not immediately follow after the saying about the sign of Jonah; instead the queen of the south is mentioned next. Thus we must consider that prediction in Luke 11.32 to have originally stood by itself.[1] This is all the more probable since it concludes with the assertion, 'and behold, something greater than Jonah is here', an assertion which sets Jesus aside from the mere analogy with Jonah, emphasizing his superiority. Hence we may assume that the comparison of Jesus with Jonah, or of Jesus' teaching with Jonah's message, was something current in the Q stratum of the tradition. It effectually served to accuse this generation, being closely linked up with the comparisons which by example of the behaviour of the generation at the times of Noah and Lot warn this generation of what may happen to them at the day of the Son of Man.

In Jeremias' view the original meaning of the *logion* on which Luke 11.30; Matt. 12.40 are based was that 'the one sent by God is legitimized by his being rescued from death'.[2] If so, this would be the only case of a saying from Q speaking in anticipation of the Son of Man's rising. Since we have seen that the announcements of the suffering and rising of the Son of Man first occur in Mark, and that the elements constituting these sayings are dependent not on Q but on the passion kerygma and the scriptural evidence adduced in connexion with it, we cannot assent to this supposition of Jeremias. We cannot assent either when considering the content of this saying. This generation is spoken of as being an evil generation because it will not listen to the teaching but demands signs instead. We cannot assume that in the opinion of the community which was aware of the reaction to the message of the resurrection this evil generation would accept the rescue from death of the one sent by God as the sign of Jonah prevailing on them to turn round in repentance; and we do not find a saying of Jesus announcing a positive reaction of this generation to his resurrection.

Matthew interpreted this *logion* in a specific way which does not concur with its original meaning. Certainly the text in Luke keeps nearer to the original meaning. In which way does Matthew use the name Son of Man in his interpretation of the *logion*?

[1] Klostermann, *Matt.*, p. 112.
[2] Jeremias in *TWNT* III, p. 413 lines 9f.

A comparison between Jonah and the Son of Man may easily have suggested paying attention not only to the teaching of both but also and even foremost to those three days which Jonah spent in the belly of a whale. This may have occurred all the more readily after the name Son of Man was connected with a phrase about rising after three days, or on the third day, in stereotyped announcements of suffering as firmly as the connexion between the three days and the name of Jonah was established in Scripture.

Hence Matthew takes the sojourn lasting three days and three nights to be the *tertium comparationis* between the sign of Jonah and the sign for this generation. Consequently he regards the sojourn in the belly of the whale as comparable with the sojourn in the world of the dead which is imagined to be located as Hades in the interior of the earth. According to that image of the world which the Bible shares with the ancient Near East, the world of the dead is inside the hollow earth and can therefore be shut off by gates and keys.[1] What is meant here, then, is the '*descensus ad inferos* in the form common to all mankind'.[2] But attention is chiefly paid not to the *descensus* but to those three days which are also firmly established in the announcements of suffering. If Matthew on the one hand found in the material transmitted to him an enigmatic saying which spoke of the Son of Man in the context of the demand for a sign and compared Jonah with the Son of Man, and if on the other hand he vividly pictured the story of Jonah, we can easily understand that for him the solution of the enigma was provided by those three days. Thus he could regard Jonah as the type foreshadowing the likeness of what had to be conceived concerning the Son of Man, namely that his resurrection after the sojourn in the heart of the earth for three days and three nights constituted the great sign given to this generation as a summons to believe and turn round in repentence.[3] Evidence adduced from the Scriptures and the formulae in the announcements of the Son of Man's suffering and rising join here to form that comparison which seems artificial to us today.[4] R. Otto thinks that Matthew is speaking here as the dogmatist of early Catholicism. We would rather not consider this to be a dogmatic enunciation in that sense but to be an argument supported by the Scriptures and by stereotyped

[1] Jeremias in *TWNT* I, p. 148 lines 24ff.
[2] Klostermann, *Matt.*, p. 111.
[3] Matt. 12.41b.
[4] Cf. Kümmel, *Promise*, p. 68.

elements of the passion announcements. It is argued that the resurrection which limits the sojourn in the world of the dead to those three days is the great sign after which the present generation is left without any excuse.

We have already had to reject when discussing above the phrase 'to rise after three days'[1] Lichtenstein's supposition that the wording 'after three days' denotes the span of time of the Son of Man's sojourn in the lower regions and that this notion is related to the concept of the concealment of the Son of Man as expressed in the book of Enoch. Here again we see that in order to form the saying in Matt. 12.40 there was no need to refer to a mythical description of the Son of Man's concealment. The combination of the scriptural evidence from Jonah with the announcements of suffering is in itself sufficient to explain why this saying should have been formed.

In the announcements of suffering Matthew uses without exception the phrase '*on* the third day'. 'The phrase in Matt. 12.40 ($\tau\rho\epsilon\hat{\iota}\varsigma$ $\dot{\eta}\mu\acute{\epsilon}\rho\alpha\varsigma$ $\kappa\alpha\grave{\iota}$ $\tau\rho\epsilon\hat{\iota}\varsigma$ $\nu\acute{\upsilon}\kappa\tau\alpha\varsigma$) is the only one which is incongruous with the $\tau\hat{\eta}$ $\tau\rho\acute{\iota}\tau\eta$ $\dot{\eta}\mu\acute{\epsilon}\rho\alpha$.'[2] This incongruity, however, appears to have been caused by the text in Jonah 1.17. Matthew obviously wished to support his argument by an exact citation from Scripture. Therefore he had to keep to the transmitted text of the narrative about Jonah. Within a reference to this text the phrase '*on* the third day' would not have made sense.

We cannot say that the designation Son of Man as used in Matt. 12.40 has a special meaning of its own. Matthew deviates from Luke and presumably from Q in not speaking here of the coming but of the rising Son of Man. But he receives the meaning of the designation Son of Man from the announcements of suffering, emphasizing a single one of their elements by relating it to the comparison with Jonah.

IV. The history of the tradition of the synoptic sayings concerning the suffering and rising Son of Man

1. Unlike the other two groups of Son of Man sayings the announcements of suffering do not occur in Q. However, they have been transmitted to Mark already from an earlier, partly Palestinian, stratum of the tradition. The following details helped to support this assumption.

(a) The word 'to be delivered', although frequently occurring in

---

[1] Cf. Chapter IV D II 3, pp. 182f.
[2] Bousset, *Kyrios*, p. 24 n. 2.

the announcements of the Son of Man's suffering (Mark 9.31; 10.33f.; 14.21; 14.41; Matt. 26.2; Luke 24.7), is not once combined with interpretative phrases from Isa. 53. This combination is, however, already present in the pre-Pauline formulae in Rom. 4.25 and 8.32. Mark himself knew the combination of the name Son of Man with an interpretative phrase from Isa. 53, as is evident from the saying in 10.45. There is no soteriological interpretation whatsoever in the sayings concerning the Son of Man's suffering. The only emphasis is on the necessity according to the Scriptures. (On Mark 10.45 see above.)

(b) Several words and phrases in the announcements of suffering are derived from the scriptural evidence which was adduced in the tradition concerning the passion; they are related to kerygmatic formulae or evidence adduced from scriptural prophecies in the Acts (Mark 8.31a; 9.12b; 10.34). It follows from this that a communication between the traditions about the Son of Man and those about the passion had already been established before Mark.

(c) Whilst the word 'to crucify' is used meaningfully and frequently in the synoptic passion narrative, it does not occur in the announcements of suffering. These speak of the Son of Man's being killed.

(d) The announcements of suffering say that the Son of Man is delivered up (by God) (Mark 9.31; 10.33; 14.41), but not that he is raised (by God). They rather speak of the Son of Man's rising, thus emphasizing his sovereign activity. Thereby they deviate from the majority of the synoptic and Pauline statements about the resurrection, expressing a special concept. The same applies to the phrase on the rising after three days which is used throughout.

(e) Mark 9.31; 14.41; 14.21 have roots in the Palestinian language area, contradicting the assumption that announcements of the Son of Man's suffering and rising originated in the Hellenistic community.

2. In the announcements of suffering Jesus speaks of himself as of the Son of Man. The sayings concerning the parousia, however, either differentiate expressly between Jesus and the Son of Man or make Jesus speak of the Son of Man as of someone different from himself. This way of speaking is invariably retained within the synoptic tradition even though those who transmit and formulate within this tradition recognize Jesus to be the coming Son of Man himself. Obviously there are heterogeneous histories of tradition lying behind

the two groups of Son of Man sayings. As we may infer from Q, the tradition of the sayings about the coming Son of Man appears to be marked by the reference to Jesus' own way of speaking. (Only Mark 13.26f. and 14.62 refer to Dan. 7.) The tradition of the sayings about the suffering and rising Son of Man, however, can be traced back to the early kerygma and the scriptural evidence adduced by the community.

This heterogeneity of the histories of tradition forbids us to regard the two groups of sayings as immediately complementing each other. We cannot conceive of the Son of Man who will suffer and rise as of the transcendent Son of Man. We cannot simply identify the sovereignty of the one who is delivered up with the sovereignty of the one who will come. Not a single Son of Man saying transfers to Jesus on earth the heavenly sovereignty of the Son of Man which is not restricted by anything existing in this world. The narrative of the transfiguration in which Jesus appears beyond all earthly restrictions is not headed by the name Son of Man. Therefore exegesis must heed the subtle difference in what has been transmitted to us, and pay strict attention to the stratum in which the respective history of tradition began, when defining what is to be understood by the respective concepts of sovereignty and humility.

3. Notwithstanding the dissimilarity of the two groups we do not consider it permissible to regard them as isolated unrelated entities. The strata in which the respective groups of sayings were handed down were not separated from each other in such a manner that the concepts current in one of them could no longer be understood in their original sense in the other. This is supported by the following considerations.

(a) Throughout the synoptic tradition, right up to Mark, Matthew and Luke, the difference between the sayings concerning the coming and those concerning the suffering Son of Man are precisely realized. If this were not the case, the sayings freshly formed by Matthew and Luke would not conform without fail to the form and structure of the earlier Son of Man sayings. In the revision of the parousia sayings which had been received, misunderstandings of their original conceptions would inevitably have turned up; no productive development would have appeared, but only a blurring of the concept of the Son of Man's parousia. Above all, it would have to be demonstrable that concepts from the two different groups had been fused, resulting in indistinct transitions and combinations of sayings. But even Luke (cf. 17.25) as well as Matthew (cf. 13.37 and 13.41) places the two types of sayings side by side without confusing them. Even while trying to correlate them, they still understand them as each having a meaning of its own.

(b) The designation Son of Man is meant to be the clamp joint which connects and is intended to connect the two groups of sayings. We shall try to elucidate this in greater detail below.

(c) There are certain common elements which pervade all three groups of Son of Man sayings. Here it is sufficient to recall the tension over against men which appears in each of the three groups.

4. Thus those who shaped the tradition of the groups of sayings were aware of and have retained their dissimilarity on the one hand and their correlation on the other. We have to consider now, in view of the differing histories of their tradition and of the differing concepts present in them, the positive means by which the sayings concerning the coming and the suffering Son of Man are connected.

We want to employ the sayings about the Son of Man's activity in the present as a bridge to understanding. They occupy a midway position, both as regards the history of tradition and as regards concepts. They do not refer to authentic sayings of Jesus, but on the other hand they already occur in Q. As we saw above, these sayings, so to speak, anticipated in their first half the name Son of Man which had been used in the second half of the parousia sayings. While in the parousia sayings the promise is given that the fellowship bestowed by Jesus will be recognized by the Son of Man, in the sayings concerning his present activity the name Son of Man is already attributed to him who bestows this fellowship on earth. In these sayings the name Son of Man is anticipated in order to emphasize what this *exousia* on earth means. By this means they obviously refer to the correlation promised in the parousia sayings between Jesus' full authority and its future confirmation by the Son of Man, stating this correlation as a fact by relinquishing the differentiation between Jesus and the Son of Man. This step, however, as we shall see below, presupposes a certain Christological understanding.

In the sayings concerning the Son of Man's activity on earth an inclusion of concepts of humility is already foreshadowed. Jesus' acting with full authority, although designated by the name Son of Man, yet is conceived as an activity which bears the restrictions of an existence on earth and the opposition of men. The fact that this unbelieving generation is endured means that one who wants to follow must also be prepared to be homeless, just as the Son of Man himself has no home amongst men. Mark 10.45a goes beyond this in saying that the Son of Man is come to serve and not in order to lay claims. The saying thus provides a bridge between the concepts in the statements about the activity on earth with full authority and those about the Son of Man's being delivered. In the latter the paradox goes even farther in saying that he who has full authority will be delivered into the hands of sinners. This understanding is expressed in Mark 9.31; 14.21 and 14.41 *et passim*. The sovereignty of Jesus' foreknowledge and of his going is emphasized by means of the designation Son of Man. Thus the message of the passion is linked up with the concept of the Son of Man.

Hence we see that the bridge connecting all three groups of Son of Man sayings is Jesus' full authority. Sayings concerning the coming Son of Man promise that he will confirm the fellowship of following and confessing which Jesus on earth bestows with full authority. Sayings concerning the Son of Man in his present activity assert that Jesus' action on earth with full authority (forgiving sins, being Lord over the sabbath, having table-fellowship with tax collectors and sinners) is an activity of the Son of Man. Sayings concerning Jesus' being delivered express that he takes the passion upon himself in full authority as the Son of Man; the rising confirms and makes the community recognize the objective reality of this authority.

We mentioned above that the tension over against men pervades and connects all three groups of Son of Man sayings. Now we can state that this tension is but the reverse side of Jesus' unique claim to authority. Just as Jesus' *exousia* is a constituting element in all three groups, so the tension over against men pervades them all as well. Jesus' full authority stands in sharp contrast to this generation's shutting themselves up against God, and this authority makes his followers stand in this tension, too.

5. When examining the sayings concerning the Son of Man's being delivered up we saw that apparently the community did not connect the Son of Man tradition with the passion kerygma either from the beginning or throughout all the groups of the community.

In the early material of the passion narrative the name Son of Man does not occur. Jesus' death is the redemptive deed which stands at the centre of the passion kerygma. His death is proclaimed as the gift of his life for many. In this way what Jesus' execution means for the authority of his eschatological teaching, of his pointing to the coming of God's reign, is not directly expressed. What can be expressed, however, is that Jesus' death means the fulfilment of Scripture.

The early narratives of the passion on the one hand do not use the name Son of Man; Q on the other hand does not refer to the passion kerygma at all. In many passages from Q what Jesus means is elucidated by means of the designation Son of Man, but there is no Q saying alluding to the Son of Man's suffering, dying and rising.

The bridge between the two spheres of concepts was already established in the Palestinian community. In Mark 9.31; 14.21; 14.41, as well as in the combination of Mark 10.45a with 10.45b, the concept of passion is connected with the name Son of Man. Had there been, before this bridge was thrown, two independent spheres in which what Jesus means was expressed in two different ways? This is the problem set before us by the result of our enquiry into the history of the tradition of the sayings concerning the Son of Man's suffering.

The two spheres of concepts were already linked up with each other when they were transmitted to Mark. He received announcements of suffering and related them not only to the passion narrative but also to material which we assign to Q, seeing it connected distinctly with the Son of Man's parousia. The latter relation is proved by the context of the Marcan announcements of suffering. Each of the three announcements is succeeded by sayings about the disciples following. It is characteristic of this relation that the train of thought leads from the Son of Man saying in Mark 8.31 to the parousia saying in 8.38, and connects the announcement of suffering with the saying pointing to the parousia by means of the sayings about following which serve as a bridge.[1] Thus Mark, too, endeavours to incorporate into his Gospel, which is entirely centred on the passion, sayings about the disciples' activity such as we find in Q.

V. Sovereignty and humility according to the announcements of the Son of Man's suffering and rising

The sovereignty of the Son of Man who will come in the parousia is completely untrammelled by this world. The statements about it have the structure of that antithesis which in the Judaism of that period was determined by the doctrine of the two aeons; this concept remained effectual in some respects for Christian thinking, too. The

[1] Chapter IV A 1, pp. 146f.

coming of the new aeon will mean the end of the old one; the two aeons cannot exist side by side or the one within the other. And when the Son of Man comes in power and glory, he will bring the old aeon to an end.

The sharp antithesis between the two aeons is the reason for the present aeon's being void of salvation. Since the new aeon can only exist as an exclusive totality, the present aeon cannot possibly participate in its gifts and powers. Because the old aeon exists, it is impossible for the bringer of salvation to appear in unrestricted glory. When he does come the restrictions of existence on earth must needs disappear.

This concept of the antithesis between the aeons and the heavenly transcendent nature of the Son of Man was not relinquished in the synoptic tradition, but was retained right up to the latest editorially formed Son of Man sayings. Yet it should not be deduced from this that the designation Son of Man would attribute to Jesus' acting and suffering on earth the sovereignty of the (Danielic, transcendent) Son of Man. The sovereignty of the Son of Man who is delivered up cannot be understood as transcendental qualities paradoxically co-existing with Jesus' activity within the restrictions of what exists on earth. The heavenly figure of the Son of Man (with his rights, attributes and functions) is not said to dwell in an historical figure in mysterious concealment. Therefore Phil. 2.6–11 cannot here lead the way for the interpretation; for here is no conception of a pre-existent Son of Man who takes upon himself obediently the utter renunciation of living as a servant even to the death upon the cross and who is exalted by God to be Lord because of this self-renunciation. Nor can the concept of a post-existent Son of Man be found here, of one who is designated to be a supra-mundane figure and thus, already filled with transcendent power, seeks utter concealment in a guise of humility. None of these concepts of obedience and self-renunciation, of disguise and concealment, are alluded to in the sayings concerning the suffering Son of Man. The authority of the Son of Man who is delivered up is of a different kind. It is the unique authority of Jesus, an authority which cannot be defined by means of traditional titles and attributes. The sayings concerning the suffering Son of Man pay special attention to the paradox that God delivers to men the one to whom he has given all authority. The one who in sovereignty bestows the fellowship of salvation which is valid before God is handed over into the hands of God's rebellious enemies.

How is Jesus seen when in his suffering he is designated as Son of

Man? He is not seen as the one who is utterly devoid of power, who surpasses all men in the thoroughness of his annihilation; instead he is always seen as the one who is marvellously aware of his course beforehand. He is not thrust into disaster unawares, but, still retaining his *exousia*, he goes and finishes his course under the power of darkness. The concept of the Son of Man's sovereignty as he goes is joined by the reference to the necessity according to the Scriptures (Mark 14.21; 8.31). Hence, when reference is made to the Son of Man's being delivered up, Jesus does not appear as one who might now be authenticated only from outside; his full authority remains with him precisely in the fact that he goes his way. The one in whom the sovereignty is inherent accepts his rejection by and deliverance to men. The Son of Man must go this way and rise after three days. In his rising his *exousia* comes to light unequivocally. His authority on earth is confirmed by his resurrection power.

V

THE MUTUAL RELATIONSHIP OF THE
THREE GROUPS OF SAYINGS CONCERNING
THE SON OF MAN

IN CHAPTERS II, III AND IV we have examined the history of the tradition and the special nature of each of the three groups of sayings. The differences between the groups are so great that it is rather difficult to elucidate their resemblance. We can only succeed in doing so by considering their respective positions within the history of the synoptic tradition. From these both the differences and the mutual relationship of the three groups will become distinguishable.

We will begin with the summary postponed above of the results of our enquiry into the sayings concerning the coming Son of Man in Chapter II.

A. THE SECONDARY CHANNELLING OF TRADITIONAL APOCALYPTIC ELEMENTS INTO THE SYNOPTIC SAYINGS CONCERNING THE SON OF MAN

Before the concept of the Son of Man appeared within the synoptic tradition, it had already existed in Jewish apocalyptic thinking. Literary evidence for this can be found in Dan. 7.13f.; IV Ezra 13 and I Enoch. There can be no doubt that there was a relationship between the apocalyptic concept of the Son of Man and the synoptic sayings. Our main task is to define this relationship more exactly. So we ask: Through which inlets were elements of the Jewish apocalyptic concept of the Son of Man channelled into the synoptic tradition?

(1) Mark

We may include amongst the definitely established facts that Mark 13.26f. and 14.62 refer—probably by way of a literary medium

—to Dan. 7.13f. The unmistakable motif of the coming with the clouds suffices to prove this. Each of the two references to Dan. 7.13f. occurs within a context which contains other references to scriptural passages as well, and the general nature of the context does not encourage us to regard it as belonging to material which probably issued from sayings of Jesus, from situations of his historical activity. Moreover, the tendency to apocalyptic description in the text in Mark 13.24–27 is inconsistent with the concepts present in Jesus' teaching; and the predominant understanding in the community of Jesus' proclamation of sovereignty before the Sanhedrin is clearly evident in 14.61ff. Thus in Mark 13.26f. and 14.62 it was the community's interest in earlier apocalyptic prophecy which induced the taking over of traditional elements of the Son of Man concept. The reason for the community's linking up with this particular concept was probably their recollection of Jesus' teaching in which the Son of Man was spoken of, although without any reference to Dan. 7. An illustration of this linking up is furnished by Mark 8.38 in which a Son of Man saying from Jesus' teaching has been secondarily extended by reference to scriptural passages in the manner of the scribes (cf. Chapter II A I c, pp. 40ff.).

Consequently we do not see in the Son of Man sayings in Mark a primary channelling of the Son of Man concept into the synoptic tradition. Ready-formed sayings using this name have been extended and supplemented here by bringing scriptural passages and traditional apocalyptic literature into play.

(2) *Matthew*

A similar procedure of secondary channelling can be observed in Matthew. Whilst the authentic sayings of Jesus keep strictly away from apcalyptic description, Matthew introduces a great number of traditional motifs; with regard to this, we may speak of a renaissance of apocalyptic elements within the synoptic Son of Man sayings (Matt. 13.41; 25.31; 24.30f.; 16.27; 19.28). Mark refers chiefly to the one biblical passage Dan. 7.13; Matthew, on his part, refers to broader streams of tradition. Some sayings formed by him are closely related to statements from the book of Enoch; Matt. 25.31 may be compared with I Enoch 61.8; 62.2; 69.27, and Matt. 19.28 with I Enoch 108.12; 96.1f.; 50.22ff., and Matt. 16.27 with I Enoch 45.3.

Such reference to apocalyptic material, which we do not find in

Luke, is obviously both in Mark and in Matthew a procedure in the manner of the scribe's erudition, an adducing of scriptural evidence from apocalyptic-eschatological scriptures, as Dodd calls them.[1]

Material from the apocalyptic concept of the Son of Man was not admitted into that stratum of the history of the synoptic tradition within which we find the Son of Man sayings in their earliest form, namely within Q. This leads us to distinguish between a primary and a secondary channelling of the Son of Man concept into the synoptic tradition. What was the nature of the primary channelling?

B. THE PRIMARY CHANNELLING OF THE SON OF MAN CONCEPT INTO THE SYNOPTIC TRADITION

Because Jesus gave the concept of the Son of Man a conspicuous place in his teaching, this concept was introduced into that material which is present in the early tradition evidenced by Q.

I. Basic elements of the primary Son of Man concept

We want to rely here on the foundation of those Son of Man sayings which we are allowed by cautious critical investigation to consider as authentic sayings of Jesus, namely the comparisons in Matt. 24.27 and par.; Matt. 24.37 and 39 and par.; Luke 17.30; the threatening saying in Luke 11.30; the admonition in Matt. 24.44 and par.; and the promises in Luke 12.8f. and par. (Mark 8.38 and par.).

1. In those parts of the above-mentioned sayings which speak of the Son of Man's coming or acting, there is no reference whatsoever to Scripture. Jesus does not look for a legitimation of his pointing to the imminent coming of the Son of Man. This accords with the sovereign certainty with which he preaches that God's reign stands at the door. There is legitimation enough in Jesus' words. Whoever believes in these words prepares for the imminence of God's reign, for the Son of Man's coming.

2. There is no apocalyptic description whatsoever of the figure or the activity of the Son of Man. He is spoken of as someone who is well known. All attention is directed to what the Son of Man's appearing will mean for men. Accordingly men are summoned to turn round in repentance and realize that the kingdom of heaven is at hand.

3. The Son of Man sayings as uttered by Jesus are both threat

[1] Dodd, *According to the Scriptures*, pp. 62ff.

and promise indissolubly linked. This may be seen most clearly in the saying on confession as it is formed in Luke 12.8f. The same structure may be seen in Jesus' teaching which summons to judgement and salvation.

4. Faced by the Son of Man's coming, all men regardless of their particular differences gather themselves into two groups. On the one side there is this generation (Luke 11.30), which is like the generation in the days of Noah and Lot; they are taken unawares by the inrush of the day of the Son of Man as by a catastrophe. The real nature of this generation comes to light at their confrontation with those who confess Jesus. To side with Jesus means to confront men, to stand in front of this adulterous and sinful generation and confess, like giving testimony in a court of law. What men demand of the disciples is obvious; they want them to deny (Luke 12.9). Assuming a solidarity, men lay a claim to the disciple which challenges what binds him to Jesus. This generation's solidarity in opposing God urges the disciples to be ashamed of Jesus and of his words (Mark 8.38). But like the generation at Noah's time which was suddenly swept away by the unexpected catastrophe of the flood, so this generation will also be found on the day of the Son of Man.

On the other side there are those who confess Jesus (not, be it noted, the Son of Man). To confess means: to bear witness to the fellowship into which one has been summoned by Jesus; to declare oneself as attached to Jesus by a legally and decisively valid bond never to be broken; to take it upon oneself to follow. To those who confess the promise is held out that the fellowship into which they entered on earth will be declared eternally valid before God. Then the Son of Man will be the guarantor (Luke 12.8; Mark 8.38). This promise accords with the reward in heaven promised by Jesus to his own. 'What is promised to the disciples as their reward (Matt. 19.27ff.) is that *God will side with them.*'[1] The Son of Man is the guarantor for God's bestowing his joy on those who confess Jesus (cf. Luke 6.23 and par.).

5. In the earliest material within the synoptic tradition no authentic saying of Jesus can be detected which would state, *I am* the Messiah, or the Son of Man, or the Son of God, etc. Jesus in his teaching *pointed away from himself*.

The sayings concerning the Son of Man's parousia accord with

---

[1] Bornkamm, *Lohn*, p. 12.

this. It is not stated anywhere in these sayings that Jesus himself would be the Son of Man. It even contradicts the structure of these sayings to interpret them in a directly Christological way. What is stated here is constructed as a soteriological correlation, not at all as a Christological continuity. Accordingly Jesus' teaching promises to those who acknowledge the new righteousness and respond to it by behaving as his followers that they will be heirs in the Kingdom of God.

To sum up: The concept of the Son of Man has been employed in authentic sayings without any particular reference to Scripture or tradition. Serving to communicate Jesus' message, this concept was conceived anew. Thus the concept of the Son of Man was primarily channelled into the material of the synoptic tradition by way of Jesus' own teaching.

II. The transition from the soteriological use of the name Son of Man in Jesus' teaching to the Christological understanding in the primitive community

The traditional concept of the Son of Man had been transformed by the use of this name in Jesus' teaching. This transformation was continued within the synoptic tradition. Sayings were formed which although linking up with Jesus' Son of Man sayings yet expressed a specific understanding. We shall mark the main steps along this road in the following section.

1. In the apocalyptic texts discussed in Chapter I the Son of Man is not yet spoken of as a finally fixed, clearly defined, self-contained concept. There is a wide range of meaning covered by the interpretations in the context of the visions in Dan. 7 and IV Ezra 13, and there are material differences in what is said about the Son of Man himself. In I Enoch the concept of the Son of Man is fixed to the relatively greatest extent; this is the form which most nearly resembles that of the synoptic tradition. At any rate that enigmatic heavenly figure, who according to Dan. 7 will take up the office of ruler only after the judgement in heaven has been concluded, is here in I Enoch more clearly defined as the eschatological Judge of the world, whilst nevertheless retaining other remarkable attributes and functions (notably pre-existence). In the Gospel of Matthew, too, the Son of Man is seen to have especially the task of carrying out the offi ce of the Judge of the world.

In Jesus' teaching the apocalyptic statements about the Son of Man are reduced to a minimum. In view of the scantiness of specific features we might be inclined to comment that in Jesus' sayings the figure of the Son of Man has again forfeited the distinction which it had laboriously achieved. And yet the Son of Man here gains a soteriological function of highest importance. He is the guarantor before God that the fellowship of following Jesus on earth will be continued in a way which will mean salvation (Luke 12.8f.).

2. Jesus' Son of Man sayings differ from the Jewish apocalyptic concepts by reason of their soteriological nature. That the Son of Man's coming will mean salvation to some, judgement to others, was already an aspect of Jewish apocalyptic thinking. But the question of who belongs to the one group and who to the other is answered anew in Jesus' teaching. According to I Enoch 45.3 the Elect One of the second Similitude, namely the Son of Man (46.1ff.), elects from men's works. What criterion does he use in electing? His criterion is without doubt the Law. However interpreted in apocalyptic thinking, the Law remains the decisive standard of judgement. According to the authentic Son of Man sayings, however, it is on the attitude towards Jesus that the decision hinges. To be attached to Jesus by following him on earth is the one decisive criterion for the future verdict of the Son of Man.

3. Jesus' speaking of the coming Son of Man does not deprive this figure in any way of its heavenly nature and transcendent sovereignty. We must fully realize this in order to resist the temptation of directly taking for traits of sovereignty of the coming Son of Man what we perceive of the full authority of the Son of Man active or suffering in the present. The figure of the coming Son of Man is not restricted by what exists on earth. We cannot say that in Jesus the Son of Man *appears*; he appears neither revealed nor concealed. Jesus does not proclaim himself as claimant to this title of dignity; he does not comport himself as the Son of Man *destinatus*. Nowhere in any of the three groups of sayings does there occur a *prolepsis* of the parousia, of the future world, of the heavenly qualities of the Son of Man.

4. The transformation of the Son of Man concept is continued by the use and development of this concept within the community. First of all, the name Son of Man is now withdrawn from use by men. It may only be uttered by Jesus. Even in the Revelation of John, the seer still avoids the direct use of the name Son of Man, although

he reproduces the old combination of Dan. 7.13 and Zech. 12.10 (cf. Rev. 1.7). According to Acts 7.56, however, Stephen *as a martyr* sees the Son of Man and may testify to this himself.

It is ineradicably impressed on the synoptic tradition that no one but Jesus may name the Son of Man. The Son of Man sayings which are newly formed, in addition to the authentic sayings of Jesus, clearly demonstrate this imprint. They are never formed as pronouncements by the community *about* the Son of Man, or as acclamations directed *towards* the Son of Man; instead, all these sayings are put in the mouth of Jesus. This indicates that words of Jesus were charismatically uttered within the early community. If Matt. 10.23 and 19.28 indeed are, as we sought to demonstrate in Chapter II, prophetic sayings that issued from the earliest, still Jewish, Christian community, then it is evident that there were men endowed with charismatic utterance who perceived the word in the spirit in such a way that it could be and had to be transmitted by reason of the authority of Jesus on earth and as his saying.

This prophetic procedure of recognizing newly formed sayings about the Son of Man to be words of Jesus on earth appears as a method throughout all the developments of the Son of Man sayings right up to those sayings which were editorially re-formulated or newly formulated by Matthew and by Luke. Did the editors merely conform to the peculiar style of the Son of Man sayings, or did they understand their own matching up with Jesus' words to be a charismatic utterance as well? Without a touch of the latter understanding, their dealing with the tradition would have to be suspected of being unauthorized and arbitrary. But obviously intent on perceiving and handing on the word of *Jesus*, and understanding the presence of the word in the spirit, they took no care to keep pre-Easter and post-Easter sayings apart.

5. We have already mentioned that peculiarity of the structure of authentic Son of Man sayings which was firmly maintained in post-Easter formulations. In all sayings Jesus speaks of the coming Son of Man as of someone different, someone in the future. We would not have expected the community to maintain this differentiating way of speaking; for, as we shall discuss in greater detail below, the community undoubtedly identified Jesus with the coming Son of Man on the basis of their assurance by his resurrection. We would have expected it even less when taking into consideration that in the sayings concerning the Son of Man's present activity on earth and

his suffering the differentiating way of speaking was abandoned without exception. Both the differentiating and the identifying way of speaking already appear side by side in Q; and in the sayings editorially formulated by Matthew and Luke Jesus is still made to point away from himself to the coming Son of Man. Consequently the two ways of speaking must have overlapped in the history of the synoptic tradition for a considerable time. We have to make this comprehensible.

6. The sayings concerning the coming Son of Man correlate the world to come with the existence on earth by assuring that the Son of Man will be the guarantor for the attachment to Jesus on earth. This soteriological correlation cannot help but illuminate Jesus' activity on earth as well. The future surety of the Son of Man includes the verification of Jesus' claim to full authority on earth. Now, in the post-Easter situation a new element enters decisively into the concept. The primitive community expected the arrival of *Jesus* as the Son of Man.[1] Expecting this, they could not but realize now that in the Son of Man sayings which had been transmitted to them Jesus himself had pointed to his arrival as the Son of Man. And considering that Jesus himself would confirm at his coming as the Son of Man his attachment to those who followed him on earth, they saw the possibility of designating his activity on earth by the name Son of Man. For the one who bestowed the fellowship on earth had now been recognized to be its future guarantor. The primitive community did take this possible step, as the sayings on the Son of Man's activity on earth in Q and in the pre-Marcan controversy dialogues show. It is not so very surprising that the name was thus transferred as soon as Jesus had been identified with the coming Son of Man. What is much more surprising is that in the sayings on the coming Son of Man the differentiation between Jesus and the Son of Man was invariably maintained. In our view, as already shown, this is comprehensible as fidelity to that way of speaking which is employed in the authentic sayings, as compliance with the authority of the formulation of words which had issued from Jesus. But in statements with which no ready-formed sayings of Jesus transmitted to them were associated, the community was already free to speak of Jesus in his earthly activity as of the Son of Man. We have to elucidate what this transformation means.

[1] Bultmann, *Theology* I, p. 33.

7. By the *soteriological* correlation in the Son of Man sayings the person of Jesus is not immediately united with the figure of the coming Son of Man; it is not expressed here that both are identical. The means by which an identification will be effected is a *Christological* judgement. It is highly significant that Christological cognition sprang up in the earliest period of the primitive community in response to Jesus' own words. The Master himself had promised to his own that their attachment to him would be guaranteed and confirmed by the Son of Man. The post-Easter community realized that these words of promise implied a continuity between the one who gave the promise on earth and the one who will come to fulfil what has been promised. Consequently they made the step to Christology. This step took them beyond what had been expressed by Jesus; and yet it was not an arbitrary one. For the authority of the one who had uttered the words of promise on earth had been confirmed by the Easter event in a way which, leading to a new understanding of his person, gave the impetus for Christological cognition. This post-Easter cognition then referred to the pre-Easter words of promise uttered by Jesus himself. The community built upon the foundation of this promise the Christological cognition that the one who gave the promise will himself be the guarantor for its fulfilment, i.e. that Jesus will come as the Son of Man. We have to stress, however—and shall develop it in greater detail below—that the event of the resurrection was prerequisite for the community's step beyond their faith in Jesus' words of promise, with their soteriological connotation, on to that Christological cognition.

Obviously the community set about expressing the Christological cognition with considerable caution. Although they have realized that none other but Jesus is the Son of Man to come they do not transfer the heavenly attributes of the Son of Man to the person of Jesus on earth. In the sayings concerning the coming Son of Man they preserve the differentiation between Jesus on earth and the supra-terrestrial figure of the one who will come. At the same time they designate Jesus in his earthly activity by the name of the one who will come; yet they do not transfer the transcendent function together with the name. Thus the Christological identification introduced by the community appears to have been accompanied by a new differentiation. There are two separate functions pertaining to different situations in the history of salvation—the one on earth and the one to come—which are not intermingled, and yet both of them are designated of the person of Jesus under the name Son of Man. As the Son of Man acting on earth with full authority, Jesus is still understood as the one who is not exempted from the restrictions of existence on earth. As the Son of Man to come, however, Jesus is understood as having unrestricted power at his disposal. This new differentiation between Jesus' functions is invariably respected in the sayings on the present Son of Man as well as in the structure of those on the coming Son of Man. To proceed in this way appears to have been possible only in a community which did not sweepingly accomplish the Christological identification, but listened to Jesus' words and complied with their authority. And nevertheless the community has stepped onto new ground when expressing the continuity between the present of Jesus' activity and the future of the Son of Man's coming. The new basis which by means of the Christological cognition of the post-Easter community was recognized as the foundation on which this continuity could be established was Jesus' *person*. The pre-eminence of soteriology in Jesus' teaching was transformed into the pre-eminence of Christology in the primitive community's message. But, as we have to emphasize over and again, the Christological conclusion (that because Jesus is the coming Son of Man, Jesus' activity on earth can already be designated by the name Son of Man) was not drawn by immediately transferring the traditional Jewish concept of the Son of Man to Jesus. That Christological cognition rather sprang up in response to the soteriological correlation in the Son of Man sayings which had issued from Jesus himself. Thanks to the impetus given by the Easter event the earliest beginnings of Christology thus sprang up from soteriology.

What we have marked here is not only the most important step on the road to the transformation of the Son of Man concept within the history of the synoptic tradition but also the location of a source from which Christology takes its rise. There are quite a number of Christological titles in the synoptic tradition; the title Son of Man is the only one, however, whose roots can be traced back to Q. We would be unable to understand the beginnings of synoptic Christology without considering this stratum of the history of tradition. So we now will turn to Q, trying to grasp its specific nature in order to get a more comprehensive view of the step from the soteriological correlation in the sayings about the coming Son of Man to the Christological continuity in the sayings about the Son of Man in his present activity.

C. THE Q MATERIAL IN ITS RELATIONSHIP TO THE
SYNOPTIC SAYINGS CONCERNING THE SON
OF MAN

I. The problem

Martin Dibelius in his essay on the Sermon on the Mount and his little book *Gospel Criticism and Christology* has pointed out the gulf which within the New Testament separates the Epistles on the one hand from the Gospels on the other hand. He regards this separation as the greatest problem in the whole New Testament. The Epistles are concerned with Christology (in the narrower sense). The foundation of their message is Jesus' death and resurrection. This they emphasize as the core of the message, and in connexion with it they also emphasize Jesus' birth and heavenly origin. But they say almost nothing about Jesus' life and for the most part equally little about his words. The Synoptic Gospels on their side of the gulf transmit narratives of Jesus' life and suffering and material parts of Jesus' teaching.

Now Dibelius shows that these two sides of the New Testament are, however, not completely separated from each other. For both the doctrine about Jesus Christ and the narratives about Jesus of Nazareth see God's revelation in him. The faith which sees in Jesus Christ God's conclusive revelation is the common ground on which both sides of the New Testament rest. Hence 'in the first generation after Jesus' death . . . a synthesis of historical tradition with theology has already come into being.'[1]

Our enquiry into the sayings about the coming Son of Man makes us aware of another separation, one which exists within the synoptic tradition. The sayings on the coming Son of Man appear to have originally pertained to the Q material. In the Gospel of Mark sayings about the coming Son of Man appear to have been rendered in a variety of ways. 13.26 occurs within the context of entirely traditional apocalyptic material; 14.62 occurs within the account of Jesus' judicial examination, yet shows distinct traces of Christological reflection in its form; whereas both in form and in concept Mark 8.38 belongs to the group of Son of Man sayings in Q as the variants from Q prove. Thus there is apparently something like a gulf between that side of the synoptic tradition in which the sayings on the coming Son of Man are deeply rooted, namely the Q material, and the other

[1] Dibelius, *Gospel Criticism*, p. 17.

side, the Gospel of Mark, which is prevailingly concerned with the passion *kerygma*, and where such sayings are more or less superficially implanted. That there is such a separation looks all the more probable in view of the fact that no passage from Q mentions the passion. We must now examine more closely in which way Q and the Gospel of Mark are separated.

Dibelius has not only demonstrated how far apart the Gospels are from the Epistles but also how near, particularly in certain aspects, the Gospel of Mark is to the theology of Paul. 'In spite of the great difference in their methods it is not hard to see the inner unity between Mark and Paul; for both of them the Passion of Jesus is the central cosmic event which from the beginning points to the resurrection and exaltation of Jesus as Lord.'[1] Whilst Paul, however, does not speak of Jesus' life, Mark is intent on expressing that already Jesus' life was the radiant path of the Son of God through this world. Thus for Mark the problem arises how the Jews could in that case reject Jesus. He solves it by means of his theory of the command to tell no man. Jesus himself willed to remain concealed, to go his way to the cross. In consequence of this theory the passion becomes the one point towards which the material in the Gospel of Mark is organized throughout.[2] The whole course of Jesus' life is a movement towards the passion; and the passion is the summit at which this course arrives. Dibelius assents to Kähler's comment that the Gospels might somewhat provocatively be called passion narratives with circumstantial introductions. 'Mark, describing Jesus' service in the light of his passion, gives a Christological meaning to Jesus' life. And this meaning is not far from what Paul has in mind when he speaks of the Jews' hardness of heart.'[3]

It has become almost an *opinio communis* to assume that the kerygma of the passion and resurrection is the centre of the synoptic tradition, thus drawing from the function of the passion kerygma in the Gospel of Mark a general conclusion for the synoptic tradition as a whole. The following statement by Dodd may represent here the view of many other scholars as well. 'Christology, it is not too much to say, is rooted in the understanding of the passion, death and resurrection of Jesus in the light of a combination of the ideas of Son

---

[1] Dibelius, *Gospel Criticism*, p. 21.

[2] The manner in which the section Mark 8.27–10.52 is composed impresses us with the intensity of the attractive power which in the Gospel of Mark directs the material towards the passion. Cf. above Chapter IV A 1, pp. 145ff.

[3] Dibelius, *Gospel Criticism*, p. 22.

s.m.–h*

of Man and Servant.'[1] We skip over the question whether it is permissible to relate Son of Man and Servant of Jehovah to the passion kerygma in Dodd's manner. We would assent to what is stated in the other part of the sentence in so far as the Gospel of Mark is concerned. But we have to examine whether this statement is valid in every respect for the Gospels of Matthew and Luke as well, or in what particular respect or restrictive sense it is valid. It is true, doctrinal reflection in the primitive community when developing the earliest beginnings of Christology started from precisely that sphere of concepts in which Paul and Mark accord with each other. But does the material in the synoptic tradition of itself thus point to the passion kerygma? Can we assume this for the material from Q? It is conspicuous enough that there was obviously not much room within the Gospel of Mark for the wealth of sayings transmitting Jesus' teaching. The decision that Mark made not to admit sayings of Jesus to a greater extent was a weighty one implying great consequences for Christology; and even the fact that Matthew and Luke admitted the substance of those sayings nevertheless did not deprive Mark's decision of its weight. Mark produced the type 'gospel', thus forming not only a literary concept but a theological concept as well which implies a certain type of Christology. It is not the central concern of a Gospel to continue to teach Jesus' teaching. A Gospel rather is concerned with giving an account of the passion which makes clear what Jesus' passion means for those who are his own. And when the community, widening its range of vision, recognize what the birth, the heavenly origin and the exaltation of the Christ mean, they can still relate all this to the event of the passion without referring to Jesus' teaching.

In view of the consequences for Christology implied in the composition of the Gospel of Mark, the conclusions we have so far drawn from our enquiry oblige us to consider the synoptic tradition in a new way. If it appears that the sayings about the Son of Man's coming and activity on earth originally pertain to the Q material which is not expressly related to the passion kerygma, but on the other hand that their formation marks the step was taken from the original soteriological structure to a Christological structure, then Dodd's statement is questionable in so far as it implies that the roots of Christology are only to be found in the understanding of suffering, death and resurrection. For if that is the case, the passion kerygma is

[1] Dodd, *According to the Scriptures*, p. 119.

not the only source from which Christology takes its rise. There is a second, independent source, then, located in the Q stratum of the tradition, as can be observed in the productive development of the Son of Man sayings. Christology as it springs up here is a Son of Man Christology.

It might be objected to our assumption of the independence of this source that a bridge does exist from this sphere of concepts to the passion kerygma by way of the sayings about the suffering and rising Son of Man. But this objection is refuted by the fact that it is these very sayings which do not occur as early as Q; they first appear in the Gospel of Mark, who had a vital interest in constructing this bridge.

So we turn to the material from Q in order to find out how it may be related with what we call a Son of Man Christology.

II. Q in recent research

(1) *Adolf Harnack*, stimulated by Wellhausen, set out in his book *Sayings of Jesus* (first published in 1907) to determine with great precision 'the second source of Matthew and Luke, which may be named Q, both in regard to its extent and its content, and to estimate its value both in itself and relatively to the gospel of Mark'.[1] He arrives at the conclusion that when considering the Q material we cannot altogether evade the impression that Q was made up of unconnected fragments. 'But as soon as one calls to mind the content of the three Gospels and compares Q with it, then Q undoubtedly appears more homogeneous than any of the three.' Compared with these Gospels the content which had to be assigned to Q is indeed homogeneous to a high degree. 'A great number of points of view and tendencies manifest in those Gospels are entirely absent here.' We rather get the impression that the compiler of Q 'is simply concerned with Jesus' commandments and aims at giving a description of his message, in which description he appears to be influenced by no special or particular bias. Perhaps we may not be mistaken in supposing that his selection was also determined by his desire to illustrate Jesus' message and his witness to himself, in their main and characteristic features, by specially striking examples.' The fact established in the introduction that Jesus is the Messiah, or Son of God, is presupposed in the compilation itself as a point no longer

---

[1] Harnack, *Sprüche*, p. iii.

subject to controversy.[1] Q appears to have been 'not a Gospel at all in the sense that the Synoptic Gospels are'.[2] It is rather 'a compilation of discourses and sayings of Jesus the arrangement of which has no reference to the Passion, with a horizon which is as good as absolutely bounded by Galilee'.[3] 'Christology' as it is understood in the compilation is presented in an unequivocal and consistent manner. To the compiler of Q it is perfectly clear that Jesus is the Messiah and instituted as Son of God at his baptism. All the sayings in the compilation must accordingly be read against this background. 'If, however, we think away this background, the resultant picture is essentially different. We now have before us a compilation of sayings in which the speaker is a teacher, a prophet, one who is more than a prophet—the final decisive messenger of God.'[4] 'In the sayings collected in Q the Messiahship is only clearly expressed under the form of the Parousia . . .; in these sayings Jesus claims faith not because he is the present Messiah—this is unthinkable—but because he works the works of God and proclaims his commandments.'[5] Finally Harnack poses the question, 'Which is the more valuable, Mark or Q?' His answer is that both Q and the Gospel of Mark must remain valid, but 'the former takes precedence. Above all, the tendency to exaggerate the apocalyptic and eschatological elements in Jesus' message, and to subordinate to this the purely religious and ethical elements, will ever find its refutation in Q. This source is the authority for that which formed the central theme of the message of Jesus—that is, the revelation of the knowledge of God, and the moral call to repent and believe, to renounce the world and to gain heaven —this and nothing else.'[6]

In recent synoptic research[7] Harnack's enquiry concerning Q has met with little attention. For it had soon appeared that the picture delineated by him was thoroughly one-sided.

[1] Harnack, *Sayings*, pp. 167f.
[2] *Ibid.*, p. 170.
[3] *Ibid.*, p. 171.
[4] *Ibid.*, pp. 243f.
[5] *Ibid.*, p. 245.
[6] *Ibid.*, p. 250.
[7] Josef Schmid in his article 'Neue Synoptiker-Literatur' in *Theol. Revue* 52, 1956, cols. 49–62, reports on new studies which critically examine the theory of the two sources of the Synoptic Gospels. In particular he deals in detail with L. Vaganay's book *Le problème Synoptique*. In this book a fresh attempt is made on a large scale to overthrow that theory. Schmid arrives at the conclusion that Vaganay's attempt is considerably less convincing than the theory of the two

(a) From the impressive consistency of the material from Q Harnack derived the conviction that the compilation had been achieved by an individual person. He spoke of an author or redactor.[1] Soon afterwards, however, the school of form-criticism in Germany reached results by which the assumption that Q had been written by such a person was rendered doubtful. So Dibelius stated that 'the present position of research into the source Q warrants our speaking rather of a *stratum* than of a *scriptum*'.[2] This stratum of tradition which appears in Q dealt with problems which had presented themselves to this particular community. We are therefore faced with the following question: What was it which urged the community to collect this particular kind of material, these particular sayings of Jesus? Even the fact that there was no individual person who acted as the author or redactor of Q does not invalidate Harnack's observation that Q when contrasted with the Gospels appears far more homogeneous. But what is the reason for this relatively great consistency of the Q material? If Q as a stratum of tradition must be ascribed to a community, it appears that a particular set of concepts was prevalent in this community. Harnack rightly stresses again and again that the concept of Jesus' passion which is present in the Gospel of Mark as his so-called Paulinism is absent in Q. How is this absence comprehensible in material which was transmitted by a community which after all must have been acquainted with Jesus' passion?

(b) Harnack reproached the critical exegesis of his time with exaggerating the apocalyptic eschatological element in Jesus' message. Subsequent research has shown that this reproach can no longer be justified. Jesus' message is indeed to a high extent of an apocalyptic eschatological nature. What has not been shown, however, is how this eschatological nature is related to the set of concepts which is present in the material collected in the Q stratum of tradition. This may be due to the fact that the theological research in Germany which is positively or negatively dependent on the school of

---

sources, since this theory solves far more problems than Vaganay's attempt does. With regard to Q Schmid states (col. 58), 'The arguments not in favour of Q (contradicting its homogeneity) remain fully valid after Vaganay's book as well. But I do not wish to imply by this that I therefore doubt that such a source (Q or Sg) did exist at some time.'

[1] Cf. Harnack, *Sayings*, p. 249.
[2] Dibelius, *Tradition*, p. 235.

form-criticism pays too exclusive attention to what is called the kerygma. The kerygma is considered to be the centre of the synoptic tradition. It integrates the material concerning the passion, i.e. the material which Q lacks. Dibelius in his *Gospel Criticism and Christology* implies that this trend in research does have something in common with the dialectic theology of the 1920s which is reproached for its too-exclusive Paulinism.[1] As attention to the unworldly message of God's grace and man's sin dominates this kind of theological thinking, attention to the particular form of Jesus' teaching and to the person of the teacher recedes into the background. The latter problems are dealt with in the material of Q and its Christological implications. In the research work done in the early days of the school of form-criticism, however, attention turned first of all to the material in the Gospel of Mark[2] which had occupied a predominant place in Dibelius' *From Tradition to Gospel*. The masters of the method of form-criticism, Bultmann and Dibelius, both established, each in his own specific way, the theological priority of the community's kerygma of the passion over the Q material.

(2) It appears to be a consequence of the trend to which research work thus conformed that *Martin Dibelius* can speak only in a rather colourless way of the original intention which may have led to the compilation of Q. He starts from the observation that there is not even the slightest indication of a passion account in the Q material.[3] To him this deficiency shows that the Q compilation of sayings cannot claim any theological significance of its own. The faith of the first Christians was that the passion and resurrection meant the beginning of the new era. Accordingly they were living in expectation of an imminent end. The point from which they took the direction of their life was exclusively what God had done at the cross and the resurrection. Only after it had become evident that the end had been delayed did the Christians realize that they needed valid moral instructions for the regulation of their life in the world. These they procured by referring back to Jesus' sayings in retrospect. So the sayings were compiled at this later stage as a secondary supplement to the unique central core, the kerygma of the passion.

[1] *Op. cit.*, pp. 13f.
[2] Karl Ludwig Schmidt, *Der Rahmen der Geschichte Jesu*, 1919; Martin Albertz, *Die synoptischen Streitgespräche*, 1921; cf. also Georg Bertram, *Die Leidensgeschichte und der Christuskult*, 1922.
[3] Dibelius, *Tradition*, p. 244.

Thus the original intention which brought about the compilation of Q was to impart not events in Jesus' life but sayings of his which were now to be observed and taught. So most of the compiled material consisted of sayings of the Lord preserved by the community merely as rules for their life. Only a few more developed passages transcend this general nature of the Q material by intending to show the identity of the one whose words were collected in the communities. The original intention, however, was to compile the sayings of Jesus merely for purposes of moral exhortation without any Christological concern. Q can be compared with the Halakha.[1]

Dibelius does go beyond this initial statement, however, when in his later essay on the Sermon on the Mount (1940) he enquires into the internal connexion between the Sermon on the Mount and the Christological message.[2] The material of the Sermon on the Mount was adopted by Matthew and by Luke from that earlier source which contained a kind of outline for a sermon.[3] 'The earliest communities, let us say about AD 50, demanded a summary of the Lord's teaching in order to have a law according to which they might live. We see from this that they believed in Christ not only as their redeemer but also as their teacher who communicated to them the new commandments for the heavenly kingdom.'[4] Thus Dibelius here connects the tradition of the Lord's sayings with the community's belief in the validity of Jesus' eschatological teaching—a step of great significance. Jesus' message that the kingdom of God is at hand was believed in this early time of the tradition, and those who heard the sayings of Jesus knew by reason of this belief, 'This is the hour of decision; only the doers will enter into the kingdom of God.'[5]

Thus it appears that the sayings of Jesus were transmitted not as general rules for life, as moral exhortation, but as Jesus' particular instructions in view of the imminent coming of God's reign. We cannot understand the tradition of these sayings of Jesus in Q if we leave this connexion out of consideration. Dibelius, however, did not pursue this line of thought any further, but was content with considering the Q material within the framework of general Christian exhortation.

[1] Dibelius, *Tradition*, pp. 245f.
[2] Dibelius, *Botschaft* I, p. 85.
[3] *Ibid.*, p. 95.
[4] *Ibid.*, p. 97.
[5] *Ibid.*, p. 98.

(3) Within the school of form-criticism in Germany it is undoubtedly *Rudolf Bultmann* who most intensively studied the material from Q, and did so marking it with the comprehensive term, Jesus' eschatological proclamation.[1] But Bultmann is the very person who has most strongly emphasized the priority of the community's kerygma over the material from Q which we mentioned above. Bultmann regarded Jesus' teaching as historically pertaining to Judaism,[2] no relevant continuity existing between his teaching and the community's kerygma. Seen from Bultmann's point of view, there must needs be a discontinuity; for to him Jesus' life was unmessianic[3] and Jesus' teaching a radical version of what Jewish prophets would proclaim.[4] It is true that the post-Easter kerygma speaks differently about Jesus. But at the first beginnings it had been understood even in the community that Jesus' life was unmessianic[5] and that Jesus' messiahship could be expected only in the future.[6] The latter statement had similarly been made by Harnack in his enquiry concerning Q. According to him it is first asserted in the sayings at the close of the Q compilation that Jesus lays claim to the messiahship, 'but only in connexion with and under the imagery of the Second Coming; He who already in his present state of existence is more than a prophet and greater than John, He who is the Son, will be the coming King as Judge'.[7] Harnack, however, had maintained that Jesus in his present state of existence was conscious of being the Son. This also was now abandoned by Bultmann. He made clear the impossibility of establishing any legitimation of Jesus' present claim. The messiahship of Jesus does not exist while Jesus is acting on earth; at this stage his messiahship is a purely future one.

Bultmann's assumption that at an early stage in the history of tradition Jesus' life was understood to have been unmessianic[8] and that at the beginning of the primitive community's existence Jesus' past activity on earth was not yet understood to have been messianic activity[9] arouses objections. Where can we get hold of evidence of a stage in the history of tradition at which this understanding was

---

[1] Bultmann, *Primitive Christianity in its Contemporary Setting*, p. 86; *Jesus*, pp. 27ff.
[2] Bultmann, *Primitive Christianity*, pp. 96f.
[3] Bultmann, *Theology* I, p. 31.
[4] *Ibid.*, p. 34.
[5] *Ibid.*, p. 31.
[6] *Ibid.*, p. 36.
[7] Harnack, *Sayings*, p. 244, cf. 245.
[8] Bultmann, *Theology* I, p. 32.
[9] *Ibid.*, p. 33.

prevalent? The only material transmitted to us which might be used to support Bultmann's assumption is the material from Q. Harnack had also assumed that what was compiled in Q could be regarded as material without any Christology if the first passages, namely those about the baptism and the temptation, were left out of consideration. But why did the community collect this material? A community which expected the coming of the one exalted to be the Son of Man, as Bultmann sees it,[1] might have been content with the voice of this exalted one. Why did they accept the authority of the words of the one on earth?[2] Obviously the motive for the collection of sayings of Jesus in Q must be elucidated.

(4) After Harnack and contemporary with the form-criticism in Germany, several exegetes studied intensively the special problems of Q. Bussmann wrote about it in his *Synoptische Studien*, Streeter in *The Four Gospels* and T. W. Manson in *The Sayings of Jesus* (1937). In the latter book the results of Harnack's, Bussmann's and Streeter's enquiries are critically taken into account. Therefore we can limit our discussion to the theses of *T. W. Manson*.

In Manson's view the kerygma of the passion was from the beginning the centre of the primitive community. 'For the primitive Church the central thing is the Cross on the Hill rather than the Sermon on the Mount, and the characteristic Church act is the Communion rather than the conference.'[3] Very soon, however, the community was faced by the problems of Christian faith and Christian life and of the relationship of the two to each other. Those who had accepted the gift of God now required teaching about the particular kind of life a Christian ought to live. 'When such instruction has to be given the natural place to which the teacher turns is the source of the Gospel—Jesus Himself. In His life and words will be found the standard and norm of Christian behaviour.' 'Some objective test was required, and it was found in the recorded acts and words of Jesus.'[4] Accordingly the motive for collecting the Q material must be seen in the Christian community's need of a norm for their way of life. In this conclusion Manson joins the view taken by Dibelius and many other scholars. He further adds other motives to the chief

---

[1] Bultmann, *Theology* I, pp. 33f.
[2] Cf. Schniewind, *Synoptikerexegese*, p. 160.
[3] Manson, *Sayings*, p. 9.
[4] *Loc. cit.*

motive of the community's need. 'We have thus four motives at
work in the compilation of the teaching: the pastoral care of the
churches, the personal interest of the disciple in the Master, the
apologetic value of such teaching in the Gentile world, and the need
of the Palestinian community to defend itself against the charge of
uttering subversive doctrines. Of these the first was probably the
most powerful.'[1] At any rate Manson clearly makes a distinction
between the material of Q which was independently transmitted in
the earliest communities and that other tradition the basic manifestation of which was the Gospel of Mark. 'We have in fact to recognize that in the earliest stages of the Christian tradition there are two
streams which eventually unite to form the Gospel as we see it in
Matthew or Luke. The one has its source in the Passion and Resurrection: its story is the story of Him who came not to be ministered
unto but to minister and to give His life a ransom for many. The
other is the record of the sayings of a Teacher who astonished the
multitudes because He taught with authority and not as their Scribes.
It is this second stream of tradition whose history we must now
attempt to trace.'[2]

Harnack, impressed with the homogeneity of Q, had raised the
question of who was the author or redactor of this document.
Dibelius, much less convinced that it must have been a self-contained
document, had considered Q to be a stratum of tradition. Manson
now arrives at the following general conclusion concerning Q:
'This document begins and ends with the thought of the coming
judgement. Its first sentences contain the eschatological preaching of
John the Baptist; its closing paragraphs consists mainly of a poem
about the coming of the Son of Man. Is this deliberate? If it is, it is a
strong argument in favour of the view, which I think antecedently
probable, that in Matthew and Luke we have preserved for us
substantially all that Q ever contained.'[3] Dibelius had objected to the
assumption that the material of Q, complete in itself, was arranged
according to a plan, his chief argument being that we cannot be sure
whether all the material was transmitted to us or not. This objection,
however, does not altogether overthrow the assumption. Of course,
we cannot prove that we possess the whole of the Q material. But
even if the question must remain open whether a complete document

[1] Manson, *Sayings*, pp. 10f.
[2] *Ibid.*, p. 11.
[3] *Ibid.*, p. 16.

did exist at all it nevertheless cannot be denied that there apparently was a plan according to which the Q material was arranged. Manson demonstrates the logic of this arrangement. In addition he compares the arrangement of the Q material in the Gospel of Luke with the arrangement of the teaching material and the material peculiar to Matthew (M) in the latter Gospel and arrives at the conclusion that 'the arrangement of this teaching material, which we shall call M, as given in Matthew corresponds at four points with the arrangement of the Q material in Luke's order'. 'The four points are Jesus' preaching, the mission charge, the speech against Pharisaism, and the eschatological speech. From this fact the inference is either that there is a scheme of the teaching older than M and Q, to which both conform, or that the M material has been incorporated into Q. The latter alternative would involve a kind of proto-Matthew hypothesis; but the former seems the more probable view. More than this coincidence in the general structure, there are also traces of coincidence in the structure of some of the speeches.'[1] 'We should not attempt to build too much on these parallelisms; but, such as they are, they allow us at least to entertain the supposition that there was a rough outline of the essentials of the teaching at an earlier stage of the tradition than is represented by Q and M. This outline, if it had a separate existence, dealt with essentials: the substance of the Christian life, the principles of Christian missionary propaganda, the defence of the new religion against Jewish attacks, and the hope of the future.'[2]

Why is there but an inconsiderable amount of narrative material in Q, and why no account of the passion? 'The most probable explanation is that there is no passion-story because none is required, Q being a book of instruction for people who are already Christians and know the story of the Cross by heart.'[3] This manner of solving the problem entangles Manson in difficulties. At first he had considered Q or the older forms to which Q might be traced back to be a very early tradition; he had located Q, about or earlier than AD 50, in the area of Antioch. Then he considered the tradition concerning the passion to be a material prerequisite for Q. If the material of Q is supposed to furnish a 'norm of Christian behaviour',[4] the step Manson took is unavoidable and yet unsatisfactory. For what is considered to be its material prerequisite is nowhere referred to in Q.

[1] Manson, *Sayings*, p. 22.
[2] *Ibid.*, p. 23.
[3] *Ibid.*, p. 16.
[4] *Ibid.*, p. 9.

Hence we shall have to question whether it will do to define Q as 'a book of instruction for people who are already Christians'.

'A third striking feature in Q is the exceedingly small quantity of polemical matter which it contains . . . ninety per cent of the document is positive religious and moral teaching.'[1] We must assent to Manson at least in so far as that form of elaborate controversy dialogue which occurs in the Gospel of Mark is entirely absent in Q. Manson assumes that the reason for the absence of this kind of material is possibly the intention 'to show the true nature of Christian beliefs and practices to the Jews'; in that case, according to Manson, 'it may well be that the compiler thought that this purpose too would be better served by positive statement than by mere disputation'.[2] This argument fails to convince us. We are not even convinced that there must have been a distinguished individual person who compiled the sayings. Moreover, we have to note that in a great number of sayings from Q the decisive tension over against the Jewish authorities and this generation is expressed. The friendly attitude towards the Gentiles which may be perceived in Q[3] no doubt implies an indirect attack on the Jewish prerogatives. Manson's argument is also contradicted by the exegesis of individual passages (cf., e.g., Luke 6.22; 7.31–35; 11.39, 42, 44; 11.46–52; 12.4, 8, 9, 10; 13.25–29; 13.34f.; 14.21ff.). Therefore we cannot assent to Manson's explanation that for reasons of diplomacy the antagonism against Israel was made to recede into the background to be replaced by the exposition of positive teaching. Yet we agree with him that in the Q stratum no special attention was paid to the development of the form of controversy dialogues, of disputations with scribes. We shall deal with this in greater detail farther on.

Thus Manson's view of the general nature of the Q material and the motives for its compilation leaves us unsatisfied mainly because from this point of view it cannot clearly be discerned how Q and the passion kerygma are related to each other. Manson, too, perceives that the material of Q cannot simply be interpreted as a 'standard and norm of Christian behaviour' without presupposing a common ground on which such norms may have been established and accepted. Consequently he ends up with postulating the passion kerygma as this groundwork in spite of the fact that it appears to

[1] *Ibid.*, p. 16.
[2] *Ibid.*, p. 16.
[3] Cf. *ibid.*, p. 20.

have been developed within the synoptic tradition later than the material of Q. But would the passion kerygma, i.e. the message of the Lord's death and resurrection, be in fact the only possible ground on which transmission of the material of Q might have taken place?

(5) *B. H. Streeter* also considered the absence of any explicit reference in the Q material to the passion kerygma to be a weighty and difficult problem. 'The absence in the Passion story of any substantial agreements of Matthew and Luke against Mark, in the view of most scholars, compels us to conclude that Q contained no account of the Passion. We must ask, Why? I think the answer must be sought in two directions. (1) The Passion and its redemptive significance could readily be taught in oral tradition. But ethical teaching implies detailed instruction which sooner or later necessitates a written document. Such a document is found in the *Didache*, which obviously presupposes a general knowledge of the central facts of the Christian story. Similarly Q was probably written to *supplement* an oral tradition. (2) Of less weight is the consideration that, while to Paul the centre of the Gospel was the Cross of Christ, to the other Apostles it was His Second Coming. Peter's speeches in the Acts show that to them, as to other Jews, the Crucifixion was a difficulty. It had been cancelled, so to speak, by the Resurrection. It had been foretold by the Prophets, and this showed that it was somehow part of the Divine Plan; but it was still one of those calamities which darken men's understanding of His purpose, rather than the one act that has unveiled the mystery.'[1]

Streeter's argument, that, as it was easier to transmit the facts and the meaning of the passion than to transmit detailed ethical instruction, Q was probably written down as a supplement of the oral tradition, cannot be verified because we simply do not know anything about an early written version of Q. At the beginning of its history the Q material, just like the other traditional material, was probably transmitted orally. We may therefore not evade the question of what impetus there was at this stage in the history of tradition to collect the material of Q. Nor are we satisfied with

---

[1] Streeter, *Gospels*, p. 292. Dibelius has challenged Streeter's understanding of Q. Streeter after having reconstructed Q arrived at the conclusion that 'Q is a document the purpose and character of which are perfectly intelligible' (p. 291). Dibelius countered (*Tradition*, p. 234 n. 1), 'That is precisely the question because of the very fact that there is no guarantee of the completeness of the list.'

Streeter's solution of the fundamental problem of how the Q material and the passion kerygma are related to each other.

III. The range of concepts and the perspective of the Q material

(1) The community's need of exhortation and the motive for the compilation of Q

If it is assumed that the passion kerygma has been the centre of the Gospel from the beginning, then the fact that there is no reference to this centre in Q will imply that the latter is a particular secondary supplement to the passion kerygma. In that case it would have to be accepted as a satisfactory explanation that a need for exhortation motivated the compilation of Q. Regarded from this point of view, however, much of the Q material cannot be understood very well or even at all.

The sections containing the 'messianic proclamation of the Baptist' and the narrative of the temptation show a Christological concern. From the point of view we have mentioned this might still be explained, since, after all, as stated by Harnack, these sections have been placed as an introduction at the head of material whose purpose differs from theirs.[1] But there are many other and earlier sections from Q which cannot be explained as having been preserved because of a concern for rules of behaviour. Some of these sections deal with Jesus' authority; for instance, the Beelzebul pericope, the sayings on the sign of Jonah, and the prophecy about Jerusalem, especially Matt. 23.39 and par., cf. Matt. 13.16f. and par.; Matt. 12.32 and par.; Matt. 11.19 and par. Other sections which cannot be understood as having an affinity with a need for exhortation are the Baptist's preaching of repentance in Matt. 3.7–10 and par.; the parts of the mission discourse in Matt. 10 which were received from Q; the woes on the Galilean cities in Matt. 11.20–24 and par.; the thanksgiving to the Father in Matt. 11.25ff. and par.; Matt. 8.11f. and par.; Matt. 11.12 and par.; the sayings against the Pharisees in Matt. 23 and par., etc.

[1] Cf. Harnack, *Sayings*, pp. 243f. To be sure, what is described in the narrative of the temptation is not specifically messianic. This narrative is not concerned with the problem of Jesus' messiahship in the narrower sense (cf. Bultmann, *Tradition*, on Matt. 4.1–11; Luke 4.1–12). But it does answer the question what is meant by saying that Jesus is the Son of God (cf. Schlatter, *Matt.*, pp. 95 and 11). So it must be understood Christologically in the wider sense because Jesus here appears—notwithstanding his being exposed to temptation like all men—uniquely as the Son of God who breaks the power of Satan in perfect faith and obedience.

It is quite possible that the material we have mentioned was secondarily seen by the community from the point of view of moral and ethical exhortation and used accordingly. In our present context, however, we wish to stress that the primary motive to preserve and collect this material appears not to have been a need of exhortation and to have been by no means dependent on the passion kerygma.

(2) *The Q material and the urge to continue to teach the teaching of Jesus*

The task before us is to render comprehensible the preservation of the individual passages of the Q material and their arrangement into larger sections. The concept of exhortation which looks to form-criticism does not suffice for this task. It appears from our enquiry, however, that there is an essential difference between the exhortatory material which complements the passion kerygma and that which is related to Jesus' teaching. The latter material, both in its form and in its concepts, is distinguished by this relation to Jesus' effective preaching concerning the coming of God's reign.

A momentous step towards an appropriate understanding of this Q material was taken by Bultmann. He realized that the primitive community gathered up Jesus' teaching and continued to teach it.[1] And, in fact, there are many passages the preservation and collection of which can easily be understood as being due to an urge to do this. Of course, this idea upsets the prevailing notion that the earliest and central message was the passion kerygma alone. Instead this idea assumes that there was a community which accepted as its central commission the communication of Jesus' teaching. Will it be possible to prove that such a community did exist?

We find encouragement for this assumption in the fact that large groups of sayings are transmitted in the Synoptic Gospels as discourses of Jesus. There was obviously an urge to transmit not only the message about Jesus Christ and the narratives about his suffering and activity in the manner of the passion kerygma but also the words of Jesus on earth as highly meaningful. The tendency to compose discourses of Jesus retrospectively can even be perceived in the Gospel of Mark (e.g. Mark 13); it appears fully in the Gospels of Matthew and Luke. It is evident that 'the long discourses composed by Matthew rest on a foundation in Q'.[2] In the Q material the narratives are completely outweighed by the sayings, the latter

[1] Bultmann, *Theology* I, p. 34.
[2] Cf. Harnack, *Sayings*, p. 180 n. 2.

apparently being understood by the community which transmitted them to be the link through which Jesus' teaching was continued. We distinguished the intention to link up in this manner in Matt. 19.28 and 10.23 also.

The material from Q allows us to discern even more distinctly the motives which brought it into being. The nature and meaning of the Q material is reflected in the mission discourse in Matthew and Luke. We wish to demonstrate now how their understanding differs from Mark's understanding.

It accords with the specific nature of the Gospel of Mark that the bestowal of *exousia* over unclean spirits is given an unbalanced preponderance in the account of Jesus' sending out the disciples in Mark 6.6–13. Likewise Mark in his revision of the Q saying on blaspheming against the Son of Man, or the Holy Spirit, understands Jesus' authority as effectual in the victory over demons.[1] Both Matthew and Luke when reproducing the Marcan text felt the need to balance out that preponderance. Matthew, still linking up with Mark, adds as a supplement to the *exousia* over the spirits the commission to heal diseases. Luke, however, corrects by stating, 'And he sent them out to preach the kingdom of God and to heal.'[2] Mark when omitting the commission to preach the kingdom of God did not do so inadvertently. In 6.12f. he describes the disciples' preaching as follows. 'They went out and preached that men should repent, and they cast out many demons and anointed with oil many that were sick and healed them.' The wording in Mark 3.14f. and in the other passages where the term 'to preach' is used supports our assumption.[3] According to Mark 13.10 the Gospel will be preached to all nations before the end. But Mark never speaks of the disciples preaching the kingdom of God.[4] His Gospel understands Christian preaching as concerned not with continuing to teach Jesus' teaching but with the gospel *of* Jesus Christ (Mark 1.1).

There is a different understanding in the pericopes containing the mission charge in Matthew and Luke. Both depend in part on material from Q. According to Matt. 10.7 = Luke 10.9 Jesus sends

---

[1] Cf. Chapter III A I b, pp. 119f., on Matt. 12.32 and par.
[2] Cf. on this Luke 9.2; 10.9; Matt. 10.7.
[3] Cf. Friedrich in *TWNT* III, p. 703.
[4] Cf. also the phrase 'for the sake of the kingdom of God', the original form of which probably is produced in Luke 18.29b (thus Bultmann, *Tradition*, pp. 110f.), which was altered by Mark to 'for my sake, and the gospel's'. Matthew says 'for my name's sake'. In addition compare Mark 8.35 with Luke 9.24 = Matt. 16.25.

out his disciples with the commission to preach that the kingdom of heaven is at hand, or that God's reign has come near to you.[1] Thus the disciples when preaching hand on the message brought by Jesus himself. A preaching concerning the kingdom of God is also spoken of in passages like Matt. 9.35; Luke 9.2; 8.1; Acts 20.25; 28.31. According to Matt. 24.14 the Gospel of the kingdom will be preached in all the world. In Luke 9.60 a man whom Jesus summons to follow him is charged to preach God's reign.[2] The wording in Matthew and Luke evinces the understanding that the commission of the disciple is to continue to teach Jesus' teaching. Mark's understanding is different. In his Gospel the passion event is presented as the real centre. All material, the sayings of Jesus included, are related to this centre. Sayings concerning the disciples' following are associated with the announcements of suffering, thus being removed from the context in which they had been transmitted in Q; no longer co-ordinated with material from Jesus' teaching, they are now subordinated to material about the passion. Discourses of Jesus are no longer presented as having a meaning by themselves. But the community which preserved the Q material for us, concentrating its attention almost exclusively on Jesus' teaching, was convinced that Jesus' pointing to the coming of God's reign had not lost its meaning in the post-Easter situation, but must be proclaimed anew. The group of the disciples was regarded as authorized to resume this teaching (Luke 10.16). The meaning of the hortatory sections, too, was not understood separately but in connexion with 'the most essential subject of our Lord's preaching, namely, that the kingdom of God is at hand'.[3] The nature of these sections is thus not determined by the passion but by the imminence of God's reign. And as late as in the Gospel of Matthew we can perceive that 'Matthew understands his rendering of the Sermon on the Mount as the transmission of nothing less than the general epitome of Jesus' preaching'.[4]

The post-Easter community, continuing to preach the message of the approach of God's kingdom, accordingly looked for the speedy coming of the Son of Man (Matt. 10.23). They founded this

[1] As shown by Kümmel, *Promise*, pp. 24f., this phrase is not intended to express that the kingdom of God has arrived, but means that it has approached.
[2] Cf. also Luke 9.62.
[3] Dibelius, *Botschaft* I, p. 98. On the difference between what is conceived by the term 'gospel' in Mark on the one hand and in the longer Gospels on the other hand cf. recently Marxsen, *Markus*, pp. 92ff.
[4] Dibelius, *ibid.*, p. 89.

expectation on Jesus' own teaching. The new prophetic sayings concerning the Son of Man's parousia which issued from the community were also linked up directly with Jesus' words (cf. Matt. 19.28 with Luke 12.8f. and par.).

(3) *The relationship of Jesus' passion and resurrection with the resumed proclamation of the teaching of Jesus*

The community which resumed Jesus' preaching concerning the coming of the kingdom must nevertheless have attributed a fundamental meaning to the events of the passion and resurrection. Without recognizing this foundation a community would not have been established at all. Considered thus it is even more conspicuous that it was not the passion and resurrection which had to be preached according to the understanding of this community. They wanted to go on preaching what Jesus had preached. But what had this to do with the passion and resurrection? As understood by this community, the passion and resurrection were not what had to be preached but what had enabled them to preach. The events of Jesus' being executed, laid under the curse of the cross and turned out of Israel could not fail to cast doubt upon the authority of his teaching. Was it possible that this man who was condemned by the lawful authorities of Israel and who was hanged had taught what would be valid before God? Might those who had followed him trust in the promise that their fellowship with him would be confirmed by the coming Son of Man? The Gospels describe the crisis to which the course of the passion events carried his followers' attachment to Jesus, and a definite conclusion is drawn: 'They all forsook him and fled' (Mark 14.50). In Luke, too, Peter, the representative of the disciples' company, does not hold on to his fellowship with Jesus but denies; nevertheless he is held by Jesus (Luke 22.54ff. and 22.31ff.). The logical consequence of Mark 8.38; Luke 12.8f.; Matt. 19.28 is that the promise is void and the threat is in force as soon as the disciples deny. With these sayings in mind, what happened after the resurrection must have been understood as the Lord's turning anew in love towards his own, as his resuming the fellowship with them. This aspect of the appearing of the risen one is emphasized several times by K. H. Rengstorf when examining John 20.1–18; John 21.15–23; Luke 24.13–53; John 21.1–14 in his enquiry about the kerygmatic meaning of Jesus' resurrection.[1] In the narrative John 20.1–18 'it

[1] Rengstorf, *Auferstehung*, pp. 51ff.

appears to be one of the points of special concern that it was Jesus who was founding anew the fellowship that had been interrupted by his death and burial, and that he was doing so in the same way in which before his death he had received men into his fellowship, namely by sacrificing himself'.[1] In the Emmaus narrative the risen one resumes the table-fellowship with two disciples. Peter, whose denial must be understood as being the typical one, is the first towards whom the Lord when he appears turns in love (I Cor. 15.5; Luke 24.34; cf. perhaps Luke 5.1ff. and John 21.1ff.). The gift of salvation with which these narratives of the resurrection are especially concerned is the renewed bestowal of that fellowship which Jesus bestowed on earth and which the Son of Man at his parousia will confirm. Seeing the resurrection thus, a community which was deeply sure of the resurrection nevertheless might follow its commission in another way than by primarily preaching passion and resurrection; for in their view the gift of salvation did not lie in these events, but had been validated by them. The fact that narratives of the resurrection occur at a relatively late stage in the history of the synoptic tradition may possibly be due to this early understanding of preaching.

Only after the redemptive significance of the death had been recognized and expounded could the passion kerygma have been presented and transmitted as the central concept. But this is the case neither in the material from Q nor in those kerygmatic formulae in the Acts which conform to the pattern: you have killed Jesus—yet God has raised him.[2] Acts 2.22ff. evinces that Jesus' authority was most trenchantly questioned by the Jews' killing him. 'Jesus of Nazareth, a man attested to you by God with mighty works and wonders and signs which God did through him in your midst, as you yourselves know—this Jesus, delivered according to the definite plan and foreknowledge of God, was caused by you to be affixed (to the cross), and slain by the hands of lawless men. But God raised him . . .' Dibelius points out that 'attested to you by God' in v. 22 is an archaic phrase.[3] It is expressed in this passage that the Jewish authorities had demonstrated by their way of acting their refusal to recognize Jesus' authorization,[4] and that this authorization was nevertheless

[1] *Ibid.*, p. 53.
[2] Cf. Acts 2.23f.; 3.15; 4.10f.; 5.30 *et passim*.
[3] Dibelius, *Acts*, p. 142; cf. Haenchen, *Apostelgeschichte*, pp. 147f.
[4] This refusal also is reflected in the controversial discourses, the point of controversy being Jesus' authorization. To vindicate Jesus' authority was a matter of

confirmed by God in the resurrection. The resurrection is God's affirmation of Jesus' *exousia*. Thereby the resurrection also is the confirmation before God of the fellowship bestowed by Jesus in his *exousia* on his own. Thus it is comprehensible why Jesus' teaching was taken up again and continued to be taught by the community; what Jesus had said had been confirmed by God. Thus it is comprehensible at the same time why he who had been teaching, who had effectually indicated the coming of the reign, was himself included in the teaching. His authorization had appeared in the resurrection. Since he himself had been affirmed by God, the fellowship bestowed by him on earth and taken up anew by his turning towards his disciples again as the risen one was also bound to be valid. The promise that the coming Son of Man will confess the confessors remained in force. But it had been Jesus himself as the risen one who had renewed the bestowal of his fellowship on his disciples. Therefore the one who will renew the fellowship in the kingdom of God, i.e. the Son of Man, can be none other than Jesus. The risen one's fellowship with the disciples can be nothing else than the fellowship which will be valid before God in eternity. Thus the continuity of the gift of salvation (the fellowship bestowed by Jesus on earth being recognized as the same as the fellowship renewed by the risen one and the future fellowship with the Son of Man) implied the identity of the giver, i.e. the identity of Jesus with the coming Son of Man.

At this point the renewed teaching of Jesus' message had to be differentiated from his authentic teaching. Christological cognition had occurred. In Jesus' own teaching no attention had been paid to Christology. Now that Christology had sprung up the material from Jesus' teaching could not be collected and formed without this cognition in mind. Its influence is indeed perceivable in the Q material. Most of the scholars hold this view, even if merely in the manner of Harnack's minimum definition that in the sayings in Q the messiahship is clearly expressed only by way of speaking of the parousia. We have seen, however, that in the Son of Man sayings from Q Jesus' *exousia* on earth was correlated with the future activity

---

life or death for the primitive community. If indeed Jesus went to Jerusalem in order to confront the city and the Jewish authorities with the necessity of declaring themselves for the coming reign of God, and if he was finally crucified by reason of the decision that this summons was unauthorized, then the central meaning of the resurrection might have well been understood as the authorization of Jesus' message and person by God.

of the Son of Man, and we have realized that the post-Easter community identified the coming Son of Man and Jesus. Thus Jesus' activity on earth had to be designated by the name Son of Man. Since Jesus was recognized as having the future task of acting as the Son of Man, he had to be recognized correspondingly as having *exousia* while acting on earth. After this recognition, the material from Jesus' teaching could not be rendered otherwise than in a manner imbued with Christological concern. Those who reproduce the material could not help emphasizing the full authority of the 'I' of Jesus.

We shall now turn our attention to the Q material in order to see whether our assumption of its being permeated by Christology will be supported. We have to remember that the early community to whom we owe the preservation of the Q material had no other intention than to collect what had been taught by Jesus in order to continue teaching it. They could not compile this material, however, without expressing in many ways their new post-Easter cognition of the *exousia* of the one who had been teaching and who would be coming as the Son of Man. With this assumption of a Christological permeation in view we shall examine the Q material in the following three sections. The first will deal with sayings concerning the disciples' attachment to Jesus and at the same time Jesus' full authority on earth (4); the next will deal with Jesus' full authority and the tension over against men in the sayings from Q (5); and the last will deal with references and allusions to Scripture in Q and their relationship to Jesus' sovereignty and humility (6).

(4) *The disciples' attachment to Jesus; the consequent understanding of the promises of the future and of Jesus' authority according to Q*

The course of our enquiry has led us to the question: How did that community which wanted to continue to teach the teaching of Jesus see the teacher, and how did it understand its attachment to him? We shall look in Q for traces of the post-Easter understanding of the teacher in view of God's affirmation of him through the resurrection and of the disciples' attachment to him.

Those who assume together with Bultmann that the early post-Easter community at first understood Jesus' significance for salvation merely in his future messiahship, his past activity on earth not having any significance for salvation since it was unmessianic, are compelled to make a curious separation between the person of the teacher and what had been taught by him.[1] Solely what Jesus will be in the future, namely the coming Son of Man, has an essential significance for faith; there is no such significance in what he was and did when he was teaching on earth. But does such a separation agree with the Q material?

The community was interested not only in the fact that the kingdom of God would come but also in participation in God's reign. According to the Son of Man sayings in Luke 12.8f.; Mark 8.38; Matt. 19.28, fellowship with Jesus on earth guarantees this participation. Hence already the one on earth who gave that fellowship which will be confirmed by the Son of Man is of fundamental significance for salvation. Jesus' activity on earth was bound to attract the maximum attention as soon as the community recognized that nobody but Jesus who had been teaching would be the coming Son of Man. This is the earliest and initial christological cognition which sprang up. It implied a specific way of understanding Jesus' activity on earth. Jesus who himself will come as the Son of Man will himself confirm the fellowship which on earth he had bestowed on those who followed him. So his summons to follow had already been an activity which had conclusive, eschatological, messianic validity. The community did not arrive at this understanding by the indirect way of first understanding themselves to be the eschatological community and then by analogy understanding Jesus' person and history. They rather arrived there by way of identifying the coming Son of Man and Jesus and recognizing what the correlation between the promise of salvation and the Son of Man meant for Jesus' activity. Those who follow have a share in salvation since Jesus has bestowed fellowship on them; the summons of the teacher is still effective when enunciated by the community (Luke 10.16). By its attachment to the teacher who is none other than the coming Son of Man, the community is the eschatological fellowship.

If there is a foundation for this assumption, the attachment to the teacher which we found expressed in the Son of Man sayings must have left traces elsewhere, too, in the Q material. For when the teacher had acted on earth in a way which opened the door to future salvation, and when the full authority of his word could go on in the community to effect this, then this had to be taken into con-

---

[1] We have already pointed out this tendency in Bultmann's view of the synoptic material when discussing Mark 8.38 in Chapter II A I c, pp. 43f. Compare on this Bultmann's argument in *Tradition*, p. 128; *Jesus*, pp. 215f.

sideration when handing on what he had taught. The Q material would have to convey the understanding that to enter into fellowship with Jesus also means to enter into the coming salvation. Can we find this expressed in Q ? Thus we ask whether and how there is expressed in Q not only the disciples' attachment to Jesus but also the Christological meaning of this attachment.

Luke 6.22f.; Matt. 5.11f. We have shown above[1] that these sayings were new formations by the post-Easter community.[2] They are affixed to the Beatitudes, the original form of which appears to have been preserved best by Luke. In the Beatitudes the plight of those with regard to whom the promises are made is denoted by the expressions poor, hungry, weeping. It is emphasized (in Luke) that those are blessed who hunger *now*. This 'now' stands in contrast to the 'to come' of God's reign.

It is a distinctive mark of the sayings newly formed by the community, Luke 6.22f. and Matt. 5.11f., that the 'now', i.e. the present situation of those who receive the promises, is defined more precisely. The tension over against men is brought out; men hate, revile and persecute. Whilst in the earlier Beatitudes (Luke 6.20f.) we read of what will be met with by everybody everywhere, namely poverty, hunger, tears, here in the later sayings the theme is what one who is attached to Jesus will meet with, and in fact will meet with for the sake of the Son of Man or, as Matthew says, 'for my sake'. This 'I' to whom 'for my sake' refers is the one who promised that whoever confesses him will be confessed by the Son of Man. It is evident that the name Son of Man in Luke 6.22 serves to emphasize the unique significance of the one for whose sake persecution will be experienced. It is exactly the attachment to him which includes the future promise. He who suffers for the sake of the Son of Man receives Jesus' promise of the reward (Matt. 19.27f.; 5.12).

Thus the Beatitudes which had been formed in a more general manner were permeated in the post-Easter situation by the more particular understanding of the attachment to Jesus. The promise of the reward in heaven was bound up with holding on to the fellowship with Jesus on earth and enduring the persecution which is the consequence of this attachment. This is a process which accords with the Son of Man Christology by reason of which, the identity of Jesus with the Son of Man being recognized, Jesus' activity on earth with

[1] Chapter III A I d, p. 123.
[2] Cf. Bultmann, *Tradition*, p. 110.

full authority can already be designated by the name Son of Man.

Matt. 7.21–23; Luke 6.46 and 13.26–27. In the form in which these sayings originally occurred in Q the relationship to the person of Jesus is strongly emphasized.[1] Jesus demands that what he says shall be done. The disciples who at the judgement appeal to the fact that they prophesied, cast out demons and did mighty works in his name (Matt. 7.22), or that they ate and drank in his presence and that he taught in their streets (Luke 13.26), will experience that no fellowship had been granted to them. The phrase 'I never knew you' expresses a trenchant excommunication, proclaiming an eternal separation.[2]

In Luke 13.26–27 we see the earlier form; here the saying is addressed to the Jews who refuse to repent, whilst Matthew applies it to the Christian community in accordance with his specific understanding of the judgement which is still ahead of the disciples in particular. In Luke, Jesus is addressed as the teacher. This is an earlier way of speaking than that in Matthew, where he who is addressed is understood to be the Judge of the world.[3] Matt. 25.31 proves that the evangelist considers the Son of Man to be the Judge of the world. But there is no synoptic text in which the name Son of Man is used for addressing the Judge.

In this passage the correlation between activity on earth and coming judgement is conceived as similar to that in the saying on confessing and denying in Luke 12.8f. The saying to the lip-disciples, however, must be heard as uttered not on earth but at the assize in heaven. In the Lucan version those who are standing before the Judge appeal to the fellowship which they had with him on earth, i.e. with Jesus. Thus the correlation here is established on that same identification of the Judge with Jesus which had sprung up from the post-Easter community's understanding of the Son of Man sayings. Before this Judge the relationship to him on earth implies the final decision. This is why appeal is made to the table-fellowship with him on earth and to the fact that he taught 'in our streets'. But the Judge will not grant any solidarity to those who did not act in accordance with his words. It is decisive, then, for recognition by the Judge whether or not there had been real fellowship with Jesus on earth. The identification, however, of Jesus on earth and the Judge to come takes place by reason of a post-Easter Christological cognition which

---

[1] Bultmann, *Tradition*, p. 116.
[2] Cf. Billerbeck I, p. 469.
[3] Cf. Matt. 25.31 with 24.42 and 24.44; Matt. 25.11, 37, 44.

emphasizes in particular what Jesus' activity on earth means for salvation.

Matt. 8.5–13; Luke 7.1–10. In this section, the narrative nature of which is uncommon in Q, the point at which the Christological exaltation of Jesus begins is evident. The Gentile centurion's faith is exceptional inasmuch as this man unconditionally trusts Jesus' word to be effectual, having recognized that Jesus is authorized to speak with full authority. As a centurion he is aware of the fact that the authority with which he is vested flows from the authority to which he subordinates himself. He clarifies by the example of his own experience that Jesus' authority is unassailable. This comparison suggests the understanding of Jesus' authority as being derived from God (cf. Luke 10.16 and par.; Matt. 11.27 and par.). The point at which Christological cognition springs up is authority. This accords with the sayings in Q and in the controversial discourses in Mark in 2.10 and 2.28 concerning the Son of Man's activity on earth.

Matt. 11.6; Luke 7.23. In the text preceding this saying Jesus' mighty works are pointed to as being self-evident signs of the coming reign. Yet the faith which is demanded is not an impersonal belief in miracles but a decision with regard to the person of Jesus. Salvation will be bestowed only on the man who takes no offence at Jesus; this means at the same time that one who refuses to believe in Jesus becomes a sinner.[1]

Matt. 8.19–22; Luke 9.57–60 (cf. Chapter III). Just as according to Luke 6.22 and par. whoever receives the promise must endure persecution from men, so according to this passage whoever follows must endure being without a home.

Matt. 10.16; Luke 10.3. It is stated here that attachment to Jesus means being authorized for a mission. He who sends and he who is sent are intimately related through this authorization.[2] The disciples are sent forth in a hostile world. They enter into the tension which exists between the Master and men. Bultmann considers this saying to be one of the 'I' sayings produced in the primitive Palestinian community. Its *Sitz im Leben* is the mission of the early community.[3]

Luke 10.16; cf. Matt. 10.40. This is another 'I' saying from the mission of the primitive community.[4] T. W. Manson has

---

[1] Cf. Arndt and Gingrich, *Lexicon*, p. 735.
[2] Rengstorf in *TWNT* I, pp. 397ff.
[3] Bultmann, *Tradition*, p. 163.
[4] *Loc. cit.*

demonstrated that probably Luke 10.16; Matt. 10.40 and Mark 9.37 refer to an identical saying which originally had been formulated in Aramaic language, the differing terms 'to hear' and 'to receive' being merely variant translations of an identical term underlying both of them. He interprets the saying as follows. 'The messengers are, in a sense, the kingdom of God itself. The solidarity is impressive. The disciple represents in the fullest sense Jesus, and Jesus represents in the fullest sense the kingdom of God. What they offer is God's offer and what they claim is God's claim. Cf. Mark 8.38, where the true text is probably "me and mine", i.e. "me and my disciples", rather than "me and my words"; and Matt. 25.31–46.'[1] This saying means much to the communal interpretation of the Son of Man. The disciples can represent Jesus in the fullest sense because they together with him are a *corpus*, the Son of Man, 'embodiment of the Remnant idea',[2] 'the organ of God's redemptive purpose in the world'.[3]

By means of this interpretation Manson can easily show the extent to which the disciples are able to represent Jesus in reality. Presupposing the concept of membership in a *corpus*, the concept of real representation is perfectly intelligible. But we do not see any synoptic saying by which the Son of Man is conceived in such a corporate manner, joined together with his members as one body.[4] In Luke 10.16 and par. it is indeed stated unequivocally that Jesus as the one who sends the disciples declares his solidarity with them; and they as those who are sent forth indeed appear to be addressed not separately as individuals but as a group. Beyond that, the saying expresses how Jesus hands on some of his authority to his disciples. Jesus' *exousia* rests on his intimate relationship with the one who sent him, and it passes over to the word uttered by the disciples. There is nothing in the text to suggest the understanding that the word thus uttered is but weak (cf. 8.5–13 and par.).

Matt. 11.25–27; Luke 10.21f. In this saying of Jesus from Q words of the risen one are spoken. This is evident from Matt. 11.27a and

[1] Manson, *Sayings*, p. 78.
[2] Manson, *Teaching*, p. 227.
[3] *Ibid.*, p. 231.
[4] As the way by which the joining is achieved Manson points out mainly the passion of the Son of Man and the disciples' following through suffering according to the arrangement of the Son of Man sayings in the composition of the Gospel of Mark. We have to object here because the sayings to the disciples were affixed to the passion kerygma only secondarily in the history of the synoptic tradition. They originally pertained to the Q material in which the passion is not mentioned at all. Cf. also Manson, *Teaching*, p. 231.

par. (cf. Matt. 28.18). The saying is intent on expressing that Jesus as the Son of the Father has no equals and is the sole mediator for those towards whom he turns to show the revelation. Here, too, as in Luke 10.16 and par., the Son involves his own in his relationship with the Father. The Son alone has direct access to the Father, and he mediates the access to his own. Jesus' authority is expressed in almost Johannine terms. The Son is the sole revealer to whom all things have been committed. Yet this saying is not absolutely alien to Q, as may be seen from the association with Luke 10.16 and par. In Matt. 11.25–27, however, to be heard as words of the risen one, the immediacy and uniqueness of the intimate relationship with the Father are expressed in an intensified manner. The Son has unique insight into the Father's plan for salvation, and utters the joyful Yea to the divine plan as the one who is intimately related to the Father. The Son knows the Father, i.e. he is related to him through election and love. According to Luke 10.16 there is an intimate relationship by reason of the mission. According to Matt. 11.25–27 this relationship is rather inherent in the Son. Christology begins with an exaltation of the revealer's person.

Luke 12.8f. and par. We discussed this Son of Man saying above in Chapter II. The primitive community appears to have understood it as implying the identification of Jesus with the coming Son of Man. This saying initiated our present consideration whether the community's understanding of what had been promised for the future was expressly associated with what could be looked back to, namely the fellowship into which Jesus on earth had summoned his own.

Luke 14.26f.; Matt. 10.37, 38. This saying illuminates the consequences arising on earth from attachment to Jesus. Jesus' claim is absolute and cannot be trammelled by natural ties.

Matt. 10.39; Luke 17.33 (Mark 8.35). That life on earth to which a man would like to cling and that true real life which the disciple will find by following Jesus are here contrasted as opposite poles. In view of the eschatological nature of Jesus' preaching and of the promise of the reward in heaven, it cannot be maintained that the true life is conceived of as merely pertaining to this world. The gain of the true life is in Luke 17.33 associated with the Son of Man's parousia, as is evident from the context Luke 17.22–37. Matt. 10.39 speaks of losing one's life 'for my sake'. These are words of an 'I' who lays the highest claims.

In order to see the way in which the disciples' attachment to Jesus was understood, we have examined so far some of the sayings from Q . We need not aim at completeness here. The sayings we have cited indicate that in the Q material the person of Jesus is distinctly in view. It must be emphasized that Jesus is in view primarily as teacher. The word of Jesus summons men to follow him; by and with the word of Jesus the disciples are sent forth; their word is recognized by Jesus to be his own. But we have found no indication that Q at the earliest stage within the history of its tradition had been concerned with Jesus' words without being concerned with Jesus himself.[1]

Wherever in the passages which we have examined attachment to Jesus was spoken of there was always mention of Jesus' acting with full authority, but never of suffering as it is regarded in the passion kerygma. This is due both to the history of tradition and to the concepts present here. Where Jesus' authority is concerned the predominant concept is the disciples' being summoned into an attachment through following which bears the promise that they will be involved in God's reign to come. Following takes place in view of the imminence of God's reign.

We will now turn to a saying which goes farther than the passages hitherto discussed in illuminating Jesus' full authority. *Luke 11.20*; *Matt. 12.28*: 'But if by the finger of God I cast out demons, then the kingdom of God is come upon you.' This saying occurs in Q in a section in which Jesus refutes the reproof that he would cast out demons with the help of the chief demon.[2] How are we to understand the statements that God's reign is already come upon the hearers of those words?

'The reign of God is an eschatological concept. It signifies the régime of God which will mean the end of the present course of the world.'[3] As we understand this saying, however, we do not find anything in it about the end of the present course of the world. The reign of God is come upon a specific group of people, namely upon those who hear Jesus' words and amongst whom he has cast out the demons. This restriction to a limited group contradicts the traditional concept of the kingdom of God. Does it also contradict Jesus' own teaching in which the Son of Man's parousia is conceived of as coming upon the

[1] Cf. Bultmann, *Tradition*, p. 128.
[2] Cf. Harnack, *Sayings*, p. 136.
[3] Bultmann, *Theology* I, p. 4.

world as a whole?[1] Must we consequently allow for two different concepts of God's reign in the words of Jesus?

Dibelius perceived this difficulty. 'Jesus never specifically re-interpreted the expression "Kingdom of God". He never said any-thing like "You have heard that it was said to them of old time: the kingdom of God will come; but I say unto you: the kingdom of God is here already". He spoke of the coming of the kingdom for which one should pray. . . . The point is not that one can disseminate the Kingdom; not one of Jesus' hearers could have entertained this utterly impious thought. The reference embodied in this picture (of the sower) is not open to doubt: it is the preaching of Jesus (and of his disciples) about the Kingdom of God.'[2] The discord between the one concept of God's reign as an absolute conclusion of the course of this world to be expected in the near future and the other concept of God's reign to be already come upon those hearers is harmonized by Dibelius as follows. 'The Kingdom has not yet appeared, but signs are visible.'[3] Until the dawn of the kingdom of God 'it lives only in the preaching and in the movement of the people affected by the preaching'.[4]

Bultmann, too, apparently perceived a similar discord. He main-tains, referring to Luke 11.20 and par., that Jesus 'sees God's reign already breaking in in the fact that by the divine power that fills him he is already beginning to drive out the demons, to whom he, like his contemporaries, attributes many diseases'.[5] Jesus has 'obviously himself understood his miracles as a sign of the imminence of the Kingdom of God'.[6] Bultmann's comments suggest that Jesus' state-ments about the breaking in of the kingdom already at present have to be imputed to his sensing an eschatological power.

The supposition that the presence of the kingdom of God is to be understood as the presence of signs deprives the statement in Luke 11.20 and par. of some of its directness. Kümmel justly objects to this procedure. His solution of the problem is that Jesus in the state-ment in Matt. 12.28 = Luke 11.20 consciously throws overboard the eschatological teaching of the Jews.[7] Contrary to this teaching, in

[1] Cf., e.g., Matt. 24.27 and par.
[2] Dibelius, *Jesus*, pp. 61f.
[3] *Ibid.*, p. 63.
[4] *Loc. cit.*
[5] Bultmann, *Theology* I, p. 7.
[6] Bultmann, *Jesus*, p. 173.
[7] Kümmel, *Promise*, p. 108 n. 10.

Matt. 12.28 'Jesus' conviction shows itself clearly that the future Kingdom of God had already begun in his activity. It follows that the proclamation of the proximity of the Kingdom of God clearly derives its *special* meaning in Jesus' mouth through this unusual proclamation of the presence of the future eschatological consummation; and it follows likewise that it is the person of Jesus whose activities provoke the presence of the eschatological consummation and who therefore stands at the centre of his eschatological message.'[1]

With this exegesis Kümmel indeed keeps more strictly to the wording of such passages as Luke 11.20 and par. and Luke 17.20f. But may we indeed say that Jesus consciously throws overboard the eschatological teaching of the Jews? There cannot be a doubt, after all, that Jesus did not destroy the concept of the coming universal reign of God which means the end of the world as a whole. How, then, do we have to conceive of the presence of God's reign when the conclusive reign of God is certainly not present yet, but is to be expected at the Son of Man's parousia?

In our view it is a questionable concept to which R. Otto has recourse when he assumes that Jesus conceived the coming *eschaton* as being effective already at present and coins the term 'dynamic post-existence'. According to this concept the energy of the kingdom of God would have to be regarded as the true *agens* whilst Jesus would have to recede, so to speak, into the metaphysical background of this kingdom which causes him to appear as its forerunner and announcer.[2] But in the synoptic texts the kingdom is not spoken of in a manner like a metaphysical potential. The energy of the coming kingdom does not enter into reality by way of Jesus, but Jesus summons the disciples to follow him and in this way, by making them do God's will, places them in that fellowship which will be valid in the kingdom of God.

So we cannot assent to the concept of the energy of the kingdom operating in anticipation and taking shape in reality as signs which as such now stand for an anticipated presence of God's reign. But how is it comprehensible that Jesus, whilst holding on to the traditional expectation of the cosmic irruption of the kingdom of God, can say that in his activity God's reign is already come upon his hearers?

As we see it, the way of speaking here is parallel to that in the Son of Man sayings from Q. When the coming Son of Man is mentioned

[1] *Op. cit.*, pp. 107f.
[2] Cf. Otto, *Kingdom*, pp. 195f. and 103f.

the reference is invariably to that transcendent universal figure of the Perfecter who is unrestricted by anything which exists on earth. Yet he is divested of the specific traits attributed to him in Jewish apocalyptic literature. Moreover, he is correlated with Jesus' activity on earth; the fellowship bestowed on earth by Jesus will be confirmed by the Son of Man. The future of the Son of Man is thus already firmly anchored in the presence of Jesus. Accordingly the future reign of God is already present in Jesus' victory over the demons in such a way as to come to a particular group of people (Luke 11.20).

As Kümmel sees the problem of the presence of God's reign, 'there remains only the interpretation that the Kingdom of God has already become effective in advance in Jesus and in the present events appearing in connexion with his person'.[1] But effective in what manner? It can hardly be enough to point to the negative effect, namely the overthrow of the demons; this is merely preparatory for something else. The reign of God embraces the affirmative gift as well. Which gift of salvation is present here and now? An answer may be found in the Son of Man sayings. God's reign is already present in the midst of men in the fellowship bestowed by Jesus on earth; for this fellowship does not pass away with this generation, but will be confirmed and guaranteed before God by the Son of Man.

We find a parallel way of speaking also in Matt. 13.38. In this passage those who are sown by the Son of Man are called sons of the *basileia*. The sphere in which they live without yet being separated from the sons of the evil one is the *basileia* of the Son of Man (13.41). Already on earth, already amidst the sons of the evil one, that *basileia* of the Son of Man is present and yet merely as a provisional entity; for admission into the *basileia* of the Father lies still ahead of the sons of the *basileia*.[2]

If we now interpret Luke 11.20 in this sense, that act of casting out the demons is an act which sets men free to follow Jesus. They are detached from what holds them back and are attached to Jesus; in

---

[1] Kümmel, *Promise*, p. 35.

[2] It is evident that here in Matthew the Church occupies exactly that position which we pointed out as occupied by the fellowship already bestowed by Jesus on earth. Matthew indeed emphasizes the Church's being a *corpus permixtum*; but also according to Matthew the sons of the *basileia* are actually in this Church. As to the fellowship with Jesus, we have mentioned in our discussion of Luke 13.26f. that it will not suffice to appeal at the judgement to the fact that there was such a fellowship on earth inasmuch as this fellowship was not a real one; so here as well the concept of separation is latently present. Cf. Matt. 7.21–23.

fellowship with him the reign of God has already reached men. This interpretation accords with the words which in Q came after those in Luke 11.20, namely, 'He who is not with me is against me, and he who does not gather with me scatters.'[1] When we compare Luke 11.20 with the Q sayings which we have discussed on the immediately preceding pages, they appear to have in common the underlying faith that to be attached to Jesus means to be involved in the salvation to come. But furthermore there appears in Luke 11.20 a complementary aspect of Jesus' acting with full authority. Whilst according to Matt. 11.19 and par. Jesus has the authority to bestow his fellowship on tax collectors and sinners and according to Matt. 11.5 and par. that to heal; what he has according to Luke 11.20 is the authority to cast out demons and thereby set his own free so that already on earth they may participate in God's reign. The exorcism of demons which plays so prominent a role in the Gospel of Mark thus also occurs in Q.

The passages discussed in this section evince that belonging to Jesus was understood to be of vital consequence. They corroborate our assumption that a Christological tendency was active in the Q material. Access to Jesus is understood to be access to the coming salvation, and Jesus is recognized to be the one who, bestowing fellowship while acting on earth, will guarantee this fellowship as the coming Son of Man before God.

We should indeed go astray if we assumed that Jesus' activity on earth was understood here in Q as having a messianic meaning in the narrower sense. In the narratives about the baptism and temptation Jesus is seen as the Son of God; but Harnack is right in insisting that the Q material must be interpreted independently of this prefixed introduction.[2] We have realized, however, that elsewhere in Q besides the introduction the earthly Jesus is seen in a prominent position. Thus a Christological exaltation begins the traces of which we have noticed again and again. The only Christological title which occurs in this connexion is the name Son of Man. Sayings are preserved in which Jesus promises that belonging to him on earth will be confirmed by the Son of Man to come; but we also find sayings in which Jesus' authority on earth is emphasized by means of the designation Son of Man. The understanding in Q no doubt is that

[1] Cf. Harnack, *Sayings*, p. 136; Klostermann, *Matt.*, p. 109; Billerbeck I, pp. 635f.
[2] Cf. Harnack, *Sayings*, pp. 243f.

Jesus and the coming Son of Man are identical. This identification which had been accepted may be called a Son of Man Christology. The manner in which the substance of Jesus' teaching was preserved, re-formulated and supplemented is distinctly influenced by this Christology. Here we only note the following two points at which this influence may be observed.

Firstly, in the arrangement of Q, sayings of the risen one interchange with sayings of the one on earth. The transitions are so smooth that we cannot help getting the impression that it did not even occur to the members of the community which collected the sayings of Jesus in Q to distinguish between pre-Easter and post-Easter sayings, it being self-evident to them that the earthly and the risen Jesus are one and the same. In Matt. 11.27 it is obviously the risen one who is speaking. In Matt. 10.16 we can hardly expect an answer to the question whether the one who sends forth is the earthly or the risen one, since it would not have made any difference to the understanding of the community. In Matt. 7.22 and Luke 10.16 the one on earth is speaking, although these sayings apparently were newly formed in the post-Easter situation; what he says, however, applies both to the situation before and to the situation after Easter.

Secondly, it is striking how often in Q Jesus appears as the teacher who acts effectively by means of his word. We have concluded from this that the community collected the Q material because they realized the urge to continue to teach what Jesus had been teaching. In Luke 6.46; Matt. 7.24ff.; Luke 10.16 the theme is explicitly Jesus' word. In Matt. 10.16 (cf. 10.7) and Matt. 7.22[1] (cf. Luke 10.16) it is presupposed that Jesus sends forth his own in order to teach. In Matt. 8.8 and par. the unconditional effectiveness of the word of Jesus is implied. The efficacy of his teaching is handed on to his disciples, as stated in Matt. 10.7f., cf. Luke 10.9; Matt. 7.22. The word as conceived here is far from being insignificant and weak.

(5) *Jesus' authority and the tension over against men in the sayings from Q*

In the course of our investigation we have stated several times that in all three groups of Son of Man sayings Jesus as the one who has full authority stands in a deep-rooted tension over against men as the adulterous and sinful generation. Jesus' *exousia* is from God. The sharpness of this tension may urge a man who holds on to Jesus to be

---

[1] Cf. Klostermann, *Matt.*, p. 70.

ashamed of the Master and of his word, to deny before men the fellowship with him. The same tension which is prevailing in the Son of Man sayings also pervades Q. It has a different structure from that antagonism which appears in the passion kerygma. According to the account of his suffering, Jesus fulfils the will of God by willingly accepting betrayal and death. He overcomes men's enmity by allowing them to reach the end they had aimed at. In Q, however, the tension over against men appears merely as having been aroused by Jesus' authority. This is evident from sayings like the following examples: Luke 6.22 speaks about men's hatred against the disciples for the sake of the Son of Man, Matt. 11.16ff. about reproaches made by this generation to the Son of Man. Luke 11.29f. speaks of this evil generation who in the face of Jesus' message demand a sign, but to whom only the coming Son of Man in his parousia will be a sign. In Luke 11.31f. we hear of the condemnation of this generation at the judgement because they have not listened, have not turned round in repentance to face Jesus' message, although in Jesus something greater than Jonah and Solomon is here. In Luke 11.50, presumably also from Q, Wisdom speaks of this generation having shed the blood of all the prophets; no doubt the community understood this saying as an accusation against that generation which kills Jesus and so proves itself guilty of murdering all the prophets there are; consequently they can expect nothing else than to be visited with affliction. Luke 12.8f. speaks of confessing and denying before men.

So in these sayings the one who is rejected is seen not as the redeemer who gives his blood for many but as the authoritative teacher who by means of his word summons men to follow him. This generation proves guilty by contradicting Jesus' fully authorized way of acting. They repudiate his message and its claim. Thus the tension here does not arise amongst men because of the difference of what will come upon them in the future (cf. Luke 6.21; 16.25). The attention is not primarily directed to the tension between the present and the future situation, but is entirely directed to Jesus' presence. His acting with full authority confronts men with the necessity to decide here and now. The future is determined by the effect of his presence.

(6) *References and allusions to Scripture in Q and their relationship to Jesus' sovereignty and humility*

The references to Scripture which prominently occur in the tradition concerning the passion are intended to show that Jesus' suffering and dying had happened according to the will of God. In the allusions to Scripture in Q the intention is different. The following brief survey will not take into consideration the pericopes up to and including the narrative of the temptation, because they hardly belonged to the early main stock of Q. The passages to be considered here, in which allusions to Scripture can be perceived, may be grouped as follows.

(a) There is a conspicuous group of passages in which allusions to Scripture occur in connexion with sayings against this generation, or Israel. The following distinction is suggested by this group.

(*a*) In three passages reference is made to Scripture in order to characterize the behaviour of that generation upon whom the Son of Man's parousia will come as affliction. These are Luke 17.26f. and par.; Luke 17.28; Luke 11.29–31 (several times). In Luke 11.50f. the behaviour of this generation is characterized by means of reproaching them for murdering the prophets.

(*b*) Luke 11.42 and par. refer to Micah 6.8 in connexion with the behaviour of the Pharisees on whom Jesus calls down woe. In Luke 10.15 and par. the depth of the fall from salvation due to Capernaum's impenitence at Jesus' coming is indicated by a reference to Isa. 14.13ff. In Luke 13.27 and par.; Luke 13.29 announcements of judgement are accompanied by scriptural allusions; they are used in 13.27 for the condemnatory address, in 13.29 to express the Gentiles' access to salvation.

(b) There is another group of passages in which Scripture is referred to in order to indicate the fact or the scope of the present fulfilment of prophecies concerning salvation. In Luke 7.27 and par. Jesus testifies that the Baptist is the forerunner to be expected according to Mal. 1. In Luke 7.22 and par. Jesus' cures, his raising of the dead, his preaching the gospel to the poor are recognized as fulfilment of prophecies in Isaiah.

(c) There are two passages with references to Scripture concerning those events in the history of salvation which in the presence of Jesus are seen in the future. In Luke 13.35 and par. threat and promise are pronounced on Jerusalem; a reference to Ps. 118.26 points to the parousia, Jesus' advent is conceived of as an event which means salvation. In Luke 13.19 and par. the greatness of the coming reign of God is illustrated by referring to the tree in Dan. 4.18ff.

(d) In Luke 12.53 and par. the sharpness with which Jesus' activity here on earth separates those most intimately attached to each other is illustrated by reference to the dissension prophesied in Micah 7.6.

When we arrange the above-mentioned allusions and references to Scripture by their chronological orientation, two groups may be distinguished. In the first the reference to the *future* salvation or loss of salvation, its advent or its nature is made. The sayings of this group are Luke 10.15 and par.; Luke 13.27 and 13.29 and par.; Luke 13.19 and par. as well as Luke 13.35 and par. In the second group which is formed by the other sayings the reference is to the *presence* of Jesus. The majority amongst these sayings are those which we have grouped above as characterizing the tension aroused by Jesus' appearing, his claim, his authority, his announcement of men's fall from salvation with regard to this generation, the Pharisees, the Galilean cities and Jerusalem. Two additional sayings adduce scriptural evidence for the positive fulfilment of prophecies concerning salvation in the presence of Jesus.

Our conclusion is self-evident: No evidence from Scripture is adduced here directed to Jesus' humility or suffering. In Q Jesus' authority, his teaching and his being rejected by those who do not acknowledge this authority is in view. Q does not speak of the *Christus humilis*.

This conclusion corroborates anew our hypothesis that there are two spheres of tradition, distinguished both by their concepts and by their history. The centre of the one sphere is the passion kerygma; the centre of the other sphere is the intention to take up again the teaching of what Jesus had taught. The Q material belongs to the second sphere. This material was preserved, collected and arranged by reason of the urge to hand on that message which had been validated by the resurrection. Jesus' full authority was expressed in this intention. The community had been assured that the promises of Jesus were not void, after all; this assurance was expressed in the hope that Jesus, who with full authority had bestowed fellowship on earth, is also the coming Son of Man who thus will guarantee and fulfil his promise. Hence the allusions to Scripture in Q which we mentioned refer in a direct or indirect way to the word of Jesus which authoritatively demands decision, which points to salvation or judgement and correlates them with the present.

In our enquiry into the Q material we met with the same motifs which we found in the Son of Man sayings.[1] We found ourselves within the same self-contained sphere of concepts in which the Christological significance of Jesus in view of his sovereignty as the coming Son of Man and of his acting on earth with full authority was dominant. The concepts of the passion kerygma remained outside this sphere. Thus the Q material proved to be an independent source of Christological cognition. From it a Christology has flowed that is clearly distinguished by the name Son of Man as used both for the coming Lord and for the Lord acting on earth. Son of Man Christology and Q belong together both in their concepts and in their history of tradition.

D. THE RECEPTION AND DEVELOPMENT OF THE SAYINGS CONCERNING THE COMING SON OF MAN AND THE SON OF MAN ACTING ON EARTH WITHIN THE Q STRATUM OF TRADITION

(1) *The relation of Matthew and Luke to the arrangement of Q*

We have not yet defined sufficiently the position of the Son of Man sayings within Q.[2] The Q material, even before Matthew and Luke used it, had been arranged thematically.[3] Both evangelists obviously saw a meaning in this arrangement—otherwise they would not have conformed to it in the main.

The changes in the arrangement of the Q material which Matthew made are to a considerable extent comprehensible as consequences of his intention to compose coherent discourses. Following this intention, however, he was nevertheless led by Q. For in Q the foundation had been provided for the Sermon on the Mount, the mission discourse, Jesus' response to the Baptist's enquiry (together with the connected material, namely the woes against the Galilean cities and the prayer of thanksgiving), the Beelzebul discourse (together with the declaration against the demand for signs), the discourse concerning the Pharisees and the discourse consisting of eschatological parables.[4] Matthew combined the parousia sayings from Q with Jesus' discourse according to Mark 13, whilst Luke did

---

[1] More precisely speaking, we met with the motifs from the group of sayings concerning the coming and the Son of Man acting in the present, but not with concepts which pertain to or distinguish the group of sayings concerning the Son of Man who is delivered up.

[2] In Chapter II B we took the arrangement of Q into consideration only in so far as it was necessary for the analysis of the sayings.

[3] Cf. T. W. Manson's conclusion, *Sayings*, p. 16.

[4] Cf. Harnack, *Sayings*, p. 180 n. 2.

not combine them. Luke rendered the Q discourse concerning the parousia at the end of the travel narrative and thus prior to the Marcan material concerning the Judean period. We can see that Luke after reproducing Mark's chapter 13 adds on the parousia discourse from Q. In Q the parousia discourse contains sayings concerning the Son of Man, and accordingly the apocalyptic discourse in Luke's rendering ends by pointing to the Son of Man and his judging (cf. Matt. 25.31).

(2) *The sayings in Q concerning the coming Son of Man*

The eschatological nature of Jesus' teaching has been preserved by Q more markedly than by any other compilation of material within the synoptic tradition. Except for the Baptist's preaching and the temptation, Q begins with the Beatitudes. They were understood by those who collected them as Jesus' promise of salvation for his own; this is evident from Luke 6.22f.; Matt. 5.11f. The promise of participation in the coming kingdom of God which occurs at the beginning of Q corresponds with the focus on the figure of the Son of Man which dominates the group of parousia sayings at the end of Q. Here the expectation of the coming reign of God becomes concrete, this expected reign having been correlated with the person of Jesus and comprehended in his coming. 'The myth has been transferred to a concrete historical person, and the consequence will be that trust will have been immeasurably strengthened.'[1]

The community continued to teach by means of the sayings concerning the coming Son of Man what had been taught by Jesus himself. But they discovered that in these sayings Jesus had spoken of his own parousia. Accordingly they now, with regard to the concept expressed in them, arranged the eschatological sayings in a group. In this group all the sayings concerning the coming Son of Man occur with the exception of Luke 12.8f. and par. and Luke 11.30 and par. (as well as Matt. 19.28; 10.23—so far as these sayings were in some form or other found in Q).

In the saying concerning the promise and threat for the confessors this state of affairs is quite intelligible. In the Gospel of Matthew this saying occurs in the group about fearless speaking; it is thus found next to the mission discourse, which to a large extent is composed of Q material.[2] Harnack has demonstrated that Matthew in his chapter 10

---

[1] Bultmann, *Theology* I, p. 34.
[2] Matt. 10.7, 8a and 10a; 10.11–15; cf. 10.16, 19, 24.

has preserved the original arrangement of the Q material better than Luke.[1] It may be concluded from this that in Q the saying on confessing was already located next to the sayings about sending forth and fearless speaking. The concept expressed in this saying then belonged here. This may also be concluded from the nature of this saying. Pointing to the parousia is not its primary intent. It speaks of confession on earth and the future confirmation of this by the Son of Man.[2]

The other saying concerning the coming Son of Man which in Q occurs outside the group of parousia sayings (Luke 11.30) is found in the declaration against the demand for signs which already in Q followed the Beelzebul pericope.[3] Here, too, attention is not primarily directed to the parousia, even though it is mentioned. The attention is rather directed toward the threat against this evil generation. This generation demands a sign regardless of Jesus' presence. Thus it comes to light that the men of this generation are evil and obdurate. Jesus declares that the sign which they seek will not be given to them where they look for it and that thence they will have nothing else to look forward to but the devastating coming of the Son of Man.

We see from this that also the sayings concerning the Son of Man were not put together indiscriminatingly in Q. On the contrary, the manner in which they are co-ordinated with the material grouped thematically shows that there was a planning and a discriminating understanding of differences. The Son of Man sayings were assigned a significant place in the arrangement of Q as a whole. Matthew and Luke have to a large extent respected this grouping.

(3) *The sayings in Q concerning the Son of Man acting at present*

In Luke 6.22 the name Son of Man is mentioned for the first time in order to emphasize the significance of Jesus on earth. If the name Son of Man did originally occur in Q at this place, then the Beatitudes had already been given a new interpretation. As uttered by Jesus, they had been meant to correlate what is now and what is

[1] Cf. Harnack, *Sayings*, p. 180.

[2] This also makes intelligible the omission of the name Son of Man in Matt. 10.32f. For Matthew, the concept of the Son of Man is distinguished by the features of the parousia and the judgement of the world; neither of them is mentioned directly in the saying reproduced in Matt. 10.32f. Shortly before these verses, namely in Matt. 10.23, the name Son of Man is used while pointing to the parousia. Matthew avoids the repetition of this name by omitting it in a passage where in his view the setting is not appropriate.

[3] Harnack, *Sayings*, pp. 137, 179.

to come. By the insertion the name Son of Man the present situation of those who receive the promise was interpreted anew. Now the promise of salvation was understood as given to him who suffers for Jesus' sake. Thus here, at the end of the introductory passage of the Sermon on the Mount or on the Plain as it occurred in Q, Jesus' authority, emphasized by the designation Son of Man, was made the key to the understanding of Jesus' own teaching. In a similar manner Jesus' *exousia* is expounded in the pericopes which follow the material of the Sermon on the Mount, namely in the narrative of the centurion of Capernaum and in the sections concerning the Baptist's enquiry and Jesus' testimony to him. In these as well the name Son of Man appears at the end (Luke 7.34 and par.).

In Q these sections were apparently followed by a group of sayings to the disciples (Luke 9.57–62; 10.1–24 in part; 11.1–13 in part). They are headed by the saying which is meant to open the eyes of a man making up his mind to follow Jesus to the fact that the Son of Man has no home (Luke 9.58 and par.). Next within this group is the material of the mission discourse and of the teaching on prayer, and after this come sayings concerning the controversy with the Pharisees, culminating in the saying that blasphemy against the Son of Man is forgivable whereas blasphemy against the Holy Spirit is not. Matthew gives this saying in its original place (12.32).[1]

Considering the respective positions of the sayings concerning the coming Son of Man and of those concerning the present Son of Man within Q, we have to assume that in several sections they stood in close proximity to each other. If Matt. 10.23 did occur in Q,[2] then it clearly came very soon after the saying concerning the Son of Man's homelessness in Matt. 8.20 and par. (cf. the proximity of Luke 9.58 to the mission discourse). The sections in Q with material about Jesus' controversy with his opponents which begins in Luke 11.14 (cf. Matt. 12.22) contained the saying about the blasphemy against the present Son of Man, in Matt. 12.32, but also sayings

[1] Luke transferred this saying, the original meaning of which seems to have been obscure to him, to Luke 12.10, immediately after the saying on confessing. Thereby he placed the two ways of using the name Son of Man (both for the parousia and for the activity on earth) directly side by side. Was this a procedure parallel to Luke 17.24–26 where a saying about the passion appears to have been interpolated into the sequence of parousia sayings with conscious intention? Or did the catch-word Son of Man prevail on Luke to link up the sayings regardless of the difference in the concepts?

[2] Did Luke perhaps omit this saying because the fulfilment of it could not be seen?

about the coming of the Son of Man, in Luke 11.30 and par.; Luke 12.8f. and par. The juxtaposition of Son of Man sayings from both groups in several sections of material in Q makes unavoidable the question which we have endeavoured to answer already above, namely, how is it comprehensible that *in the same stratum of tradition* the name Son of Man designates at one time Jesus' parousia and at another time Jesus' activity on earth and that nevertheless these two groups of Son of Man sayings are neither fused nor assimilated? In view of this juxtaposition within Q Bultmann's supposition that the two groups of sayings belong to two different strata of tradition which are separated from each other by ceasing to be understood[1] can no longer be maintained. With regard to Q we will summarize here again the answer which we have given earlier.

1. The community which collected the sayings of Q was giving again the teaching of what Jesus had taught. Urged by Jesus' authority, they felt bound to hand on the sayings of the coming Son of Man in conformity to their traditional structure. Thus the community retained the differentiation between the 'I' of Jesus and the coming Son of Man.

2. The community had come into existence thanks to the risen one's once more turning towards them in love. He had restored that bond of faithful and obedient following of Jesus which the disciples had broken. Out of this sprang the confidence that the promise of a confirmation of fellowship with Jesus by the Son of Man before God had not become void after all, but that Jesus who has re-established this fellowship as the risen one is also the one who will be the eschatological guarantor of it, i.e. the coming Son of Man.

3. The community's faith in the identity of the one who is risen with the one who was on earth and the one who is to come did not induce them to abolish the differentiation between Jesus' activity on earth and to come. They also designated his earthly activity by the name Son of Man. But still they differentiated between the works done on earth and the consummation to come. The transcendent attributes of the coming Son of Man were not transferred to Jesus when his earthly activity was in view.

4. The community did not look back to Jesus' acting on earth with full authority as to something which had ended in the past. What had happened in the past continued to have a meaning to them which they emphasized by designating this activity by the name

[1] Bultmann, *Theology* I, p. 30 *et passim*.

Son of Man. Since the broken fellowship is restored by him who is risen, following Jesus is just as possible after Easter as before. The one who is risen—as well as the one who was on earth—made his own look forward to the promised fulfilment of fellowship with him at the coming of the Son of Man. Opposition to Jesus' acting on earth with full authority was considered by the Christians who looked back to this activity to be forgivable. But opposition to the Spirit after Easter was considered to be unforgivable (Matt. 12.32 par.), since the post-Easter community is the eschatological community. It is the eschatological community because the fulfilment of the promises of him who had been teaching on earth began when the risen one once more turned towards them in love. All that the community was looking forward to was Jesus' advent as the Son of Man in heavenly authority.

E. THE SAYINGS CONCERNING THE SON OF MAN'S ACTIVITY ON EARTH IN THE SYNOPTIC TRADITION OUTSIDE Q

Sayings in which Jesus is designated as the Son of Man with regard to his activity on earth do not exclusively occur in Q. Two sayings concerning the Son of Man's *authority* on earth occur in the controversy dialogues which Mark received from an earlier tradition (Mark 2.10, 28). There are two more sayings concerning the Son of Man's *mission* on earth, namely Luke 19.10 and Mark 10.45a. Matt. 13.37 also belongs here.

The sayings about the Son of Man's activity on earth which occur in the controversy dialogues are closely related to the sayings of this group from Q. In Matt. 11.19 and par.; 12.32 and par. the Son of Man appears as one who is exposed to reproaches. In Luke 6.22 and Matt. 8.20 and par. the disciples who follow Jesus appear as those who are afflicted and cast out by men. The same situation is in view in the controversy dialogues. Here Jesus' authority is both challenged and declared. These dialogues issued from a community whose members had to vindicate their authority in the face of Jewish opponents. In order to vindicate their own activity, they referred to Jesus' full authority. In doing so they designated Jesus as the one acting with full authority on earth by the name Son of Man.

This way of speaking of the Son of Man's activity on earth is proved to have early and widespread roots in the synoptic tradition by the fact that sayings of this kind occur both in Q and in the pre-

Marcan compilation of controversy dialogues. No such proof can be adduced for speaking of the Son of Man's mission. Sayings of this kind lack a typical mark of those other sayings which speak of the authority and vulnerability of the Son of Man on earth, namely the tension over against men, or this generation. The sayings about the mission are intended to enunciate exclusively and positively the form of Jesus' activity on earth. The Son of Man is come to seek and save what was lost; he is come to serve (Luke 19.10; Mark 10.45a). These considerations do not, however, support the assumption that the two sayings mentioned are Hellenistic products. In the case of Mark 10.45a this is out of the question,[1] and in the case of Luke 19.10 it is improbable.

It is remarkable that all the different kinds of sayings concerning the Son of Man's activity on earth contain the thought that Jesus' authority implies his turning in love towards sinners. In Matt. 11.19 and par., hence in Q, the Son of Man is called a friend of tax collectors and sinners. In Mark 2.10 it is declared that the Son of Man has authority to forgive sins. In Luke 19.10 there is the statement that the Son of Man is come to seek and save what was lost. This focusing of Jesus' authority on sinners will have to be taken into account when considering what is meant by the transition from the teaching about the Son of Man's authority to the message about his giving his life for many (cf. Mark 10.45). Here we reach the problem of how the sayings concerning the Son of Man who is to come and has authority at present are related to what is conceived by the passion kerygma.

F. THE FORMATION OF THE SAYINGS CONCERNING THE SUFFERING AND RISING SON OF MAN OUTSIDE THE Q STRATUM OF TRADITION

In the passion kerygma of the Palestinian community it has already been recognized that Jesus' death has a soteriological significance, since he gave his life for many (Mark 10.45; 14.24). It is all the more striking that the sayings concerning the Son of Man's suffering and rising do not express this awareness. They do speak of the necessity of the Son of Man's being killed according to the Scripture, but they do not express the conviction that this death by itself means salvation for many. Attention rather is directed at once to the rising after three days; with that moment in mind the positive

[1] Cf. above Chapter IV D III d, p. 203.

meaning of the passion event is to be understood. In the context of a
passion announcement the rising means first of all the legitimation
of the one who was delivered by God himself into the hands of sinners. This is how we must interpret Acts 2.22f.; this is how we must
expound those formulae in the Acts in which it is not said that the
death in itself means salvation, but merely that the Jews killed Jesus
and that God has raised him up, which means that God legitimated
Jesus in his *exousia*; this, finally, is how we must explain why the
evangelist Luke, too, could still refrain from expressing the concept
of a 'direct soteriological significance drawn from his suffering or
death', as Conzelmann has shown.[1] Luke, as opposed to Matthew,
omits Mark 10.45, thus refraining from rendering just the one Son
of Man saying in the Gospel of Mark in which the concept of the
Son of Man's mission is brought into relation with the concept of
atonement by death.

The sayings concerning the Son of Man's suffering and rising
make their first appearance within the synoptic tradition in the
Gospel of Mark, who used them to lead up to the passion account.
But Mark did not form the sayings himself. The earliest of them
originated with the Palestinian community. Before Mark used them
they had been combined with scriptural evidence adduced in order
to affirm the necessity of the event of the passion. Obviously there
were groups within the primitive community which demonstrated
to the Jews by means of scriptural evidence the necessity of Jesus'
suffering without expounding that this death means atonement and
salvation. We see from the combination of the Palestinian sayings
about the Son of Man being delivered up with parts of such scriptural
evidence that these groups were in the first place intent on affirming
the legitimacy of Jesus' activity and the validity of his *exousia*. Considering this intention it is understandable that Ps. 118.22 in particular was referred to. The announcements of suffering may have
originated within these groups in the primitive community. Mark
received the announcements into his Gospel where he brought them
into relationship with the passion account. In the same way he reproduced in Mark 10.45 a saying which related the concept of the Son of
Man to the soteriological concept of Jesus' death as meaning salvation,
a concept which existed in the tradition concerning the Lord's Supper,
as is evident from Mark 14.24.

The announcements about being delivered up are linked up with

[1] Conzelmann, *Theology of Luke*, p. 201.

the sayings about the Son of Man's activity on earth, which are transmitted in the Gospel of Mark and already occur in Q, inasmuch as in both groups the name Son of Man is used to designate Jesus on earth and in both groups, too, Jesus' *exousia* is emphasized. Yet these announcements also show that an essentially different cognition has sprung up. In the sayings about the activity on earth Jesus in his *exousia* confronts with his claim this evil generation; he stands on God's side, acting with a mission from God. But in the sayings about being delivered the distinctive statement is that the Son of Man who has full authority is delivered by God himself into the hands of men. By means of this paradoxical statement the community, confronted with the enigma of the death on the cross and challenged by the Jews, express their faith. They maintain against the Jews that the delivering up has been announced beforehand by the Scriptures and thus conceals within itself the true will of God. Moreover, they point to the free and sovereign way of the delivered one as he goes where God willed him to go. He who is delivered appears not only as one passively subjected to the action of another but at the same time as one himself actively going the way of which he is aware, right through to the resurrection.

Thus Jesus' authority here is conceived as not invalidated by his being delivered up—however much it may be concealed by men's will which in opposition to God reaches the end it had aimed at. The announcements of suffering combine the concept of Jesus' humiliation with that of his authority, thus producing the paradoxical coordination and unity of sovereignty and humility which has been given full expression in pre-Pauline and Pauline material, in the Gospel of John and in the Epistle to the Hebrews. The recognition that the Son of God in all his authority willingly suffers humiliation becomes the great theme of Christology. We may not overlook, however, that Jesus' authority undergoes a Christological interpretation which differs from that peculiar to the Q stratum of tradition.

G. THE JUXTAPOSITION OF THE THREE GROUPS OF SAYINGS CONCERNING THE SON OF MAN IN THE COMPOSITION OF THE SYNOPTIC GOSPELS

In Q only the two groups of sayings concerning the coming and the present Son of Man had been integrated. The Synoptic Gospels added the sayings of the third group, those concerning the suffering

Son of Man, and related them to the other groups. This was done by the evangelists from different points of view.

(1) *In the Gospel of Mark* the pivotal point is Peter's confession at Caesarea Philippi. It is a long-debated question whether this is merely a turning-point in Mark's book or in fact an historical event by which what followed in Jesus' life and interpretation of himself was deeply determined. An answer to this question implies consequences for the consideration of the relationship between the groups of sayings concerning the suffering and the active Son of Man.

It is often assumed that stages in the historical course of events in Jesus' life, such as the failure of the mission of the Twelve (Mark 6.6b–13), the withdrawal into the region of Tyre (Mark 7.24ff.) and the appearing of Jesus at Caesarea Philippi, led to the inception of a new teaching which concerned the suffering Son of Man (Mark 8.31). If, assenting to this assumption, we consider the arrangement of the Gospel of Mark to be historically correct, and if consequently this composition is considered to be the foundation on which to establish an interpretation of the Son of Man sayings before and after Peter's confession, then the sayings in Mark 2.10 and 2.28 must be interpreted as typical for the early activity and self-interpretation of Jesus whilst the sayings concerning the Son of Man's suffering must be interpreted as late statements valid after the event at Caesarea Philippi. This is the argument of Albert Schweitzer and the scholars who share his view. Recently it has been argued thus, for instance, by Vincent Taylor.[1] In this view the relationship in the Gospel of Mark between these two groups of Son of Man sayings was achieved in conformity to the historical sequence in Jesus' life. T. W. Manson, who also ascribes a fundamental significance to Peter's confession, modifies this view by interpreting Mark 2.10 and 2.28, in accordance with Wellhausen and Bultmann, as belonging 'to the class of which it can most plausibly be said that the term "Son of Man" in them represents a misunderstanding of an original Aramaic *bar nāshā*'; consequently, these sayings being left out of account when the Son of Man sayings in the Gospel of Mark are considered, there is no relationship at all between the two groups.'[2]

Within the limits set for our investigation we cannot discuss the general question whether the way in which the Gospel of Mark is

[1] Taylor, *Names*, p. 34.
[2] Manson, *Teaching*, p. 214.

composed conforms in the main to the historical course of Jesus' life.[1] We will confine ourselves to the more particular problem whether the way in which the evangelist Mark understands the Son of Man sayings is influenced by their occurring before or after Peter's confession.

When it is assumed that Mark understood the situation at Caesarea Philippi to be the first revelation in history of Jesus' messiahship, the earlier use in 2.10 and 2.28 of a title of sovereignty in its full sense as a self-designation of Jesus must be disregarded. In this case the supposition mentioned above suggests itself that in these two Son of Man sayings nothing but 'man' must be read. We cannot assent to this supposition.[2] If, however, Mark understood the situation at Caesarea Philippi to be the first revelation of the true meaning of Jesus' messiahship, namely of the mystery of suffering, then it would be permissible to conclude that Mark received and reproduced the name Son of Man in 2.10 and 2.28 in the same way that he let the title Son of God be heard already before Caesarea Philippi, namely that he expected the reader to understand that the true meaning of the name would be revealed only when used in the announcements of suffering which would make the disciples realize the mystery of Jesus. In Mark's view the Son of Man sayings in Mark 2.10 and 2.28, when expressing the sovereignty of Jesus' activity on earth, did something provisional which would give place to the real expression of what the designation Son of Man meant as revealed by Jesus at Caesarea Philippi when he spoke of the suffering of the Son of Man. We cannot doubt that Mark thus understood the Son of Man sayings about Jesus' activity on earth as provisional with regard to the passion; Mark 10.45 proves this. The central position which Jesus' passion and giving his life as a ransom for many occupies when seen from Mark's point of view accounts for Mark's specific use of the

[1] The results of the form-critical examination of the Gospel material forbid us to found our interpretation on the assumption that in the main the Gospel of Mark is composed in conformity to history; for this examination leaves no doubt that Mark has adapted earlier material to his own composition and that this composition itself is dominated by theological points of view. This does not of course mean that there is no possibility left that certain traits in the composition of the Gospel of Mark do conform with the historical course of events. We have already shown above in Chapter III (cf. especially B I 1 c, p. 132) that Mark 2.10 and 2.28 belong to pre-Marcan material and are out of harmony with the composition of the Gospel. So we cannot assent to making the interpretation of these passages depend on an historical chronology relative to the confession at Caesarea Philippi.

[2] Cf. Chapter III B I 1 a, pp. 126f.

Son of Man sayings. The sayings which express nothing but Jesus' acting on earth with full authority are given no prominence in the composition of the Gospel of Mark. Mark's omission of the name Son of Man in the saying about blaspheming against the Spirit in Mark 3.28f. which we discussed above[1] corroborates what we have assumed here.

It appears to be a consequence of Mark's strict concentration on the passion kerygma that he does not emphasize as much as Matthew and Luke do the sayings concerning the Son of Man's parousia. The coming of the Son of Man as the saviour is mentioned only once, namely in 13.26f. within the apocalyptic discourse of Jesus, and this mention probably was suggested by the material which Mark received.[2] When we compare the arrangement of the Q material with the composition of the Gospel of Mark, we notice at once the difference in the weight of the *parousia* sayings in the one and the other.

Thus Mark, although he does reproduce Son of Man sayings from all three groups, yet turns his attention by preference to the sayings concerning the Son of Man's being delivered, killed and rising. The other sayings appear to have been adopted rather incidentally through material transmitted to Mark.

(2) *In the Gospel of Matthew* essential differences in the understanding and composition over against the Gospel of Mark are already evident from the way in which the Son of Man sayings are used. Matthew takes over the Son of Man sayings from the Gospel of Mark and mostly leaves them in the context they had there, but there is a shift of emphasis. The sayings from Q about the Son of Man's parousia are stressed considerably by Matthew and their number is increased by newly formulated editorial sayings (13.41; 25.31).

It was not only the source material which Matthew used that made him proceed in this way, but also and fundamentally the theological understanding which is expressed in his Gospel. G. Bornkamm has demonstrated in his essay 'Tradition and Interpretation in Matthew' the extreme care with which Matthew interpreted theologically the traditional material compiled and arranged by him. Matthew succeeds in bringing out the main points of the Son of Man Christology from Q in spite of the fact that the Christological understanding

[1] Cf. Chapter III A I b, p. 120 and n. 3.
[2] Cf. Chapter II A I a, pp. 33ff.

current in his community was somewhat modified. Some brief indications of this must suffice here.

According to Bornkamm there is a specifically Matthean Christology expressed in the first gospel. By this Christology Jesus in his messianic *exousia* is conceived of as the teacher. A tension exists between the Pharisees and scribes on the one side and on the other side this teacher who as a second Moses on the Mount, the true exponent of the law, gave as his commandment the new 'exceeding' righteousness according to God's primeval and ultimate will. By this Christology the concept of the Law is intimately connected with the concept of following. And, finally, by this Christology Jesus is centrally conceived of as the Judge of the world, most of all for the Church. These features follow exactly in the steps of the Son of Man Christology which we have shown. The sayings about the Son of Man's parousia are further developed according to Matthew's concept of the Judge of the world by means of which Matthew brings out more distinctly than the other evangelists Jesus' judicial function as the Son of Man. This chimes in with Matthew's concept of the Law by means of which he expresses the understanding that Jesus' acting on earth with full authority is the teaching of the exceeding righteousness, that Jesus is the authorized interpreter of the Law; for it is just this exceeding righteousness taught by Jesus which contains the criteria which the Son of Man, who is also King and Judge of the world, will use when pronouncing his verdict on each man's behaviour (25.31ff.; 16.27). In Matthew's understanding of Jesus' activity on earth the miracles are assigned a place in the second rank, as Bornkamm has demonstrated. This again corresponds to the understanding expressed in the Q material and in those Son of Man sayings which are part of this material. The point at which Matthew deviates from the understanding of Q is the following. According to Q the Master who claims confession to himself and summons men to follow him does so in sovereignty and full authority without referring to anything which might have been provided beforehand to support his claim. According to Matthew, Jesus is the legitimated teacher; his message is primarily understood as teaching. Yet he also sees Jesus as the one who preaches with full and effectual authority, as the one who already on earth is to be designated by the name Son of Man and sows the good seed, his disciples, into his *basileia* (c.f. 13.37).

A detail may elucidate further how closely Matthew follows the main concept in the Son of Man sayings from Q. Matthew uses the designation *Kyrios* as a title of highest sovereignty and in striking parallelism to the designation Son of Man. Not only is the coming Judge of the world named both Son of Man and *Kyrios* (cf. Matt. 24.42 and 44), but also Jesus' sovereign activity on earth is designated in both ways. The Son of Man as he acts on earth is the one who teaches with full authority, the Master who has *exousia* to summon tax collectors and sinners into fellowship with him as well as the one who can promise that this fellowship will be valid in the judgement before God. The *Kyrios* who is sovereign on earth is likewise, as Bornkamm has demonstrated, the Saviour with full authority to whom prayer for mercy and salvation is directed. Thus both titles are conceived by Matthew in a parallel structure correlating what is on earth and salvation. Because of this structure each of the two can be used alike to designate the coming Judge of the world as well as the one who acts on earth with full authority.

However, Matthew does not only know the material of Q and its concepts, but also the passion kerygma. He knows the Gospel as written by Mark. Therefore he has the task of combining the concepts pertaining to Jesus' passion and humility with those pertaining to Jesus' acting on earth with full authority. He achieves this combination by means of the specifically Matthean concepts which join with that concept of unequalled authority, namely the gentleness and compassion of the Messiah and his humility and obedient lowliness. Matthew makes clear that Jesus is not pushed into humility and suffering, but is by reason of himself and his commission the humble and obedient one, condescending to those who are lowly.

(3) *The Gospel of Luke* incorporates the Son of Man sayings both from Mark and from Q. Luke, like Matthew, abandons Mark's plan, which had placed Jesus' passion and its redemptive meaning in the centre and thereby made Jesus' teaching and its meaning for salvation of marginal significance. Conzelmann has demonstrated that Luke understood Jesus' activity on earth as a special period of salvation and accordingly stressed the unique significance of this period as seen within the sequence of stages in the history of salvation. When Luke takes over sayings of Jesus he does so because they have originated during that period of salvation which is constituted by Jesus' presence on earth, and so are authorized to claim to be valid expressions of the norm that endures beyond all time.

Luke's view differs from that of Q in so far as he has realized that 'the period of Jesus, like the present, is not yet the last'.[1] But neither Jesus' teaching as a whole nor his eschatological message in particular are invalidated by this. Luke adopts the sayings concerning the Son of Man's parousia, understanding them indeed not in the sense of imminent expectation but applying them to the period which will only come after the period of the *ecclesia pressa*. Certainly Luke, too, considers Jesus' teaching on earth to be action with full authority; yet what he gives as Jesus' preaching 'does not contain teaching but a reference to the function of miracle'.[2] In teaching and in miracle Jesus' *exousia* is effectual in his activity on earth (Luke 4.16–22). The door to salvation is accessible not only by way of Jesus' passion.

Thus we can understand that in the Gospel of Luke the function of the material from Q is quite prominent. Luke like Matthew stresses the Son of Man sayings about the parousia and the activity on earth. He also takes over sayings about the Son of Man's suffering and being killed—but he omits Mark 10.45. Comparing the Gospel of Luke with that of Mark and with Q, it can be perceived that Luke even reinforced the groups of sayings about the Son of Man's parousia and the activity on earth by inserting both 21.36 and 18.8b as well as 19.10.

[1] Conzelmann, *Theology of Luke*, p. 37.
[2] *Loc. cit.*

VI

THE ABSENCE OF THE ELEMENTS OF PRE-EXISTENCE AND EXALTATION IN THE SYNOPTIC SAYINGS CONCERNING THE SON OF MAN

IT IS QUITE natural that there is a tendency in Jewish apocalyptic literature to combine the concept of the heavenly Man as the eschatological saviour with the concept of pre-existence.[1] While Daniel does not refer to a primeval existence of the Man who in chapter 7 comes after the kingdom of the beasts, the author of the Similitudes 'combines the eschatological saviour and the primal Man, his pre-existence in eternity and his ultimate purpose'.[2] In the vision in IV Ezra 13 the tempest brings the Man up from the heart of the ocean (13.3). This feature of the description does not yet unambiguously show whether it is a reference to the concept of pre-existence or not. But this concept is unmistakably alluded to in the interpretation of the vision in 13.26 and 52. Apart from its occurrence in combination with the concept of the Son of Man the concept of pre-existence also occurs in several motifs in the Old Testament and in the later literature of Judaism, expressed in a more or less elaborate manner.[3]

When we call to mind how quickly the conviction spread in the primitive community that Jesus is the pre-existent Son of God who became man, it is surprising that there is not a single Son of Man saying within the synoptic tradition which links up with the concept of pre-existence from apocalyptic literature. 'The possibility of

[1] Cf. Staerk, *Soter II*, pp. 415f.
[2] Volz, *Eschatologie*, p. 190; cf. I Enoch 48.3; 48.6; 62.7; 39.6; 40.5.
[3] Cf., for example, the references Mowinckel adduces in *RGG* IV, col. 1384; Sjöberg, *Menschensohn*, pp. 83ff.; Sjöberg, *Verborgener Menschensohn*, pp. 96 and 41ff.; Billerbeck II, pp. 334f., 353ff.; Volz, *Eschatologie*, pp. 205ff. and 190; Bousset, *Religion*, pp. 342–5 and 352.

introducing the concept of pre-existence and the setting for it were in fact provided when the designations Son of Man, Messiah, Son of God, Logos and others were used for Jesus.'[1] Yet the synoptic Son of Man sayings have nothing to do with this concept. Those who transmitted them were intent on continuing the teaching of Jesus. In this teaching the concept of pre-existence was as absent as the concept of an itinerary by means of which an eschatological figure would have been described as proceeding in his course leading the way to salvation, according to the pattern of IV Ezra 13. The immunity of the synoptic Son of Man sayings from the concepts of pre-existence and itinerary cannot be explained more conclusively, so far as we see, than by assuming that these sayings are dependent on Jesus' preaching.

Can we be as sure that the synoptic Son of Man sayings likewise have nothing to do with the concept of exaltation? In Luke 24.26 it is stated as clearly as possible that the *Christ*'s course leads through suffering into glory. Encouraged by this passage, Bousset considers Luke 22.69 as expressing 'the concept of the exaltation of the earthly Jesus of Nazareth to the dignity of Son of Man, a concept which the Jewish doctrine concerning the Son of Man had naturally enough not been able to conceive in advance'.[2] According to Lohmeyer, the concept of Jesus' *kyrios*-ship, or lordship, namely the concept of Jesus' existence as the exalted one, would actually be the centre of the Son of Man concept current in the primitive Galilean community.[3] It might also be considered a natural combination to conceive of Jesus' installation as Son of Man with the help of the concept of adoptianism. The argument might then run as follows.

---

[1] Bauernfeind in *RGG* IV, col. 1385.

[2] Bousset, *Kyrios*, p. 14, cf. pp. 16ff. Together with E. Schweizer, *Erniedrigung*, p. 93 n. 401, we miss a more precise statement here how Bousset conceives of exaltation, since 'no passage in the New Testament speaks of an exaltation *to* Son of Man'. This conclusion of Schweizer cannot be contradicted with regard to the synoptic passages. We certainly have to distinguish precisely between the *act* of enthronement by which the Son of Man is given the authority of co-regent with God and a *state* of exaltation preceding the parousia which is recognized and conceived of as a lengthening period of time. The latter concept is, in fact, expressed in Luke 22.69, whereas in Mark 14.62 such a state is not conceived; the latter passage does not speak of the act of enthronement either, but merely announces that he who will come at the parousia will come with the authority of one who sits at God's right hand. In what follows we shall take exaltation to mean not the act of enthronement but the state of exaltation in the lengthening period preceding the parousia.

[3] Lohmeyer, *Galiläa*, p. 92 *et passim*.

The primitive community with the background of the Easter event believe that the prophet Jesus raised by God is by the resurrection installed by God as Son of Man in heaven. The martyr Stephen, indeed, sees Jesus as Son of Man standing at God's right hand and addresses him as *Kyrie Jesu*.[1] But may we introduce the concept of adoptianism into the sphere of the Son of Man concept? There is no synoptic Son of Man saying which perceptibly reflects on the act of installation to Son of Man. In the Lucan passages cited, Luke 22.69 and Acts 7.56, the Son of Man is seen in a state of exaltation at God's side.

It is evident from the conclusions mentioned above how readily the present-day scholar, too, adopts a view which cannot conceive of the Son of Man's coming without first conceiving of his exaltation. A scholar would be definitely obliged to assume a state of exaltation as soon as he consciously or unconsciously presupposes that all Christological titles have to be conceived of according to the pattern of an itinerary. We do not consider the concept of exaltation appropriate for the synoptic Son of Man sayings. Nowhere but in Luke 22.69 is it distinctly presupposed that the Son of Man exists in a state of exaltation during the period of the post-Easter Church. In this saying Luke, actuated by his specific understanding of eschatology, omitted that part of the citation from Dan. 7 which mentions the coming of the Son of Man (cf. Mark 14.62 and par.).

We do not intend to dispute here the fact that in the Palestinian primitive community Jesus was conceived of as the exalted one. What we are discussing now is rather the problem whether the concept of exaltation is associated with the sayings about the coming Son of Man and whether it is originally connected with them. We will leave aside also the problem whether and how far the resurrection is considered to be identical with the exaltation or whether the exaltation is an independent aspect additional and subsequent to the resurrection. There is no stereotyped and clear expression of the concept of exaltation to be found in the synoptic texts, not even in Luke, whose way of thinking had an affinity to this concept (cf. 22.69), but who nevertheless described the ruling function of the exalted one indirectly rather than directly by pointing to his activity in the post-Easter present.[2]

Eduard Schweizer, in his book *Erniedrigung und Erhöhung bei Jesus*

[1] Acts 7.56 and 59; cf. on this also Rom. 1.3f.
[2] Cf. Conzelmann, *Theology of Luke*, pp. 176ff.

und seinen Nachfolgern, uses the concept of Jesus' *course* as the thread running through his train of thought and interpretation, and also where the synoptic texts are concerned. In Schweizer's view Jesus himself understood his course with the succession of humiliation and exaltation in an analogy to the course of the suffering and triumphant righteous man in Judaism; the post-Easter community understood Jesus' course according to his own understanding of it.[1] The only place within the synoptic tradition where the concept of exaltation was clearly preserved, as Schweizer sees it, is in the Gospel of Luke, namely in 22.69; 9.51; 24.26; it also appears in 24.51, since, according to Schweizer, in this passage the ascension is transferred to Easter Day.[2] It is not these passages which decide how the concept of exaltation must be understood, but some passages from Acts. In Schweizer's view the concept of exaltation in Acts 2.33; 2.36; 5.31 serves to interpret the concept of raising; the meaning of the latter concept therefore is the installation as Lord and Christ, as Son; it includes the enthronement at God's right hand. According to what is stated in Peter's sermons, it must be regarded as a consequence of this installation of Jesus as Lord that he pours out his Spirit on the community (Acts 2.33) and offers to all the world the possibility of repentance and forgiveness. 'Thus his being the ruler over his community as over the "Church" is clearly meant.'[3]

Schweizer's argument gives us the impression that, suggested by the concept of an itinerary, the concept of exaltation which occurs in Acts is presumed to underlie what occurs in the synoptic tradition.[4] We cannot consider it permissible to ascribe the specific concept of exaltation occurring in the Lucan writings to the synoptic texts in general. That Lucan understanding of the exalted one's ruling over the community at present is not expressed anywhere else in the synoptic texts, least of all in the sayings from Q and the sayings about the coming Son of Man.

Some scholars do indeed maintain that in Matt. 28.16–20 the risen one as the exalted Son of Man is speaking to the community. Schniewind, for instance, argues for this view as follows. 'But now at the resurrection Jesus is installed in the power and dominion of the

[1] Schweizer, *Erniedrigung,* e.g. pp. 35, 44, 73.

[2] Schweizer, *Erniedrigung,* p. 61. Perhaps Mark 16.19 can also be adduced here, and certainly *Barn.* 15.9.

[3] Schweizer, *Erniedrigung,* p. 71.

[4] Cf. Schweizer, *Erniedrigung,* where Mark 14.62 and 8.38 are unjustifiably referred to as supporting this assumption.

Son of Man. Our saying adopts Dan. 7.14, only leaving out the expression (sc. Son of Man).'[1] In this view Luke 22.69 and Acts 7.56 would not be alone in speaking of the exalted one as the Son of Man. Lohmeyer somewhat modifies this view. To him the allusion to Dan. 7.14 is not the main support for the assumption that Matt. 28.18 contains a statement about the Son of Man. He maintains that Matt. 28.16–20 is rather an expression of Jesus' lordship, i.e. of his being the *Kyrios*. He considers this to be a central element of the Son of Man concept. The designation Son of Man and the title of *Kyrios* being indissolubly bound up together, Matt. 28.18 too is to be considered, according to Lohmeyer, as an expression of an element from the sphere of the Son of Man concept. In Lohmeyer's view, the concept of *Kyrios* is actually the centre of the tradition concerning the Son of Man.[2]

It is not improbable that there is, in fact, an allusion to Dan. 7.14 in Matt. 28.18. But what is alluded to? It is the enthronement alone, not the concept of the Son of Man; for if an allusion to this concept had been intended, it would not have been possible to omit the name Son of Man.

Our assumption is corroborated by the way in which Matt. 28.18 deviates from Mark 14.62 and Matt. 26.64. In Matt. 28.18 the risen one himself speaks about his installation as Lord which has already happened; no immediate connexion with his parousia is indicated. In Mark 14.62 and Matt. 26.64 the dominion is regarded instead as an integral part of the parousia; the parousia is announced by Jesus as an event to come, and the post-Easter community also sees the parousia in the future. Matt. 28.18 proclaims the dominion which already exists at present and addresses a community which prays to the risen one as to its Lord. The one who is acclaimed in this way is never designated by the name Son of Man—he is designated by the title *Kyrios*. Thus used, the title of *Kyrios* acquired a special significance in the early Hellenistic community. The Christians may be specified as those who call on the name of the Lord Jesus Christ.[3] Even earlier than Paul it is the title of *Kyrios* which is used in confession.[4] The title occurs as the name of the one who is invoked in prayer, e.g. in II Cor. 12.8. According to Acts 1.6 the earliest community

[1] Schniewind, *Matt.*, p. 279.
[2] Lohmeyer, *Markus*, pp. 98, 101.
[3] I Cor. 1.2; cf. Acts 9.14, 21; 22.16; II Tim. 2.22.
[4] Phil. 2.11; Rom. 10.9.

addresses as Lord the risen one who by his appearance and what he says proves himself to his disciples to be the living one. Thus it is evident that the title of *Kyrios* is a feature of statements which exhibit quite a different structure from the sayings concerning the Son of Man. We therefore have to take care not to interpolate the concept of the Son of Man into passages which neither mention the Son of Man explicitly nor occur in contexts within which Son of Man sayings occur elsewhere. So we cannot assent to the suppositions of Schniewind and Lohmeyer which we have cited.

The attempts at interpretation which have been discussed indicate that indeed the concept of Son of Man verges on the concept of *Kyrios*. Bultmann maintains that 'in place of the titles "Son of Man" and "Christ" = Messianic King which are dying out, there appears in the Hellenistic congregation the title κύριος, Lord'.[1] This statement is irrefutable, but does not exhaust the problem, for the concept of Son of Man and the name *Kyrios* occur side by side already in the Palestinian sphere of tradition. This is clearly evident from the way in which Matthew uses the name *Kyrios*. Bornkamm has demonstrated that when Jesus is spoken of and addressed as the *Kyrios* in the Gospel of Matthew this name has, in fact, the nature of a title of divine sovereignty[2] (7.21f.; 25.11; 25.37 and 44). Comparing Matt. 24.42 and 24.44 we see that pointing to the coming *Kyrios* and pointing to the coming Son of Man means the same; here in exhortation both names perform the same function. As understood by Matthew the two titles converge in certain spheres of meaning whilst the spheres of application remain differentiated;[3] when Jesus or the Judge is *addressed* the name of Son of Man is never used. Thus it is comprehensible why the frequency of the use of the title of *Kyrios* gradually outweighs that of the name Son of Man. A community which calls on its Lord and knows that it is addressed by him needs a title which is suitable for epiclesis. The name Son of Man cannot be applied in this way. In Jesus' teaching this name pointed to the consummator of salvation. But since in the post-Easter situation instruction given by the risen one existed, since this risen one was recognized as speaking to and acting with the community, the need for a name which might be invoked was bound to arise. The name *Kyrios*, suitable

---

[1] Bultmann, *Theology* I, p. 124.
[2] Bornkamm, 'Expectation', pp. 42f.
[3] We have already shown above that the two titles are analogous in their twofold use both for the coming one and the one acting on earth as the Saviour.

S.M.–K

for epiclesis, met this need. Matthew's use of this name links up with the concept of Son of Man; not only is the coming Judge of the world addressed as *Kyrios*, but this name can finally also be used in a statement like Matt. 24.42 as a designation of the coming Judge uttered by Jesus. In the latter use this name even replaces the designation Son of Man in its specific original function.

At least one of the reasons for which the name *Kyrios* became current can be traced back to the sphere of epiclesis. This is corroborated by the use of the name *Kyrios* in the Gospel of Matthew where the earthly Jesus is called on.[1] Addressed in this way, the earthly Jesus is often enough called on as the Saviour who has full authority: Lord, have mercy, save, command![2] Epiclesis assuming a more and more central place in the life of the community, which is undoubtedly the case in public worship, the use of the name Son of Man has to move over to a more marginal place. In the course of this process of the replacement of the name Son of Man Matthew's use of the name *Kyrios* apparently represents an early stage; for here the latter is not yet used to call on the exalted Lord of the Church as the one who is recognized to be already acting as the ruler in his community during this still continuing period of the world.[3] Matthew understands the *Kyrios* to be in particular the coming Judge of the world, thus conforming in his use of this name to the specific nature of the Son of Man concept.[4] Luke on his part expresses distinctly enough in Acts that he understands the *Kyrios* to be already at present the ruling Lord of the community, i.e. to be exercising the functions of the exalted one in the narrower sense.

If we now apply to Matt. 28.18 what we conclude from the preceding considerations, we are cautioned against all the attempts to interpret Matt. 28.18 as a statement about the *Kyrios* or even the Son of Man. The title of *Kyrios* is used by Matthew where the coming Judge of the world is addressed; but 28.18 refers primarily to that installation which is already effective as exaltation. This verse may be interpreted as an expression of Jesus' being the *Kyrios* only on

[1] Hence we must co-ordinate the Aramaic formula of prayer *maranatha* with the pre-Hellenistic Palestinian understanding of the name *Kyrios* as it can be seen in the Gospel of Matthew; we cannot co-ordinate this formula with the name Son of Man which is never used as a form of address in a prayer.

[2] Cf. Bornkamm, 'Expectation', p. 42.

[3] Cf., e.g., Matt. 15.22; 17.15; 8.25; 14.28–30.

[4] This corresponds exactly to what we found in Matt. 13.37, 41, which speaks of the sower on earth and the coming Lord of the Church, not of the Lord acting as the ruler in the post-Easter Church.

condition that to this interpretation the comment is added: the understanding of the title *Kyrios* which is expressed here does not occur elsewhere in the Gospel of Matthew, but certainly occurs in Luke's writings. Consequently we certainly cannot assume that the concept of installing in the dignity of Lord (Matt. 28.18) evolved directly from the concept of Son of Man. In Luke's writings the concept of exaltation certainly has considerable influence culminating in the formulation of Luke 22.69, but this concept nevertheless did not obscure the original meaning of the designation Son of Man. The Christology of exaltation as expressed by Luke springs from a different source from the Christology expressed in the sayings about the coming Son of Man. The Christology of exaltation is not immediately directed toward the continuation of preaching the kingdom of God as Jesus had preached it, but is intent on explaining that the resurrection and the subsequent appearances mean that Jesus was raised to be the Lord who even during the present period of the *ecclesia pressa* is active as the ruler over his Church. However, Luke himself demonstrates in 24.26 that in his understanding the entry into glory is not implied in the Son of Man concept. Even though distinctly referring to the announcements of suffering, Luke does not use the name Son of Man, but formulates, 'Was it not necessary that the *Christ* should suffer these things and enter into his glory?'

Our conclusion is as follows. The concept of exaltation does not belong to the sayings about the coming Son of Man as a Christological element specific to them. It is mostly absent from these sayings. Where its influence can be seen in the Son of Man sayings—Luke 22.69—the concept of exaltation has been adopted from a sphere of Christological cognition which is not immediately connected with the Son of Man concept. The title of *Kyrios* is in the main coordinated with that other sphere of Christological cognition; in the Gospel of Matthew, however, this title is used in such a way that it can converge with and even replace the name Son of Man in some contexts, especially that of addressing the Judge of the world or the miracle-working Saviour on earth.

All this makes comprehensible why the use of the name Son of Man quickly moved over to a more marginal place. It has to move aside as soon as the transmission of Jesus' preaching concerning the kingdom of God is no longer directly understood as the central task. According to the Matthean theology the use of the name Son of Man might have retained its central place by reason of Matthew's specific concept of Jesus as the fulfiller of the Law and the Son of Man as the Judge to come who will validate Jesus' teaching; but even in the Gospel of Matthew the title of *Kyrios* can be observed gaining ground, since epiclesis plays an ever greater part in determining the life of the community. In Luke the name Son of Man is not given up as a designation for the coming Lord of the End-time; but the consciousness of the bond with the Lord already active as ruler over the community, who is experienced in this function as the exalted one, looms larger than the prospect of his coming.

CONCLUSION

IN VIEW OF the imminence of God's reign Jesus had summoned his disciples to follow him. The breaking in of the kingdom of God which he proclaims is the indicative which is the basis of this summons. Jesus himself is the sole guarantor for the truth of his statement that this is God's conclusive word to men. Accordingly Jesus claims that the disciple should confess him and gives to the confessor a promise valid in God's world to come. So Jesus actually exercises a comparable authority by bestowing on his own even now the fellowship that comes through following him and by promising them participation in the salvation to come. His authority is seen in two ways: he is the giver both of the bond by which the fellowship through following comes into existence and of the promise that this bond will be recognized as valid before God.

The Jews disputed Jesus' authorization by executing him. The disciples did not stand by Jesus; they fled, denied him and broke the fellowship which he had bestowed on them. But the Easter event forged anew the bond which had been broken. So this event caused a new understanding of the word and the person of Jesus to appear amongst the disciples. Instead of the general breaking in of the kingdom of God, there took place a particular action of God towards the one who had been executed. By the Easter event a new light was thrown both on what was to be expected in the future and on what the significance of Jesus had been. While in the pre-Easter situation there had merely been Jesus' sovereign promise of the salvation to come given without adducing any support from existing authorities, the post-Easter faith realized that Jesus was vindicated by God himself, who thus had invalidated all contradiction by men and all that men had been able to see. Jesus was now recognized as possessing full authority. From this, then, resulted what we will call a Christological understanding.

The nature of a Christological statement is that it expounds the significance of the giver of salvation for the gift of salvation. Such statements appear in the post-Easter situation. Jesus himself had in his teaching pointed to salvation, but he had not expounded what he himself meant for salvation. Jesus' sayings about the Son of Man and what he meant to his followers are of a soteriological and not of a Christological nature. Christological understanding sprang up out of what Jesus himself had said. The new Christological understanding of the soteriological correlation stated in the parousia sayings was then expounded. Jesus had bestowed on those who followed him on earth the promise that the Son of Man would guarantee the validity of this fellowship before God. After Easter there sprang up in the community the Christological understanding that Jesus himself would also be the eschatological guarantor and thus the Son of Man. Where there was faith in Jesus' identity with the fulfiller to come, there was also a deeper recognition of the authority of the one who had given the fellowship on earth. Before Easter this authority had appeared as a sovereign claim for which there was no existing reason. After Easter it appeared as determined by the community's looking forward to Jesus as the coming Son of Man. Christological understanding and recognition of Jesus' authority are thus most intimately connected. Where Christological understanding springs up the step is taken from seeing Jesus' sovereign claim without seeing any logical reason for it to recognizing that there does exist a logical reason for it.

Considering how closely the earliest Christological understanding (that Jesus will be the coming Son of Man) is linked to Jesus' own soteriological statements concerning the coming of the Son of Man, we cannot but perceive that this Christology does not conform with a prevalent assumption about the structure of Christological statements. The assumption to which we cannot assent is that Christology consists in transferring to Jesus titles of dignity in that stereotyped form which these titles had already been given before; it is supposed either that Jesus himself effected this transfer or that the post-Easter community did so. It is supposed, for example, that the primitive community which expected Jesus to arrive as the transcendent Son of Man transferred the myth of an unreal heavenly Son of Man to the real historical person of Jesus. We have indeed seen that Mark and Matthew took over directly the Jewish concept of the Son of Man—they referred back to Dan. 7 and I Enoch; but we have seen as well that this transference was a secondary procedure. Christological understanding primarily referred to the sayings of Jesus, thus accepting that meaning of the name Son of Man which it had been given when this title was taken up to serve in Jesus' teaching. Jesus had assigned to the Son of Man the function of being the eschatological guarantor of attachment to Jesus on earth. This function remained the distinguishing mark of the title when the post-Easter community identified Jesus with the Son of Man. The content of the community's Christological understanding was determined by Jesus' soteriological word. In spite of the conflict with the whole tradition, the community designated Jesus as the one who acts on earth with full authority by the name Son of Man because Jesus himself had correlated the guarantee of the Son of Man with his own earthly activity.

There is a prolepsis of the designation Son of Man in the sayings about the activity on earth; but this prolepsis took place within definite limits. The sovereignty which the name Son of Man signifies may be understood as consisting of the elements of legitimacy, validity, legal authority ($\dot{\epsilon}\xi o\upsilon\sigma\iota\alpha$);[1] seen with this understanding, the intimate relationship between Jesus on earth in his full authority and the Son of Man can be emphasized. If, however, the sovereignty of the Son of Man is seen as an exercise of power ($\delta\upsilon\nu\alpha\mu\iota\varsigma$), the disparity between Jesus on earth and the Son of Man appears. Accordingly the community did not transfer the transcendent *dynamis* of the Son of Man to the earthly Jesus when designating his activity on earth by this name. The Christological understanding of Jesus' activity on earth definitely referred to the *exousia*.

The difference between this Christology and that which is expressed in Phil. 2.6–11 is not to be overlooked. In the psalm about the Christ cited by Paul, Christ's complete humiliation is emphasized; there is no mention of acting with full authority. And yet the motif of *exousia* is not missing. By the attribution to Christ of pre-existence, an unsurpassable authority is expressed which is seen as pertaining to his person and irremovably attending him on his course; even in so far as he does not exercise this authority he still retains it.

Christological doctrine has been developed in Protestantism mainly with regard to the concepts expressed in Phil. 2. The synoptic texts were interpreted to conform to this passage. Accordingly the synoptic statements could not be understood otherwise than in this predetermined way; the one who has preached on earth could only

[1] Campenhausen, *Amt*, p. 5 n. 5.

be seen as the transcendent person, the pre-existent Son of God, or the heavenly Son of Man, and Jesus' acceptance of earthly restrictions could only be understood as humiliation. This understanding had, to be sure, to allow for heavenly glory to shine again and again through the *Christus humilis*.

In the course of this investigation we have arrived at the conclusion that there is a Christology in the synoptic tradition the basis of which is not a Christological concept of Jesus' *person*. This Christology conceives of Jesus' *authority on earth*. It does not conceive of a transcendent person, the Son of Man, as immanent in Jesus. If our conclusion is correct, new tasks have been set for Christological and dogmatic investigation. It will be necessary to investigate how the early Christology of *exousia* in Q and in other strata of the tradition is related to the Christology in Phil. 2 or in Paul's writings. We shall have to take into consideration that the continued transmission of Jesus' teaching in view of the divine authorization of the teacher does not appear from the same source and with the same meaning as the passion kerygma but has a source and a meaning by itself. The old task of expounding the relationship between *Jesus'* gospel and the gospel *of* Jesus is thus set anew, as is the task of investigating how the different post-Easter Christologies which appear side by side in different thought-worlds are correlated.

EXCURSUS I

Discussion of Erik Sjöberg's book *Der verborgene Menschensohn in den Evangelien*

ERIK SJÖBERG has offered in his book *Der verborgene Menschensohn in den Evangelien* a new interpretation of the synoptic Son of Man concept. The peculiarity of this interpretation is that in the first place the concept of the pre-existence and the heavenly concealment of the Son of Man in the book of I Enoch is understood to be the historical reason for the messianic secret in the Gospels, and furthermore this messianic secret is understood to be the means by which the synoptic Son of Man sayings can be made comprehensible.

We shall consider Sjöberg's argument by first summarizing important conclusions of his earlier monograph *Der Menschensohn im äthiopischen Henochbuch* (A) and then discussing critically his statements about the synoptic Son of Man concept which particularly concern our enquiry (B).

A

1. The Son of Man was not a mere fortuitous visionary phenomenon which occurred solely in I Enoch, but a heavenly reality whose existence was accepted as a fact in the apocalyptic circles from which the Similitudes issued. The name Man or Son of Man was completely adequate to designate this heavenly figure as the one Judge of the sinners and saviour of the righteous at the end of time.[1]

2. The Son of Man is not co-ordinate with but subordinate to God. However, he is associated with God in a unique manner not to be compared with that of other heavenly beings; he is nearer to God than any other being. Therefore God commits to him the divine function of eschatological judgement.[2]

3. There is a close connexion between the Son of Man and the community. But the Son of Man does not appear as a personification of the community.[3]

4. There is no sufficient support for J. Jeremias' assumption that the Similitudes connected the Son of Man concept with the concept of the suffering *Ebed Yahweh*. Neither in IV Ezra nor in I Enoch are there

[1] Cf. Sjöberg, *Menschensohn*, pp. 59f.
[2] *Op. cit.*, p. 82.
[3] *Op. cit.*, p. 101.

any traces of a concept of a *suffering* Son of Man.[1] The figure of the Son of Man is also completely different from the figure of the Messiah-King of the seed of David at the consummation.[2]

5. In I Enoch the concept of the real pre-existence of the Son of Man is expressed. It serves to indicate the Son of Man's lofty position at God's side.[3]

6. The Son of Man has been brought into existence for the purpose of being revealed and acting in the eschatological situation. He already exists before this moment, 'preserving the lot of the righteous' (I Enoch 48.7), but otherwise he remains inactive. Thus he exists before the eschatological situation in complete concealment. In agreement with R. Otto, Sjöberg thus sees the concept of the heavenly concealment of the pre-existent Son of Man underlying the messianic secret in the Gospels. 'If there is a historical reason for the so-called messianic secret in the Gospels, this secret will have to be understood as connected with that concept.'[4]

B

In his book *Der verborgene Menschensohn in den Evangelien* (1955) Sjöberg combines the concept of the Son of Man's concealment with the messianic secret and makes this combination the leading idea running through the whole enquiry.

1. Sjöberg wishes to demonstrate first that the messianic secret in the Gospels is not an isolated phenomenon. According to him the concept that Christ and the salvation he brought mean the revelation of a divine secret, which had hitherto been concealed but is now revealed, is a thread running through the whole New Testament. This concept is said to have been present already from the beginning in the Palestinian community.[5] They did not see Jesus' life on earth as unmessianic; they rather saw that during Jesus' activity on earth his messianic glory was concealed from the people and only indirectly revealed to a small group. They received the gospel as the secret which had been revealed. According to Sjöberg the scattered statements about Jesus' life on earth which occur outside the Gospels are also characterized by the contrast between the concealment on earth and the enthronement in glory of the Messiah, Jewish concepts about the Messiah being presupposed in these statements.[6]

2. Sjöberg further asserts that the meaning of what is transmitted in

---

[1] *Op. cit.*, pp. 128, 139.
[2] *Op. cit.*, p. 146.
[3] *Op. cit.*, pp. 90–93.
[4] *Op. cit.*, pp. 102, 115; cf. R. Otto, *Kingdom*, pp. 192, 233f.
[5] Cf. Sjöberg, *Verborgener Menschensohn*, pp. 1, 40.
[6] *Op. cit.*, p. 40.

the Gospels about the concealed Son of Man can only be explained
when it is connected with the messianic secret as it is generally conceived in primitive Christianity.[1] In I Enoch the concealment is not an
incidental but an essential element of the Son of Man concept.[2] And
in IV Ezra, too, a concealment of the Son of Man is conceived of which
precedes his appearance at the consummation.[3] If concealment is
understood to be not complete but partial, then a double revelation
is the resulting concept: 'now a special revelation to the elect of what is
still concealed, (but) at the consummation the appearance before the
whole world of what had been concealed'.[4] By means of this concept
of a double revelation Sjöberg then expounds how the sayings concerning the Son of Man who suffers on earth and the sayings concerning the
coming heavenly Son of Man are related to each other. The apocalyptic
literature only knew the pre-existent Son of Man concealed in heaven.
Jesus, however, acted and announced his future parousia on earth. It
followed from this that the apocalyptic concept of the double revelation
had to be transferred to Jesus, that indeed Jesus himself if he understood himself to be the Messiah had to refer back to this concept. Now
the concealment of the activity on earth was spoken of instead of the
concealment in heaven. Thus Jesus in the sayings about the Son of
Man being delivered up initiated the narrower circle of his disciples into
the secret of his coming passion. The secret remained concealed from
the world, but was revealed in principle (not in fact) to the faithful.[5]
After the concealment on earth there was to follow the revelation visible
to all which was spoken of in the sayings about the Son of Man's
coming. Only by reason of Jesus' coming as the *concealed* Messiah or
Son of Man was it possible that the period of mercy and repentance
could still last, that Jesus could fulfil his mission with regard to sinners,
that he could understand himself as the suffering Servant of God and
finally that he could combine into a consistent unity the concept of
the imminent coming of God's reign and that of its having come already.[6] Thus the messianic secret belonged 'as an integrating factor
to the image of the Son of Man already acting on earth before the last
judgement' and 'to the historical reality of Jesus' life as that of the
Son of Man'.[7] Mark in his theory about the messianic secret assumed
that Jesus 'made arrangements to prevent his messiahship from becoming known'; Jesus, although he did not do what Mark assumed, 'did

---

[1] *Op. cit.*, p. 1.
[2] Cf. Sjöberg, *Menschensohn*, pp. 102f.
[3] Cf. Sjöberg, *Verborgener Menschensohn*, pp. 46f.
[4] *Op. cit.*, p. 46.
[5] *Op. cit.*, pp. 128f.
[6] *Op. cit.*, pp. 243–5.
[7] *Op. cit.*, p. 246.

not proclaim his messiahship publicly either but let it shine through his words and deeds without speaking about it. His messiahship was concealed, it was a secret which nobody could come to know at will. Jesus did not make his messiahship known by means of special instruction and proclamation; yet he did not want it to remain unknown. His words and deeds called on those who heard and saw them to think about them. In this call the messiahship was indeed implicit.'[1]

3. We have to examine whether the statements which we have cited are in accordance with the synoptic Son of Man sayings. Sjöberg speaks of a 'tradition concerning the concealed Son of Man'.[2] But does such a tradition, in fact, exist? Is the motif of concealment clearly expressed in the Son of Man sayings? Sjöberg further speaks of a transference of the concept of the concealment of the pre-existent Son of Man as expressed in I Enoch to the earthly Jesus. Is this permissible? If pre-existence and concealment were originally conceived as a unity, the one motif would have to be accompanied regularly by the other in the synoptic Son of Man sayings. Consequently we must examine these sayings to see whether the combination of the motifs of pre-existence, concealment and messianic secret which Sjöberg assumed are present.

(a) The motif of pre-existence is a prerequisite for the concept of the concealed Son of Man.[3] But even Sjöberg states that this motif is entirely inconspicuous in the Synoptic Gospels. Nevertheless Sjöberg is inclined to assume that Jesus himself combined the motif of pre-existence with the name Son of Man. In Sjöberg's view Jesus conceived of the Son of Man in a manner closely related to that religious understanding which had been expressed already in the motif of pre-existence, namely in so far as for Jesus, too, the Son of Man is God's representative. We cannot share this view. The religious understanding that the Son of Man is God's representative is by no means bound up with the motif of pre-existence. This is evident from the fact that in Dan. 7.13f. and IV Ezra 13 the motif of pre-existence is not present. Even the secondary interpretation of the sixth vision in IV Ezra 13 does not speak of pre-existence but of the concealed origin of the Man. Moreover, it is not methodologically permissible to proceed in the way that Sjöberg does when, because of the contact between the concepts of Son of Man and pre-existence in I Enoch, he presupposes the concept of pre-existence in the synoptic Son of Man sayings also, in spite of the fact that it cannot be distinguished in the synoptic texts. The only valid proof that Jesus conceived of his messiahship essentially according to the categories of the apocalyptic Son of Man concept[4] would be evidence in the synoptic texts themselves.

[1] *Op. cit.*, pp. 229f.
[2] *Op. cit.*, p. 1.
[3] Cf. *op. cit.*, pp. 96, 99; *Menschensohn*, pp. 90–93.
[4] Cf. Sjöberg, *Verborgener Menschensohn*, p. 241.

(b) Is the motif of the Son of Man's concealment expressed in the synoptic texts? Sjöberg relies mainly on the Son of Man saying in Matt. 11.19 and par., supposing it to provide evidence when understood in the context of the section 11.16–19 for the 'fact of the concealed Messiah'.[1] In our view this saying is a rather unreliable support for Sjöberg's assumption. In this text the name Son of Man designates Jesus as the one who is rejected by men just as the Baptist is. The analogy between Jesus and the Baptist demonstrates that at any rate the motif of the specifically messianic secret is not present here. Men refuse to acknowledge Jesus, not because his mission and person is concealed from them, but simply because the Baptist and Jesus do not correspond with their will. This is plainly expressed by means of the comparison with naughty children who complain that their playmates have not responded to their suggestions. Sjöberg's interpretative rendering of Matt. 11.19 and par., 'yet truth has been acknowledged by all her children',[2] makes no difference; for those who naughtily stand off because their claims are not fulfilled are not the children who acknowledge truth. Thus here the theme is not the concealment of Jesus' activity but the fact that men refuse to acknowledge it because of their wilful obstinacy.

So we do not see the motif of concealment in sayings from the group of those about the Son of Man's activity on earth. Might there be support for Sjöberg's assumption in sayings concerning the Son of Man's suffering? It seems possible to regard suffering as some kind of concealment and the necessity of suffering as an enigmatic secret. Yet the announcements of suffering do not speak of concealment at all. It is only Mark's editing which combines them with that 'concept of the revelation of the secrets to the more intimate circle' which Sjöberg has indicated.[3] And the secret of the suffering of Jesus is not dependent on the concept of the concealment of his messiahship; the necessity of suffering has its reason in the paradox that God delivers the one to whom he has given authority into the hands of sinners.

In Sjöberg's view some of the sayings about the coming Son of Man express the same relationship between secret and revelation which is present in apocalyptic literature. The parousia sayings undisputably point to a conclusive and definitive revelation of the Son of Man. What might be disputed is only whether they contain the motif of concealment. Sjöberg attempts to demonstrate that they do. He has to presuppose, however, 'the understanding prevalent amongst scholars today' that Jesus considered himself to be the Messiah.[4] Now Sjöberg states that the parousia sayings with the exception of Mark 14.62 do not express the identity between

[1] *Op. cit.*, p. 181.
[2] *Op. cit.*, p. 181.
[3] *Op. cit.*, p. 128.
[4] *Op. cit.*, pp. 240f.

Jesus and the Son of Man. He concludes from this statement that a secret relationship between the two is thereby intimated which is alluded to particularly in Mark 8.38 and which shows that the concept of the messianic secret is presupposed.[1] We are not convinced by this argument. Even if it had been proved that Jesus understood himself in his earthly activity to be the Messiah, it would still have to be demonstrated in which way he related this consciousness of being the Messiah to the concept of the coming Son of Man. Sjöberg obviously considers the concept of Messiah and the concept of Son of Man as identical, leaving out of consideration the weighty differences both between those concepts and between their respective histories of tradition. We have to object that it cannot be demonstrated even in the apocalyptic literature of Judaism that a merging of the two titles had been effected. There are, to be sure, some sections in I Enoch and IV Ezra in which both titles occur not very far apart from each other. Owing to the procedure of compilation, however, discrepant passages often occurred side by side. Hence there is not even a probability that in those sections, either as received from the previous tradition or as edited in their present form, a co-ordination of the two titles had consciously been established. Consequently we do not think it permissible to employ the title interchangeably. This applies equally to the Synoptic Gospels. The title of Messiah does not occur in the Q material, and the concept of the suffering Son of Man does not occur in the early passion account which begins with Jesus' arrest. So we cannot assent to Sjöberg's combining the Son of Man sayings with the concept of concealment which pertains to the sphere of concepts connected with the title of Messiah. Nor can we assent to his identifying the concept of the transcendent Son of Man who will come at the parousia with the concept of the Messiah on earth. Sjöberg combines and identifies unreflectingly, thereby making it necessary to introduce the motif of concealment.

We have to draw the following conclusion from our critical discussion. Neither the concept of pre-existence nor the concept of the messianic secret can be found expressed in synoptic Son of Man sayings. There is no tradition in the Gospels concerning the concealed Son of Man. It is not permissible to transfer the motif of the concealment of the pre-existent Son of Man from I Enoch to Jesus' activity on earth. The pre-existent Son of Man is inactive, whilst Jesus' existence on earth involves acting in supreme authority and with a decisive meaning for participation in the coming kingdom of God. Inactive pre-existence and active existence have no congruity by which both concepts might be subordinated to the concept of concealment.

[1] *Op. cit.*, p. 237.

EXCURSUS II

Discussion of the concept of the heavenly Son of Man in Acts 7.56

THE BOOK of Acts gives an account of a vision of Stephen using the following terms: Stephen, full of the Holy Spirit, gazed into heaven and saw the glory of God and Jesus standing at God's right hand; and Stephen said, 'Behold, I see the heavens opened and the Son of Man standing at the right hand of God.' In Mark 14.62 and par. conforming to Ps. 110.1 the expression '*sitting* at the right hand' of God is applied to the Son of Man. It is only Acts 7.55f. which speaks in this context of Jesus' or the Son of Man's *standing*. What does the phrase in this form mean?

Haenchen in his commentary on Acts[1] records three explanations which have been given. (1) Jesus has risen to welcome Stephen; (2) Jesus has risen to enter upon his messianic office; (3) Jesus was originally imagined to be—like the angels—standing before God. Haenchen expresses no preference among these explanations. Bauernfeind[2] with the majority of commentators considers the first explanation to be the most appropriate when Stephen is regarded within the actual course of historical events. For 'the actual vision deviates sooner from the traditional picture than does the literary vision'. Hence the 'striking feature in v. 56 is explained by the fact that Stephen spoke in these terms and not otherwise'.

The first and the third explanation mentioned above would set the saying in Acts 7.56 far apart from the synoptic Son of Man sayings; for in these, with the exception of Luke 22.69, each statement about the heavenly Son of Man refers to his parousia or his acting as the guarantor at God's last judgement. The explanation that Jesus *like the angels* is standing near God appears to be preferable when Acts 7.56 is regarded as a recurrence of that combination of Ps. 110.1 and Dan. 7.13 which occurs in Mark 14.62 and par., and, in fact, accords with the rendering of those passages in the LXX. The phrase 'at the right hand' is then regarded as taken over from Ps. 109.1. The phrase here in Acts, unlike that in Mark 14.62 and par., was not associated in the Jewish manner with a paraphrase for God, but was formulated directly, 'at God's right hand'. The term 'standing', however, could be taken over from Dan. 7.13 LXX. Neither in the Aramaic form of this passage nor in the translations of the LXX and of Theodotion is a *sitting* of the Man mentioned, whilst the LXX

---

[1] Cf. Haenchen, *Apostelgeschichte*, p. 249 n. 5.
[2] Cf. Bauernfeind, *Apostelgeschichte*, p. 120.

does speak in an unexpected phrase (a misunderstanding by the translator or a corruption in the basic manuscript?) of the *bystanders*, the angels.

According to the second explanation Jesus has risen to come at the parousia.[1] The most important parallel passage is said to be the Assumption of Moses 10.3, where it is stated that the heavenly one rises from his royal throne and goes forth from his holy habitation. However, it is rather doubtful whether this passage should be adduced to explain Acts 7.56. Ass. Mos. speaks of God himself, not of the Son of Man. Moreover, it is a feature which occurs quite often in the Old Testament that Yahweh rises; he rises to set the poor in safety (Ps. 12.5), to intervene against his enemies (Ps. 3.7; 7.6; 9.19 *et passim*), to terrify the earth (Isa. 2.19, 21), against Babylon (Isa. 14.22 *et passim*). Hence we do not see why Acts 7.56 should be regarded as referring to Ass. Mos. 10.3 in particular.

In view of these exegetical disagreements we will begin by examining the first part of Acts 7.56, 'Behold, I see the heavens opened', in order to find out whether this is a concept which belongs to the sets of themes connected with the parousia and which might thus link this saying to the synoptic Son of Man sayings. In the book of Acts itself the motif of the opened heaven has no connexion with the parousia. In Acts 10.11 (cf. 10.16 and 11.5) Peter sees in a vision heaven opened and a vessel descending from it and going up into it again. In the synoptic accounts of the baptism the motif of opened heavens has nothing to do with the parousia either, cf. Mark 1.10; Matt. 3.16; Luke 3.21. The same applies to John 1.51. In Rev. 19.11 the motif of the opened heaven is clearly part of the *form* of the vision, as is evident from the basic passage Ezek. 1.1, cf. the Syriac Apocalypse of Baruch 22.1 and Rev. 4.1. Nevertheless what is seen in the vision in Rev. 19.11 is indeed described as something which might be understood to be the parousia. We cannot overlook, however, that in the description the dominant features are those which in the Old Testament tradition are associated with the expectation of the Messiah.

The preceding survey merely allows us to conclude from the first part of Acts 7.56 that the description of Stephen's vision makes use of a traditional motif. Heavens are opened above what happens, but this opening can be perceived only by the seer of the vision himself. The preponderant majority of the passages cited does not allow us to consider the motif of opened heavens as bearing an affinity with the concept of the irrupting parousia. The opening of heaven enables Stephen to gaze into it, seeing in faith the *doxa* of God and Jesus.[2]

---

[1] H. P. Owen holds this view in 'Stephen's Vision in Acts VII 55–56', in *New Testament Studies*, 1955, pp. 224–6. O. Cullmann in *Christology*, pp. 157f., 183, considers Acts 7.56 to express the understanding that Jesus is a *witness* at the court and is therefore standing. This explanation is not improbable but hardly provable.

[2] Cf. Traub in *TWNT* V, p. 530 lines 8f., with reference to Bultmann, *Johannes*, p. 75.

We have to notice further that amongst the synoptic Son of Man sayings only the saying in Luke 22.69 speaks of the Son of Man's *remaining* with God and does not refer to the imminent irruption of the parousia. Since Luke in 22.69 closely follows the Marcan account, we cannot assume that here a specifically Lucan tradition is adopted. We have to assume instead that Luke varies the Marcan account. Hence it seems possible to conclude that the concept expressed in Acts 7.56 is peculiar to Luke himself. Yet this conclusion proves to be impossible when the differences between vv. 55 and 56 are taken into consideration. There is a singular, 'heaven', in v. 55,[1] and a plural, 'the heavens', in v. 56. This change indicates at least in part a pre-Lucan formulation.

When assuming that Acts 7.56 is predominantly a pre-Lucan formulation we have to distinguish this formulation clearly from the set of concepts present in the synoptic tradition. In the Synoptic Gospels the designation Son of Man appears without exception as uttered by Jesus, while in Acts 7.56 the designation is uttered by somebody else, namely by Stephen. In view of this difference from the synoptic Son of Man sayings we no longer see any possibility of assuming that in Acts 7.56 the parousia theme is already present; as this is regularly combined in the synoptic sayings with the concept of the heavenly Son of Man, it would have provided a link between the synoptic Son of Man sayings and Acts 7.56. The way in which the name Son of Man is used here, and, in fact, here alone, cannot lead to an understanding of the synoptic sayings. The pre-Lucan understanding of the name Son of Man in Acts 7.56 remains uncertain. Accordingly we have throughout our investigation merely referred to Luke's understanding of Acts 7.56 as it can be deduced from the comparison with Luke 22.69. So we cannot share the view that there is a pre-Lucan tradition underlying both Luke 22.69 and Acts 7.56 which would complement and render comprehensible by the concepts expressed in it the synoptic tradition concerning the Son of Man.

[1] The singular accords with the Lucan usage; cf. Haenchen, *Apostelgeschichte*, p. 249 n. 3.

EXCURSUS III

Discussion of the concept 'fellowship with Jesus'

IN THE history of devotion the idea of 'fellowship with Jesus' has been represented in a variety of forms. We shall not refer to these historical forms, but only to some synoptic texts from which we wish to derive the elements of this concept as we have used it in the course of our investigation.

A

I. What made us introduce this concept into our investigation was Jesus' saying on confession in Mark 8.38 and par.; Luke 12.8f. and par. The warning against denying and the admonition to confess him before men imply a fellowship which precedes denying and confessing. G. Bornkamm in his essay, 'Das Wort Jesu vom Bekennen',[1] has dealt with the nature of this preceding fellowship. The characteristics of homology, i.e. of being faithful to the word which has been given, are always the following: 'Confessing means to give a *legally binding* word; the one who confesses (like the one who denies) commits himself publicly.' 'Homology always concerns what is *decisive* for the relationship to the other.' 'Thus the disciples are asked whether or not they will admit the fact that they belong to Jesus and are ready to maintain their loyalty to him.'[2] Belonging to Jesus is, as the saying on confessing shows, a unique relationship. It means being involved in the conflict with 'this adulterous and sinful generation'; the term 'men', which refers to those before whom the confession to Jesus is to be made, does not denote a vague generality of mankind but the actual public in the existing world who lock themselves up in the solidarity of opposing God. The world's opposition springs from Jesus' claim. By reason of Jesus' claim men summon the disciple before their tribunal, confronting him with that claim which they have established as valid. Thus the confessing and denying essentially takes place before a judge who is authorized by the public and consequently can offer to the disciple the possibility of being once more involved in solidarity with the world's opposition to God on condition that he denies.

The disciple who is ready to maintain his loyalty to Jesus not only takes upon himself the tension over against men, but is also given the assurance that the Son of Man will confess him before God. As the

---

[1] In *Monatsschrift für Pastoraltheologie* 34, 1938.
[2] *Op. cit.*, pp. 113ff.

disciple holds on to Jesus, so the Son of Man preserves and seals in the judgement this fellowship which has been established and kept on earth. Hence those who confess may be assured that God himself will be on their side and let them partake of his joy (Matt. 5.12).

Thus Bornkamm has demonstrated that in the saying on confessing the attachment to Jesus is of fundamental significance. If this fellowship is kept on earth, it will be continued as the fellowship with the Son of Man before God. The fellowship to which both threat and promise point is itself the real gift of salvation. There will be no salvation for one who is unmasked at the judgement as having been a lip-disciple by the *Kyrios'* disclaiming all fellowship with him. The sentence of expulsion 'I never knew you' as it occurs, for example, in Matt. 7.23 is addressed in particular to those who appeal to the fact that they were together with the *Kyrios* on earth, prophesying, driving out demons and performing miracles in his name. But the *Kyrios* denies that they belonged to him. The fellowship which he recognizes and confirms was not kept by them on earth.

II. Trying to enquire further into the nature of this fellowship, we find a helpful clue in the variant reading in Luke of the passage concerning the expulsion of the lip-disciples (13.26f.). The disciples who seek to be recognized by the judge say to him: We ate and drank in your presence and you taught in our streets. That they may obtain mercy from the judge they appeal to their table-fellowship with Jesus and to their listening to his teaching.

Table-fellowship thus appears to be a concrete expression of belonging to Jesus. No one can appropriate this fellowship for himself; Jesus bestows it. Table-fellowship attaches vitally. It causes sorrow that the traitor is one who sits at table with Jesus (Luke 22.21; Mark 14.18–20 and par.). 'The gospel tradition has given apt expression to the unity of deed and word in Jesus' teaching and activity, by choosing the scene of a feast, significantly and not fortuitously, for many of the Lord's sayings. . . . Of course there is no historical importance in their setting. And yet the frame is not unimportant, but is a true and unmistakable indication that what the parables say actually happens in Jesus' fellowship with other people.'[1]

When table-fellowship is bestowed, the guest is accorded recognition. In the etymological derivation of the term *berit* L. Koehler has shown that originally a communion effected by having a meal in common was conceived of by this term, more particularly 'table-fellowship, which a healthy person offers to a sick person, one therefore who because of his sickness is socially and religiously suspect'. Thus it is a fellowship between two unequal partners.[2] J. Jeremias elucidates this concept in the same sense. 'Orientals, to whom symbolic actions mean more than to us,

---

[1] Bornkamm, *Jesus*, p. 81.
[2] L. Koehler, *Old Testament Theology*, p. 62; cf. L. Koehler, *Lexicon*, p. 152.

immediately understood that the admission of the outcasts to table-fellowship with Jesus meant an offer of salvation to the guilty sinners and the assurance of forgiveness.'[1]

By bestowing table-fellowship Jesus recognizes the worth of many who should never have been given such recognition according to the Law. He does not consort with the devout, but draws upon himself the reproach, 'Behold, a glutton and a drunkard, a friend of tax collectors and sinners' (Matt. 11.19, cf. Mark 2.15ff.). Jesus goes beyond the limits which cannot be crossed by Jewish piety, and he does so by reason of his mission. He is come to call the sinners (Mark 2.17; Luke 19.10). Thus to give table-fellowship is part of Jesus' acting with full authority. This way of acting is unprecedented and shocking in so far as it does not stop short before it reaches tax collectors and sinners, but bestows on them a new status before God. Thereby it reaches out into the sphere of God's sovereignty. God alone can forgive sins (Mark 2.7). It is for this reason that the Phari-sees and scribes rebel against Jesus: 'This man receives sinners and eats with them' (Luke 15.2).

Being called into table-fellowship means that a barrier has been removed which separated the tax collector and sinner from God and God's own. Thus the gift of table-fellowship is a gift of salvation. The nature of this fellowship with Jesus becomes fully clear when the intimate correlation is perceived which exists between bestowing table-fellowship and preaching the kingdom of God. 'Jesus' parables show that fellowship of the table is, as it has been from ancient times, a symbol of the closest fellowship with God, and a picture of that joyful age brought in by the Messiah (Matt. 8.11; Mark 2.15ff.; Luke 14.16ff.; Matt. 22.1ff.).'[2] Table-fellowship with Jesus is not a fellowship which only exists on earth; it has an eschatological aspect, too.[3] It exists as already related to the meal in heaven (Luke 22.16, 18; Mark 14.25 and par.).[4] Jesus promises to those who have stood by him in his temptations that they will eat and drink at his table in his kingdom (Luke 22.30). And conversely, according to Luke 13.26 those disciples who are not admitted suppose that they can appeal to the fact of their having eaten and drunk in Jesus' presence. This fact makes them expect, though wrongly, that they will eat the meal anew with him in God's kingdom (cf. Matt. 26.29; Luke 14.24).

[1] J. Jeremias, *Eucharistic Words*, p. 136 and n. 2.

[2] Bornkamm, *Jesus*, p. 81.

[3] In the Manual of Discipline (1QS) there occur concepts comparable with Jesus' table-fellowship with his disciples, the Last Supper, and the continuation of table-fellowship in the primitive community. Cf. Kuhn, 'Abendmahl', p. 519 and n. 45 ('Lord's Supper', p. 84, note omitted), and *ThLZ*, 1950, col. 403 n. 2.

[4] Cf. for the concept of a messianic meal Isa. 25.6; Eth. Enoch 60.7f.; 62.14; IV Ezra 6.52; Syr. Baruch 29.4; Rev. 3.20; 19.9; Matt. 8.11; Luke 22.69f. See Lohmeyer, *Markus*, pp. 304f.; Billerbeck IV, pp. 1154–65; Bultmann, *Tradition*, p. 109 n. 1.

III. The fellowship with Jesus on earth is more precisely expressed in the relationship of following him. It appears to be necessary to distinguish between table-fellowship with Jesus and fellowship through following Jesus. 'The tax collectors and sinners with whom Jesus sits at meat are not asked first about the state of their moral improvement, any more than is the prodigal when he returns home.'[1] There are no prerequisite conditions for Jesus' bestowal of his table-fellowship. He bestows it independently and sovereignly. On those who have been given the fellowship falls the light of heavenly joy over finding what was lost. The fellowship through following Jesus is spoken of in a different manner. Certainly the accounts of the calls of the disciples show that here, too, the first thing to happen is Jesus' calling them. First of all it is Jesus who decides for someone in particular. But what results then is the concern of the sayings on following. These sayings make clear what it means to follow Jesus. He who follows must go where Jesus has been going, he must take upon himself Jesus' homelessness (Matt. 8.19f.) and deny himself (Mark 8.34). According to Luke 22.28, he takes part with Jesus in the conflict by standing by him throughout his temptations.[2] This applies in particular to a fellowship of disciples whom Jesus keeps especially close to himself, thus distinguishing this fellowship from his adherents in general.[3] This special fellowship is intimately attached to him and commissioned to serve in preaching the kingdom of God. Thus belonging to Jesus here, and, in fact, especially here, is due to the imminence of God's reign, and the promise based on this attachment is directed toward its coming. It is in this sense that Matt. 19.28 is formulated. The fellowship through following Jesus will be continued by the Son of Man when he sits on the throne of his glory.

The sayings on confessing, on table-fellowship and on following directly presuppose fellowship with Jesus. There are certain characteristics of this fellowship which occur throughout these sayings.

1. Wherever there is a relationship with Jesus, Jesus has taken the initiative. He bestows table-fellowship, he calls into the fellowship created by following, he thus brings about the situation in which confession may take place.

2. Whenever fellowship is granted by Jesus, ultimate decisions come with it to that one who stands up for or denies this fellowship granted to him. Such ultimate seriousness is inherent in it because it has a part in the coming of God's reign. This fellowship does not pass away with this world, but is confirmed and renewed before God. The Son of Man will stand up for those who have stood by Jesus on earth (Luke 12.8f.; Mark 8.38), he will have prepared a place for those who have followed

[1] Bornkamm, *Jesus*, pp. 83f.
[2] On this cf. n. 3 in Chapter II, p. 62.
[3] Bornkamm, *Jesus*, pp. 135f.

(Matt. 19.28). Between the fellowship through following Jesus on earth and participation in the meal in the kingdom of God there is a soteriological correlation.

Thus fellowship with Jesus shows that by its very nature it is the gift of salvation. What relationship does this fellowship with Jesus establish amongst those who may give thanks for this gift? Does their partaking of a meal in common mean that they communicate in the manner of the relationship existing in a corporate group? What significance could be assigned to this corporality? How should we conceive of it with regard to the concept of the Church?

B

I. The 'communal interpretation' proposed by T. W. Manson and others implies that in Jesus' time it was impossible to conceive of calling a follower without conceiving of this follower being set in a corporate group. The concept of the Remnant in Israel, the corporate idea of the Son of Man in the book of Daniel, the bond between the Son of Man and a community surrounding him in the book of Enoch, the Pauline concept of the body of Christ, the disciples' being linked with Jesus' suffering and lastly the fact that primitive Christianity understood itself to be the eschatological community represented by the Twelve as eschatological rulers and to be the true Israel—all this suggests the conclusion that Jesus, too, calls followers into a corporate body. In this body he himself is the head and the followers are set together as an *organism*. This conclusion would allow the assumption that the post-Easter understanding of the Church linked up directly with this corporate fellowship, the Church thus being conceived of as the continuation among his followers of the relationship which had been inaugurated by Jesus.[1]

At first sight this interpretation looks convincing. At a second glance, however, difficulties become visible. When we enquire into the synoptic sayings which tell of the relationship between Jesus and his disciples as it existed in history, we cannot perceive anywhere that his followers are distinctly and emphatically designated as a corporate entity. It is their attachment to Jesus, in view of the coming reign, that always and completely constitutes the relationship amongst them. Nowhere are the adherents of Jesus set apart as a holy remnant or corporate body locked away from everyone else; on the contrary the doors stand open for the tax collectors and sinners, for those who were lost.

T. W. Manson's interpretation is of considerable consequence for the understanding of Jesus' person. According to Manson, Jesus' mission would culminate in his having come to create the Son of Man, i.e. to establish the final eschatological corporate body; this, however, is not an essentially new entity, but merely the ultimate expression in a sequence of

[1] Cf. T. W. Manson, *Teaching*, p. 233.

concepts in which the remnant and the Servant of Jehovah have occurred before. The Son of Man thus is in Manson's view an embodiment of the Remnant idea.[1] When Jesus appears he can only fulfil what is already conceived and expressed in prophecy. It is thus no longer comprehensible why the disciples' following is so distinctly and exclusively related to Jesus' person. We do not see any other way of bringing out fully the peculiar nature of the pre-Easter fellowship with Jesus as it can be gathered from the texts than to abandon Manson's interpretation and instead to assume that the eschatological community is being created by the risen one.

II. W. G. Kümmel and N. A. Dahl in their investigations concerning the primitive community's understanding of the Church have taken into consideration that the Church was thus conceived as being created by the risen one.[2] Both scholars, however, also emphasize that there is not really a break between the disciples' fellowship with Jesus when he was on earth and the Church fellowship in the primitive community 'because the fellowship of the disciples who surround Jesus, the concealed Messiah, constitute the germ of the coming Church in the same manner as in history the primitive community surrounded as their core the personal disciples of Jesus after these had become witnesses to the resurrection'.[3] Thus it was not Jesus on earth who instituted his disciples into being the *ecclesia*. 'And yet the concept of an *ecclesia* has deep roots in Jesus' activity.'[4]

The situation in which the relationship between the disciples exists is the expectation of the coming kingdom into which Jesus calls men by summoning them to follow him. The Twelve as a more intimate circle have the special function of service in preaching the kingdom of God; at the same time they represent Jesus' call to the nation as a whole.[5] 'The position of the disciples is distinguished by their expectation of the kingdom of God.' The kingdom of God 'will bring not only fellowship with God but also a fellowship amongst those who partake of the salvation (Matt. 22.1ff.; Matt. 25.10, 21, 23), a table-fellowship with Abraham, Isaac and Jacob (Matt. 8.11 Q).'[6] So here, too, as with T. W. Manson, the fellowship with Jesus is conceived as a relationship amongst the partakers of salvation. Yet Dahl and Kümmel agree in emphasizing that belonging to Jesus is the fundamental and prevailing element of this concept and cannot be subordinated to the concept of the Remnant.[7] This is in agreement also with the results of this enquiry into the concept of fellowship with Jesus. The peculiarity and applicability of this concept in the sense in which we have used it in our investigation is thus illustrated by the two scholars.

[1] T. W. Manson, *Teaching*, p. 227.
[2] Kümmel, 'Kirchenbegriff'; Dahl, *Volk Gottes*, cf. bibliography.
[3] Kümmel, 'Kirchenbegriff', p. 42.   [4] Dahl, *Volk Gottes*, p. 166.
[5] Cf. Kümmel, 'Kirchenbegriff', p. 31.   [6] Dahl, *Volk Gottes*, p. 147.
[7] Dahl, *Volk Gottes*, pp. 159f.; Kümmel, 'Kirchenbegriff', p. 30.

EXCURSUS IV

Discussion of J. Wellhausen's exegesis of the saying concerning the blasphemy against the Spirit

JULIUS WELLHAUSEN concluded from the comparison of the variant forms of the saying concerning the blasphemy against the Spirit that the form in Mark (3.28f.) must be considered as prior to that from Q (Matt. 12.31f.; Luke 12.10). Many scholars did and still do consider the forms of the saying according to Wellhausen's supposition. When examining the saying above in Chapter III A I b, we were led to a contrary conclusion. Hence we will pursue here Wellhausen's argument step by step.

A

Wellhausen's view is determined by the following assumptions.

1. In the second edition of his *Einleitung in die drei ersten Evangelien* Wellhausen in 1911 expressed his conviction that a general 'priority of age' over Q must be conceded to the Gospel of Mark. He assumed that both sources originated in the community at Jerusalem and therefore are closely dependent on each other. Whilst in the Gospel of Mark the contradictions between tradition and dogma are not yet covered up, there predominates in Q 'in the main as well as in detail an artistically correct literary form'. The inconsistencies which are not yet obscured in the Gospel of Mark are made consistent in Q 'by a fusion of tradition and Gospel in which the concepts change colour'.[1]

Thus delineating the relationship between the two sources in the history of tradition Wellhausen assigned the priority to the Gospel of Mark. Within this delineation the examination of the saying on blasphemy against the Spirit also takes place. Wellhausen searches for an original form of the saying from which the modified form transmitted to us in the Gospel of Mark as well as the form in Q can be derived. He assumes that the form in Q is dependent on the form which it originally had with Mark and which Wellhausen supposes to have contained a singular 'to the man' conceiving of man in a general sense. In the Marcan text as it is transmitted to us the singular number of the original form has been replaced by the plural number.

2. According to Wellhausen it had been stated in the original form of the saying that 'all can be forgiven the son of man (i.e. a man)'. In this statement the singular 'the man' turned out to be open to misinterpre-

[1] *Op. cit.*, pp. 162, 167.

tation as being the Messiah. Wellhausen assumes that with the intention of excluding the misunderstanding that sins would be forgiven the Messiah the singular number was changed into 'the plural τοῖς υἱοῖς τῶν ἀνθρώπων, which is appropriate in concept but unheard-of in form'.[1]

3. Wellhausen uses Mark 2.10 and 2.28 as a proof that the presumed misunderstanding of the saying was likely to occur in the early community. As Wellhausen sees it, it is evident from the context of the two passages that originally merely the human individual was conceived by means of a normal expression rendering the Aramaic *bar nāshā*.[2] 'Since it was natural to think that only the Messiah might forgive sins and disregard the sabbath' the expression *bar nāshā* came to be misunderstood quite early as a self-designation of Jesus. Already the community in Jerusalem distinguished a specifically messianic understanding of this expression from a normal understanding of it.[3]

Thus it is evident to Wellhausen from Mark 2.10 and 2.28 'how the Christians came to make Jesus utter this mysterious substitute for "I" '. From the abnormal understanding suggested in these passages the Christians 'could then deduce that Jesus was in the habit of replacing "I" by "the Son of Man", i.e. the Messiah, and could put to further use what they had thus deduced'.[4]

4. According to Wellhausen, the messianic understanding of the expression man or son of man threatened to give an undesirable meaning to the saying on blasphemy in its original form. So Wellhausen assumes that the replacement of the original singular by the plural 'to men' was intended to make unmistakably clear that a messianic understanding had never been implicit in this saying.

5. In Q there was no longer—as seen by Wellhausen with regard to his delineation of the history of tradition—any check on this messianic misunderstanding. 'Instead of "all can be forgiven the son of man (i.e. to a man)", it now stated that "all that is spoken against the Son of Man (i.e. against Christ) can be forgiven".'[5] The wording in Q is nearer to the original *bar nāshā* than the wording transmitted to us in the Gospel of Mark. But the expression 'to blaspheme' was secondarily changed in Q because it did not agree with the understanding that the one who is spoken about is the Messiah.

6. In more recent research the supposition has been put forward that the messianic misunderstanding of *bar nāshā* arose when this expression was translated into Greek.[6] Wellhausen had supposed, however, that the

---

[1] *Op. cit.*, p. 67.
[2] *Op. cit.*, pp. 123 and 129.
[3] *Op. cit.*, pp. 129 and 130.
[4] *Op. cit.*, p. 129.
[5] Wellhausen, *Einleitung in die drei ersten Evangelien*, 1905, pp. 75f.
[6] For example Bultmann, *Theology* I, p. 30.

distinction between the specifically messianic understanding and the normal understanding of *bar nāshā* had already arisen in the community in Jerusalem.

B

We must raise the following objections to Wellhausen's assumptions. On (1): a. The assumption that both Mark and Q originated in the community in Jerusalem and are immediately dependent on each other has not held good during the course of research since Wellhausen. So we must leave it out of account when trying to solve our problem.

b. There is no variant form of the saying to be found in the manuscripts which might corroborate Wellhausen's assumption that an original text of the Gospel of Mark had used the singular number 'the man' in the saying on blasphemy.

On (2), (3) and (4): Our enquiry into Mark 2.10 and 2.28[1] led us to the conclusion that neither saying speaks of the authority of man in general. Thus they cannot serve to support Wellhausen's assumption, since, when seen from our point of view, a transition from an original unmessianic understanding of the expression 'the man' to a later messianic understanding of it is not evident from these sayings.

On (5): Wellhausen states that the *wording* in Q is near to that earliest form of the saying in which a *bar nāshā* had been used. He also states that the expression Son of Man was used in Q as a title of sovereignty. He disputes, however, that the form in Q was the original form. What he disputes we, however, have to assert on the following grounds:

a. The saying on blasphemy occurs both in Q and in Mark within the context of Jesus' discourse refuting the reproach that he is in league with Satan. Jesus' contest with the demons had been taken as the reason for this reproach. Consequently an opposition to the authority peculiar to Jesus is presupposed in the saying on blasphemy; the saying is concerned with the possibility of forgiving this opposition. It is already evident from the fact that demons cannot be overcome by man in general that the opposition must have been conceived in this saying as directed against a special authority.

b. The text in Mark corroborates what we have assumed. Mark appends to the saying on blasphemy an explanation: 'for they had said, he has an unclean spirit' (Mark 3.30). Mark thus confirms that opposition to Jesus is spoken of. In the first part of the saying (Mark 3.28) it is not distinctly stated against whom this might be directed. We have assumed in our investigation[2] that speaking thus of blasphemy against the Son of Man must have been considered by Mark as offensive, since he understood the name Son of Man as a designation both for the transcendent

---

[1] Cf. Chapter III B I 1 a to c, pp. 125–33.
[2] Cf. Chapter III A I b, p. 120 and n. 3.

figure on the one hand and also for the one who suffered for the many, but not for the one who was teaching with full authority. Hence it is comprehensible that he altered the statement about blasphemy in 3.28. By this alteration the saying has lost its distinct outlines. Both the recipients and the content of the blasphemies are no longer distinguishable. So the meaning of the saying has become obscure. It appears from the history of exegesis that this saying caused great difficulties and necessitated again and again the deduction of a meaning for it from the context. Obviously Mark perceived these difficulties himself. By adding the explanatory statement (3.30) he associated the altered saying again with that context within which its meaning had been clear, the context within which it occurred in Q and which also predominates in the passages preceding this saying in Mark. Thus the text in Mark itself supports our assumption that the saying is concerned with a reproach against Jesus' authority in particular.

c. Wellhausen assumes that in the form in Q the expression 'to blaspheme' was changed secondarily because it did not agree with the Son of Man about whom it is used here. We see linguistic evidence, however, which unequivocally contradicts his assumption.

In the form in Mark only the expression 'to blaspheme' is used. In the form from Q there occurs the expression 'to speak a word against'. Matthew takes over from Mark the expression 'to blaspheme' in Matt. 12.31, but in Matt. 12.32b he uses the expression from Q instead. Luke obviously follows the wording in Q in the first part of Luke 12.10; in the second part of Luke 12.10 he gives the meaning by using a participial construction with the expression 'to blaspheme'.

It can easily be seen that the expression 'to blaspheme' is not likely to have been used in the earliest formulations of the saying. Within the synoptic tradition this expression did not become a meaningful term in itself until the later strata. The word is not used in Q. Mark makes use of it several times, namely in 2.7; 3.28; 3.29; 7.22 (in a list of vices); 14.64; 15.29. Matthew takes over the word from the Marcan passages cited with the sole exception of Mark 3.29. We cannot explain this exception otherwise than by assuming that Matthew here depended on Q. Matt. 26.65a, moreover, shows that the editor of this Gospel was inclined to use the word 'to blaspheme' even more often than Mark. Luke takes over the word from Mark directly in a single passage, Luke 5.21. But he is familiar with the concept of blasphemy; he uses it in the summary statement in Luke 22.65 and, by an alteration of the text in Mark, in Luke 23.39, the verse introducing the account of the two robbers which is part of the material peculiar to Luke.

It is evident from this survey that the expression 'to blaspheme' does not occur in the earlier strata of the synoptic tradition.[1] The evangelists,

---

[1] Cf. on Mark 2.7 Dibelius, *Tradition*, pp. 66f., and Bultmann, *Tradition*, p. 15.

however, use it and do so with increasing frequency and emphasis. The concordance shows that it was a current and meaningful term in primitive Christianity. Its occurrence in the list of vices in Mark 7.22 and par. indicates that it was used as a technical term.

This linguistic evidence accords with another observation. The root βλασφημ- in the LXX does not have a regular equivalent in the Hebrew original.[1] So the word βλασφημέω became a current term with a stereotyped meaning during the course of primitive Christian history, but had not been such a term before.

The expression 'to speak a word against' is on the contrary firmly rooted in the Palestinian sphere of language. Evidence of the crime of blasphemy which was punishable by death 'was considered to have been furnished when any one had been "speaking insolently against the Torah", Siphre Num. 112 on 14.30'. In the Zadokite Document 5.11ff. it is said of the enemies of the New Covenant, 'They have desecrated the holy spirit within them and with mocking tongue have opened their mouths against the statutes of God's Covenant.'[2] Billerbeck goes so far as to formulate, 'To speak against the Holy Spirit would have meant the same as to speak insolently against the Torah. This sin was reckoned amongst the unforgivable sins.'[3]

Within the synoptic tradition the fact of blasphemy is stated only once, namely in the saying from Q in Matt. 12.32; Luke 12.10, by means of that expression 'to speak a word against'. The reference to the way in which the expression had been used in passages like those cited above is evident. The opposition against the Son of Man, however, takes the place of speaking insolently against the Torah. In the later strata of the synoptic tradition the expression no longer occurs. It has been replaced by the term 'to blaspheme'. So we do not see any possibility at all of assuming with Wellhausen that the precise term current in primitive Christianity, 'to blaspheme', was re-translated from the Marcan text into the expression 'to speak a word against' in the text from Q.[4] The linguistic evidence which we see and have cited above shows that the trend was in the opposite direction.

Moreover, we must note that the Marcan form of the saying presupposes that 'to blaspheme' is a precise term. In its first part there is no definite statement at all about what sort of blasphemies are concerned and against whom they are directed—against God, against the Law, against Jesus? 'To blaspheme' must have had a meaning in itself already;

[1] So Beyer in *TWNT* I, p. 620 lines 33f.; cf. also Schlatter, *Matt.*, pp. 229, 408, 409, 760; and Billerbeck I, pp. 1008ff.

[2] Cited from T. H. Gaster, *The Scriptures of the Dead Sea Sect*, 1957, p. 76.

[3] Billerbeck I, p. 637, cf. also the evidence cited on pp. 636ff. and Schlatter, *Matt.*, p. 409.

[4] Cf. Wellhausen, *Matt.*, p. 62.

otherwise the Marcan form of the saying would not have been conceivable. So the usage of the expression 'to blaspheme' supports the assumption of a priority of the form from Q.

d. Two problems remain to be considered. Can we expect Christological reflection as intricate as that which is present in Matt. 12.32 and Luke 12.10 in as early a stratum in the synoptic tradition as in Q? And did the use of the name Son of Man to designate the one on earth here in this saying originate in a later stratum after all?

The second problem is one of the subjects examined in Chapter III. In any case it is evident from Matt. 11.19; Luke 7.34 and Matt. 8.20; Luke 9.58 (and perhaps Luke 6.22) that the name Son of Man was used to designate the one on earth elsewhere in Q as well. It is further evident from Mark 2.10; 2.28 and also 10.45 that the name Son of Man was used in the same way in pre-Marcan material. There is no reason which might hinder us from including Matt. 12.32; Luke 12.10 in the group of sayings using the name Son of Man in this particular way. This particular use of the name Son of Man to designate the one on earth cannot be used as an argument against the priority of the form of the saying on blasphemy in Q.[1]

As regards the first problem, we cannot say that there is Christological reflection of such intricacy in the form of the saying in Matthew and Luke as would be expected only from a generation later than that in which Q was compiled. The opposition to Jesus during his ministry by men, namely by the Jews, was a fact well known to every Christian. Hence the community was bound to ask whether this opposition to Jesus might be forgiven; the actual situation of the early community must have made this question an urgent one. A. Fridrichsen, also assuming the priority of the Q version,[2] interprets this saying as having issued from the earliest Christian mission which addressed men who had repudiated Jesus during his life on earth. The concept that the opposition which Jesus had met with amongst the Jews was forgivable occurs elsewhere, too, in the kerygma, e.g. in Acts 3.17–21; Acts 13.27ff.; cf. Acts 17.30 and Luke 23.34. When in our saying the assurance is given that opposition is forgivable, it is indeed already implied that the attitude towards Jesus before Easter is of a different nature from the attitude towards the Lord after Easter or the decision with regard to the Holy Spirit. Certainly we can perceive here the beginnings of reflection and the drawing of distinctions in Christology and the history of salvation which find expression in later strata of the tradition. But this is far from convincing us of a priority of Mark 3.28 over the form in Q of the saying on blasphemy. The form of the saying in Q emphasizes Jesus' sovereignty. Jesus is named the Son of Man by

[1] E. Percy in his book *Die Botschaft Jesu*, Lund, 1953, pp. 253–6, likewise concludes that the Q version of the saying is the earlier one.

[2] In *Revue d'Histoire et de Philosophie Religieuses* 3, Strassbourg, 1923, p. 369.

the reason of authority peculiar to him which makes opposition to him mean the same as blasphemy which by its nature is directed against God. It is not a matter of course that such opposition can be forgiven; this requires a particular assurance which is given to those who opposed Jesus during his life on earth.

EXCURSUS V

Discussion of O. Cullmann's interpretation of the Son of Man concept in *The Christology of the New Testament* Part II Chapter 6

CULLMANN CONSIDERS *Ebed Yahweh* and Son of Man to be the most important of the Christological titles. With regard to them he carries through exhaustive enquiries culminating in the statement that each of the titles goes back to Jesus himself. He considers that the combination of the two titles was decisive for Jesus' self-consciousness and represents his really new contribution. For him the Son of Man concept comprises in itself or attaches to itself the concept of *Ebed Yahweh*.[1]

It is Cullmann's intention to investigate the Christological titles phenomenologically and to use for this 'phenomenological investigation' an 'analytical method'.[2] He further intends to combine the different titles and to enquire into their inner connexion. On the strength of this combination of titles he draws conclusions as far-reaching and in as daring a manner as Ernst Lohmeyer alone amongst recent exegetes has done in his book *Gottesknecht und Davidssohn*—though, of course, on a different line of reasoning. Cullmann penetrates to a comprehensive view of primitive Christianity's understanding of the Christ event extending from pre-existence to eschatology. He thinks that from here the sheer mass of monographs, such as Kittel's *Wörterbuch* displays, can be overdone[3] and is convinced that his conclusions have a direct significance for theology. At the end of the voluminous chapter on 'Jesus the Son of Man' he expresses the sincere wish that a modern theologian would build a Christology entirely on the basis of the New Testament concept of the Son of Man. Thus Christology would rest completely on the New Testament, would go back to Jesus' self-designation and would lastly transpose the problem of how the two natures in Christ are correlated, which cannot be solved logically, to a level where the solution of this problem becomes visible. The solution is that the pre-existent Son of Man who is with God even at the very beginning and whose existence as God's image is contemporaneous with God is *by his very nature* divine man already. According to Cullmann the laborious discussion in the early Christological controversies would

---

[1] Cullmann, *Christology*, pp. 81, 175, 183f.
[2] *Op. cit.*, pp. 9, 6f.
[3] *Op. cit.*, p. 9. On Cullmann's methodical intentions see also p. 68.

turn out in the light of this understanding to have been somewhat super-fluous.[1]

It is impossible within the limits of this excursus to go with any degree of completeness into Cullmann's exceedingly far-reaching discussion. We will confine outselves to those statements of Cullmann which concern directly the *synoptic* Son of Man sayings. Amongst them, however, there are some that indicate the pivotal point of Cullmann's view of the comprehensive significance of the Son of Man concept. By scrutinizing these we can thus make a critical contribution to the whole of Cullmann's solution of the Son of Man problem.

A

Cullmann makes a surprisingly quick decision about the vigorously debated question whether Jesus used the name Son of Man as a self-designation. He makes the decision that Jesus without doubt expressed by means of the title Son of Man his consciousness of fulfilling the work of the heavenly man and of doing so in two ways, ultimately at the end of time in glory, but first amidst sinful men in the humility of incarnation; the latter way was completely new to any preceding concept of the Son of Man.[2] Since Jesus when using the title to designate his person and function thus conceived not only of the Son of Man's coming on the clouds of heaven, but at the same time of his first coming in humility to suffer and to die an atoning death, it may be assumed—seen from Cullmann's point of view—that he understood his work *also* in the light of the intention which God pursued when creating man to be God's image. Cullmann accordingly combines the concept of the eschatological heavenly man (Son of Man in the terminological sense) with the concept of the first man, Adam, as both concepts have their roots in the one concept of *bar nāshā*. In both man is conceived of as destined to be God's image.[3] The problem of how to conceive of the relationship between Son of Man and Adam, which had already been treated in Judaism, was given a Christian solution by Paul, in precise correspondence to Jesus' self-consciousness.[4] This far-reaching assumption which at the same time establishes an intimate relationship between Jesus' self-consciousness and Paul's Christology is supported by Cullmann's discussion of three Pauline texts, namely I Cor. 15.45–47; Rom. 5.12–21; Phil. 2.5–11.[5] In Rom. 5.12ff.

---

[1] *Op. cit.*, p. 192.

[2] *Op. cit.*, p. 164.

[3] When summarizing his considerations Cullmann lays great stress on the idea 'that Christ was already the Son of Man in his pre-existence and that at his return he will appear as the Son of Man in his post-existence as well'. He emphasizes that 'in this sense the designation Son of Man means the same as the assertion that Jesus is the "image of God" ' (p. 192).

[4] *Op. cit.*, pp. 166, 181.

[5] *Op. cit.*, pp. 164–81.

Paul combines the concepts of Son of Man and of *Ebed Yahweh* most closely by placing the main emphasis on the work of atonement fulfilled by the man Jesus. 'This is extremely important, as we have seen, because Jesus himself made the same connexion. *Barnasha* and *Ebed Yahweh* are the Christological titles which go back to Jesus himself, and their connexion represents what is decisively new about him Christologically. The unprecedented thing is Jesus' assertion that the Son of Man who appears on the clouds of heaven in divine majesty must suffer many things.'[1]

What we have cited shows that for Cullmann all depends on the presupposition that Jesus did in fact designate himself by the title Son of Man, combining this concept at the same time with the concept of *Ebed Yahweh*. It is all the more regrettable that Cullmann does not substantiate in detail this prerequisite assumption.[2] He deals only summarily with the objections to this assumption which have arisen in recent exegesis, by referring briefly to Bultmann's view.[3] He considers Bultmann's conclusion to be dependent on the unproved supposition that all predictions of Jesus' suffering are *vaticinia ex eventu*. Bultmann certainly holds this view. But in that passage of Bultmann's *Theology of the New Testament* from which Cullmann cites, Bultmann also considers the problem whether Jesus designated himself as the Son of Man, reasoning in a way which convinces us far more. We will mention three of Bultmann's points.

(a) Bultmann states that in the parousia sayings Jesus speaks of the Son of Man in the third person without identifying himself with him, but that in the sayings concerning the earthly activity and the suffering of the Son of Man Jesus openly identifies himself with the Son of Man. On this Cullmann merely comments that a scholar who recognizes the authenticity of Jesus' sayings concerning the coming Son of Man and nevertheless asserts that Jesus when using this designation does not have himself but another one in mind raises more problems that he solves.

(b) Bultmann states that in the sayings concerning the suffering and earthly activity of the Son of Man no account at all is taken of the transcendent nature of the coming (Danielic) Son of Man; the name Son of Man here is only related to Jesus' activity on earth and receives its meaning only from there.

(c) Bultmann states that the three groups of sayings concerning the Son of Man differ as regards the place of their origin within the history of the tradition. The parousia prophecies are older than those of the passion and resurrection; Q knows only the former and not yet the latter.

The difference in origin, the difference in concept and the difference in formal structure (self-identification with the Son of Man by Jesus in the sayings concerning his suffering and activity on earth, absence of it in the

[1] *Op. cit.*, p. 171.
[2] *Op. cit.*, pp. 155 171.
[3] *Op. cit.*, p. 156 n. 4.

parousia sayings), all fit in with each other. This is what makes Bultmann's argument convincing to us.[1] Cullmann skips over Bultmann's points. Not heeding any difference between the groups of sayings concerning the Son of Man, he sees no problem in connecting them with each other. He carries over the reference to Isa. 53 which occurs in Mark 10.45 to the Marcan announcements of the Son of Man's suffering,[2] and combines the Son of Man concept with the *Ebed Yahweh* concept with reference to Jesus' self-consciousness. He answers the question whether or not Jesus already ascribed to himself the function of Son of Man during his life and activity on earth not on the grounds of detailed exegesis but on the grounds of general considerations, assuming that Jesus understood the kingdom of God to have been introduced already with his own person and that he therefore had to designate his own person by the name Son of Man.[3] Cullmann's argument, however, relies on some support that is somewhat unreliable.

(a) What is indicated by the statement that the kingdom of God has already been introduced with the person of Jesus is still a point of controversy. No unequivocal conclusions can be drawn from it. Recent exegesis has been endeavouring to arrive at an appropriate understanding, without so far achieving a conclusive interpretation.

(b) The relationship between the concept of the kingdom of God and the Son of Man concept has not been much elucidated so far. No conclusions can be drawn yet from this relationship for Jesus' self-consciousness. Cullmann presupposes on logical grounds that there existed a relationship between the two concepts adduced by him and draws his conclusions from this local presupposition, looking for detailed exegetical evidence in the synoptic texts only partially and without sufficiently heeding the location of the various pieces of evidence in the history of the synoptic tradition.

The following train of thought leads Cullmann to the conviction that Jesus designated himself as the Son of Man.

1. Son of Man was not a current designation for Jesus in primitive Christianity. The synoptic evagelists expressed neither a Christology of the *pais* nor a Christology of the *anthropos*. Nevertheless they used the title Son of Man and emphasized the *Ebed Yahweh* concept whenever they presented Jesus as uttering sayings himself. Cullmann considers this as the proof that the Son of Man sayings expressed not the theology of the community but reminiscences of the historical facts.[4]

2. The evangelists themselves never call Jesus the Son of Man; they

---

[1] We have discussed Bultmann's argument critically during our enquiry into the Son of Man sayings in question; cf. especially Chapter III and Chapter IV.
[2] *Op. cit.*, p. 160.
[3] *Op. cit.*, p. 159.
[4] *Op. cit.*, pp. 173, 154f.

never let a person with whom Jesus is speaking address Jesus by the name Son of Man. Only where they present Jesus as speaking himself do they use the title Son of Man in his utterances. This limitation of the use of this title is incomprehensible if it is assumed that the evangelists on their part have been the first to attribute to Jesus this self-designation; it is comprehensible only when it is assumed that the evangelists handed on the precise memory that Jesus alone gave himself this name.[1]

We must scrutinize this train of thought. Before doing so, in section C, we will examine in section B some assumptions made by Cullmann which for him are connected with what we have just been discussing. These assumptions concern the history of primitive Christianity and the history of the synoptic tradition.

B

When the synoptic evangelists express their own faith in Jesus they use the name Christ or Son of God.[2] They do not use the name Son of Man in passages for which they have no transmitted material to rely on. Nor does the primitive community use the name Son of Man to designate Jesus. Considering the history of the synoptic tradition thus, Cullmann has to assume that the memory of Jesus' statements that he was the Son of Man was preserved by a separate group and transmitted by them to the evangelists. This group must have understood that the designation Son of Man was the solution of the problem of Christology. By preserving this understanding they preserved Jesus' own understanding of his person and his work more faithfully than the synoptists. Cullmann identifies this postulated separate group with the 'Palestinian Hellenists'.[3] The passage which leads him to make this identification is Acts 7.56. To Cullmann it is evident from the mention of the Son of Man in this passage that there was a reliable early memory transmitted in that early stratum of the tradition which concerned Stephen, the Palestinian Hellenist, since he is the only one in the whole book of Acts who is allowed to speak of the exalted Jesus as of the Son of Man.[4]

According to Cullmann it is of utmost consequence for an understanding of the history of primitive Christianity to explore this group of the Palestinian Hellenists. They presumedly were not Jews who used the Greek language, but Jews who lived in the Greek style. They were designated Hellenists for lack of an appropriate term to denote syncretistic-Hellenistic Judaism. Cullmann assumes that the group of 'Hellenists' were connected with those esoteric circles of Judaism with which we may become acquainted in the books of Enoch and in the Qumran texts.[5] He

[1] *Op. cit.*, p. 155.
[2] *Op. cit.*, pp. 137, 164, 184, 290ff.
[3] *Op. cit.*, pp. 165f.
[4] *Op. cit.*, pp. 183, 165f., 155 n. 3.
[5] *Op. cit.*, pp. 183f.

moreover assumes that the concepts current in this group as connected
with esoteric Jewish circles were those which Jesus himself had shared;[1]
thus this group must be considered as the link between the Jewish esoteric
circles and certain primitive Christian movements.

The observation that in the esoteric circles of Judaism the expectation
of the Son of Man had already been cultivated almost as a secret teaching,
together with Acts 7.56 from which passage it is evident that the Son of
Man concept was familiar to Stephen, lead Cullmann to conclude that it
was the circle of the 'Hellenists' within which the Son of Man Christology
was cultivated.[2] But since Jesus also spoke of the Son of Man, it must be
concluded, according to Cullmann, that the group of the 'Hellenists' which
cannot have arisen suddenly out of the void after Jesus' death joined
company with the Master while he was still living. This accounts for the
'Hellenists'' understanding of Jesus' person and work which Cullmann
assumes to have been more reliable than that of the synoptists.[3] Cullmann
concedes that Luke and John give a faint idea of the significance of this
group. He sees in John 4.38 an attempt to uphold the honour of those
'Hellenists'; he associates with this passage Acts 8.4ff., 'which reports that
the Hellenists were the founders of the Christian missionary activity,
whereas the Twelve only subsequently sanctioned their work'.[4] From this
assumption that the Gospel of John stands up especially for the Hellenists,
Cullmann concludes that it probably originated within a circle closely
connected with theirs. He sees this probability confirmed by the fact that
the concepts expressed in the Gospel of John appear to be related to that
esoteric Judaism which Cullmann connects with the 'Hellenists', and had
also been shared by Jesus. Cullmann can then understand by reason of
this apparent relationship that the Son of Man Christology must have a
much greater significance for the Gospel of John than it has for the
synoptists. In view of this necessity the fact that the title Son of Man occurs
twelve times in the Gospel of John and sixty-nine times in the Synoptic
Gospels cannot cause any disturbance. The synoptists reproduce what has
been transmitted to them; the fourth evangelist, however, takes a much
greater share himself in the formulation of the discourses. The passages in
which he uses the title and the concept of Son of Man being decisive ones,
this idea must have been especially familiar to him. Thus Cullmann arrives
at a clear comprehensive view by combining the four components:
esoteric Judaism, Jesus, the Hellenists and the Gospel of John.[5]

Within this sequence, by means of Jesus' self-consciousness, the Son of
Man concept acquires a decisively new stamp. By means of the Son of Man

[1] *Op. cit.*, p. 155 n. 3.
[2] *Op. cit.*, pp. 183f.
[3] *Op. cit.*, p. 165.
[4] *Op. cit.*, p. 184.
[5] *Op. cit.*, pp. 184f.

Christology the closest connexion with Jesus' self-consciousness was preserved amongst the 'Hellenists' and in the Gospel of John. Finally the Son of Man concept was given its particular depth by Paul.[1] For the apostle then solved the Jewish problem of the relationship between the eschatological Son of Man and the original Adam in entire agreement with Jesus' self-consciousness by identifying the Son of Man with the historical man Jesus, thereby bringing out clearly and contrasting with the Jewish speculations what had become radically new.[2]

C

After this survey of Cullman's view of the history of the Son of Man concept we will now scrutinize Cullman's view of the concept itself as outlined at the end of section A.

I. Cullmann assumes that the designation Son of Man for Jesus was not currently used in primitive Christianity. Considered thus the group of the 'Hellenists' and the Gospel of John are to be excluded from primitive Christianity in this connexion. They are the bearers of the Son of Man Christology, but must be considered as a separate group. Notwithstanding this separation they must have transmitted to the synoptic evangelists the knowlege of Jesus' Son of Man consciousness. By way of this group's mediation the evangelists were able to know that from the beginning the title which had been used by Jesus was not in current use otherwise.

There is a serious objection to Cullmann's assumption in the fact that the Q material occurs in the Synoptic Gospels as part of the material which had been handed on within the primitive community. It has largely been recognized by scholars that Q can be traced back to the Palestinian community.[3] Q contains Son of Man sayings both concerning his coming (Matt. 24.27 and par.; Matt. 24.37–39 and par.; Luke 17.28–30; Luke 11.30; Matt. 24.44 and par.; Luke 12.8f. and par.) and concerning his present activity (Matt. 11.19 and par.; Matt. 12.32 and par.; Matt. 8.20 and par.; and perhaps Luke 6.22). Hence we cannot assume otherwise than that the designation Son of Man was current in the primitive Palestinian community and that it was mostly from the material handed on within this community that the synoptists adopted the name Son of Man and the way in which to use it. Cullmann himself, by emphasizing that the synoptists use the name Son of Man without exception as uttered by Jesus himself, supports this assumption which contradicts his own. The rule to which the synoptists conformed is broken only in Acts 7.56, where Jesus is designated as the Son of Man by Stephen. When the synoptic evangelists knew 'that from the beginning the title used

---

[1] *Op. cit.*, p. 188.
[2] *Op. cit.*, pp. 166f.
[3] Cf. Bornkamm, *RGG* 3rd edition Vol. I, col. 758.

by Jesus was not in current use otherwise',[1] they were not connected with but separated from that 'old stratum of the tradition about Stephen' and the 'Hellenists' by means of this knowledge with which the way in Acts 7.56 of using the name Son of Man does not agree. So there is no support in the title Son of Man for Cullmann's assumption of an especially close connexion between a separate group of 'Hellenists' and Jesus' own understanding of his person and his work.

II. Cullmann assumes that the synoptic evangelists, maybe no longer fully understanding the Son of Man concept, did no more than merely hand it on.[2] There are also facts, however, which disprove this assumption. A reference to our enquiries in Chapter II C and D, Chapter III B I, Chapter IV A, B and C and Chapter V G must suffice here. We have endeavoured to demonstrate that each of the three evangelists had his own way of understanding the Son of Man concept and of emphasizing it within the framework of his writing. Each of them also paid attention to the differences between the three groups of sayings concerning the coming, the activity and the suffering of the Son of Man. There is no support at all for the assumption that any of the synoptic evangelists might have been no longer sure whether he still understood the concept. Certainly the synoptic evangelists do not allow themselves the same independence in relation to the transmitted material as the fourth evangelist does. And yet they do interpret on their own by their own less conspicuous ways of editing and composing the Son of Man sayings which were transmitted to them, linking up to these transmitted sayings with apparently full understanding in sayings which they formulate anew.

III. Cullmann observes correctly that the synoptic evangelists introduce the title Son of Man when Jesus himself is speaking. He concludes from this observation that thus to limit the use of the title would be incomprehensible on the assumption that the synoptists themselves were the first to attribute this self-designation to Jesus. He assumes instead that the synoptists 'knew that from the beginning the title used by Jesus was not in current use otherwise'.[3] Whence did they receive this knowledge of how this title was used from the beginning? According to Cullmann, they must have received it *via* the Palestinian 'Hellenists' who within their circle cultivated the Son of Man Christology and preserved Jesus' own understanding of his person and work more faithfully than the synoptists. This is contradicted precisely by Acts 7.56.[4] So we must endeavour to find another way to make the limitation of the use of the title Son of Man

---

[1] *Op. cit.*, p. 182.
[2] *Loc. cit.*
[3] *Loc. cit.*
[4] This passage is the only one in which it is not Jesus who expresses an understanding of his person and work by using the name Son of Man, since it is Stephen who utters the name here.

comprehensible. When the evangelists allow no one but Jesus to utter the name Son of Man they follow those sayings concerning the Son of Man which have been transmitted by way of Q. Hence we do not see any support whatever for Cullmann's conclusion that the evangelists can have let Jesus utter the title Son of Man as a self-designation by reason of a community's theology. Whether or not Jesus designated himself by the title Son of Man may be decided only after enquiry into the Son of Man sayings in the earliest strata of the synoptic tradition. We have drawn two conclusions from this enquiry: first that in none of the sayings in Q an identification of Jesus with the coming Son of Man is explicitly stated and also that Jesus himself promised the coming of the Son of Man. These conclusions enable us to answer Cullmann's question why the evangelists limited the use of the name Son of Man to Jesus himself. Our answer is that they strictly followed the understanding present in the Q stratum of the tradition that the threat and promise of the coming of the Son of Man was bound up with the authority of the word of Jesus. Only Jesus himself may promise to his own that the Son of Man's coming will mean salvation for them, that the Son of Man will stand up and go surety for them before God in judgement on the basis of their fellowship with Jesus on earth.

To those who received the promise given by Jesus to his own when they heard his preaching on earth the name Son of Man was not distinguishable as a self-designation. The name was understood in this sense, however, after the resurrection had made the community realize that Jesus himself would be coming as the Son of Man. In consequence of this post-Easter identification of Jesus with the coming Son of Man, the designation Son of Man could be applied in a new way, namely to Jesus on earth, in the sayings concerning his activity and suffering. But even in this post-Easter application only Jesus himself was allowed to utter the name Son of Man. Thus the community both conformed to those sayings which had been formed earlier and also placed the sayings under the specific authority of Jesus. It is evident, for instance, in the synoptic apocalypse in Mark 13, where Jesus is made to utter earlier traditional material, or in the composition of the discourses in the Gospels of Matthew and John, that there was a keen desire thus to found on the authority of Jesus what one had to say as a Christian.

D

In Cullmann's chapter 'Jesus the Son of Man' there is a wealth of combinations established on complex hypotheses. We cannot discuss them, but must be content to state that the fundamental assumptions on which this construction rests apparently fail to agree with the Son of Man sayings in the Synoptic Gospels. Our main objection is that Cullmann hardly notices the history of the tradition from which the Synoptic Gospels arose, ignores the significance of Q for the discussion of the Son of Man problem and sees nothing of the differentiations within the synoptic concept of the Son of Man. He deals with the Son of Man concept as though it were throughout the New Testament a uniform and self-contained entity; and in Jewish apocalyptic literature, too, he largely overlooks the variant forms in which this concept appears.

As regards the problem of the combination between the Son of Man concept and the *Ebed Yahweh* concept, it suffices here to state that Cullmann assumes this combination to have taken place in Jesus' self-consciousness;[1] since in our view Jesus did not designate himself as the Son of Man, Cullmann cannot convince us that Jesus combined the two spheres of Christological understanding in his own understanding of himself.

[1] More detailed considerations of this problem giving the objections to the assumption of a combination between the concepts of Son of Man and of *Ebed Yahweh* can be found in our enquiry in Chapter IV D II 1, pp. 159ff. and 168f. and in Chapter IV D III d, pp. 203ff.

EXCURSUS VI

Discussion of Ph. Vielhauer's concept of the coming Son of Man in 'Gottesreich und Menschensohn in der Verkündigung Jesu'

VIELHAUER IN his thoughtful and highly significant essay enquires into the relationship as conceived in Jesus' preaching between the eschatological figure of the Son of Man and the coming of the kingdom of God. His conclusion is that 'the concept of God's reign in its strict sense excludes any possibility that Jesus expected the coming Son of Man or went as far as identifying himself with this figure'.[1] Even the earliest of the synoptic sayings concerning the coming Son of Man were formed in the primitive community. Faith in the Son of Man was the point at which Christology began its course. This faith objectivized and isolated a particular element of Jesus' preaching, and thus is, according to Vielhauer, as uncertainly founded but nevertheless as necessary as any Christology.[2]

After precisely stating and defining the problem (I), Vielhauer first demonstrates (II) that in none of the synoptic Son of Man sayings is God's reign spoken about and that the evangelists for their part as well as the material transmitted to them did not distinctly connect the kingdom of God and the Son of Man. Vielhauer then (III) derives from the synoptic texts his arguments against the assumption that the sayings concerning the coming Son of Man are authentic. He leaves out of consideration the sayings concerning the suffering Son of Man and the one who has come by reason of their pertaining to later strata. 'There is a probability verging on certainty that none of the sayings concerning the coming Son of Man originated with the historical Jesus.'[3] In the following section (IV) Vielhauer enquires into the relationship between the kingdom of God and the Son of Man according to the eschatological expectation of Judaism in order to demonstrate that the two concepts do not by their origin have anything to do with each other. Thus their combination was not suggested to Jesus by his religious background either. In the concluding section (V) Vielhauer assumes that what Jesus did was to connect the concept of the kingdom of God with the concept of the aeon to come, and that he did so by using the *olam* terminology when speaking of the kingdom of God and in this terminology replacing the coming *olam* by the kingdom of God.

---

[1] Vielhauer, 'Gottesreich und Menschensohn in der Verkündigung Jesu' in *Festschrift für Günther Dehn*, 1957 (pp. 51–79), p. 77.

[2] *Op. cit.*, p. 79.

[3] *Op. cit.*, p. 71.

Vielhauer assumes that there had been no room in such eschatology for the figures of the Son of Man and the Messiah, nor for the speculation about the date of the End, nor for imaginary descriptions of the future world. In the post-Easter community, however, the concept of the Son of Man was regarded, according to Vielhauer, as 'best suited to be used to elucidate the identity of the one on earth with the exalted one and his eschatological significance'.[1] Thus Son of Man sayings were formulated for Christological reasons. The hope of the imminent irruption of the kingdom of God spoken of in Jesus' preaching was now superseded or substituted by the expectation of the arrival of Jesus as the Son of Man. 'This is the reason for the unconnected juxtaposition of the kingdom of God and the Son of Man in the synoptic tradition.'[2]

So Vielhauer excludes any possibility that the expectation of the kingdom of God and the expectation of the Son of Man might be considered, as they are by Bultmann,[3] as having occurred side by side with almost the same meaning in Jesus' preaching. Vielhauer considers the two concepts as having been separated, not only by the difference between their respective origins but also by an objectivizing element which is inherent in the concept of the Son of Man from the time of its origin[4] and which is apparently not inherent in Jesus' concept of the kingdom of God. They are, moreover, separated, according to Vielhauer, by a personal element appearing in the futuristic form of eschatology in which the Son of Man concept is expressed but apparently not in agreement with the concept of the kingdom of God. In a community whose faith was a faith in Jesus' *person*, the point at which Christology could begin had to allow for this person. That was the case in the Son of Man concept, the concept of the person of a transcendent bringer of salvation beside God.

We shall discuss Vielhauer's statements in the following order.

(A) The background provided for the occurrence of the concepts of kingdom of God and of Son of Man in Jesus' preaching and in the synoptic tradition as regards the history of religion (cf. Vielhauer's sections II and IV).

(B) The problem of the authenticity of the sayings about the coming Son of Man in Jesus' preaching (cf. Vielhauer's section III).

(C) The meaning of the Son of Man concept in Jesus' preaching and in the primitive community's Christology (cf. Vielhauer's section V).

A

Vielhauer's investigation starts from the observation that in the synoptic tradition the Son of Man sayings are never connected with

---

[1] *Op. cit.*, p. 79.

[2] *Op. cit.*, p. 79.

[3] Bultmann, *Theology* I, pp. 5ff., and *Tradition*, p. 122; cf. G. Bornkamm, *Jesus*, pp. 66–69; Kümmel, *Promise*, pp. 36f. *et passim*.

[4] *Op. cit.*, p. 79.

statements about God's reign.[1] This observation prompts the question whether the concepts of kingdom of God and Son of Man have by their origin anything to do with each other. Vielhauer answers in the negative. Evidence adduced from Judaism proves that 'where the Son of Man is an *individual figure* and has an active function, the kingdom of God is not mentioned'.[2]

What is that evidence which Vielhauer adduces able to prove? (a) As regards rabbinic literature, Vielhauer relies in particular on Kuhn's enquiries into the concept of kingdom of God.[3] Kuhn demonstrates that the concept of the kingdom of heaven occurs in rabbinic literature 'comparatively seldom and has not nearly as much theological significance as it has for example in Jesus' preaching'.[4] Its occurrence is more or less limited to two phrases. The first is 'To take upon oneself the yoke of the kingdom of God'. This phrase denotes confessing the monotheistic belief of Judaism and can even mean reciting the *Shema*. The second phrase is 'Manifestation of the kingdom of God in this world'. Here the concept of kingdom of God is an eschatological concept in the strict sense.[5]

Kuhn is especially intent on demonstrating that the concept of kingdom of heaven is sharply distinct from the expectation of the messianic King. The latter concept 'is certainly never an eschatological one in the strict sense. In Judaism the "coming of the Messiah" always is conceived of as an event *before* the eschaton.' 'Thus the two concepts are entirely heterogeneous.' 'They are nowhere brought into an inner relationship to each other.' 'The possibility of such an association with the concept of the Messiah is completely excluded by the concept of *malkuth shamaim* in its strict sense.'[6] We have to note here that the heterogeneity which Kuhn speaks of distinguishes the concepts of kingdom of God and of Messiah from each other; he does not speak of a heterogenity between the expectation of the kingdom of God and the expectation of the Son of Man. As Kuhn sees it, the reason why an inner relationship cannot exist is the fact that a national Jewish Messiah is inconceivable in a strictly eschatological manner, but can only be conceived of as pertaining to a time *before* the eschaton. We cannot consider it permissible to replace in Kuhn's argument the figure of the national Messiah by the figure of the universal Son of Man, since the latter in Kuhn's view is an eschatological figure in the strict sense.[7]

[1] *Op. cit.*, p. 53.
[2] *Op. cit.*, p. 76.
[3] Cf. Kuhn in *TWNT* I, pp. 570ff.
[4] Kuhn, *op. cit.*, p. 571 lines 15ff.
[5] Kuhn, *op. cit.*, pp. 571f.; cf. also Volz, *Eschatologie*, pp. 166f.
[6] Kuhn, *op. cit.*, p. 573.
[7] Cf. Vielhauer, *op. cit.*, pp. 76f.

(b) As regards Jewish apocalyptic literature, Vielhauer mainly relies on the three Son of Man texts (Dan. 7.13f.; IV Ezra 13; I Enoch) which are to prove that no relationship exists between the concept of Son of Man and the concept of kingdom of God. When proof with regard to the Son of Man as an individual figure is required Dan. 7.13f. cannot be cited, because the Son of Man is not conceived of either in the vision or in its interpretation as an individual heavenly person, judge or saviour, but is conceived of as a symbol for the eternal heavenly kingdom.[1] Thus only I Enoch and IV Ezra 13 remain. As to the kingdom of God, the concept is absent throughout the Similitudes and is absent in the description of the action itself in the Son of Man vision in IV Ezra 13.

Are these two texts a basis which is able to support the assumption that Jesus' background as we see it from the history of religion did not prompt him to associate kingdom of God and Son of Man, or even the assumption that the concept of God's reign in the strict sense excludes any possibility of such an association?[2] Both Kuhn and Volz stress the fact that the concept of kingdom of God seldom occurs in rabbinic literature, especially seldom in the strictly eschatological sense.[3] So it is not unexpected that this concept does not occur in its terminologically strict sense in I Enoch and is not used in the Son of Man vision in IV Ezra. There are only very few passages in Jewish apocalyptic literature where the expected eschatological future, the new aeon in Vielhauer's view, is spoken of as God's reign, namely Dan. 2; Sib. III 767; Ass. Mos. 10.1ff.[4] We cannot really consider it permissible to deduce from these passages an interpretation of Jesus' preaching.

(c) According to Vielhauer, the assumption that there cannot have existed a relationship between the concepts of kingdom of God and of Son of Man in Jesus' preaching, since there did not exist any such relationship in his background as regards the history of religion, is corroborated by the fact that 'the evangelists hardly established a relationship between the two traditions (sc. concerning the kingdom of God and concerning the Son of Man), even by their own method of composition'.[5] Is this a methodically permissible procedure? In our view evidence to prove whether or not the concepts of kingdom of God and of Son of Man were associated by Jesus should above all—before adducing it from the composition of the Gospels which happened relatively late within the history of tradition—be adduced from earlier strata, without regard to which, indeed, the evangelists' method of composition often remains incomprehensible. Since those sayings concerning the coming Son of Man

---

[1] *Op. cit.*, p. 73.
[2] *Op. cit.*, p. 77.
[3] Kuhn in *TWNT* I, p. 571 lines 15ff.; Volz, *Eschatologie*, pp. 166f.
[4] Vielhauer, *op. cit.*, p. 76.
[5] *Op. cit.*, p. 53.

which we have assumed to be authentic occur almost exclusively in Q, it is from there that we should primarily adduce evidence.

Both concepts, that of Son of Man and that of kingdom of God, occur in Q. The kingdom of God is spoken of, for example, in the following sayings in the Lucan order:

Luke 6.20 = Matt. 5.3 (the first beatitude).

Luke 7.28 = Matt. 11.11 (the least in the kingdom of God is greater than the Baptist).

Luke 10.9 = Matt. 10.7 (the disciples who are sent forth are to preach that the kingdom of God is come near).

Luke 11.2 = Matt. 6.10 (the second petition of the Lord's prayer: Thy kingdom come).

Luke 11.20 = Matt. 12.28 (Jesus declares that the kingdom of God is come upon his hearers already in his casting out demons by the finger of God).

Luke 11.52 = Matt. 23.13 (Jesus reproaches the Pharisees for shutting up the kingdom of heaven against men; the variant in Matthew is closer to the original form in Q than is Luke 11.52).[1]

Luke 12.31 = Matt. 6.33 (Jesus summons his disciples to seek first of all the kingdom of God).

Luke 13.18f., 20f. = Matt. 13.31f., 33 (parables concerning the kingdom of God: the mustard-seed and the leaven).

Luke 13.28, 29 = Matt. 8.11f. (in Q the table-fellowship with the patriarchs in the kingdom of God was probably mentioned).

Luke 16.16 = Matt. 11.12 (the saying concerning the men of violence).

Luke 22.29f. cf. Matt. 19.28 (the promise to those who follow Jesus that they shall partake of his kingdom to come or, in other words, of the Son of Man's kingdom).

The coming Son of Man is spoken of in Q in the sayings which now follow, again in the Lucan order:

Luke 11.30 = Matt. 12.40, in Jesus' refusal of the demand of a sign.

Luke 12.8f. = Matt. 10.32f., in the admonition for the disciples to confess openly, in Q probably appended to the mission charge.

Luke 12.40 = Matt. 24.44, as the application of the crisis parable about the thief at night.

Luke 17.23f. = Matt. 24.26f., in the sayings concerning the day of the Son of Man.

Luke 17.26f. = Matt. 24.37–39, in the sayings concerning the day of the Son of Man.

Luke 17.28–30, no parallel in Matthew, in the sayings concerning the day of the Son of Man.

As to Matt. 10.23, it remains doubtful whether this saying occurred in

[1] Cf. Klostermann, *Matt.*, p. 184.

Q; and as to Matt. 19.28 = Luke 22.28–30, it remains doubtful in which form it occurred in Q.

Three of the Son of Man sayings which we have cited occurred in Q within the same section dealing with a particular theme. The other three sayings occurred in different sections of Q which apparently were independent of each other.

It is evident from the above list of sayings that in Q, a compilation which the community could use in proclamation and instruction, both concepts occur. There are sayings about the kingdom of God as well as sayings about the coming Son of Man. A fusion between them is not attempted anywhere. But is it permissible to conclude from the absence of any fusion that the respective groups of the Lord's sayings were transmitted in separate strands? Both groups of sayings pertain to the same compilation, to the same stratum in the history of tradition. It appears to us that to expect the establishment of a relationship between two groups of sayings is something which cannot be expected from compilers. The compilers of Q did not directly relate the sayings about the Son of Man's activity on earth (Luke 6.22; Matt. 8.20 and par.; Matt. 11.19 and par.; Matt. 12.32 and par.) to those about the coming Son of Man within their compilation; just as little have they related the sayings about the Son of Man to those about the kingdom of God. The evangelists conformed to the procedure of the compilers of Q. There is only one passage, Luke 17.23ff., in which Luke attempts a co-ordination between sayings about the day of the Son of Man and one about the suffering Son of Man by means of making them follow each other directly. We share Vielhauer's view that neither in Q nor in the Synoptic Gospels has a definite relationship between the concepts of kingdom of God and of Son of Man been established; we do not share Vielhauer's conclusions. Nothing indicates that the compilers of Q or the evangelists saw any difficulty in the fact that the groups of sayings occurred in unconnected juxtaposition. We do not read from the synoptic texts that in the course of the history of their tradition the one group of sayings competed with the other or ousted it.[1] If we wished to deduce from the historical development of the synoptic tradition what must have been the case in Jesus' preaching, we could not find evidence excluding the possibility that there, too, both concepts might have occurred side by side.

Thus, assuming that the unconnected juxtaposition of the two concepts within the synoptic tradition does not indicate their mutual exclusion, we also arrive at a different conclusion as regards the relationship between the Son of Man statement in Matt. 19.28 and the *basileia* statement in Luke 22.28–30. Both statements are concerned with a promise given to the followers. Matt. 19.28 promises participation in the Son of

[1] Cf. Vielhauer, *op. cit.*, p. 79.

Man's reign; in Luke 22.28–30 what is promised obviously has the same meaning, but is denoted by a different term, namely by that of partaking in the *basileia* appointed for Jesus by God. Vielhauer's assumption that the two concepts are mutually exclusive[1] cannot convince us here. If that were so, we do not see why both concepts should have been combined within one of the variants of this saying. The original wording of the saying cannot be reconstructed with certainty. So we have to be content with the fact that participation in the Son of Man's reign and partaking of the *basileia* appointed for Jesus by God[2] have a similar meaning within the context of the respective variants. Each of the evangelists, Matthew as well as Luke, depended in his respective formulation of the saying on a text transmitted to him. Hence we must assume that the possibility of using either term to express much the same meaning had existed at an earlier stage within the history of tradition than that at which the evangelists composed their Gospels.

Vielhauer remarks, in connexion with the fact that the Son of Man saying in Mark 8.38 is directly followed by the kingdom of God saying in Mark 9.1, that 'the juxtaposition of the two sayings does not even show how Mark conceived of the relationship between Son of Man and Kingdom of God'. He intimates that as Mark understood them the two concepts could not be related.[3] But is this conclusion a necessary one? Can we presuppose that he would have related them had he seen a possibility of doing so? We should rather conclude from the fact of the juxtaposition of the sayings about the coming of the kingdom of God and the coming of the Son of Man in Q as well as in the earliest Gospel that what was spoken of in the two groups of sayings was not regarded as alternative.

As to Luke, Vielhauer concludes from the train of thought in Luke 17.20ff. that 'in Luke's understanding the Kingdom of God breaks in with the day of the Son of Man'.[4] According to this understanding, Luke makes the parable of the fig-tree announce that imminence of the kingdom of God (21.29–31), the sign for which is the coming of the Son of Man (21.25–28). And from the mission charge Vielhauer concludes that 'in Matthew's understanding the arrival of the Son of Man (10.23) which means the end to preaching and tribulation is the τέλος (24.14), the συντέλεια τοῦ αἰῶνος τούτου (13.39f., 49; 24.3; 28.20), which is the same as the dawn of God's reign (13.43)'.[5] We, however, draw the following conclusion: the juxtaposition of the concepts of kingdom of God and Son

---

[1] *Op. cit.*, p. 61.
[2] Cf. Luke 22.29f. with Matt. 6.33 and Luke 12.31; cf. Luke 22.30 with Matt. 8.11 and Luke 13.29.
[3] Vielhauer, *op. cit.*, p. 54.
[4] *Op. cit.*, p. 54.
[5] *Op. cit.*, p. 55.

of Man in both Luke and Matthew is parallel to their juxtaposition in
Q ; the concepts could be related in Luke's and Matthew's understanding;
therefore the juxtaposition which is already conditioned by the tradition
which Luke and Matthew adopted cannot have excluded the possibility
of relating them.

This conclusion does not make it necessary to identify the two concepts.
They undoubtedly differ as to elements which they contain. But both
concepts occur side by side in the strata of the history of tradition, and
each apparently conceives of the same eschatological event. To expect
that the two concepts should have been expressly connected does not do
justice to the nature of the writings in question. Q and the Synoptic
Gospels are compilations, a literary form in which the initiative of the
editor was confined to quite definite and narrow limits—within which, of
course, the editor had to do his work of composition with theological
understanding. Thus we cannot conclude with Vielhauer that the concept
of God's reign in its strict sense would exclude the possibility that Son of
Man sayings may have issued from Jesus' preaching.[1]

(d) We have also to examine here Vielhauer's assumption that Jesus
connected the concept of the kingdom of God with that of the aeon to
come and did so by using the *olam* terminology when speaking of God's
reign but replacing within it the coming *olam* by the kingdom of God.
According to Vielhauer there cannot have been room in such an eschatology for the figures of the Son of Man and the Messiah.

Vielhauer appeals to Volz for support for this assumption. We do not
see, however, that he can find support there.[2] Volz has stressed that in
rabbinic theology a more and more distinct differentiation arose between
the messianic period as an intermediate time and the coming *olam* as the
ultimate eternal salvation.[3] So there was no room in the concept of the
universal aeon to come for the expected national Messiah. The concept of
the Messiah was too strongly determined by the nation and kingdom of
Israel which it had in view; what was conceived here always remained an
earthly figure, however much its marvellous traits were enhanced. There
was room in the concept of the aeon to come, however, for the expected
transcendent figure of the universal leader to salvation, the Son of Man.[4]
If Vielhauer is right in assuming that Jesus connected the concept of the
kingdom of God with that of the aeon to come, we can assent to his conclusion that the figure of the Messiah did not fit in with Jesus' preaching
concerning the kingdom of God, but as we disagree with Vielhauer we have
to conclude that the figure of the heavenly Son of Man did do so.

[1] *Op. cit.*, p. 77.
[2] *Op. cit.*, p. 77 nn. 140 and 141.
[3] Volz, *Eschatologie*, p. 72.
[4] Kuhn in *TWNT* I, p. 573; Volz, *Eschatologie*, pp. 72f.; Bousset, *Religion*,
p. 259; cf. Sjöberg, *Menschensohn*, p. 146.

B

After examining the Son of Man sayings in the material peculiar to Luke and Matthew (Luke 17.22; 18.8; 21.36; Matt. 13.37; 13.41; 16.28; 25.31) and in the Gospel of Mark (13.26f.; 14.62; excepting 8.38), Vielhauer arrives at a conclusion similar to that at which we arrived after our enquiry in Chapter II, namely that the Son of Man sayings mentioned are not to be regarded as words of the historical Jesus. Differences between Vielhauer's view and ours do not appear until the Son of Man sayings from Q are dealt with. We will consider these sayings now.

Vielhauer leaves open the question of the authenticity of the Son of Man sayings in Matt. 24.37–39 and par., since he does not find any clue for an answer either in these sayings themselves or in their contexts. With regard to the sayings in Luke 17.23f./Matt. 24.26f. as well as Luke 12.39f./Matt. 24.43f. and Luke 12.8f./Matt. 10.32f. in connexion with Mark 8.38, however, Vielhauer gives an answer to the question of their authenticity. Whereas we answered in the affirmative, Vielhauer answers in the negative. So these sayings will be decisive when we are considering whether or not we may assume that there exist sayings which originated with Jesus on earth. Unfortunately Vielhauer drops Luke 11.30 out of the discussion far too soon.[1]

(1) *Luke 17.23f./Matt. 24.26f.* As Vielhauer sees it, the connexion between Luke 17.23 and Luke 17.24 presupposes that the titles Messiah and Son of Man here must be considered as identical; this saying means an attack on a certain manner of expecting the appearance of the heavenly Son of Man which here is conceived of identically with the appearance of the earthly Messiah. Since there had not been a fusion of the concepts Son of Man and Messiah in Judaism, the identification in Luke 17.23f. must have been achieved by the primitive community which understood both the Messiah and the Son of Man to be Jesus.[2]

It is indeed possible in the Lucan context of the saying to consider it as a warning against going out to see the *Son of Man*. But as demonstrated by Vielhauer himself, the naming of the Son of Man in Luke 17.22 occurs in a formulation by Luke and thus had not been part of Q. We cannot be certain what in Q preceded Luke 17.23f./Matt. 24.26f. It is probable, however, that this saying occurred at the beginning of a section containing Son of Man sayings.[3]

Bultmann considers Luke 17.23f. and par. to be a variant of the preceding saying in Luke 17.20f. and considers both sayings as equally

---

[1] Vielhauer, *op. cit.*, p. 53 n. 13. Cf. our enquiry, Chapter II B I 2, pp. 52ff.
[2] Vielhauer, *op. cit.*, p. 68.
[3] Cf. our enquiry Chapter II B I 1, p. 49.

original; both dispense with apocalyptic calculations and are in such contrast to the typical prophecies concerning the End that a Jewish origin is hardly probable for them.[1] Had Luke 17.20f. already occurred in Q the parallelism of Luke 17.21 and 17.23 (ἰδοὺ ὧδε ἢ ἐκεῖ / ἰδοὺ ἐκεῖ, ἰδοὺ ὧδε) would have indeed to be taken into consideration for the interpretation as thoroughly as it is by Bultmann. We do not see, however, why Matthew should have omitted the saying in Luke 17.21. So we prefer to assume that Luke, who by his formulation in 17.22 had added something to the transmitted material as well, in his editing made the phrases in 17.21 and 17.23 conform to each other.

The text in Matthew, being more precise than that in Luke 17.23 and 24a, may also for this reason be nearer to the formulation in Q. In this form the text can be considered as clearly referring to the 'idea of the concealed Messiah'.[2] This is made possible also by the direct linking of Matt. 24.26f. and Matt. 24.23–25. Did, then, the section in Q begin with a warning against believing in messianic figures about whose obscure activity rumours are heard? And did the section continue by pointing to the Son of Man whose arrival is 'characterized as able to be seen instantly and simultaneously everywhere?'[3]

If so, we have to object against Vielhauer that in Q the verse which is reproduced in Luke 17.23 did not speak of *Son of Man* pretenders[4] and that consequently the pair of verses in Luke 17.23 and 24 = Matt. 24.26 and 27 did not presuppose an identity of Messiah and Son of Man.[5] The saying probably sets the consolation of pointing to the Son of Man whose arrival will be manifest everywhere against the disturbing belief in a Messiah who might possibly arrive in concealment, so that one could miss the opportunity of attaching oneself to him. Here the concept of the Son of Man is not so much fused with a concept of the Messiah as trancending and superseding it.

This assumption does, in fact, correspond to the material from Q throughout. Nowhere in this material is there a fusion of the Son of Man concept with the Messiah concept. Nowhere in Q is Jesus designated as Messiah. So we cannot consider it permissible to cite the fact that outside Q Jesus is designated as Messiah in order to prove by it that the saying in Luke 17.23, 24 must have been formulated by the community, since the community was the first to see both the Messiah and the Son of Man in Jesus and therefore as identical. So we are not convinced by Vielhauer that the Son of Man saying in Luke 17.24 was formulated first by the community.

[1] Bultmann, *Tradition*, pp. 122, 125.
[2] Klostermann, *Matt.*, p. 194.
[3] Klostermann, *Matt.*, p. 195.
[4] Vielhauer, *op. cit.*, p. 67.
[5] *Op. cit.*, p. 68.

(2) *Luke 12.39f./Matt. 24.43f.*, the parable concerning the thief at night which points to the uncertainty of the hour at which the Son of Man will come, is treated by Vielhauer very briefly. He considers that it conceives of the Son of Man's coming in a 'fundamentally Christological' way and presupposes that the parousia has been delayed.[1] But we see with Jeremias that the saying in the form in which it is transmitted to us was bound to be understood by Jesus' hearers as a summons to watch in view of the imminence of the eschatological catastrophe, thus having its nearest parallels in other Son of Man comparisons.[2]

We fully agree with Vielhauer's assertion that the reference to the Son of Man was part of the parable from its origin. We cannot agree, however, with his presupposition that this parable is 'fundamentally Christological'[3] when discussing the question of its authenticity. Had it been proved in all other passages as well that the name Son of Man was exclusively used as a post-Easter and hence as a Christological designation, it might be permissible to use the fact of the occurrence of this name as evidence disproving the authenticity of this passage. We cannot see with Vielhauer that a delay of the *parousia* is the necessary presupposition for the summons to be constantly ready with regard to the uncertainty of the hour at which both the thief and the Son of Man will come.[4]

(3) *Luke 12.8f. and par./Mark 8.38*, the saying on confessing, is first discussed by Vielhauer with regard to the question whether the designation Son of Man was originally used in the second part of the double saying in Luke (12.9) also, or whether in the first part (Luke 12.8), in analogy to Luke 12.9, the judge originally was also spoken of as God himself. In the latter case it would have to be concluded that the designation Son of Man was introduced later and displaced the mention of God. 'This would be a Christological interpretation of the saying by the community which saw in Jesus the Son of Man and the eschatological Judge, a proceeding which was carried to its logical conclusion in Matthew's version of the saying.'[5] Vielhauer leaves the question open. We have to note that the sole variant of Luke 12.9, the Marcan version of the saying, does contain the name Son of Man, obviously without being dependent on a version in Q. Kümmel's supposition, substantiated by other means, that Luke 12.9 is to be considered as having contained the name Son of Man as well, is thus corroborated by Mark 8.38.[6]

[1] *Op. cit.*, p. 66 and n. 79.
[2] Matt. 24.37–39; Luke 17.26; cf. Jeremias, *Parables*, p. 39; Bornkamm, *Jesus*, p. 67.
[3] Vielhauer, *op. cit*, p. 66 n. 79.
[4] Cf. also Kümmel, *Promise*, pp. 55f.; Bultmann, *Tradition*, p. 152 n. 1, and *Theology* I, p. 29.
[5] Vielhauer, *op. cit.*, p. 69.
[6] Cf. Kümmel, *Promise*, p. 45 n. 86, cited by Vielhauer, pp. 68f.

Vielhauer raises the following objections to the authenticity of this saying. The usage of the expression 'to confess' and 'to deny' shows that the saying about the eschatological meaning of such behaviour towards Jesus is unique. Within the synoptic tradition, denying Jesus is mentioned in no more than two connexions, namely in connexion with Peter's denial and in this saying. The expressions 'to confess' and 'to deny' (Luke 12.8f. and par.) as well as 'to be ashamed of' (Mark 8.38 and par.) are used with a forensic meaning. What is spoken of in the beginning of each of the two parts of the double saying is thus a situation before human tribunals, a decision for or against Jesus, confession or denial, being demanded in this situation of a judging on earth. 'During Jesus' lifetime such a situation arose only at his passion, and was acute only for Peter. If this had been an authentic saying of the Lord, then Jesus would have foreseen and foretold here that instead of the message of the kingdom of God, the imminence of which was the subject of his preaching, he himself would become the subject of preaching, and that the disciples would therefore meet with distress, this attitude to his person becoming the decisive criterion both for the judgement on earth and for the Last Judgement. The confession and denial of Jesus "before men" presupposes, however, the disciples' being persecuted for Jesus' sake (Luke 6.22f.; Matt. 5.11f.). Hence what is foretold here is not eschatological tribulation in general. The saying thus belongs, together with Luke 6.22f. and par. and analogous sayings, to a stratum of the tradition which can no longer be traced back to the historical Jesus.'[1]

(a) The idea underlying this argument thus appears to be that the situation which is presupposed in this saying did not yet exist at the time of the historical Jesus' preaching. This means that Vielhauer's argument is dependent on a certain interpretation of the saying. Vielhauer intimates that the subject of preaching at the time when this saying was issued was no longer the imminence of God's reign, but already the one who had been preaching this imminence.[2] We have to raise the following objections to Vielhauer's interpretation.

We cannot see with Vielhauer that by the promise given to the confessor according to Luke 12.8 it is presupposed that the subject of preaching is already Jesus instead of the message about the kingdom of God. In Vielhauer's view, of course, this must be seen as a support for his assumption that the expectation of the arrival of the Son of Man superseded the hope of the imminent irruption of the kingdom of God which had been the subject of Jesus' preaching.[3] The wording of the saying, however, does not suggest this interpretation to us. As we read it, the promise (or threat) concerns a certain attitude, a confessing (or denying), towards Jesus on

[1] Vielhauer, *op. cit.*, p. 70.
[2] *Op. cit.*, p. 70.
[3] *Op. cit.*, p. 79.

earth. The promise itself, that the Son of Man will confess to the confessor before the angels of God, does not mention Jesus at all; this part of the saying concerns the Son of Man. We do not see where preaching Jesus instead of the message of the imminence of God's reign comes in. Vielhauer when arguing against the authenticity of this saying refers to the post-Easter fact of the community's identifying Jesus with the coming Son of Man and does not allow for the possibility that a pre-Easter fact of the absence of such an identification might be expressed here. It will be sufficient to refer to Bultmann's warning which he often repeats: '. . . . in no circumstances could one follow the evangelist's idea that the identity of Jesus and the Son of Man is self-evident, but one must first prove the point.'[1] We must take into consideration that the wording of the saying in Luke as confirmed by Mark 8.38 differentiates between the 'I' of Jesus and the Son of Man before we decide whether or not this saying might have been uttered at the time of Jesus' preaching. Then it appears that it is not a Christological identification which constitutes the structure of this saying, but a soteriological correlation, the correlation established by the promise between the confessor's fellowship with Jesus on earth and the Son of Man's fellowship with this confessor before God, or the correlation established by the threat between denying and being deprived before God of this fellowship.[2]

(b) Vielhauer assumes that denying or confessing with regard to Jesus was not conceivable before Easter or at any rate before Jesus' passion. At the same time he does not dispute that 'Jesus saw himself indissolubly related to the kingdom of God and its coming', that he uttered a unique claim which is already implicit in his way of 'expounding the new aeon to be God's reign, announcing its imminence and summoning men to turn round in immediate repentance', since he did this 'with self-evident authority'.[3] Vielhauer considers Luke 11.20; 10.18; 10.23f. as being authentic sayings of Jesus; hence he recognizes that Jesus in his attitude towards law and tradition claimed a 'higher authority than that of Moses to whom Judaism had ascribed the function of a supreme court of appeal', that Jesus understood 'himself to be God's conclusive word to men'.[4] He also cites the saying from Q in Matt. 11.6, 'Blessed is he who takes no offence at me', as significant for Jesus' preaching. Could not these sayings about Jesus' claim convince Vielhauer that circumstances in which confessing or denying might take place could have existed before the time of the passion? It can, after all, hardly be disputed that Jesus summoned disciples to follow him. The personal relationship of following provides the

[1] Bultmann, *Tradition*, p. 152; cf. *ibid.*, pp. 112, 127, 128, *Theology* I, pp. 28f.; Kümmel, *Promise*, p. 45 n. 86.
[2] Cf. our enquiry in Chapter II B I 4 a, pp. 55ff., and Chapter II A I c, pp. 41f.
[3] Vielhauer, *op. cit.*, p. 77.
[4] *Op. cit.*, p. 78.

possibility of that denying which is spoken of in Luke 12.9/Matt. 10.33. Schlier, referring to this saying, states that the actual way in which denying takes place is unwillingness to respond throughout one's life to Jesus' summons to confess to him by way of following him.[1] Vielhauer's intention to confine the usage of the expression 'to confess' and 'to deny' to the forensic situation in the strictest sense seems to us to be called in question already by the passages which he himself adduces as evidence supporting his assumption; in Mark 14.66, 68, 70 Peter denies before a servant girl.[2] Those who followed Jesus and those on whom Jesus bestowed table-fellowship could not help finding themselves in circumstances in which denying or confessing might take place, since there existed a conflict between Jesus, who infringed hallowed precepts, and the Jewish authorities.

Jesus' claim and the disciples' attachment to his word and his person inevitably brought into existence that tension between them and 'men' in which those who followed Jesus were urged to stand up for their attachment to Jesus or to deny it. The Baptist's death was well known to Jesus' generation. Vielhauer further states that 'Jesus understood and claimed obedience or disobedience to his word and so to his person to be decisive for his hearers' salvation or loss of it'.[3] Such obedience, however, required a man to stand up in confession to his Master or to do the opposite, namely to follow the summons uttered by men and to deny him.

There is a certain one-sidedness in Vielhauer's emphasizing the forensic nature of the expressions 'to confess' and 'to deny' as well as ἔμπροσθεν, which according to Michel, whom he cites, is a 'stereotyped expression for standing before the judge'.[4] Michel, on his part referring to G. Bornkamm,[5] states that in the context of the saying on confessing in Luke 12.8/Matt. 10.32 'ὁμολογεῖν denotes a public pledge which expresses in a binding and legally valid form the concretely existing attachment of a man to Jesus'.[6] Thus when confining the meaning of the expressions in question to a legal technical term Vielhauer is supported as little by Michel as he is by Bornkamm and Schlier.[7] So we cannot accept the evidence either from linguistic usage or from historical evolution which Vielhauer adduces to disprove the authenticity of the saying in Luke 12.8f. and par./Mark 8.38.

Vielhauer refers to Käsemann's assumption that the saying in Luke 12.8f. and par. is one of those enunciations of principles of 'sacred law' by

[1] Schlier, *TWNT* I, p. 470 lines 2f.
[2] Cf. also the way σκανδαλίζεσθαι and ἀπαρνεῖσθαι succeed each other in Mark 14.29, 30, 31.
[3] Vielhauer, *op. cit.*, pp. 69f.
[4] *Op. cit.*, p. 70, cf. n. 105 there.
[5] Bornkamm, 'Wort Jesu', especially pp. 112f.
[6] Michel, *TWNT* V, p. 208 lines 14ff.
[7] Cf. Schlier, *TWNT* I, p. 470; Bornkamm, 'Wort Jesu', pp. 112f.; Michel, *p. cit.*, p. 208 lines 4f.

which the 'eschatological *jus talionis*' was established in the community and thus must be considered by reason of its form as a prophetic saying first uttered within the community. But the pattern of the *jus talionis* can be found also in sayings outside the group of the primitive community's prophetic sayings, so it cannot be a criterion by means of which an unequivocal distinction could be made between sayings uttered by Jesus and sayings uttered by the primitive community's prophets. Moreover, our acquaintance with the verbal style of such enunciations is rather limited and unreliable.[1]

(c) The saying on confessing in Luke 12.8f. and par./Mark 8.38 is of crucial significance for our understanding of the Son of Man concept in the Synoptic Gospels. Being attested both in Q and in Mark in independent variants, it has been transmitted to us with a remarkable degree of agreement throughout the synoptic tradition. Its formal structure, the differentiation between Jesus and the Son of Man, offered the criterion which we used to distinguish the strata in the history of the synoptic tradition. Distinguishing marks which might help to decide whether a saying issued from Jesus or from the primitive community are constantly looked for, but apparently scarce. So the utmost care must be taken when enquiring into that possibility of drawing distinctions which appeared to exist in Luke 12.8f. and par./Mark 8.38. When considering Vielhauer's conclusions we are guided by what we found in this saying.

Vielhauer stresses that the concept of the Son of Man was first made use of by the community, which saw in it an appropriate means to express their Christological understanding, and not by Jesus himself. According to Vielhauer this Christology was the understanding that Jesus' person is the centre of faith. If Vielhauer is right, the Son of Man sayings must be concerned with establishing an identification between the Son of Man and Jesus' *person*. We do not see that they are. Vielhauer himself observes that Mark 14.62 is the only statement 'in which Jesus identifies himself expressly with the Son of Man'.[2] Here the account of the passion 'was determined by and formulated according to the faith in Christ and confession of Christ of the community'.[3] If all the sayings about the Son of Man owe their origin to the community's intention expressing their Christological understanding, Vielhauer ought to be able to explain why the other statements concerning the coming Son of Man do not contain such an express identification. He ought to be able to explain why the identification of Jesus with the Son of Man does not take place in the group of sayings about the coming Son of Man while it already pervades without exception both the sayings in Q about the Son of Man's activity on earth

---

[1] Käsemann, 'Sätze heiligen Rechtes im Neuen Testament', *New Testament Studies* I, 1954/55, pp. 248–60.

[2] Vielhauer, *op. cit.*, p. 64.

[3] *Op. cit.*, p. 65.

and also those about his suffering also. He ought to explain what made him
state that the Christological interpretation of the saying on confessing in
Luke 12.8f. when carried to its logical conclusion resulted in Matthew's
version of the saying,[1] that is to say, in that version of the saying in which
the name Son of Man is omitted and Jesus speaks directly of himself in
both parts. Vielhauer appears to have perceived that in the beginning
Jesus and the Son of Man had not been conceived of as identical; otherwise he could hardly have intimated that a Christological identification
was the end result. Vielhauer does not deal with these questions. In the
main he expounds the sayings about the coming Son of Man as if they
expressed the identification of Jesus with the Son of Man. But the wording,
especially of Luke 12.8f. and Mark 8.38, does not identify but differentiates.

C

The above considerations have shown that we cannot concur with
Vielhauer's objection to the authenticity of the synoptic Son of Man sayings
in question. Since we recognize as authentic the sayings in Luke 12.8f. and
par.; Mark 8.38; Matt. 24.44 and par.; Luke 17.23f. and par., we must
decide that the sayings Matt. 24.37–39 and par. are authentic as well.
Vielhauer did not decide in the latter case.[2] In addition we recognize
Luke 11.30 as authentic.[3]

Vielhauer's weighty investigation has the merit of having posed
thoroughly and impressively the problem of whether the concepts of the
kingdom of God and the Son of Man are related to each other. Both concepts stand side by side in all strata of the synoptic tradition. We now ask,
what connects them?

1. First of all we see the two concepts connected by the motif of crisis.[4]
When Jesus speaks of hoping for God's reign he apparently implies that
the crisis is going on already. Since the appearance of the Baptist the
kingdom of God is even now on the way (Matt. 11.12 and par.). Satan
has fallen from heaven like lightning (Luke 10.18ff.). Jesus casts out demons
by the finger of God (Luke 11.20 and par.). Seeing the things which
Jesus' disciples see is called blessed (Luke 10.23). Now is the time for
rejoicing (Mark 2.18f.). The signs of the times make it possible to perceive
the great crisis, the ultimately decisive turning-point. Bultmann is right in
saying that Jesus on the one hand adopts the apocalyptic concept of the
future and thus the concept of the crisis of the aeons, but on the other hand
proclaims with full certainty, 'The End is here'. God's reign is breaking in.
Therefore the time to make one's decision is now.[5] The judgement stands
at the door (Luke 11.31f. and par.). It will be terrible for those who are

---

[1] *Op. cit.*, p. 69.   [2] *Op. cit.*, p. 54.
[3] Cf. our enquiry Chapter II B I 2, pp. 52ff.
[4] Cf. Bornkamm, *Jesus*, pp. 59–62.
[5] Bultmann, *Theology* I, pp. 5ff.

lost (Luke 10.14 and par.; Matt. 11.24), but will bring salvation for those who have been found (Luke 6.20ff.). So the motif of crisis undoubtedly pertains to Jesus' preaching concerning the coming of God's reign. But this motif pertains to the Son of Man concept as well. This is evident from the passage from Q in Luke 11.29–32 and par. and also from the parables of crisis which show the intention 'to arouse a deluded people and their leaders to a realization of the awful gravity of the moment'.[1] Kümmel rightly emphasizes with regard to Matt. 10.14 and par. and 10.15 and par. and Matt. 11.21 and par. that 'the present time, being marked out by Jesus' actions and message, stands out in a *particular* relation to the coming day of judgement. Besides this, that day will undoubtedly coincide with the entry of the Kingdom of God.'[2] The day of judgement also coincides with the day on which the Son of Man will reveal himself (Luke 17.30; Matt. 24.37–39). There is a correlation between Jesus' activity and preaching and the coming day of judgement as well as between Jesus' teaching and the appearing of the Son of Man (Luke 11.29ff.).

We cannot say that Jesus stripped the concept of the kingdom of God of the highly coloured features with which it had been decked out in Jewish apocalyptic literature, but adopted the concept of Son of Man inclusive of all its traditional features. On the contrary, the thorough toning down of all tendencies toward elaboration in apocalyptic fashion is another connexion between the two concepts which we see expressed in the Son of Man sayings from Q and in the sayings concerning the coming of God's reign.[3] A connexion appears, moreover, when we consider the relationship of the approaching kingdom of God and the coming Son of Man to Jesus' own word and person. By the reference to the kingdom of God as well as to the Son of Man, the summons is given to turn round in repentance immediately (Mark 1.15; Matt. 24.27–39 and par.). In both cases Jesus' teaching is the last sign (Matt. 11.5 and par.; Luke 11.29f. and par.), the conclusive notification summoning to turn round in repentance before it is too late to do so. In both cases it is Jesus himself with reference to whom even now 'the decisions take place which pertain to the ultimate end to come' (Matt. 11.6 and par.; Luke 10.23f. and Luke 12.8f.; Mark 8.38). In both cases the same 'interlacing of statements about the future and the present' appears which interferes with 'the time-scheme of the doctrine concerning the aeons'.[4] In neither case does it happen that Jesus in his own person—apart from all titles of sovereignty by which he is designated—supersedes the subject of his own preaching.[5]

---

[1] Jeremias, *Parables*, p. 52.
[2] Kümmel, *Promise*, p. 37.
[3] Cf. our enquiry in Chapter II B II, p. 66.
[4] Vielhauer, *op. cit.*, pp. 77f.
[5] Bornkamm, *Jesus*, pp. 66f., 90f.

So we see a close parallelism in concept and structure between the sayings concerning the kingdom of God and the sayings concerning the Son of Man's coming. We are thereby urged to recognize both groups of sayings side by side as having issued from Jesus' preaching. Thus we have to assume that Jesus expressed his expectation of what was to come in a personal form, too; this is evident from the concept of the Son of Man as God's eschatological 'partner'. Why should we assume that Jesus did not use this mode of speech as well?

2. We agree with Vielhauer's view that the name Son of Man was of central significance for the beginnings of Christology in the primitive community. So Vielhauer's conclusions concerning the nature of this earliest Christology are of special interest to us.[1] Vielhauer states, first, that the disciples lived in the faith that Jesus' death and resurrection means that the *eschaton* has dawned. In view of this event Jesus as the one who had been preaching became the one who was to be preached. Since that Jesus, with whom was bound up the decision concerning eternal salvation or loss of it, was in God's glory, he had to be looked upon as the Son of Man, judging and saving at the end of time. The expectation of Jesus' return as Son of Man superseded the hope of the imminent irruption of the kingdom of God as preached by Jesus. Yet Vielhauer states that Jesus' preaching about the kingdom of God was still transmitted.[2] Why? If it has to be assumed that the community was not able to reconcile it with the expectation of the Son of Man, there is no reason why the community should have transmitted the preaching about the kingdom of God. According to Vielhauer, this preaching had to be transformed by the transmitting community so that through it the newly understood meaning of Jesus' death and resurrection as the dawn of the *eschaton* and so of Jesus' person could be expressed. This transformation was brought about, according to Vielhauer, by means of the Son of Man concept as it was current in traditional Jewish eschatology. 'The concept of the Son of Man was best suited to elucidate the identity of the one on earth with the exalted one and his eschatological significance, especially since the exaltation of a man to be the Son of Man had already been formulated earlier in the book of Enoch (chapter 71).'[3] This sentence occupies a key position in Vielhauer's most thoughtful argument and hence requires further consideration.

In what way was the concept of the transcendent Son of Man best suited to express the identity of the one on earth with the exalted one? This question is hard to answer. According to Vielhauer, Jesus on earth did not speak of the Son of Man at all. Why, then, did the community apply the concept of the *transcendent* Son of Man to the *earthly* Jesus? How is the identity of the one on earth with the *exalted* one elucidated by this proceed-

[1] Vielhauer, *op. cit.*, p. 79.
[2] *Op. cit.*, p. 79.
[3] *Op. cit.*, p. 79.

ing? Vielhauer relies on the only evidence available in Jewish apocalyptic literature as a possible link, namely the exaltation of Enoch to be the Son of Man as formulated in the highly controversial chapter 71 of the book of Enoch. We cannot regard this chapter, however, as a presupposition of the synoptic Son of Man sayings. I Enoch 71 narrates how the exaltation and installation as the heavenly Son of Man, as the central figure in the world above, has happened—a motif which is entirely absent in the synoptic Son of Man sayings. Nowhere is there even a hint at the occurrence of an exaltation and enthronement of Jesus as Son of Man; always—with the exception of Luke 22.69 and, outside the Synoptic Gospels, Acts 7.56—reference is to the parousia.[1] Considering that what is expressed in the synoptic Son of Man sayings is the concept not of an exalted one but of a coming one (the Son of Man in I Enoch 71 does not come at the *parousia*), and considering that in Vielhauer's view Jesus on earth did not speak of the Son of Man, we do not see a possibility for Vielhauer to assume that the Son of Man concept was suited in any way to express an 'identity of the one on earth with the exalted one'. One might consider the concept of *Kyrios* much better suited to perform this task.

If one does not wish to commit oneself already from the start to the concept of exaltation, one can only assume that the community regarded Jesus after Easter as the coming Son of Man. This particular Christological identification apparently was concerned with expressing not what was meant by 'what Jesus did in the past' but 'what Jesus was expected to mean in the time to come'.[2] The meaning of Jesus' activity on earth can be found expressed by means of the title Son of Man primarily in the sayings about this activity rather than in the sayings about the coming Son of Man. This group of Son of Man sayings lay outside the limits which Vielhauer had set for his investigation. In our view it has appeared that the decisive step to express the identification of the one on earth with the one to come was taken with the shift from the sayings about the Son of Man's parousia to the sayings about his activity on earth. We have concluded from our enquiry that by reason of the understanding that Jesus is identical with the one to come, the name Son of Man was used already in Q and in pre-Marcan material (Mark 2.10; 2.28; Luke 6.22; Matt. 11.19 and par.; 8.20 and par.; 12.32 and par.) to designate by it that activity to which the first part of the saying on confessing in Luke 12.8f. and par./Mark 8.38 refers, namely Jesus' acting with full authority. The Christological understanding of Jesus' activity on earth thus led to the deeper understanding of Jesus' *exousia* and found here the continuity between the one on earth and the one to come.[3]

[1] Cf. on this our enquiry in Chapter II and Excursus II.
[2] Bultmann, *Theology* I, p. 36.
[3] Cf. our enquiry Chapter V B II, pp. 230f.

EXCURSUS VII

Discussion of A. J. B. Higgins' book, *Jesus and the Son of Man*

A. J. B. HIGGINS' book *Jesus and the Son of Man* appeared in 1964 after the translation of our book was complete. In his brief statements of 'the more outstanding recent contributions to the debate', Higgins gives to Tödt the honourable place at the end (pp. 24f.). Reading on p. 20 of the acceptance which the contributions mentioned have won with Higgins: 'the conclusions to be drawn from our study, if correct, render all these solutions untenable', and reading on pp. 14f. Higgins's prediction: 'It is not to be expected that the suggestions put forward in the following pages and chapters will be any more successful in winning acceptance than previous studies of this complex and fascinating subject', we felt naughtily tempted just to combine the two statements. But after having read the rest of the book, we could not help accepting Higgins's suggestions—even if that is contrary to Higgins's expectation.

Higgins presents a survey of the whole New Testament material about the Son of Man, and he does it in a form which gives the reader excellent help in finding his way through the texts. He marks the three groups of Son of Man sayings with A ('earthly activity'), B ('sufferings') and C ('glory') (p. 26), and lists the sayings, thus grouped, at the beginning of the chapters. After having dealt with the sayings occurring in Mark and with those peculiar to Luke and to Matthew, Higgins deals with the Q sayings and ends this chapter with the following sentences: 'The full significance of the two types of sayings in Q, however, can only be assessed in relation to the other synoptic evidence. This will be undertaken in chapter 8, where the results of the preceding studies will be co-ordinated, and suggestions will be offered towards a solution of the problem of "Jesus and the Son of Man". But first, in the next two chapters, we must consider the Son of Man concept elsewhere in the New Testament and in the Fourth Gospel' (p. 142). This had a rather startling effect on us, as we could not but remember our own wording at the end of our Chapter II. At the beginning of his chapter 8, Higgins, when tabulating the A, B and C sayings, explicitly refrains from referring to the Fourth Gospel, since 'it makes no positive contribution to the problem of Jesus and the Son of Man' (p. 185, cf. the concluding sentence on p. 25: Tödt 'does not deal with the Fourth Gospel. The Johannine Son of Man tradition, however, is very important, and is fully treated in chapter 7'). So Higgins, exactly like ourselves, bases his conclusions in the main on the two types of sayings in Q. Nobody will expect us to reject conclusions of our own when we read them in Higgins's book. In fact, we take for an implicit appraisal what Higgins says on p. 193: Most scholars' views 'come to grief through failure to take seriously the possibility that Jesus never used the title Son of Man as a self-designation. It is with understandable reluctance that I venture to differ from eminent predecessors in this field, and am impelled by what I take to be the evidence of the texts to abandon widely accepted assumptions.' We even, in spite of p. 20 and pp. 14f., cannot help finding solutions we suggested accepted by Higgins. The problem of Jesus *and* the Son of Man 'can only be understood correctly when his *non-identification* with the Son of Man is brought into the centre. The crucial passage is Luke 12.8f.' (p. 200). Luke 12.8f. indeed supplied the decisive impulse for our considerations of the problem of Jesus and the Son of Man. If what we learnt by starting from that point and investigating what we called the 'Son of Man Christology' of Q really is backed by truth, it is there for everybody to take it as self-understood, and we feel honoured by those who like Higgins—a scholar to whom the literature concerning our problem is perhaps better known than to anybody else (cf. p. 9)—do so. May we venture to add that a few more references to Tödt at crucial points could have been of help for Higgins's readers? Those who realize that they do not fully understand what is briefly stated in Higgins could turn to Tödt for more detailed discussion. Our team of translators has tried to find a more easily readable wording than we fear our book had in the German form which Higgins used. Maybe Higgins like others shied away from our analysis of the Marcan announcements of the Son of Man's passion and resurrection. We cannot explain otherwise what caused Higgins' conviction that he disagrees with us when (on p. 25) he disagrees with a theory that 'the passion narrative reacted on an already existing Son of Man tradition containing sayings of groups A and C, of which the latter includes some authentic sayings, but not the former, and led to the production of the passion sayings in group B. Probably, however, only the C category existed at the beginning of the process of development, because it alone includes authentic utterances of Jesus', and when (on p. 192) he doubts that the passion narrative 'as such was a very powerful factor in the development of the passion predictions in group B', since 'Jesus speaks as the Son of Man for the last time on the *threshold* of the passion story'. But we gladly accept a suggestion which Higgins gives us by his way of treating Mark 10.45, as compared with Luke 22.25–27, and Matt. 12.38–42, as compared with Luke 11.29–32. In both cases those to whom we owe the text were not disturbed by the logical inconsistency which can be demonstrated in it (cf. p. 136). In both cases there is mention in the same breath both of teaching which can be followed by men—the men of Niniveh acted on to what Jonah had preached—and of something beyond all earthly comparisons which in Mark 10.45b and in Matt. 12.40 is associated with the Son of Man's passion. Jesus' action (teaching human beings how to act on earth) and Jesus' passion can be spoken of as a unity when seen in the light of what the term 'Son of Man' stands for. We pointed out that by the use of the term the post-Easter community focused attention on Jesus' full authority, both in his activity and in his passivity on earth; there is no end to this authority Godward, as comes to light in the resurrection, even when man's hostile authority makes an end of it on earth by killing Jesus. With this accords what is further developed in the Fourth Gospel, where, as we learn from Higgins, 'the passion is subsumed under the glory', for instance by using the same verbs to express both (cf. p. 156). There is another interesting suggestion of Higgins' concerning a further inconsistency. Jesus must have spoken about the coming Son of Man in a way which was 'inconsistent, at least formally'; for the heavenly function of the Son of Man is both that of the Judge of the world and that of an advocate for those who follow Jesus on earth. Higgins suggests that the Son of Man is seen as Judge when there is a reference 'to a climacteric conclusion to the period during which he has acted as an advocate or witness' (p. 187). Luke, who in 12.8f. preserves the saying in which the Son of Man is seen as advocate, uses in the section 17.22–30 both the plural and the singular of 'day' in connexion with the Son of Man, a fact which Higgins interprets as denoting both a period and the final culmination of a period (cf. p. 88). It is worth while listening to Higgins when he associates the Son of Man's function understood as that of an advocate with the concept of exaltation. Luke's special interest is to reflect on what happens *before* the ultimate end. Accordingly he speaks less of what the Son of Man will mean at the end, as the Judge of the world (which is Matthew's special interest), and more of what the Son of Man means at the present time, as bringing before God what Jesus' followers are doing on earth. In this way Jesus is regarded as the one who is *now* the 'glorified and exalted Lord' (cf. p. 188). There is apparently a possibility that both what Luke stresses and what Matthew stresses are equally true in spite of the incompatibility which exists between the functions of advocate and of judge when justice is administered on earth. We tried to take account of this possibility by avoiding as far as we could the evaluation of the evangelists' specific modifications of the Son of Man sayings in terms of superiority or inferiority.

Higgins adds to the conclusions we have in common a combination of the Son of Man Christology with the Son of God Christology. Like the former, the latter arose 'despite the absence of explicit statements by Jesus that he was God's Son', but things are different here, 'for Jesus certainly believed God to be his Father in a unique and special sense' (p. 202). We see that the concept of 'Sonship' needs special consideration. But we do not see that the findings in Higgins' book necessitate his assumption of Harnack's point of view that Jesus on earth already believed himself to be the Son of God (cf. p. 202), or necessitate his conclusion that as such Jesus presupposed (p. 207) his performing Son of Man functions in the future and spoke of the Son of Man 'in inverted commas' meaning 'the Son of God exercising his intercessory or judicial functions' (p. 202). The point of view we share is most clearly expressed by Ferdinand Hahn in his book *Christologische Hoheitstitel*, 1962, pp. 287, 292, 308, 319, and 332f.

ABBREVIATIONS

BZNW	Beihefte zur *ZNW*, Giessen
ET	English translation
EvTh	*Evangelische Theologie*, Munich
GGA	*Göttingische Gelehrte Anzeigen*
KEKNT	Kritisch-exegetischer Kommentar über das Neue Testament, begründet von H. A. W. Meyer
JTS	*Journal of Theological Studies*, Oxford
RGG	*Die Religion in Geschichte und Gegenwart* I–V², 1927–31
ThBl	*Theologische Blätter*, Leipzig
ThLZ	*Theologische Literaturzeitung*, Leipzig
ThR	*Theologische Rundschau*, Tübingen (1898ff.; Neue Folge: 1925ff.)
TWNT	*Theologisches Wörterbuch zum Neuen Testament*, ed. G. Kittel, Stuttgart, 1932ff.
ZKG	*Zeitschrift für Kirchengeschichte*, Gotha
ZNW	*Zeitschrift für die neutestamentliche Wissenschaft*, Giessen
ZThK	*Zeitschrift für Theologie und Kirche*, Tübingen

BIBLIOGRAPHY

Bold type indicates the short titles by which works are cited. English translations have been used where available, but have been slightly emended where it seemed necessary.

ALBERTZ, MARTIN: *Die synoptischen Streitgespräche*, 1921.
Die **Botschaft** *des Neuen Testaments*, 1946.

ARNDT, W. F., and GINGRICH, F. W.: *Greek-English* **Lexicon** *of the New Testament*, 1957.

BARRETT, C. K.: *The Holy Spirit and the Gospel Tradition*, 1947.

BENTZEN, AAGE: *Daniel* (Handbuch zum Alten Testament I 19), 1937.
Messias, Moses redivivus, Menschensohn, 1948; ET, *King and Messiah*, 1955.

BERTRAM, GEORG: *Die Leidensgeschichte und der Christuskult*, 1922.

BORNKAMM, GÜNTHER: 'Das **Wort Jesu** vom Bekennen', *Monatsschrift für Pastoraltheologie* 34, 1938, pp. 108ff.
Der **Lohn***gedanke im Neuen Testament*, 1947.
'Die Verzögerung der Parusie', *In memoriam Ernst Lohmeyer*, 1951, pp. 116ff.
'Matthäus als Interpret der Herrenworte', *ThLZ* 79, 1954, cols. 341ff.
'Enderwartung und Kirche im Matthäus-Evangelium', *The Background of the New Testament and its Eschatology*. (Studies in honour of C. H. Dodd), 1956, pp. 222ff.; ET, 'End-**Expectation** and Church in Matthew', G. Bornkamm, G. Barth and H. J. Held, *Tradition and Interpretation in Matthew*, 1963, pp. 15ff.
Jesus von Nazareth, 1956; ET, **Jesus** *of Nazareth*, 1960.

BOUSSET, WILHELM: **Kyrios** *Christos*[2], 1921.
Die **Religion** *des Judentums im späthellenistischen Zeitalter*, 1927.

BULTMANN, RUDOLF: *Jesus* (Die Unsterblichen I), 1926; ET, **Jesus** *and the Word*, 1935.
Die Geschichte der synoptischen Tradition[2], 1931; ET, *The History of the Synoptic* **Tradition**, 1963.
'Die Frage nach der Echtheit von **Matt. 16.17–19**', *ThBl* 20, 1941, pp. 266ff.
Das Urchristentum im Rahmen der antiken Religionen, 1949; ET, **Primitive Christianity** *in its Contemporary Setting*, 1956.
Das Evangelium des **Johannes** (KEKNT 11), 1950.
Theologie des Neuen Testaments, 1948–53: ET, **Theology** *of the New Testament* I–II, 1952–5.

BUSSMANN, W.: *Synoptische Studien* I, 1925.

354   BIBLIOGRAPHY

CADBURY, H. J.: 'The Titles of Jesus in the Acts', in Foakes Jackson and Lake, *The Beginnings of Christianity* I, 5, 1933.

CADOUX, C. J.: *The Historic Mission of Jesus*, 1941.

CAMPENHAUSEN, HANS FREIHERR VON: *Die Idee des* **Martyriums** *in der alten Kirche*, 1936.
Die **Askese** *im Urchristentum*, 1949.
Kirchliches **Amt** *und geistliche Vollmacht in den ersten drei Jahrhunderten*, 1953.

CONZELMANN, HANS: *Die Mitte der Zeit* (Beiträge zur historischen Theologie 17), 1954; ET, *The* **Theology** *of St* **Luke**, 1960.

CULLMANN, OSCAR: *Die Christologie des Neuen Testaments*, 1957; ET, *The* **Christology** *of the New Testament*², 1963.

DAHL, N. A.: *Das* **Volk Gottes.** *Eine Untersuchung zum Kirchenbewusstsein des Urchristentums*, 1941.
'The Parables of Growth', *Studia Theologica* 5, 1952, pp. 132ff.

DALMAN, GUSTAV: *Die Worte Jesu*², 1930; ET, *The* **Words** *of Jesus*, 1902.

DIBELIUS, MARTIN: *Die* **Formgeschichte** *des Evangeliums*, 1933; ET, *From* **Tradition** *to Gospel*, 1934.
Gospel Criticism *and Christology*, 1935.
*Jesus*², 1946; ET, **Jesus**, 1949.
Aufsätze zur Apostelgeschichte, 1951; ET, *Studies in the* **Acts** *of the Apostles*, 1956.
Botschaft und Geschichte I (Gesammelte Aufsätze), 1953.

DODD, C. H.: *The Parables of the Kingdom*, 1935.
According to the Scriptures, 1952.

EBELING, H. J.: *Das* **Messiasgeheimnis** *und die Botschaft des Markusevangelisten*, 1939.

FASCHER, ERICH: 'Theologische Beobachtungen zu δεῖ', *Neutestamentliche Studien für Rudolf Bultmann* (BZNW 21), 1954, pp. 228ff.

GLASSON, T. FRANCIS: *The Second* **Advent**, 1947.

GOGUEL, MAURICE: *La foi à la résurrection de Jesus dans le christianisme primitif*, 1939.

HAENCHEN, ERNST: *Die Apostelgeschichte* (KEKNT 10), 1956.

HARNACK, ADOLF VON: **Sprüche** *und Reden Jesu*, 1907; ET, *The* **Sayings** *of Jesus*, 1908.

HAUCK, FRIEDRICH: *Das Evangelium des* **Lukas**, 1934.

HÉRING, JEAN: *Le royaume de Dieu et sa venue*, 1937.

HIGGINS, A. J. B.: *Jesus and the Son of Man*, 1964.

HÖLSCHER, GUSTAV: 'Die Apokalypse Mk 13', *ThBl* 12, 1933, pp. 193ff.

HOLTZMANN, H. J. (editor): *Hand-Commentar zum Neuen Testament* I, 1: *Die* **Synoptiker**², 1901.

IBER, GERHARD: **Uberlieferung**sgeschichtliche Untersuchungen zum Begriff des Menschensohnes im Neuen Testament, Diss. Heidelberg, 1953.

JEREMIAS, JOACHIM: '**Erlösung** und Erlöser im Spätjudentum und Urchristentum', Deutsche Theologie 2, 1929.
Jesus als Weltvollender, 1930.
'Das **Lösegeld** für Viele (Mk 10.45)', Judaica 3, 1947, pp. 249ff.
Die Abendmahlsworte Jesu², 1949; ET, The **Eucharistic Words** of Jesus, 1955.
'Der Gedanke des "Heiligen Restes" im Spätjudentum und in der Verkündigung Jesu', ZNW 42, **1919**, pp. 184ff.
Die Gleichnisse Jesu², 1952; ET, The **Parables** of Jesus, 1954.
and W. ZIMMERLI: 'Pais Theou', in TWNT V, pp. 663–713; ET, The **Servant** of God (Studies in Biblical Theology 20), 1957.

JOHNSON, SHERMAN E.: 'Jesus and First-century Galilee', In memoriam Ernst Lohmeyer, 1951, pp. 71ff.

KÄSEMANN, ERNST: 'Zu H. W. Wolff, Jes 53 im Urchristentum', Verkündigung und Forschung, 1949/50, pp. 200ff.

KLOSTERMANN, ERICH: Das **Matthäusevangelium**², 1927.
Das **Lukas**evangelium², 1929.
Das **Markus**evangelium³, 1936.

KOEHLER, LUDWIG: **Lexicon** in veteris testamenti libros, 1953.
Theologie des Alten Testaments², 1953; ET, Old Testament Theology, 1957.

KRAELING, C.: **Anthropos** and the Son of Man, 1927.

KROLL, JOSEPH: 'Gott und Hölle', Studien der Bibliothek Warburg 20, 1932.

KUHN, K. G.: 'Die Abendmahlsworte', ThLZ⁵, **1950**, pp. 399ff.
'Uber den ursprünglichen Sinn des **Abendmahls**', EvTh 10, 1950/1, pp. 508ff.; rev. ET, 'The **Lord's Supper** and the Communal Meal at Qumran', The Scrolls and the New Testament, 1958, pp. 65ff.
'Jesus in Gethsemane', EvTh 12, 1952/3, pp. 260ff.
'Πειρασμός—ἁμαρτία—σάρξ im Neuen Testament und die damit zusammenhängenden Vorstellungen', ZThK 49, 1952, pp. 200ff.; rev. ET, 'New Light on **Temptation**, Sin and Flesh in the New Testament', Scrolls and NT, pp. 94ff.
'Die beiden Messias Aarons und Israels', New Testament Studies 1, 1954, pp. 168ff.; rev. ET, 'The two Messiahs of Aaron and Israel', Scrolls and NT, pp. 54ff.

KÜMMEL, WERNER GEORG: Verheissung und Erfüllung², 1953; ET, **Promise** and Fulfilment (Studies in Biblical Theology 23), 1957.
'Kirchenbegriff und Geschichtsbewusstsein in der Urgemeinde und bei Jesus', Symbolae Biblicae Upsalienses 1, 1943.

LICHTENSTEIN, ERNST: 'Die älteste christliche Glaubensformel', ZKG 63, 1950/2, pp. 51ff.

LIETZMANN, HANS: *Der Menschensohn*, 1896.

'Der **Prozess** Jesu', *Sitzungsbericht der Berliner Akademie der Wissenschaft*, 1930.

LOHMEYER, ERNST: **Galiläa** *und Jerusalem*, 1936.

Das Evangelium des **Markus** (KEKNT 11), 1951.

Die Offenbarung des Johannes (Handbuch zum Neuen Testament)[2], 1953.

Gottesknecht *und Davidssohn*[2], 1953.

LOHSE, EDUARD: **Märtyrer** *und Gottesknecht*, 1955.

McCOWN, C. C.: 'Jesus, Son of Man', *Journal of Religion* 28, 1948, pp. 1ff.

MANSON, T. W.: *The* **Sayings** *of Jesus* (being Part II of *The Mission and Message of Jesus*, 1937), 1954.

The **Teaching** *of Jesus*[2], 1955.

MANSON, WILLIAM: *Jesus the* **Messiah**, 1943.

MARXSEN, WILLI: 'Der Ursprung des Abendmahls', *EvTh* 12, 1952/3, pp. 293ff.

Der Evangelist **Markus**, *Studien zur Redaktionsgeschichte des Evangeliums*, 1956.

MAURER, CHRISTIAN: '**Knecht Gottes** und Sohn Gottes im Passionsbericht des Markusevangeliums', *ZThK* 50, 1953, pp. 1ff.

MEYER, RUDOLF: *Der Prophet aus Galiläa*, 1940.

MICHAELIS, WILHELM: *Herkunft und Bedeutung des Ausdruckes* '**Leiden** *und Sterben Jesu Christi*', 1945.

Die Erscheinung des Auferstandenen, 1944.

MICHEL, OTTO: *Der Brief an die* **Römer** (KEKNT[10]), 1955.

NOTH, MARTIN: 'Zur Komposition des Buches Daniel', *Theol. Studien und Kritiken* 98/99, 1926, pp. 143ff.

'Die Heiligen des Höchsten', *Gesammelte Studien zum Alten Testament*, 1957.

OTTO, RUDOLF: *Reich Gottes und Menschensohn*, 1934; ET, *The* **Kingdom** *of God and the Son of Man*, 1938.

PERCY, ERNST: *Die Botschaft Jesu*, 1953.

PREISS, THÉO: *Le* **fils** *de l'homme* (Etudes théologiques et religieuses), 1953.

REITZENSTEIN, RICHARD: *Das iranische* **Erlösungsmysterium**, 1922.

RENGSTORF, KARL: *Die* **Auferstehung** *Jesu*, 1952.

SCHELKLE, KARL HERMANN: *Die* **Passion** *Jesu in der Verkündigung des Neuen Testaments*, 1949.

SCHILLE, GOTTFRIED: 'Das Leiden des Herrn', *ZThK* 52, 1955, pp. 161ff.

SCHLATTER, ADOLF: *Der Evangelist* **Matthäus**, 1929.

Die **Geschichte** *des Christus*, 1923.

Der **Glaube** *im Neuen Testament*, 1927.

Jesu Gottheit und das Kreuz, 1901.

SCHMIDT, KARL LUDWIG: *Der Rahmen der Geschichte Jesu*, 1919.

SCHNIEWIND, JULIUS: 'Zur **Synoptikerexegese**', *ThR* 2, 1930.
Das Evangelium nach **Markus**, 1949.
Das Evangelium nach **Matthaus** 5, 1950.
'**Messiasgeheimnis** und Eschatologie', *Nachgelassene Reden und Aufsätze*, 1952.

SCHÜRER, EMIL: *Geschichte des jüdischen Volkes im Zeitalter Jesu Christi* I–III⁴, 1901–9; ET, *A history of the* **Jewish People** *in the Time of Jesus Christ*², 5 vols., 1893–1900.

SCHWEITZER, ALBERT: *Das Messianitäts- und Leidensgeheimnis*², 1956; ET, *The* **Mystery** *of the Kingdom of God: the Secret of Jesus' Messiahship and Passion*, 1925.
*Von Reimarus zu Wrede: eine Geschichte der Leben-Jesu-Forschung*⁵, 1933; ET, *The* **Quest** *of the Historical Jesus*², 1911.

SCHWEIZER, EDUARD: **Erniedrigung** *und Erhöhung bei Jesus und seinen Nachfolgern*, 1955; abridged ET, *Lordship and Discipleship* (Studies in Biblical Theology 28), 1960.

SJÖBERG, ERIK: *Der* **Menschensohn** *im äthiopischen Henochbuch*, 1946.
Der **verborgene Menschensohn** *in den Evangelien*, 1955.

STAERK, WILLY: *Die Erlösungserwartung in den östlichen Religionen.* **Soter II**, 1938.

STRACK, H. L., and **Billerbeck**, PAUL: *Kommentar zum Neuen Testament aus Talmud und Midrasch* I–IV², 1956.

STREETER, B. H.: *The Four* **Gospels**⁸, 1953.

TAYLOR, VINCENT: *The* **Names** *of Jesus*², 1954.
'The Origin of the Marcan Passion-Sayings', *New Testament Studies* 1, 1954/5, pp. 159ff.

VEIT, M.: *Die Auffassungen von der Person Jesu im Urchristentum nach den neuesten Forschungen*, Diss. Marburg, 1946.

VIELHAUER, PHILIPP: '**Gottesreich** und Menschensohn in der Verkündigung Jesu', *Festschrift für Günther Dehn*, 1957.

VIOLET, BRUNO: *Die* **Apokalypsen** *des Esra und des Baruch in deutscher Gestalt*, 1924.

VOLZ, PAUL: *Die* **Eschatologie** *der jüdischen Gemeinde im neutestamentlichen Zeitalter*², 1934.

WEISS, JOHANNES: *Die Predigt Jesu vom Reiche Gottes*², 1900.

WELLHAUSEN, JULIUS: **Einleitung** *in die drei ersten Evangelien*², 1911.
Das Evangelium Marci, 1903.
*Das Evangelium Matthaei*², 1914.

WERNER, MARTIN: *Die Entstehung des christlichen Dogmas*², 1953.

WOLFF, H. W.: **Jes**aja **53** *im Urchristentum*², 1950 (ed. 3, 1952).

WREDE, WILLIAM: *Das* **Messiasgeheimnis** *in den Evangelien*, 1901.

INDEX OF AUTHORS

INDEX OF BIBLICAL REFERENCES

OLD TESTAMENT

NEW TESTAMENT

EXTRA-CANONICAL WRITINGS

INDEX OF SON OF MAN SAYINGS

I APOCALYPTIC WRITINGS

II MARK